FIGURES OF THE PRE-FREUDIAN UNCONSCIOUS FROM FLAUBERT TO PROUST

An original, wide-ranging contribution to the study of French writing in the nineteenth and early twentieth centuries, this book examines the ways in which the unconscious was understood in literature in the years before Freud. Exploring the influence of medical and psychological discourse over the existence and/or potential nature of the unconscious, Michael R. Finn discusses the resistance of feminists opposing medical diagnoses of the female brain as the seat of the unconscious, the hypnotism craze of the 1880s and the fascination, in fiction, with dual personality and posthypnotic crimes. The heart of the study explores how the unconscious inserts itself into the writing practice of Flaubert, Maupassant and Proust. Through the presentation of scientific evidence and quarrels about the psyche Michael R. Finn is able to show the work of such writers in a completely new light.

MICHAEL R. FINN is Emeritus Professor of French in the Department of Languages, Literatures and Cultures at Ryerson University in Toronto. He has written widely on the connection between literature and medicine, including the books *Proust, the Body and Literary Form* (Cambridge, 1999) and *Hysteria, Hypnotism, the Spirits and Pornography* (2009), as well as an extensive range of articles.

FIGURES OF THE PRE-FREUDIAN UNCONSCIOUS FROM FLAUBERT TO PROUST

MICHAEL R. FINN

CAMBRIDGE
UNIVERSITY PRESS

CAMBRIDGE
UNIVERSITY PRESS

University Printing House, Cambridge CB2 8BS, United Kingdom

One Liberty Plaza, 20th Floor, New York, NY 10006, USA

477 Williamstown Road, Port Melbourne, VIC 3207, Australia

4843/24, 2nd Floor, Ansari Road, Daryaganj, Delhi – 110002, India

79 Anson Road, #06–04/06, Singapore 079906

Cambridge University Press is part of the University of Cambridge.

It furthers the University's mission by disseminating knowledge in the pursuit of education, learning, and research at the highest international levels of excellence.

www.cambridge.org
Information on this title: www.cambridge.org/9781107184565
DOI: 10.1017/9781316882153

First published 2017

Printed in the United Kingdom by Clays, St Ives plc

A catalogue record for this publication is available from the British Library.

Library of Congress Cataloging-in-Publication Data
NAMES: Finn, Michael R., author.
TITLE: Figures of the pre-Freudian unconscious from Flaubert to Proust / Michael Finn.
DESCRIPTION: 1 Edition. | New York : Cambridge University Press, [2017] | Includes bibliographical references and index.
IDENTIFIERS: LCCN 2016059633 | ISBN 9781107184565 (Hard back)
SUBJECTS: LCSH: Subconsciousness–History. | Psychology–History.
CLASSIFICATION: LCC BF315 .F525 2017 | DDC 154.2–dc23 LC record available at https://lccn.loc.gov/2016059633

ISBN 978-1-107-18456-5 Hardback

For Clara Mary Elizabeth Raeburn and
Carroll Bernard Finn

Contents

Acknowledgements

There are a number of professional and personal friends to whom I owe much for their help in bringing this study to fruition. My appreciation goes to Margot Irvine and Clive Thomson, who were close and careful readers of parts of the manuscript. A number of the ideas for this study were developed in the series of 'Convergences' seminars that were organized by them at the University of Guelph. My colleague at Ryerson University, Kathleen Kellett, has been an indefatigable source of good advice, and idea exchange over the years with Rachel Mesch has always been thoughtful and rich. When I needed to be set straight in the world of nineteenth- and twentieth-century medicine, I could always count on the erudition and wit of Angus McLaren. And I salute my friend John Cook, who, without fail, arrived at every lunch with enthusiasm, appetite and a new, just-begun volume for discussion under his arm. Though many, many miles away from Toronto, Cathey Baker has been a constant support.

Research for this volume received a crucial boost from an Insight Grant awarded by the Social Sciences and Humanities Research Council of Canada. Among other things, the grant permitted consultation of the marvellous resources of the Bibliothèque interuniversitaire de médecine and the Bibliothèque nationale de France in Paris. My article, 'Physiological Fictions and the Fin-de-Siècle Female Brain', is reproduced (revised) from *Nineteenth-Century French Studies* with permission from the University of Nebraska Press, copyright 2011.

My sincere thanks to Dr Linda Bree, Senior Executive Publisher and Head of Humanities at Cambridge University Press, for her cordial, helpful professionalism and her assistance in moving this project forward. Thanks also, at Cambridge University Press, to Tim Mason and Becky Jackaman.

This book would not have been quite the same without the encouragement, grace and sure-footed advice of Elizabeth Ann Park.

Introduction

The prestige and penetration into culture of Freud's ideas present the current-day reader with what appears to be a coherent topography of the unconscious. All was not so clear in the latter years of the nineteenth century, however, as psychological and neurological studies of the mind and the brain only gradually began to unravel the workings and locus of speech, memory, vision, etc., and hysteria research opened up more questions about the psyche than it answered. In France, well-publicized experiments in medical hypnotism seemed to liberate a second personality in patients, a visible proof that the unconscious existed. But was it, as some thought, a 'reflex unconscious', a quasi-muscular entity, embedded in our system of physical reflexes? Was it a 'cerebral unconscious', located (but unlocatable) in the physical brain? Was the unconscious simply a locus of amoral instincts and drives that the rational intelligence and willpower must contain and repress, or could it function, as a few suggested, as a reservoir of creative images and intuitions?

It is these two main currents – the unconscious as static and/or as an unstable source of danger and the unconscious as aesthetically productive – that I wish to trace, first in French medico-psychological discourse of the late nineteenth century, and then as they migrated outward and were challenged by or adapted into the discourse of fiction and into the creative stance of a number of French writers. Awareness of and anxiety about the unconscious materialized in a number of phenomena, figures that point to but do not really acknowledge the unconscious as we know it today: the mindset of the hysteric; posthypnotic suggestions and crimes; the double, or dual/multiple personality; the unknowable female psyche; even late nineteenth-century degeneration theory, which has been called an imaginary explanation of the unconscious overtaking the will.

In this works I explore the impact that medico-psychological thinking and theories about the unconscious had on the thematics and creativity of both major and secondary French writers from 1850 to 1920. Although my initial focus will be the question of how various forms of mental duality were interpreted by doctors and psychologists, the bulk of my study interrogates how medicalized human duality began to show up in the fiction and in the creative theory of writers, particularly Flaubert, Maupassant and Proust. Critical work on the unconscious as a medico-psychological phenomenon is ubiquitous, but there is a gap in criticism connecting the unconscious and fiction, a gap that this study is intended to fill, at least in part.

The authoritative, encyclopaedic study of the history of the unconscious, both for the French and in the Anglo-Saxon world, remains *The Discovery of the Unconscious* (1970) by the Swiss medical historian Henri Ellenberger. The work is particularly good on pre-Freudian, nineteenth-century theory and luminaries, the latter including Drs Jean-Martin Charcot and Pierre Janet, both key characters in my project, and a further set of Ellenberger's essays, *Beyond the Unconscious* (1993), contains important French-oriented material as well. Mark Micale's *Approaching Hysteria* (1995) is also a significant contribution to the field. However, given French preoccupation with their own medical history in the nineteenth century – and a rich history it is – there are important French-language works that offer useful background to the study I propose. These include texts such as Élisabeth Roudinesco's now-classic *Histoire de la psychanalyse en France 1, 1885–1939* (1994), Marcel Gauchet's *L'Inconscient cérébral* (1992), Gauchet and Swain's *Le vrai Charcot* (1997), and Pierre-Henri Castel's *La Querelle de l'hystérie* (1998). More focused work on hypnotism and the unconscious has been done in Jacqueline Carroy's twin volumes *Hypnose, suggestion et psychologie* (1991) and *Les Personnalités doubles et multiples* (1993). Serge Nicolas' *Histoire de la psychologie française* (2002) is but one of a series of substantive studies, nineteenth-century reeditions and commentaries produced by this author in recent years.

Some aspects of the unconscious in fiction have received enough critical attention that I will not attempt to reexamine them in my own study. The dream and the fantastical tale are aspects of late-century French literature about which more than a little has been written. Jean Le Guennec has authored two studies on the irrational and the unconscious in the fantastical tale, *États de l'inconscient dans le récit fantastique 1800–1900* (2002) and *Raison et déraison dans le récit fantastique au XIXe siècle* (2003). Dreams and their interpretation have been examined in a plethora of authors, Nodier, Balzac, Gautier, Baudelaire, Hugo, Nerval, Rimbaud and Proust, to name just some. The figure of the double in Maupassant and European literature at large has drawn substantial essays from Wladimir Troubetzkoy in

La Figure du double (1995) and *L'Ombre et la différence. Le double en Europe* (1996), though in a largely Freudian interpretation.

What has received only tangential treatment, and what represents a largely unresearched area that I will be exploring, is the permeability of French fiction, pre-Freud, to theory and doxa about the unconscious and about unconscious creativity. My objective is to provide a broader, better contextualized picture than now exists of the attentiveness of literature and its authors to evolving French medico-psychological theory concerning the structure of the psyche and the mind. The few studies that have touched on this subject include Pierre Citti's somewhat hostile *La Mésintelligence. Essais d'histoire de l'intelligence française du symbolisme à 1914* (2000), where (in chapter 14) he looks briefly at the figure of the double in Jean Lorrain, Marcel Schwob and Huysmans, and Jean Pierrot's classic *L'Imaginaire décadent 1880–1900* (1977), which has a chapter on sex and the unconscious. A recent study by Bertrand Marquer, *Les 'Romans' de la Salpêtrière: Réception d'une scénographie clinique: Jean-Martin Charcot dans l'imaginaire fin-de-siècle* (2008), on the impact of Charcot's public demonstrations and of the Salpêtrière's presence in the fin-de-siècle literary imagination, has been useful especially as background to Chapter 3, on Maupassant.

Chapter 1 begins with the emergence of theorizing about a spinal, 'reflex' unconscious, discussed by the British physiologists William Carpenter, Thomas Laycock and others in the 1830s and 1840s. Their research[1] suggested that because the brain is directly connected to the spinal column, the various cerebral centres must be subject to automatic, reflex action similar to that noted in the spinal column. The consequences of this apparently limited idea were to be significant. If automatism and reflex action enjoyed a physical link to the brain, the traditional, absolute role of the intellect and willpower in guiding human action was irresistibly called into question.

The chapter also examines other avatars of the late-century unconscious, the 'subliminal self' and what was called 'unconscious cerebration',[2] the latter widely spoken of and apparently understood as an activity in the brain that was exclusively physiological rather than involving the psyche. The morphology of the brain also intrigued researchers and encouraged some 'to envision the mind as somehow spatially congruent with the brain'.[3] Could the unconscious be lodged, for example, in one of the brain's halves? Or was the cerebellum, the backmost, lowest part of the brain and closest to the spine, thus directly connected to our 'lower body functions'? Was it the seat of sexual function? Chapter 1 continues with an extended discussion of the 'Quarrel of the Unconscious', that is, the debate involving doctors, physiologists, philosophers and newly minted psychologists as to whether the unconscious existed and, if so, how it functioned. The final section is a coda tracing the French resistance, headed by Dr Pierre Janet, to Freudian thought.

Flaubert, the subject of Chapter 2, died in 1880, at the dawn of a decade that was to interrogate dualities and dualisms of every type, dual and multiple personalities, hysterical duality, the second selves visible in the hypnotized and mediums, etc. The sense of two selves we encounter in Flaubert is immediately visible in his admission that he was creatively conflicted, at once drawn to oversized, lyrical, emotional themes and subjects, yet chastened by a quasi-obsessive need to gather documents and objective facts. Of course, in the Romantic tradition, which so influenced Flaubert's youth, genius was androgynous, and in that sense the bi-gendered artist was not a newcomer on the scene, nor was the claim, made both by Baudelaire and Flaubert, that they themselves were hysterics. I reexamine Flaubert's claim to hysteria and bi-genderdness from two points of view: that of feminist criticism, which has accused Flaubert of 'critical cross-dressing' and 'male lesbianism', but also through the lens of major hysteria theorists of the mid-nineteenth century who all noted that the male hysteric did exist. I pay special attention to Dr Hector Landouzy because of Flaubert's close reading and annotation of his *Traité complet de l'hystérie*. I also engage, in this chapter, with the ideas of Mark Micale, Jan Goldstein and Benjamin Bart on the question of Flaubert and hysteria.[4]

The phenomenon of Flaubert's various dualities thus seems a natural entry point for an investigation of his writing stance. The hallucination offers yet another image of the writer as subject to dual states. It is now fairly well agreed that Flaubert suffered epileptic attacks characterized by vivid, hallucinatory visual effects. His contemporary Hippolyte Taine was aware of this as he gathered material for discussion of second states in his *De l'intelligence* and questioned Flaubert in 1866 in a set of letters about his experience. I explore the question of the hallucination, as an element of Flaubert's physical makeup, as a theme in his fiction and as a figure in his style, and argue that the invasion of self that occurs in the hallucinatory state is reconverted and redirected, in his writing, into a half-conscious openness to absorption into external phenomena.[5] Adam Watt's idea of 'le délire de la lecture' ('reading as delirium') in Proust will be tested as possibly applicable to compositional delirium in Flaubert.[6]

Chapter 3 engages with a question that has been a subject of interest and conjecture on the part of many critics, that is, the impact that the encounter with Jean-Martin Charcot's hysteria research had on Maupassant and his literature. Élisabeth Roudinesco maintains that the structure of duality in Maupassant's writings is visible in the differing treatment afforded by his novels (detailed realism) as compared with his short fiction (wild hallucinatory swings). It is the encounter with Charcot and the doctrines of La Salpêtrière hospital, she argues, that triggered this hallucinatory current.[7] Maupassant is said to have attended Charcot's lectures from 1883 to 1886[8] and to have been diplomatically excluded from them in late 1887 and early 1888, because of criticisms of Charcot and behavioural problems of which Charcot had been informed.[9]

A major purpose of the Maupassant chapter is to provide a clearer and more exact medico/cultural context to Maupassant's fiction and to his famous story *Le Horla*, than we have seen to date. *Le Horla* owes more to the hypnosis research of the Nancy school under Dr Hippolyte Bernheim than it does to the practices at La Salpêtrière where, in the mid- to late 1880s, Charcot and his assistants were turning away from posthypnotic suggestion in part because of Dr Bernheim's contention that Salpêtrière-style hysteria was itself a suggested, cultivated behaviour.[10]

In Chapter 3, I document the society-wide infatuation with apparently paranormal phenomena by focusing on the furor created in 1885–86 in the French medical and scientific communities by the successful experiments in what appeared to be mental telepathy carried out by Pierre Janet and a colleague in Le Havre. Not yet a medical doctor, Janet would later distance himself from these experiments, but the behaviours he induced in his famous patient Léonie included clairvoyance, and in particular an ability to 'see' objects held behind her back. Maupassant's Mme Sablé in *Le Horla* is invested with similar psychic powers. I also review, as a contemporary pendant to Maupassant's stories, paranormal fiction by Dr Charles Richet (under the pseudonym of Charles Epheyre).[11] In addition, I explore a so far unexamined aspect of Maupassant's fascination with the paranormal, his interest in the powers, hypnotic and perhaps psychic, of itinerant 'magnétiseurs' active in the 1880s, including in particular the Belgian Pickmann, whose impact on the Maupassantian psyche may have been as powerful as that of the more prestigious Charcot.

What figure represents most aptly the idea of the unconscious in Maupassant? This subject has been treated with ingenuity by a number of critics. I end the chapter confronting the viewpoints on this question of Jean-Louis Cabanès, Sandra Janssen and Pierre Bayard.[12] These critics perceive the Maupassantian unconscious variously as a malevolent force, personified and feared as the Horla itself; a kind of depossession of the soul; a voracious parasitism in the brain; and perhaps, most interestingly, a psychic strangeness characterized by its undecidability.

How the female herself became a figure of the unconscious in the nineteenth century is the subject of Chapter 4. She was perceived as governed by whim, caprice and emotion, and the application to her of the label 'inconsciente' ('thoughtless', 'unconscious') was a commonplace of male discourse in the late nineteenth century, both socially and in literature. It was principally medical discourse that, noting the reduced size and thus physiological inferiority of the female brain compared with that of men, stipulated in addition that her brain functioned inefficiently. I examine here the claims of hysteria experts Pierre Briquet, Jean-Louis Brachet and others[13] who theorized that extreme sensibility and impressionability meant that the female brain was subject to a stream of continuous sensations to which it unfailingly reacted, leaving her unable to 'reflect'. Her exaggerated stimulus/response mechanism also suggested that her behaviour was related to the reflex, automatic unconscious.

Another aspect of this medical doctrine was that if adolescent girls or young women, saddled with this highly reactive and exhausting cerebral function, attempted too much intellectual work, they could damage their childbearing abilities. In a woman, went the watchword, a fertile mind always led to physical sterility, and vice versa. Here, the chapter follows the migration of physiological theory into the debate over female education that characterized the 1880s and 1890s, a debate strongly coloured by the failing French birth rate[14] and male fear of women displacing men from male careers. I explore the ideas on female non-educability of philosophers such as Alfred Fouillée, of philosopher and self-appointed sociologist Jean-Marie Guyau, of Sorbonne education chair Henri Marion and Harvard education professor Edward H. Clarke (who argued in the 1870s that Vassar students were headed for procreational grief), and of the politician Henri Thulié, who stated baldly that political involvement for the female caused sterility.[15]

The chapter concludes with a discussion of four women who actively – and sometimes confusedly – agreed with medical doxa about female intellectual inferiority. These women based their reasoning on their own interpretation of ambient medical thinking and illustrated those judgements in their writing. Three of the women are novelists and one a medical doctor. In Georges de Peyrebrune, who authored some thirty-five novels, I examine an implied theory of female mental and emotional (in)capacity. I analyze the novel *Névrosée* by Daniel Lesueur (Jeanne Lapauze, née Loiseau), which paints the damning portrait of an ambitious protagonist whose overly intense education causes her hysteria, miscarriage and suicide. Georgette Déga defended a medical thesis that appears to argue the exact opposite of the message of *Névrosée*: Déga felt that a young girl's 'native' inability to concentrate could be reversed only by an intense education, preferably in mathematics, and that such an ability to concentrate would *prevent* her from becoming a hysteric. The third novelist is Rachilde (Marguerite Eymery), who reflected cogently on the powerful role the unconscious played in her ability to create fictional narratives, but who remained unconvinced that women possessed the intellectual and emotional stability to reason like men.[16]

The impact of experimental, medical hypnotism on French fiction and on thinking about dual personality and the unconscious is the subject of Chapter 5. In Paris in the mid-1880s not only Charcot at La Salpêtrière but Dr Jules Luys at La Charité hospital and Amédée Dumontpallier at La Pitié welcomed students, foreign visitors, the press, writers and fellow medical men to observe the behaviours of hypnotized subjects. In Nancy Dr Hippolyte Bernheim and his team received a similar range of visitors. One particular aspect of such behaviours that caught the attention of doctors, the newspaper-reading public and writers of fiction alike was the experimental or suggested crime, that is, a criminal action committed posthypnotically. Observers were fascinated to learn that, hypnotized and under suggestion, subjects seemed to slip into a second personality and blindly followed instructions they had been given, even if the latter were eccentric or illegal. Subjects would also carry out suggested actions in the future at the time and place prescribed, but have no memory of what they had done when returned to a normal state.

I study first how the debate over whether posthypnotic suggestion could actually override a subject's sense of right and wrong became a subject of bitter disagreement between the Charcot school and the Nancy group. The arena in which this debate took place was often the courtroom, and I examine a number of court cases, including the famous murder trial of Michel Eyraud and his hypnosis-attuned accomplice Gabrielle Bompard, which brought the full forces of medical reputations into play. Bernheim's representative at the trial, Jules Liégeois, a lawyer who strongly believed in suggested crime,[17] lost this court debate to the defenders of Salpêtrian views. But at the same time Bernheim was also insisting ever more tellingly that the multistage, Charcot-defined hysteria attack was a cultivated behaviour produced by either unconscious suggestion or actual coaching on the part of Charcot's staff.

Crime was a significant element in scientific and societal thinking in the 1880s with the creation of Alexandre Lacassagne's *Archives de l'anthropologie criminelle* (1886) and the French translations of a number of Cesare

Lombroso's works, *L'Homme criminel* (1887), *L'Homme de génie* (1889) and *La Femme criminelle et la prostituée* (1896). Fiction that highlighted dualities of personality and suggested crimes flowered during the decade, and this chapter analyzes a three-stage development of such works. I begin with *La Faustin* (1882) by Edmond de Goncourt, a kind of predecessor of the novel of dual personality presenting an actress whose roles begin to inhabit her and displace her everyday personality. An impressive number of novels juxtapose hypnosis and crime. When the hypnotist/doctor figure is evil, characters are often rescued by a benevolent figure with similar hypnotic gifts. *Jean Mornas* (1885) by Jules Claretie and *Alphonsine* (1887) by Adolphe Belot, both set in a highly medicalized frame where actual doctors are juxtaposed with fictional characters, are classics of this novel of mind control, but other second-drawer novelists provide far-fetched, often exhilarating examples of hypnosis, alter egos and crime. I end the chapter with a focus on the 1890s where, in the novels of Paul Bourget and Marcel Prévost, second personality in the hypnotized is replaced by psychological dualities, the latter a more realistic plot pivot that looks forward to the conscious versus unconscious dualism that characterizes Proust's Narrator in *À la recherche du temps perdu*.

The subject of Chapter 6 is Marcel Proust, who famously described *À la recherche du temps perdu* as 'a series of novels of the unconscious'. He was a man of prodigious intellectual abilities and at the same time someone very wary of intellectualism. An initial part of the chapter assesses Proust's position in the wave of anti-intellectualism that swept over France as the nineteenth century turned to the twentieth. Here, I investigate the attack on so-called intellectuals (or supporters of Dreyfus) led by conservative anti-Dreyfusard writers such as Maurice Barrès and Ferdinand Brunetière. The Dreyfus Affair provides one reason for the devaluation of the term 'intellectual'. But as critics such as Pierre Citti have pointed out,[18] at the turn of the century the word 'intellectual' took on, quite independently, the connotation of something not profound but rather artificial. Writers like Valéry, Gide and Proust prized not the intellectual but what was more dynamic and unpredictable, and thus authentic, something intuitive and unconscious.

The final years of the nineteenth century saw a flurry of publications focused on the connection between the unconscious and creativity, a theme that would form the centerpiece of Proustian aesthetic theory. In this segment, I investigate works focused on the capabilities of the unconscious by a philosopher/psychologist, a medical doctor, a writer and journalist, and a mathematician. Théodule Ribot's *Essai sur l'imagination créatrice* (1900) made a direct connection between the dynamic operations of the unconscious and individual creative abilities; Proust had already read with great admiration Ribot's *Les Maladies de la volonté* (1883). The medical thesis of Dr Paul Chabaneix, *Le Subconscient chez les artistes, les savants et les écrivains* (1897), polled a cross-section of artists and scientists about the role of the unconscious in their writing (writers such as Paul Adam, Sully Prudhomme and Rachilde responded). Already known as a writer in whose work the unconscious plays a key role, Remy de Gourmont reviewed Chabaneix's work very positively in his essay 'La Création subconsciente'.[19] Most interestingly, the mathematician Henri Poincaré argued strenuously for the importance of the unconscious in scientific thinking in works such as *La Valeur de la science* (1905) and *Science et méthode* (1908).[20]

It is often forgotten that Proust's early, unfinished novel *Jean Santeuil* provided a kind of mystical underpinning for the mature work, in that nature, natural scenes, sunbathed moments, etc. drew from Jean's unconscious impressions and memories of moments already lived but obscured. About nature-based inspiration, Proust wrote, 'Seule, en nous faisant sentir ce que nous avons senti une fois, [la nature] nous mène droit à quelque point de ce monde fabuleux de nos souvenirs qui est devenu le monde de la vérité'[21] ('[Nature] alone, by allowing us to feel what we have felt before, leads us directly to some point in that fabulous world of our memories which has become the world of truth.') I explore in this chapter the way the diminished but still powerful prestige of nature is preserved in Proust's discussions of certain natural scenes. Here as well, I investigate the impact that the reading of Maurice Maeterlinck's essays had on Proust, focusing in particular on a text from *L'Intelligence des fleurs* (1907), which offers a key to the steeples and trees theme in *À la recherche*, and on a chapter titled 'La Chance' from *Le Temple enseveli*[22] in which, in very Proustian style, Maeterlinck insists on the need to plumb the depths of the deep, unconscious self and describes the magical prestige and appeal of the past. For Proust, Maeterlinck's style is, very much like his own, 'irrational', by which he means instinctively, metaphorically apt, yet unexpectedly, magically allusive.

Memory, the involuntary and the unconscious, elements so integral to Proust's own aesthetic system, were viewed by at least one late-century psycho-philosophical school not only as specifically incapable of generating creativity but as part of a syndrome that pathologized the individual who depended on them. In the preface to the second edition of his authoritative philosophy thesis, *L'Automatisme psychologique*, Pierre Janet noted that his study was focused on identifying, in human mental activity, the difference between the creative and the non-creative, the opposition between the inventive and the 'reproductive' or automatic. Towards the end of the same work, he analyzes examples of this automatism, each labelled an 'inferior mental activity': lack of attention or lack of concentration; instinct; passion; habit, to which he equates memory (463). Although Proust would have agreed with this negative categorization of habitual, conscious memory, involuntary memory and these other 'inferior' activities of the mind constitute fundamental pillars of creativity in the aesthetic theory rolled out in Proust's *À la recherche du temps perdu*. Interestingly, Proust's novel was brought to Janet's attention in the 1920s, and he judged the work to be pathologically emotional.

Even in 1914, a year after the publication of *Du Côté de chez Swann*, Théodule Ribot noted that many doctors and psychologists still denied the existence of 'affective' (involuntary) memory. When, therefore, Proust defines the essence of his creative position as the distinction between the voluntary (unproductive) and the involuntary (authentic and rich, because arriving from the unconscious), his is not only an aesthetic statement but a defiant volley in an ongoing medico-psychological debate. For Proust, the unconscious is what is deep, behind, within, beyond. Above all, what arrives involuntarily from an unconscious layer of the mind bears with it an imperative: its obscure message must be converted into an equivalent, perhaps first a bodily, mimetic gesture, then a metaphor, and finally language. The language of everyday reason and logic is helpless to effect such expression. The unconscious is a set of deeply personal, individual structures in the mind of each of us, but without articulation and elucidation they remain forever mute.

CHAPTER I

Before Freud
The Quarrel of the Unconscious in Late Nineteenth-Century France

Works such as Henri Ellenberger's monumental *Discovery of the Unconscious*[1] have attempted to document the history of thinking about the unconscious across European countries, especially from about the late eighteenth century forward. The ambition of this chapter is more circumscribed – it is an attempt to understand the 'French unconscious' before Freud – and even so the task has not been straightforward. I have been surprised not so much by the dissension, among French philosophers, doctors, psychologists and psychiatrists, as they tried to define the nature of the unconscious, as by the fact that not a few of them refused to credit the idea of an unconscious at all.

One current but incorrect assumption, for example, is that before Freud, the unconscious, for philosophers, designated what was not conscious, what was outside of consciousness. On the contrary, we will see that for many philosophers and the psychologists who followed their lead, all thought was by definition conscious, and it was thus ludicrous to speak of an unconscious. Others felt that the unconscious was a place of reflex activity, repeated automatic impulses, not a space where instincts and impressions might interact dynamically. How was one to account, I asked perhaps naively, for the movement from this science-based questioning or outright denial of the unconscious to a statement like that of Proust, who pictured *À la recherche du temps perdu* as 'a set of novels of the unconscious'?[2]

What seemed especially intriguing was that doubts about or denials of the existence of the unconscious were being voiced at the same time as intensive French research on hypnotism and hysteria demonstrated that there existed various kinds of second mental states and divided personalities. One objective of this initial chapter would therefore be to track the high points in the debate over the existence and nature of the unconscious until the early years of the twentieth century. In this debate Pierre Janet, a doctor of philosophy and a medical doctor, played a significant role.

Clearly, there was a change in perspective on the unconscious around 1900; a number of psychologists and some doctors, artists and writers began to express resistance against the positivist belief in the decisive roles in human mental life of reason and willpower. Works such as *Essai sur l'imagination créatrice* (1900) by Théodule Ribot and *Le Subconscient chez les artistes, les savants et les écrivains* (1897) by Paul Chabaneix took the idea of the unconscious powers of the mind in a decisive, new, creative direction. Adepts of the new unconscious began to be referred to as anti-intellectual by old-school positivists.

Perhaps in part because of cultural adherence to the Gallic rule of clarity and precision, 'ce qui se conçoit bien s'énonce clairement' ('what is clearly thought out will be clearly expressed'), the idea of a part of the mind shuttered off from conscious oversight and decision-making was neither appetizing nor logical for some. This traditional view of consciousness was very cut and dried: 'everything psychic is a priori conscious and hence ... an unconscious mental process is an absurdity and a contradiction.'[3]

Most critics seem to agree that nineteenth-century interest in the unconscious came late, if not reluctantly, to France. Yet it seems somewhat simplistic to write off the second half of the nineteenth century as dominated by reason and willpower, while the automatic, the reflex and the spontaneous were labelled as manifestations of mental alienation. Jacqueline Carroy suggests that interest in the unconscious came obliquely via an appreciation of mental duality, which one could observe in somnambulists, mediums and hysterics. This convergence she calls a culture of the unconscious.[4] Lancelot Whyte argues that the French paid little attention to the unconscious until the 1870s, decades after the Germans and the English. He points to the fact that it was a Swiss francophone, the philosopher and diarist Henri-Frédéric Amiel, who is credited with introducing the noun 'inconscient', in the sense of what is not conscious, into the French language.[5] Musing about how dreams transform straightforward realities, Amiel wrote in 1861: 'Le développement de notre nature inconsciente suit les lois astronomiques du Ptolémé. Tout est changement, cycle, épicycle et métamorphose.'[6] ('The development of our unconscious nature is subject to Ptolemy's laws of astronomy. All is change, cycle, epicycle and metamorphosis.')

Eduard von Hartmann's study *Die Philosophie des Unbewussten* (1869) attracted great interest when translated into French as *La Philosophie de l'inconscient* in 1877, but in a revised edition of the *Dictionnaire de l'Académie française*, published one year later, the term 'inconscient' is still listed as an adjective only.[7] By way of contrast, by the 1770s, men such as

J. H. Fichte, Schelling, Kant, Goethe and Schiller were using the term as a noun.[8] The philosopher Ernst Platner is widely credited with the first use of the term *Unbewusstsein* (unconscious) in his *Philosophical Aphorisms* (1776).[9] Still, Anne Harrington argues that most of the interest in the 'double brain', that is, in its physical and psychic duality, was centred in France in the 1860–1900 period, rather than in England and Germany,[10] and one of the potential dualities that was increasingly proposed was certainly the conscious/unconscious divide. Among French thinkers of the early nineteenth century, Maine de Biran was one of the few who articulated the notion that we unconsciously acquire affective impressions that, he felt, our fully conscious mind might normally repress. He spoke of the human being having two modes of existence in terms which suggest that, for Biran, the unconscious was not purely organic but that there was a psychic element to it:

> Dans l'un [de ces modes] nous vivons, sentons et agissons avec la conscience ou le sentiment intime de notre existence, de nos impressions, et de nos actes, tandis que dans l'autre nous vivons, sentons et agissons, souvent par les mêmes organes, et en apparence de la même manière, sans conscience, sans *moi*, sans souvenir, et en demeurant comme étrangers dans l'un de ces états ou modes d'existence, à tout ce que nous avons éprouvé, senti, ou fait dans l'autre.[11]
>
> In one [of these modes] we live, feel and act conscious of, or with the intimate sensation of, our impressions, our acts, whereas in the other we live, feel and act, often using the same organs, and apparently in the same way, unconsciously, without our *moi*, without memory, remaining as strangers, in one of these states or modes of existence, to everything we have experienced, felt or done in the other.

Anne Devarieux (82) notes that Janet saw in Biran a precursor in the field of experimental psychology and that Freud cites him in his *Interpretation of Dreams*.

Before turning to what I have called the 'Quarrel of the Unconscious' itself,[12] let us examine briefly a few key concepts and theories that relate to the emergence of a belief in an unconscious function of the mind. For my part, it is in the most general sense of 'what is not conscious' that I will employ the term 'unconscious'.

1.1 Reflex Action, Unconscious Cerebration, Subliminal Self

The concept of a reflex response centred in the spine was not a French discovery, but it would have an important impact on French theorizing about the unconscious.[13] The idea was developed separately by the Englishman Marshall Hall and the German Johannes Müller in the early 1830s,[14] well before the research of French physicians such as Jules Luys and Valentin Magnan, whom we will discuss shortly. Although Hall carefully assigns reflex action strictly to the spinal column, his contention that the brain was not the overseer/regulator of such action was a shock to many physiologists.[15] In 1855, Thomas Laycock became chair of medicine at the University of Edinburgh. Already in 1840, at age twenty-eight, he had begun to speak of unconscious cerebral activity, an idea that had far less immediate impact than the discovery of medical hypnotism, but major implications for the shift in understanding of the unconscious as the century advanced. In 1845, Laycock followed up with an article[16] in which he argued that because the centres in the brain are directly connected to the spinal column, those centres must be subject to automatic, reflex action similar to that noted in the spine. This insistence on the fact that the complete spinal/cerebral/nervous system was subject to reflex, automatic activity opened the way for a different view of the mind. According to such a theory, there now existed a cerebral area that was outside the purview of consciousness. In Marcel Gauchet's view, there was no turning back: if automatism and reflex action were part of a continuous physical chain that ended at the brain, the absolute role of consciousness and willpower in guiding human action was irremediably called into question.

Conscious willpower, according to the traditional view, had been seen as the instigator of all mental activity, and thus when 'cérébration inconsciente' ('unconscious cerebration') found its way into French medical terminology, there was a reluctance to admit that some part of the mind acted autonomously. Instead, such mental activity is described, reassuringly, as a useful helpmate to consciousness, but at the same time, there is a warning: keep the unconscious under tight control. In the entry on delirium in the *Dictionnaire encyclopédique des sciences médicales*, authors Antoine Ritti and Benjamin Ball point out, very much like Dr Valentin Magnan will do, the proximity of the automatic and reflex to the pathological:

> Il existe un certain nombre de phénomènes de l'activité cérébrale ... qui constituent ce qu'on a appelé la *cérébration inconsciente* et se distinguent des phénomènes cérébraux conscients et volontaires en ceci qu'ils s'accomplissent *automatiquement* ...
>
> L'automatisme cérébral est un mode d'activité intellectuelle qui vient en aide au travail conscient et lui prête un secours des plus précieux; mais il faut éviter soigneusement de lui laisser prendre le dessus, sa prépondérance serait l'anarchie, ce serait le délire.[17]

> There exist a certain number of phenomena within cerebral activity ... which constitute what has been called *unconscious cerebration*; they are distinct from conscious and voluntary cerebral phenomena in that they take place automatically ...
>
> Cerebral automatism is a mode of intellectual activity that helps in conscious work, affording it precious assistance; but one must carefully avoid allowing it to take over, for its preponderance would be anarchy, it would be delirium.

Michel Foucault's discussion of a radical change in the nineteenth-century understanding of madness provides a useful context to this expressed concern about automatism and reflex action. Foucault credits publications by Dr Jules Baillarger around 1850 with creating a new psychiatry no longer focused, like that of the *aliénistes*, on identifiable manifestations of madness such as hallucinations or false beliefs, but simply on the presence of the voluntary and the involuntary in human action. Behaviours involving the automatic, the reflex, the spontaneous, the instinctive, the intuitive and the involuntary are potentially demented. And thus the great change, as Foucault saw it, was that mental normalcy and abnormalcy would henceforth be identified using an axis of voluntary/involuntary, in which relative distance from a norm of voluntary behaviour would be a measure of the abnormal. Thus, Foucault reasoned, all human behaviour became a psychiatric subject.[18]

It was in the mid-1870s that Laycock, William Carpenter and Henry Maudsley duelled over credit for discovery of unconscious cerebration. Laycock, generally viewed as its discoverer, published a memoir on the question in the year of his death, 1876, with a title intended to set the record straight, 'Reflex, automatic and unconscious cerebration. A history and a criticism'.[19] Two years earlier, in 1874, William Carpenter had published his *Principles of Mental Physiology* in which chapter 13 was titled 'Of unconscious cerebration'.[20] He argued there in part that the cerebrum could act upon reflex impressions transmitted to it and develop intellectual results, 'without any consciousness on our parts' (515). Consciousness, he wrote, was still thought of by many as the basis of all strictly mental activity (516); the position of philosophers was that consciousness was a whole, a unit, the total of everything we have ever known, and thus consciousness, as we have noted, contains the unconscious. Perhaps Pierre Janet's refusal to admit the existence of the unconscious – a subject to which we will return – can be related to this philosophical concept and to his academic qualifications as a professional philosopher. Carpenter concluded that, just as many centres in the body have reflex actions taking place without mental instigation, so the brain works on impressions and sensations sent to it, both during sleep and when the attention is focused elsewhere. 'The best judgements', he wrote, 'are often mentally delivered, in difficult cases, by the unconscious resolution of the difficulties' (531). Carpenter seems to open the debate to the notion that the mind has some capacity for unconscious activity that is dynamic, independent and creative.

What was the French reaction to Carpenter and Laycock? A review article from 1876 speaks to the tenor of the times.[21] In spite of the fact that the experience is common to many, Léon Dumont refutes as conjecture Carpenter's idea that unconscious activity finds solutions to problems or creates new ideas. He seems particularly affronted by the suggestion that unconscious activity can develop intellectual ideas totally unknown to the self. Another reflection in Dumont's text situates it clearly in its mid-1870s context: he suggests that unconscious activity in the brain might be related to that part of the cerebrum being starved for blood (30).

The concept of unconscious cerebration seems to have been both poorly understood and intellectually unwelcome. Writing as late as 1910, and in spite of the fact that Carpenter had demonstrated that unconscious activity could produce solutions to problems left unsolved, Isador Coriat, cited in part earlier, claimed that unconscious cerebration was exclusively physiological:

> all subconscious manifestations, such as hysteria, automatic writing, the subconscious solution of mathematical problems, are merely pure nerve processes unaccompanied by any thought whatsoever. According to Münsterberg, the subconscious is not psychical at all; he would interpret it as a physiological process.[22]

One encounters the term 'cérébration' in French medical and fictional texts, though its meaning appears subject to slippage. Charcot and Paul Richer used the expression 'unconscious cerebration' in an 1883 article they published in English (Gauchet, 119), and Paul Chabaneix uses it in his volume on the subconscious (13, 41). There was also a scattering of court cases where the term surfaced. One doctor defends the accused, Ulysse, by arguing that he was unaware of committing a crime. What did this mean? His actions were simply '[des] scènes d'automatisme et de cérébration inconsciente'. The impressive terminology had its effect on the judge. Ulysse was acquitted.[23] Similarly, Dr Paul Garnier was convinced that a young man accused of robbery had acted in a state of unconscious automatism. He wrote, 'C'est aux manifestations de cette cérébration inconsciente que nous devons ... accorder le premier rang.'[24] ('We must ... accord greatest importance to the manifestations of this unconscious cerebration.')

When writers of fiction used the term 'cerebration' its original meaning was often obscured or twisted. In the novel *L'Automne d'une femme* by Marcel Prévost,[25] Dr Daumier (possibly based on Pierre Janet) diagnoses the cause of a young woman's depressive decline as 'la consomption de la vie par le dedans, sous l'influence d'une cérébration' (294) ('a life consumed from the inside, under the influence of a cerebration'). The term seems to mean here an unconscious secret. What the woman needs to articulate, to return to health, and in this Daumier helps her, is the fact that she loves a young man who does not return her affections. In another novel, *Suggestion*,[26] overwrought with references to hysteria, hypnotism, second states, dual personality, etc., the term's meaning is deflected even further. A friend of the main character, Lebarrois, suggests that he suffers from a 'cérébralité intermédiaire' (145): here a version of the word seems to mean a half-conscious state that might lead him eventually to possess special psychical powers. Later, as Lebarrois declines mentally, an obsessional idea he cannot get out of his head is called 'une cérébration stupide' (335).

'Subliminal self' was an expression popularized by Frederic Myers, whom some dictionaries present as one of the non-spiritualist members of the British Society for Psychical Research, founded at Cambridge University in 1882. The phrase denoted initially 'that part of the personality which is normally beneath the "threshold" (*limen*) separating consciousness from unconsciousness'.[27] But like some philosophers, certain schools of psychology with a physiological focus could not accept the idea of an unconscious under any name. The Harvard psychologist Arthur H. Pierce attacked the concept of a subliminal self by attempting to argue that most instances of apparent secondary consciousness were caused by cerebral pathway clogging. Other so-called subliminal phenomena were instances of barely remembered events reusing nerve paths that had become unfamiliar.[28] The expression 'subliminal self' had no more afterlife than 'unconscious cerebration', but it is interesting to consider its development in Frederic Myer's thought. In his posthumous *Human Personality and Its Survival of Bodily Death* (1903), Myers pictured the subliminal self, almost in a Jungian, collective sense, as part of a vast psychic reservoir not bound up with the earthly life of the individual human being.

Terminology regarding the unconscious was for a long time fluid. A number of researchers followed Pierre Janet in using the term 'subconscient'.[29] In his *Essai sur l'imagination créatrice*, the psychologist Théodule Ribot waffles on terminology: sometimes he speaks of the 'inconscient', sometimes of the 'subconscient' and at other moments of the 'moi subliminal'. Not surprisingly, 'subliminal self' was an expression appreciated by spiritualists. The astronomer and prominent spiritualist Camille Flammarion notes in his memoirs that in his youth he felt he was in contact with the spirit of Galileo. As a much older man, he reflects that this type of communication must result from auto-suggestions produced by 'our subconscious being, our subliminal self'.[30] And he adds that for the spiritualist, there must exist beyond the human unconscious some additional occulted power at play. Myers' lesson regarding the subliminal self was thus not entirely forgotten.

1.2 The Double Brain and Cerebral Topography

In her study of cerebral duality, Anne Harrington reminds us of a perspective on brain physiology that also influenced thinking about an unconscious part of the mind. She stresses that various theories about cerebral topography showed a willingness 'to envision the mind as somehow spatially congruent with the brain'.[31] Was the unconscious thus locatable, and if not, could its functioning be explained in physical terms? The liberation of a second personality, usually through hypnotism, but also occurring naturally, as in the famous case of Félida, a woman with multiple personalities, dovetailed with late nineteenth-century research on the topography of the brain, research that was accelerated by Dr Paul Broca's discovery that the seat of speech was in the left frontal cerebral lobe. In 1875 Charcot delivered a set of lectures entitled *Leçons sur les localisations dans les maladies du cerveau*. The studies of Dr Jules Luys related to brain structure were not atypical of the period; they tended to convert physical characteristics of the organ into moral or psychological characteristics of the individual. In an 1879 essay, he writes that although the unity of personality is guaranteed by the physical links between the cerebral hemispheres, the asymmetry and unequal weights of the brain lobes suggest that 'l'être humain [est] divisé en deux sous individualités indépendantes et insubornées'[32] ('a human being [is] divided into two independent and insubordinate sub-individuals').

A thesis by a student of Luys, Gabriel Descourtis, *Du fractionnement des opérations cérébrales et en particulier de leur dédoublement dans les psychopathies*, follows up on this reasoning, demonstrating how brain structure could be used to explain deviant behaviour, an idea that was easily superimposed onto the idea of a mind divided into consciousness (good) holding in check the unconscious (instinctive, criminal).[33] Because of the splitting of brain functions, one could imagine competing functions, or dysfunctions caused by competition.

If blood stopped flowing or its flow was reduced to certain parts of the brain, Descourtis reasoned, irrigation was arrested and those parts became non-functional. And an oversupply of blood in one sector or another created an overactivity, 'un état d'éréthisme de tel ou tel groupe de cellules, qui devient par cela même un foyer d'activité morbide' (10) ('a state of erethism of one or another group of cells, which thus becomes a place of morbid activity'). Dreams were explained in a similar manner. After a day of work, the brain like the body was tired and we therefore slept. A dream happens when certain brain cells become irritated by an afflux of blood, while the others, half shut down after strenuous daytime activities, are 'resting'. Thus dreams themselves are a discordant effect, a product of 'imbalance', which sets them on the path to the pathological.

This speculation, a metaphorical modelling of the physical without the ability to obtain physical data, Descourtis employs as a natural transition for the examination of special psychopathic states (12). He mentions individuals who suffer from 'la lésion de la volonté', that is, they understand and recognize that there is something they must do, but they don't have the willpower to make themselves do it. Conversely, there are those who find the temptation to do something they should not do irresistible; they cannot prevent themselves. He connects this operational splitting, or competition within the brain, to the activities of certain criminals who cannot prevent themselves from committing an act they know to be morally wrong. For his part, thesis director Luys proposed that cerebral dissociation might be the origin of the famous Félida's dual personality.[34] The view of her doctor, Eugène Azam, was that individual activity of the cerebral hemispheres also involved the question of brain nutrition. He believed that the onset of a second personality in Félida was caused by an impediment, blocking the flow of blood to one hemisphere and temporarily cancelling access to the memories stored there.[35]

The 'insubordination' of two functions can create aberrant behaviour. Such affected individuals are the unbalanced, 'les déséquilibrés', contends Luys (*Études sur le dédoublement*, 25), and this Luys imagines in physical terms. In a reversal of what is healthy, the right lobe of the unbalanced person weighs more than the left; the right lobe 'a absorbé à lui seul la sève et l'activité nutritive de l'encéphale' (27) ('has itself absorbed the vigour and nutritional activity of the brain').

We will see throughout this study the research of Dr Jules Luys constantly downgraded, partly because of the eccentric nature of much of that work – his experiments in thought transfer between hysterics, for example – but also because he employed Dr Gérard Encausse, alias Papus, founder of the modern version of the esoteric Martinism movement, who had already published a number of occultist works even before he received his medical degree in 1894. But it is also possible, somewhat paradoxically, to see Luys as a perfectly rational scientist determined, like his materially oriented generation, to understand and explain psychic phenomena in a concrete manner without preconceptions as to the origin of the forces at play:

> Luys n'avait rien d'un farceur. Il était au contraire l'éminent représentant français de la réflexologie la plus rigoureuse, et un positiviste convaincu, décidé à expulser par l'usage obstiné de la méthode expérimentale toute velléité de spiritualisme dans l'appréhension des phénomènes mentaux.[36]

> Luys was no jokester. On the contrary, he was the eminent French representative of the most rigourous reflexology and a convinced positivist determined to expunge, by the dogged application of the experimental method, any vague attraction to spiritualism in the apprehension of mental phenomena.

Marcel Gauchet does in fact credit Luys with an early (French) recognition of reflex activity in the brain, quoting texts such as this:

> il y a parmi les phénomènes de l'activité cérébrale toute une série de manifestations tant normales que pathologiques qui sont de nature *réflexe.* [Elles] sont en tous points comparables aux manifestations similaires dont la moelle épinière est le siège, et ... elles s'exercent d'une façon automatique et la plupart du temps en dehors de la volonté et de la *personnalité consciente.*[37]

> among the phenomena of cerebral activity there are a whole series of manifestations, both normal and pathological, that are of a *reflex* nature. [They] are, in every way, comparable to similar manifestations centered in the spinal column and ... they function in an automatic way and, most often, beyond the will of our *conscious personality.*

This text is from 1874, but, strangely, it refers not to Laycock or Carpenter but rather solely to articles on reflex action by the French doctor Ernest Onimus. Luys also made the daring suggestion, for his time, that the influence of conscious personality and willpower on our speech was not at all as absolute as one might think (Gauchet, 114).

But the question of the bilateral potential of the brain remained: were its two hemispheres functionally independent? Hemi-anaesthesia was a fairly significant aspect of Charcot's work, as was the transfer of physical sensations or affective moods from one side of the body to the other. Assessing the numerous 1880s experiments in hemi-hypnosis, Anne Harrington has shown that many simply suppressed the activity of one hemisphere. But she has resuscitated some very interesting research on this question, which shows that Dr Amédée Dumontpallier and his student Edgar Bérillon conducted more sophisticated experiments.[38] A typical example is the following. Dumontpallier plants two quite different suggestions in a hypnotized subject's mind. In one ear, he whispers that she should imagine a tranquil, relaxing country scene. With that ear blocked, the researcher then suggests in the other ear that she is witnessing a bloody wild boar hunt. The result is an expression of fear on one side of the subject's face and one of contentment on the other (Harrington, *Double*, 193).

An intriguing subset of this question of brain topography, nutrition and the unconscious involves the disagreement, in France at least, over the role played by the cerebellum ('cervelet' in French). One has the sense that certain medical men saw the difference between 'superior brain functions' and 'inferior brain functions' translating itself into a three-dimensional, physical hierarchy. The 'cervelet' is the back-most, dorsal part of the brain, tucked beneath the two hemispheres and in close connection with the spinal column. Although researchers had already determined that an important function of the cerebellum was control of motor functions, the phrenologist Franz Joseph Gall was famous for his claim that it was the organ of the reproductive instinct. David Ferrier's *The Functions of the Brain* (1876) was known and discussed in France as soon as it was published,[39] and his conclusion was also that the cerebellum was the likely seat of conditions such as satyriasis and nymphomania. As late as 1892, according to one disciple of Gall, the cerebellum was understood to be the seat of 'the amative function'.[40] But already in 1889 the psychiatrist Henri Beaunis had denounced this residue of Gallism, observing that the sexual drive subsists even when the cerebellum is absent or has been removed.[41]

Nevertheless, the sexualized cerebellum caught the imagination of writers of fiction, particularly in the fin-de-siècle period, and we encounter references to it as the home of erotic instincts in Huysmans and, most interestingly, in the female novelist Georges de Peyrebrune, who, writing in the same year Ferrier's study appeared, attributed the low sex drive of women like herself to an undernourished cerebellum. I will explore further Peyrebrune's essay on this question, *Les Vierges de feu et la décroissance de la population*, in Chapter 4, which examines the female and the unconscious. Huysmans' hero Des Esseintes wears himself out with sex, but when he recovers his forces, 'soon his cerebellum re-awakened and called him back to action'.[42]

Certain other examples of brain research, or rather theorizing, were just as fanciful as what writers like Huysmans and Peyrebrune could imagine. In 1885, Dr Valentin Magnan delivered a paper in which he divided degenerates into four categories according to what he imagined to be the locus in the brain of their sexual thinking.[43] Those who had the most ethereal, idealized images of the loved one were 'les cérébraux antérieurs', those cerebralists whose reflections on love took place in the frontal portion of the brain. Their thinking was pathological but harmless. At the opposite end were the spinal, in whom the erotic trigger, and orgasm, were simply a spinal reflex without ratiocination. Next to them, one step up the spine, were the 'spinaux cérébraux postérieurs', individuals barely able to control their sexual instincts because of the positioning of their thought, right at the cerebellum. The explanation of their behaviour was the following: '[La région cérébrale postérieure ...] n'est autre que le substratum organique des appétits et des instincts, que le siège de l'automatisme cérébral'.[44] (['The posterior cerebral area ...] is nothing less than the organic substratum of appetites and instinct, it is the locus of cerebral automatism'.) In this work of an influential psychiatrist such as Magnan, therefore, we find confirmed the suggestion that the frontal part of the brain is reserved for ideas and that its organic, automatic, reflex activity – in other words what passes for its unconscious action – is centred in its lowest, back-most part.

1.3 Hallucination and Hypnotism

Much has been written about early nineteenth-century dissension regarding the nature of hallucination. It seemed clear enough that because hallucination was a verifiable feature of the behaviour of the insane, the phenomenon must in itself be pathological. Yet some extreme positions developed in connection with this argument. In what one critic has described as the first foray into retrospective medicine, Socrates (because of his visions) and Pascal (because of his hallucinations) were declared insane by Dr Louis-Francisque Lélut. While some congratulated Lélut on the 'courage' of his position, other doctors such as Brierre de Boismont mocked such conclusions.[45]

The idea of drug-induced hallucinations was introduced by Dr Jacques-Joseph Moreau in his *Du hachisch et de l'aliénation mentale* (1845). Moreau believed it was imperative to understand from the inside the mental state of the insane. Writers like Balzac, Gautier, Baudelaire, Nerval and Alphonse Karr sampled hashish and opium alongside medical men[46] during the meetings of the Club des Hachischins on the Île Saint-Louis in the 1840s. The juxtaposition of hallucination, mental alienation and the exalted inspirational state of poets and creative writers did much to characterize genius, for a long period in the nineteenth century, as a form of madness. Writing, it is true, about monomanias, Moreau captures the bizarre, eccentric, even apparently deranged mind states of artists, musicians and writers in moments of inspiration. He quotes, in English, what a British author has said about such individuals: 'They are certainly cracked; but the crack let in light.'[47]

We will see, in the next chapter, that the hallucination played a significant role in what have been diagnosed as Gustave Flaubert's epileptic seizures and that he was questioned closely by Hippolyte Taine on these attacks as Taine researched the question of non-standard mind states for *De l'intelligence*. Our object in that chapter will be to examine how these visions and the emotional aura that surrounded them are converted and deployed in Flaubert's writing style and become a radiant but perhaps not quite conscious aspect of his prose.

At mid-nineteenth century, the Faculty of Medicine at the University of Edinburgh found itself a powerful force in European medicine. Before Laycock had become chair there, James Braid, a Scottish surgeon who had studied at Edinburgh, published a study on hypnosis[48] that was to influence profoundly medical studies, psychological research and, as we will see, the popular novel, particularly in France, for the rest of the century. Never mind that the trigger for Braid's thinking was attendance at a few stage performances by the itinerant Swiss magnetizer Charles Lafontaine. Braid examined onstage some of Lafontaine's hypnotized subjects and confirmed for himself that they were in an altered mental state. Intrigued, he subsequently learned to hypnotize patients himself and was able to employ hypnotism on a number of them for therapeutic purposes.

If Braid can be said to have rescued hypnotism from its origins in mesmerism and animal magnetism, and from its history of having been declared charlatanism by medical commissions, hypnotism required an active apostle. It found that in Jean-Martin Charcot, whose astute decision was to connect hypnosis to the treatment of the most visible and spectacular of 1880s maladies, hysteria.[49] Hypnotism induced multistage behaviours similar to hysterical attacks, he contended; thus, by employing hypnosis doctors could better understand the nature and treatment of hysteria itself. Moreover, he argued, only the most serious of hysterics could be hypnotized, and for this reason the practice must remain firmly within the exclusive province of doctors. Charcot's success in winning over the medical community, given hypnotism's history, was a stunning tour de force.[50]

Fascination with hypnotism was at its peak during the 1880s in France. The rivalry between La Salpêtrière and its hysteria theories and the work of the Nancy school under Hippolyte Bernheim was a very public phenomenon, written about widely. And the medical community was unsuccessful in its bid to rescue hypnotism from high-profile, sideshow magnetizers. The latter flourished and not a few lay observers remarked that the doctors had learned their techniques from the magnetizers they were trying to vilify.

If many of Charcot's experiments and those of Dumontpallier and Bérillon demonstrated the brain's apparent functional asymmetry, another specific lesson of hypnotism created unease in the public mind and would inspire a long list of fictional texts. Posthypnotic suggestion was presented as a kind of mind control exercised over hypnotized individuals who could be instructed to carry out strange acts sometimes long after the suggestion had been planted in their minds. These suggestions appeared to show that each of us had the potential for a second, darker personality – perhaps it was an image of the unconscious itself – that could be directed into any number of dubious acts. We will see in Chapter 3 on Maupassant and Chapter 5 on the popular novel the extent to which fascination with this aspect of hypnotism permeated 1880s French society and preoccupied writers of fiction.

1.4 The Quarrel of the Unconscious

If one were to focus on just one of the seminal French manifestations of interest in the unconscious that preceded that decade of hypnotism and dualities, the 1880s, it would have to be the text of Hippolyte Taine, *De l'intelligence*.[51] There, in the very first pages, the theme of psychic 'dédoublement' ('splitting') is broached in telling language. For Taine, the explanation of human intelligence goes well beyond an exploration of the characteristics of the conscious mind:

> Dans cette recherche, la conscience, qui est notre principal instrument, ne suffit pas à l'état ordinaire. (I, 3)
>
> La plus grande partie de nous-mêmes reste hors de nos prises et . . . le moi visible est incomparablement plus petit que le moi obscur. (I, 7)

> In this search, consciousness, which is our principal instrument, is of no help in ordinary circumstances.
>
> The greatest part of ourselves remains beyond our grasp and . . . the visible self is incomparably smaller than our obscure self.

He predicts, rightly and prophetically, that in the years ahead dreams, somnambulism, hypnotism, illusions and hallucinations (even morbid ones) will all have to be explored to understand the human mind. Spiritualism itself offers objects of examination for the researcher. The automatic writing of the medium while she focuses her conscious mind on other subjects, even conversing with others, demonstrates 'cette pluralité foncière du moi' (I, 16), and provides a firm image of 'deux personnes morales juxtaposées dans le même cerveau' (I, 17).[52]

To a large extent, the doctors who practised hypnotism on hysterics and who wrote about it and demonstrated it to the public were the source of public skepticism about the nature of modern hysteria because, in order to establish hysteria as a historical phenomenon, they revived, but then constantly discredited, stories of demonic possession.[53] Charcot's interest in the baroque and in medieval demonology and possessions was public knowledge. Already in 1882, a Maupassant character had voiced suspicions about the master's expertise because of his attraction to religious explanations, saying, 'ne pouvant toujours comprendre ce qu'il voit, [Charcot] se souvient trop peut-être des explications ecclésiastiques des mystères'[54] ('not always able to understand what he is witnessing, [Charcot] is perhaps overly reminded of ecclesiastical explanations of these mysteries'). In 1887, Charcot would publish jointly with his student Paul Richer *Les Démoniaques dans l'art*,[55] a study of artistic depictions of demonic possessions. Charcot's fascination with the visual diagnosis of hysteria has been pointed out frequently, but it is less well known that his attraction to hallucinations and images of possession may spring from an 1853 experiment with hashish in which, recounting his visions, he set language aside and began simply to sketch what he had seen.[56]

One can justifiably argue, I believe, that preoccupation with the second personality seen in hysterics, and freed up in other individuals via hypnotism, retarded French interest in and acceptance of the main tenets of Freudian theory. For many, any tangible demonstration of psychic duality actually revealed '*the* unconscious', and in that sense, the hypnotized state *was* the unconscious. A similar exemplar was the case of the second state of mediums, cited, as we have seen, by Taine: while engaged in an automatic writing exercise, a medium might well converse normally with those around her, oblivious to her own writing. She too was exhibiting a duality, the conscious and unconscious states. More important, however, in the minds of certain French doctors and psychologists, the submissive behaviours and apparently reduced faculties of hypnotized individuals supported the view that the unconscious was far inferior to the rational state.

In an important article dating from 1889, Dr Jules Héricourt wrote that the hypnotic state consists of:

> une réduction, une diminution, une paralysie – une inhibition comme on dit aujourd'hui – de l'activité cérébrale supérieure qui constitue la personnalité consciente, et, parallèlement, en un grossissement, une excitation de l'activité cérébrale inconsciente.[57]
>
> a reduction, a diminution, a paralysis – an inhibition as we say today – of the superior cerebral activity which constitutes the conscious personality and, in parallel, of an increase, an excitation of unconscious cerebral activity.

The consequence, according to Héricourt, was this: since the unconscious state is 'inferior' to consciousness, if an individual is in a state of full mental equilibrium, the portion of brain activities that is unconscious is as limited as possible (ibid., 268).

As well as an overview of the unconscious question, Héricourt's article was a review of Pierre Janet's influential philosophy thesis, *L'Automatisme psychologique*, which had appeared some months previously.[58] The days of belief in cerebral duality – that is, that the two brain hemispheres were each home to a separate personality, or home one to consciousness and the other to the unconscious – are over, notes Héricourt. Yet the 'proof' offered against topographical duality of the brain, if arithmetically logical, is somewhat surprising: it is that some individuals demonstrate two, three or four personalities.

Héricourt's essay strongly reinforces the negativity attached to the unconscious. That is, the unconscious is 'of obviously inferior quality' to its colleague consciousness, and the article is full of references to the way hypnotism shows this to be true. A reference to Théodule Ribot's *Les Maladies de la personnalité*[59] is employed to argue that the influence of the unconscious on the conscious mind can lead to maladies of the personality. (This may well be true, but if so, as we will see in Chapter 6 on Proust, Ribot's understanding of the unconscious and its capabilities had undergone profound changes by the time he published his *Essai sur l'imagination créatrice* in 1900.)

Héricourt reveals the impact Janet's philosophy thesis has made, not only at the Sorbonne but in medical circles. However, his assessment is not entirely uncritical for he notes the overemphasis in Janet's study on the linkage of the subconscious to malady:

> comme [Janet] conclut surtout d'observations faites sur des hystériques et sur des sujets hypnotisés, il est fort possible que les personnalités secondaires qu'il a pu évoquer soient, comme on le verra par la suite, le résultat artificiel de l'expérimentation ou le produit naturel de la maladie (259).
>
> Given that [Janet] bases his conclusions mainly on observations regarding hysterics and hypnotized subjects, it is quite possible that the second personalities he has produced are, as we will see, the artificial result of experimentation or the natural product of malady.

This criticism that Janet's patients were in fact afflicted individuals on whom one could not base predictions about a healthy unconscious would be leveled at him for most of his career.

In defending himself against such accusations a few years later (in the preface he provided for the translation of the American Joseph Jastrow's work *La Subconscience*[60]), an irritated Janet admits that he indeed was investigating sick and abnormal subjects in *L'Automatisme psychologique*, that the term 'subconscient' was used in that context, and that it is unrelated to the unconscious, whose existence and creative potential he will continue to mock. Janet's reluctance to admit mistakes was well known. It was only in 1923 that he averred that Bernheim's theory about Charcotian hysteria was correct: 'L'hypnotisme à trois phases de Charcot, comme M. Bernheim l'a très bien remarqué dès 1884, n'a jamais été qu'un hypnotisme de culture, c'est lui qui a gagné la bataille.'[61] ('Charcot's three-stage hypnotism, as Bernheim noted as early as 1884, was never more than a cultivated hypnotism, it is he who won the battle.')

Morbid or normal, the duality of the human psychic activity is recognized, and it is the hysteria/hypnosis conflation that best demonstrates that duality. But where immoral actions are concerned, insists Héricourt, the conscious personality is always capable of resistance and of controlling the unconscious. Posthypnotic suggestions cannot lead to the commission of real crimes. If hypnotized individuals are told to commit a robbery or murder, they will follow up only if their conscious mind knows that it is an experiment. There were widely differing views on this subject, which we will explore in detail in Chapter 5.

A study from 1892, *La Philosophie de l'inconscient* by Théophile Desdouits, reprised Hartmann's title and some aspects of his metaphysics, but in arguing that the unconscious had only an automatic function and no role in *active* intellectual life, the work can be seen as a confirmation of

Janet's view of conscious versus unconscious phenomena. Reviewing the book, the philosopher Léon Brunschvicg wrote that Desdouits was trying to show that consciousness offers a complete explanation of intellectual life, and he summarized, 'l'inconscient agit seulement en "sous-ordre", pour l'exécution mécanique des décisions du libre-arbitre, ou "par délégation" pour la reproduction de certains actes qui nous sont devenus habituels'[62] ('the unconscious acts only as "second in command", in the mechanical execution of certain decisions of our free will, or "by delegation", so as to reproduce certain acts which have become habitual for us'). Even when we sleep, or when a second personality seems to appear in us, Desdouits argues that an obscure consciousness subsists, the subconscious. His adoption of this term marks the headway Janet's arguments were making in contending that there was no part of the mind that was fully unconscious.

What Brunschvicg perceives in Desdouits' work is also, although he does not dwell on the point, that his colleague sees a metaphysical justification for his analysis: consciousness and rationality are identified with God (Brunschvicg, 406), but Brunschvicg insists that what underlies Desdouits' position is a societal theme of the period, the fear that the unconscious could be autonomous and take over rationality, and thus Desdouits invests the concept, not unlike other participants in the debate, with mistrust, restrictions and denial.

The French fin de siècle showed a marked resistance to entertaining the idea of a dynamic unconscious, a place where unusual, perhaps even surprisingly novel, combinations of thoughts and memories might take place autonomously. Responsibility for this must go in part to Pierre Janet and the impact made initially by *L'Automatisme psychologique*. Although his case studies were of hysterics, his work appeared to suggest that, for any individual, the 'subconscient' was the part of the mind that carried out only automatic, mechanical processes. Janet noted specifically that his study was focused on identifying, in human mental activity, the difference between the creative and the non-creative: 'C'est cette opposition entre l'activité créatrice de l'esprit et l'activité reproductrice qui mérite vraiment le nom d'automatisme que nous avons essayé de préciser' (*L'Automatisme*, ix). ('It is this opposition between the creative activity of the mind and the copying activity which truly merits the name of automatism that I have attempted to elucidate.') Towards the end of the volume, Janet analyzes four examples of this automatism, each labelled an 'inferior mental activity': 'ce sont les phénomènes de la distraction, ceux de l'instinct, de l'habitude et de la passion' (463). Many creative personalities would and did challenge the view that distraction (absentmindedness, day-dreaming) and instinct were inferior activities of the mind. And when Janet specifies that memory is a 'synonym' of habit, he adds to his list of low-level automatic activities a complex function that would sit at the heart of the creative system of a writer like Marcel Proust. Nonetheless, Janet remained a leading if not the leading figure in French psychology. 'Prior to World War I, in short', writes Lawrence Rainey, 'the intellectual paradigm of automatism established by Janet was unchallenged and widely diffused across the spectrum of well-educated cultural life.'[63]

Janet continued to deny those who believed in dynamic, creative, unconscious activity, and he was not above ridiculing the naiveté of his opponents' views:

> On a désigné par ce mot [= inconscient] des activités merveilleuses qui existent, paraît-il, au-dedans de nous-mêmes, sans que nous soupçonnions leur existence[;] on s'en est servi pour expliquer des enthousiasmes subits et des divinations du génie . . . Je me garde bien de discuter des théories aussi consolantes et qui sont peut-être vraies.[64]

> This term [= unconscious] has been used to designate marvelous activities which exist, apparently, within ourselves, without our suspecting their existence[;] the term has been employed to explain the sudden enthusiasms and divinations of genius . . . I don't get involved in discussing such consoling theories, which are perhaps true.

Janet's views on the unconscious would be central to his quarrels with Freud. The reality of late-century French thinking about the unconscious, some of it tainted by degeneracy theory, seems to have been that after a century of studies of abnormal psychology, of *aliénisme*, from Esquirol to Valentin Magnan and even to Janet himself, whose subjects were confirmed hysterics, it was difficult to see the unconscious zone of mental life as something other than a place of pathology. Janet was unapologetic on this subject: he observed that he had chosen his experimental subjects among those who presented the most vivid symptoms of the question he wished to study. That these individuals might be sick or troubled made no difference.[65]

Janet's misgivings or diffidence about the existence of a creative, dynamic unconscious have been related to his early involvement in experiments with mental telepathy, an episode that will be discussed in detail in Chapter 3 on Maupassant. Henri Ellenberger feels that the unscientific and sensationalist interest of others in those experiments in Le Havre involving Janet's patient Léonie gave the careful Janet a lasting suspicion of parapsychological research.[66] Janet confirms this in a later article where he counts himself among those '[qui ont] conservé des doutes sur la réalité actuelle des phénomènes métapsychiques'[67] ('[who have remained] dubious about the reality of metapsychic phenomena').

Janet is still regarded, writes the medical historian Mark Micale, as the 'most sensitive and original thinker in early French depth psychology',[68] and he points to a reevaluation of Janet's research on hysteria, dissociative states and traumatic psychopathology.[69] Ellenberger, who had known Janet, has been at least partly responsible for that reevaluation because of his chapter on Janet in *The Discovery of the Unconscious*; he argued that Janet had a huge influence on modern psychiatry and on Jung and Adler in particular.[70]

Comparing patient care in Freud's and Janet's systems, Ian Hacking places Janet on a superior plane.[71] He argues that since Freud saw trauma as involving people's acts, such human action must be interpreted. By contrast, Janet viewed trauma as impersonal, the result of things encountered in the world. What treatment did each employ? Janet would convince his patients, through hypnotism or whatever persuasive means at hand, that their trauma had not happened, or he would replace the thing that made them anxious by another imagined object that was non-threatening. He would in effect lie to them. In contrast, Hacking sees Freud as a rigid theoretician who, in dealing with patients' trauma, 'probably fudged the evidence in favour of theory' (195).[72]

For anyone who has undergone a lengthy, barely interactive Freudian-style psychoanalysis, it is tempting to agree with Hacking that for Freud, 'the obligation of the analyst [was] to lead each patient to a self-knowledge that squared with theory', while Janet focused more precisely on helping his patients rid themselves of their problem (197). It is not so easy, however, to follow Hacking when he lauds Janet, without evidence, as a far more honourable man than Freud, the latter labelled 'an entrepreneur who annihilated Janet's reputation' (44). We will see later in this chapter that what Hacking sloughs off as Janet's 'childish remarks' about his rival in an infamous paper he gave in 1913 were very much an attempt to destroy Freud's reputation.[73]

Elisabeth Bronfen is among those female readers who admire Janet's treatment of his patient Madeleine, recounted in *De l'angoisse à l'extase*, because the psychiatrist descended from the medical pulpit and a real dialogue ensued in which Janet realized that certain *idées fixes*, especially types of religious obsessions and hallucinations, could bring joy and consolation.[74] On the French side of the ledger, Élisabeth Roudinesco is almost unsparingly critical of Janet, while French psychologist Serge

Nicolas writes more dispassionately that from the 1920s forward Janet's work was simply eclipsed by that of Freud. Other critics feel Janet demonstrated 'passablement de perfidie' ('a good deal of nastiness') in criticizing Théodule Ribot for taking too theoretical an approach in his writing. They also feel that Janet's focus on distraction, habit and passion as inferior mental activities revealed a moralistic rather than a scientific side of the man.[75]

One does encounter many cautionary notes about Janet's view of normalcy. Any study of mediums was, for him, part of 'l'étude psychologique du névropathe'.[76] His contemporary Charles Richet wrote that Janet was far too inclined to treat hysterics as sick people and that there were infinite gradations of supposed imbalance. The unconscious was not morbid, but a place of creativity: 'Le talent de l'inconscient a plus de variétés encore que le talent du conscient.'[77] ('The unconscious has many more varieties of talent than consciousness.') As we will see in the final chapter, Janet read at least some of Proust's *À la recherche*: perhaps predictably, he found the author abnormal.

We have sampled portions of the debate regarding the existence of the unconscious occasioned by the publication of *L'Automatisme psychologique* in 1889. Twenty years later, in 1909, and then ten years after that, in 1919, we encounter clear signs that the debate is still ongoing. A discussion of a meeting of French philosophers and psychologists at the Société française de philosophie illustrates just how murky were French perspectives on the unconscious in 1909.[78] The participants included, among others, the psychologist Alfred Binet and philosophers Henri Bergson, Alphonse Darlu (Proust's respected philosophy teacher at Lycée Condorcet), Jules Lachelier (who was also, according to Jean-Yves Tadié,[79] an important influence on Proust's thought), Léon Brunschvicg and Dominique Parodi. Binet refused to admit the existence of the unconscious, while Bergson spoke of what Jeremy Stubbs interprets as the preconscious. Parodi sat on the fence, but expressed much skepticism:

> Je constate, d'après l'échange d'observations qui vient d'avoir lieu, que, si le mot et la notion d'inconscient semblent tenir une place sans cesse grandissante dans la psychologie contemporaine, non seulement on n'en conçoit pas l'idée d'une manière plus claire qu'autrefois, mais même on ne s'entend pas sur le genre d'existence qu'il faut lui attribuer.[80]
>
> I note, based on the exchange of views that has just taken place, that although the term and the notion of the unconscious seem to occupy an ever-expanding place in contemporary psychology, not only is it not understood more clearly than in the past, there is no agreement on what kind of existence should be attributed to it.

Writing at about the same time, philosopher and columnist Alfred Fouillée also denied the existence of an unconscious. All thought had at its base, he argued, what he called, in opposition to Schopenhauer and others, 'une volonté de conscience' ('the will to consciousness'): that is, willpower is directly attached to intelligence and these two are the triggers and initiators of thought and action. He opposed the 'mutilation' of the human intellect by theorists like Ribot, William James and Bergson. They would divide consciousness into two parts and have us believe that there exists 'une vie affective pure, autonome, indépendante de la vie intellectuelle, qui a sa cause en bas, dans les variations de la cénesthésie, qui est elle-même une résultante des actions vitales'[81] ('a pure, autonomous emotional life independent of intellectual life, which has its cause in the depths, in variations in cenesthesia, which itself results from our vital functions').

A further ten years went by before Parodi authored his influential *La Philosophie contemporaine en France*,[82] in which he observes that although French acceptance of the unconscious is broader than ever, little progress has been made in understanding its nature. Gone are the days when the unconscious was imagined as a corporeal reflex or a simple residue of a former conscious thought, nor is it, as some used to argue, linked to mental imbalance. Parodi appears nostalgic and puzzled at the severing of this sensible link: 'l'inconscient ne paraît plus comme lié à des troubles psychiques, il devient la source normale et féconde où s'alimente notre vie intérieure' (102) ('the unconscious no longer appears linked to mental problems, it is becoming the moral, fertile source of our internal life'). But Parodi's main sentiment is regret that the rational is being displaced: 'l'admission d'un inconscient absolu et la large part qui lui est faite dans la vie intérieure, semblent une invitation à limiter le rôle de la raison ou de la pensée proprement dite'[83] ('the acceptance that an absolute unconscious exists and the important role it is afforded in internal life seem an invitation to limit the role of reason or of thought itself'). All 'thought' is part of conscious rationality, he wants to remind his reader. He sees the early years of the twentieth century as a period of anti-rationalism or at least of anti-intellectualism.[84] In the chapter on Proust, we will again take up, but in some detail, the question of fin-de-siècle and early twentieth-century anti-intellectualism. The erudite intellectual Proust was particularly concerned that the intellect not be credited with an exaggerated role in the creative process.

Contemporaries of Parodi could be far more critical of French dithering on the subject of the unconscious. Writing in 1919, the same year as Parodi, Dr Gustave Géley scoffed at the reduction of the unconscious to some version of Janet's automatism and summarized in the following way what he saw as the still extant, blindfolded, 'classical' French view of the unconscious:

> D'après [la majorité des psychologues contemporains], tout ce qui, au point de vue psychologique, n'est pas dans la moyenne, relèverait de la maladie. Les capacités subconscientes seraient des produits morbides; l'hypnotisme serait assimilable à une névrose; les manifestations des personnalités multiples résulteraient de désintégrations pathologiques du moi; les phénomènes supranormaux ne seraient que des symptômes d'hystérie; quant à l'inspiration supérieure et le génie, ils seraient simplement des fruits de la folie.[85]
>
> According to [the majority of contemporary psychologists], everything, from a psychological point of view, that is not in the mean is morbid. Subconscious abilities would thus be morbid products: hypnotism could be assimilated to a neurosis; the manifestations of multiple personalities are the result of pathological disintegrations of the self; paranormal phenomena are simply symptoms of hysteria; as for high-level inspiration and genius, they are nothing but the products of madness.

Though a medical doctor, Géley cannot be counted on for a purely scientific view of the unconscious, since he wrote on reincarnation and spiritualism. However, his assessment of hidebound French medical views of the unconscious in 1919 seems both refreshing and largely accurate.[86]

Dominique Parodi's observations about the building anti-intellectualism in fin-de-siècle France merit a closer look, because among those 'anti-intellectuals' in French society were a number – *pace* Lawrence Rainey – who disagreed with Janet's notion of a static unconscious and its automatisms. Let us try to identify some of the various directions from which assertions of a dynamic unconscious were flowing.

The social psychologist Gustave Le Bon dedicated his 1895 volume *La Psychologie des foules* to Théodule Ribot, and at least one aspect of the study looks forward to Ribot's *Essai sur l'imagination créatrice*. On the one hand, although Le Bon owed something to Pierre Janet's theory of the psychological automaton, on the other his image of the unconscious can definitely appear at odds with that of Janet, who saw what is below the level of normal consciousness as a conglomeration of *idées fixes*, habitual and repeated phenomena that are essentially undynamic. Le Bon's perspective on the unconscious recalls more that of Leibnitz; that is, it is not static but rather a place of mixing, of new combinations. He saw this dynamism reflected in the crowd:

> Dans l'agrégat qui constitue une foule, il n'y a nullement somme et moyenne des éléments, il y a combinaison et création de nouveaux caractères, de même qu'en chimie certains éléments mis en présence ... se combinent pour former un corps nouveau.[87]

> In the aggregate constituted by a crowd, the constituent elements are in no way a sum total or an average, instead there are combinations and the creation of new characteristics, just as in chemistry certain elements, when brought together ... combine to form a new body.

Moreover, what is striking in Le Bon's theory is the almost negligible role he grants to the rational not only in the behaviour of crowds but in the everyday life of individuals:

> Ce n'est pas seulement dans la vie organique, mais encore dans le fonctionnement de l'intelligence que les phénomènes inconscients jouent un rôle tout à fait prépondérant. La vie consciente de l'esprit ne représente qu'une bien faible part auprès de sa vie inconsciente. L'analyste le plus subtil, l'observateur le plus pénétrant n'arrive guère à découvrir qu'un bien petit nombre des mobiles inconscients qui le mènent. (ibid., 16)

> It is not only in the life of our organs, but in the operation of the intellect that unconscious phenomena play a totally preponderant role. The conscious life of the mind represents but a small portion compared to our unconscious life. The subtlest analyst, the most insightful observer succeed in discovering just a bare few of the unconscious motives that drive them.

In a crowd, a group unconscious develops that negates personal willpower in its members who exhibit the aboulia of a hypnotized subject, a subject who becomes 'l'esclave de toutes les activités inconscientes *de la moelle épinière*, que l'hypnotiseur dirige à son gré' (ibid., 19; emphasis added) ('the slave of all those unconscious activities of the *spinal column*, which the hypnotist controls as he wishes'). What we might call this 'automatic' reference to hypnotism and the companion allusion to the spinal column demonstrate that reflex activity theory still underlies the understanding of the unconscious, be it dynamic or not. Crowds make of a person, writes Le Bon, 'un automate que sa volonté ne guide plus' (ibid., 20).

Interest in crowds had also drawn literary commentary from Charles Baudelaire in the 1850s and 1860s. He would presumably have rejected Le Bon's idea that a crowd member becomes a slave of group willpower. Baudelaire's crowd participant is the poet who adores immersion in crowds but at the same time revels in an incognito status within them that enables him to live vicariously off the group's electricity and unpredictability. The crowd takes one out of oneself, but not to be coopted or unconsciously cowed by the energy of others; rather, it provides an exotic *déplacement* out of self into a free world of the unexpected and the yet unknown.[88]

The survey became particularly popular in France after Jules Huret's *Enquête sur l'évolution littéraire* (1891) and a few years later Dr Paul Chabaneix's questionnaire-based inquiry titled *Le Subconscient chez les artistes, les savants et les écrivains* identified dozens of artists, writers and scientists whose creative moments surfaced from their unconscious in the form of dreams, hunches, second states or involuntary memory. Chabaneix's study has been accused of lacking philosophical coherence,[89] but what seems more important is that here we have a doctor with a creative bent (he also wrote novels and poetry under a pseudonym, Jacques Nervat) contributing to an important, expanding current of psychological investigation by devoting his medical thesis to the range of formats in which unconscious inspiration reaches the creative person. We will examine Chabaneix's study more closely in Chapter 6 on Proust.

Other doctors supported the idea of a creative unconscious. The physiologist and psychologist Henri Beaunis, who also wrote poetry, short stories and plays, differentiates in a Proustian manner between ideas that arrive from the unconscious and willed conscious activity. Suddenly, writes Beaunis, what he calls 'une idée-mère' appears in his consciousness, and he begins to work on the offshoots of that idea. But there is a difference between the unwilled and the willed:

> cette frondaison, elle est soumise à ma volonté, elle se produit et se développe sous l'influence d'une activité mentale dont j'ai conscience et que je dirige à mon gré; mais pour l'idée-mère, ... elle surgit dans ma conscience sans que je sois pour quelque chose dans son apparition'.[90]
>
> these offshoots are subject to my willpower, they are produced and develop under the influence of a mental activity that I am conscious of and which I direct as I wish; but as for the parent-idea ... it wells up in my consciousness without any involvement on my part.

He notes that when he deliberately tries to summon up these ideas, they are unattainable. Thus, his parting advice is: 'Laissez travailler l'inconscient: il ne se fatigue jamais' (ibid., 40). ('Let your unconscious do the work: it never gets tired.')

Published in 1900, Théodule Ribot's *Essai sur l'imagination créatrice*[91] was almost Proustian in its relegation of the rational intelligence to an organizational rather than an instigative role in the creative process. And some ten years before Remy de Gourmont's own essay on the unconscious, 'La Création subconsciente', he had remarked of his novel *Sixtine*, 'l'inconscience joue un si grand rôle dans les opérations intellectuelles; – je crois même qu'elle joue le premier de tous, celui d'impératrice-reine!'[92] ('the unconscious plays an important role in our intellectual operations; – I believe in fact that it plays the number one role, that of empress and queen!)

It was probably to be expected that a century that applauded science and medicine so enthusiastically would see a counter-movement that prized the intensely personal and intuitive, the spiritual and the paranormal. As the cultural historian Christophe Prochasson has written:

> Le merveilleux connut comme un regain au sein même de la science ... L'essor du rationnel, qui semble incarner l'ascension de l'esprit scientifique, s'accompagne inévitablement d'une montée concomitante du paranormal. Tout se passe comme si l'effacement progressif du divin des perspectives et des pratiques intellectuelles avait pour contrepartie l'épanouissement des sciences de l'irrationnel et du féerique.[93]

> The supernatural experienced an upswing within science itself ... The progress of the rational, which seems to embody the ascension of the scientific spirit, is inevitably accompanied by a related surge in the paranormal. It is as if the gradual erasure of the divine from intellectual perspectives and practices has as compensation the blossoming of the irrational sciences and the magical.

Pierre Citti has looked at fin-de-siècle skepticism about the intelligence in his already mentioned *La Mésintelligence. Essais d'histoire de l'intelligence française du symbolisme à 1914*. The question of the secondary role of the intellect and of willpower is one that traversed Marcel Proust's entire intellectual life; it is especially evident in his unfinished *Contre Sainte-Beuve* where the first line of one fragment reads, 'Chaque jour j'attache moins de prix à l'intelligence.' Chapter 6, on Proust, is therefore the appropriate place to examine Citti's theses and to trace the fortunes of the term 'intellectual' at the fin de siècle, including during the Dreyfus Affair. This will include examining the disagreement between Daniel Halévy and Proust regarding Halévy's signing of the 1919 manifesto 'Pour un parti de l'intelligence'.

Without any claim to completeness, it seems logical to end this first chapter by discussing the main aspects of the debate between Pierre Janet and Sigmund Freud over the unconscious. Janet, with his dual background as a philosopher and doctor and his skittishness about the paranormal, would defend the idea of a subconscious that is simply a lower level of consciousness. Freud and his supporters would begin to export into France and the world the layers of Freudian theory, with its disturbing emphasis on sexuality.

1.5 The French Unconscious, Janet and Freud

As we will see, the presence of Freudian theory in France was not felt in any significant way until the mid-to-late 1920s. The index of Parodi's

1919 tome records only one reference to Freud: Dr Emmanuel Régis of Bordeaux is said to be working on 'naturalizing' Freud's notion of repression to fit the French context.[94] Nor were literary milieus especially well informed about psychoanalytical theory. One of the first Freudian investigations of *À la recherche du temps perdu* appeared only shortly before Proust's death, in 1922, when René Rousseau, buoyed by a reading of Freud's *Interpretation of Dreams*, wrote a long, incisive essay in the *Mercure de France* on Freudian themes in *À la recherche*.[95]

More than a few critics have mused about the lengthy impermeability of French thinking to Freudian influence. The French defeat of 1870–71 and the annexation of Alsace-Lorraine; World War I, German defeat, German loss of Alsace-Lorraine; French revanchism, German revanchism: all these painful events and feelings and the bitterness that resulted from them make difficult any dispassionate analysis of Franco-German disagreements about the nature of the unconscious. That enmity certainly disturbed the ongoing scientific investigation into the idea of the unconscious mind. Another disruptive factor, it has also been argued, is that the anti-Semitic furor of the Dreyfus Affair exacerbated French xenophobia and French distaste for Freudian theories.[96]

The legacy of Charcot's neurological research and the growing importance of Janet meant that in the early years of the twentieth century there was the notion of an unconscious *à la française* that could be held up as a corrective to Freudian theory. But part of the Franco-German dispute hinged also on the personal relationship between Pierre Janet and Freud: Sigmund Freud, Jewish, German-speaking, with hesitant French but a background in Charcot's research; Janet, one of the main inheritors of Charcotian eminence who had learned German as a child but had a phobia about its use probably because his mother was Alsatian born, intensely patriotic and Catholic.[97] The exchanges between and about these two men mirror the evolution of French thinking regarding the unconscious up until the mid-1920s when studies by Dr Emmanuel Régis and his student Angelo Hesnard brought a version of Freudian psychotherapy (a somewhat amputated version) formally into French practice.[98]

One significant aspect of the Franco-Freudian quarrel was the across-the-board French denial of the sexual aetiology of neuroses and of infant sexuality. In our current age of exacerbated interest in sexuality, this denial may seem strange, but of course the resistance to Freudian sexual interpretations was not limited to France. An argument can certainly be made that Freud was just as reviled in Vienna as by the French in Paris. That is, Vienna was a city with its own puritan strain and certain Viennese reviled

Freud as a traveller who had brought back a sexual infection from dirty, degenerate France (Roudinesco, *History*, 87–91).

Contrasting forces were at work in French fin-de-siècle culture. On the one hand, sexuality has never been perceived as foreign to the French psyche. The authors of a recent encyclopaedia of erotic writing place the French national output in the field at the top of their list: 'French and Francophone writers', they write, 'have contributed more than any other linguistic culture to the development of the erotic genre.'[99] On the other hand, how could the fin-de-siècle French medical community, made up of well-off, educated men of generally conservative tastes, accept the normalization of infant sexuality and sex-based diagnoses given the bourgeois investment in female virginity before marriage and the official, inviolable prudery of the marriage bed?

Certainly, if writers of fiction seemed apparently obsessed by sex, a large part of the credit must go to the French sexology movement of the latter years of the nineteenth century, to medical researchers who have been characterized as 'fascinés par la puissance du sexe, où ils cherchent le secret des passions et de la décadence des civilisations'[100] ('fascinated by the power of sex in which they seek the secret of passions and of the decadence of civilizations'). Indeed, the French sexological tradition saw sexual 'excess', and this included any sexual practice other than heterosexual intercourse, as degenerate, pathological and leading normally to madness and death. To leaf through some of these sexually oriented studies is to be awakened. Dr Benjamin Ball's *La Folie érotique* (1888) addresses the madness of exhibitionism, nymphomania, satyriasis, necrophilia and pederasty. Dr Alexandre Cullerre in *Les Frontières de la folie* (1888) has chapters on anomalies of the sexual instinct, genital perversions and other sexual aberrations. Dr Paul Moreau's manual *Des aberrations du sens génésique* (1880) provided material on masturbation, orgasm and 'post-connubial madness' (a kind of quasi-epileptic attack experienced by the just-married after initial sex), which the writer Paul Bonnetain copied verbatim into his novel of masturbation *Charlot s'amuse*. Jean-Louis Dubut de Laforest plagiarized material on satyriasis and bestiality from the same manual for his novel *Le Gaga*.[101] A novel of homosexuality by Verlaine's friend Henri d'Argis, *Sodome* (1888), has its hero snap because of his obsessive attraction to men and begin to experience paralysis and fits of madness, the standard preliminaries (according to sexologists) for lunacy and death that face those suffering from degenerate mind states. If Bonnetain's hero Charlot commits suicide, it is because his creator has listened to Dr Paul Moreau's prognosis concerning sexual deviants: 's'ils n'ont pas assez de courage pour mettre un terme à une existence si malheureusement remplie, la démence incurable s'en empare et les conduit rapidement au tombeau'[102] ('if they are not courageous enough to end a life filled with such unhappy things, incurable insanity is their lot and they rapidly end up in the grave'). Perhaps it was not so surprising that the French medical community resisted Freudian theory so consistently: the claims about a sexual aetiology for the neuroses of mature people had to be resisted given the context of belief about the relationship between perverted sex and degeneracy.

Although a certain bourgeois resistance to too much sex talk may also have played a role in French reactions, Élisabeth Roudinesco suggests that Janet's complete avoidance of addressing sexual issues was part of a rigorous insistence on a positivistic approach: 'Il s'agit d'un évitement systématique du sexe, étayé par un rationalisme scientifique' (Roudinesco, 25) ('The approach was a systematic avoidance of sex, justified by scientific rationalism'). What Janet desired – and no doubt this was in part what French psychologists desired – was to eliminate from Freudianism the conjectural and the metaphysical and be left with an ideal, Gallic clarity. Sticking to a scientific and rational approach meant avoiding the murky world of sexual drives and erotic attractions. It also meant remaining within conservative medical bounds. Charles Richet admitted the dangers of being too open-minded as a scientist when he spoke of his own very early experiments (beginning in 1873) with hypnotism/magnetism:

> Quand je m'en suis occupé (avec une grande ardeur), j'étais presque forcé de me cacher, pour ne pas exciter la raillerie, dédain ou pitié. On me disait que c'était me perdre, tomber dans le domaine des charlatans ou des songe-creux.[103]
>
> When I was involved with it (in a really intensive way), I was almost forced to go into hiding so as not to arouse mockery, contempt or pity. I was told that I was ruining myself and entering the domain of charlatans or dreamers.

But as far as Janet's rationalistic diffidence about sexuality is concerned, Freud felt that this was the man's Achilles heel. Writing to Jung in 1907, Freud granted that Janet had a finely tuned intelligence but he was certain that without recognizing the importance of sexuality his theories could advance no further.[104]

I have mentioned the name of Dr Emmanuel Régis, who, according to his colleague Parodi, was working at 'naturalizing' the Freudian concept of repression to fit the reality of the French makeup. Régis was not alone in his diffidence about repression. We see the writer and critic Edmond

Jaloux make the following comment just a few years later, in 1924, about the 'racial' basis of repression:

> Je ne crois pas que l'on ait insisté, autant que cela le mérite, sur les différences que présentent au point de vue de l'inconscient les divers groupes de races. Il me paraît évident que chez les races latines – les Français en particulier – les manifestations inconscientes sont infiniment plus faibles et dans un certain sens plus rares que dans les groupes germaniques, anglo-saxons, slaves et scandinaves ... Si les médecins ont refusé si longtemps d'adhérer aux idées de Freud, c'est que, à la lettre, ils n'ont pas pu toujours les vérifier. Il y a peu de refoulés en France, où la tolérance générale laisse aux êtres une relative liberté d'action et crée rarement autour des manifestations sexuelles cette atmosphère d'angoisse et contrainte qui est si sensible dans les cas étudiés par Freud ou par Havelock Ellis.[105]

> I don't believe that there has been appropriate emphasis on the differences related to the unconscious of the various racial groups. It seems obvious to me that in the Latin races – the French in particular – the manifestations of the unconscious are infinitely less pronounced and, in a certain sense, more rare than among German, Anglo-Saxon, Slavic and Scandinavian groups ... If doctors have refused for so long to accept Freud's ideas, it is precisely because they have not always been able to verify them. There are few repressed people in France, where generalized tolerance affords people relative freedom of action and rarely creates around things sexual that atmosphere of anxiety and constraint which is so evident in the cases studied by Freud or by Havelock Ellis.

Régis' study, *La Psychoanalyse des névroses et des psychoses: ses applications médicales et extra-médicales*, while critical of Freud, argues strongly against French xenophobic opposition to Freud's 'germanisme scientifique'. But the Régis work went to press just before the outbreak of World War I. How much more difficult it became, during and after the war, to defend the cause of 'German psychoanalysis'. Freud's ideas were depicted in the preface to the second edition of the Régis work (1922), written by his colleague Dr Hesnard, as possessing a 'caractère outrancier' ('outrageous character') and demonstrating 'des aspirations mystiques'.

Alain de Mijolla's study, *Freud et la France*, tabulates and assesses French writing about and knowledge of Freud year by year from his first visit to France in 1885 and his earliest publications.[106] It presents in arresting detail the reasons it took so long for the French to accept him: some ridiculed the notion of repression, as we have seen, proposing in effect that the French were, sexually speaking, irrepressible; others scoffed at the idea of infantile sexuality ('une obscénité') and deplored Freud's pan-sexualism; there were the usual claims that the Freudian structure of the unconscious was conjectural and unscientific; and unfortunately, there were also constant reminders that Freud was both a Jew and a 'Boche'.

In the end, however, it may have been the stance of Pierre Janet vis-à-vis the unconscious that inhibited French acceptance of Freud. Janet, the philosopher, psychologist and medical doctor, was in many ways the champion of early to mid-twentieth-century French psychotherapy. His objections to Freudian psychoanalysis are summarized most completely in a famous paper given at the Seventeenth Annual International Congress of Medicine in London in 1913;[107] that paper is also viewed by many as the beginning of the decline of his reputation.[108] As a general principle, Janet argued that Freud's ideas had largely been borrowed from himself and renamed. Conversion, transfer and displacement he categorized as vague terms, novel but not meaningful, and though the reality of repression was accepted, Janet saw it as mostly a conscious activity: it would not affect the unconscious of a 'normal person' (72). The mental state of those neurotics who were his patients was always categorized as one of weakened psychological tension, 'une conscience rétrécie' (67), ('a reduced consciousness), a 'subconscience par désagrégation psychologique' ('a subconscious the result of psychological disintegration'), a kind of psychic exhaustion (psychasthenia) that leads to dissociation, to 'des esprits malades et déjà dédoublés' (76) ('minds that are sick and already split').

There is some initial basis for Janet's claims when one appreciates how close were the ideas of Charcot, Janet and Freud in 1892 as Freud with Breuer was preparing the preliminary communication on their *Studies on Hysteria*, 'On the Psychical Mechanism of Hysterical Phenomena'. Marcel Gauchet sees this article and *Studies on Hysteria* itself as set in a Charcotian framework, with references to Charcot's hysteria stages, Binet's *Les Altérations de la personnalité* and Janet's *L'Automatisme psychologique*. Freud, almost quoting Charcot, sees the unconscious as 'le rudiment, plus ou moins organisé, d'un second conscient, d'une condition seconde'[109] ('the rudimentary part, more or less organized, of a second consciousness, of a second state'). Freud also uses a term that would be key to Janet's work, 'dissociation', relating it to the abnormal. Relations between Janet and Freud were quite cordial in the early to mid-1890s as Janet acknowledged Freud and Breuer's references to his own work in the 1894 edition of his *L'État mental des hystériques*: 'Le travail le plus important qui soit venu confirmer nos anciennes études est sans contredit l'article de MM. Breuer et Freud, récemment paru dans le *Neurologisches Centralblatt*.'[110] ('The most important work to have confirmed our earlier studies is without doubt the article by MM Breuer and Freud, recently published in the *Neurologisches Centralblatt*.')

As one gathers, however, in reading Janet's 1913 article, Janet and Freud differ in their view of psychological energy and feebleness. Gauchet sees Freud as impressed by the excess force of emotion that hysterics display, which leads him to the idea of defence mechanisms and repression. Janet, on the contrary, sees a deficit of strength in his patients, and thus his basic doctrine is of psychological weakness. Hence the conclusion that 'l'émotion liée à l'idée fixe provoque la dissociation de la personnalité, la "désagrégation mentale", faute d'énergie suffisante pour opérer et maintenir la synthèse personnelle'[111] ('the emotion attached to the idée fixe causes the dissociation of the personality, "mental disintegration", because of lack of sufficient energy to operate and maintain personal synthesis'). But this latter analysis leads inevitably to categorizing all people suffering from forms of fixed ideas as mentally troubled if not on the road to madness.

Élisabeth Roudinesco pictures Janet's performance in London as a catastrophe, an attempt by a lone French scientist at Gallic rhetoric and wit before a critical, even hostile audience of adepts of a new psychotherapeutic method that was taking the world by storm.[112] Encouraging patients into a lengthy talking cure Janet ridiculed as simple blabbing, a 'procédé naïf et médiocre'. But it is in the second part of his long talk, devoted to the sexual, that Roudinesco sees Janet's fatal mistake, the error of stepping outside his persona as the leading French specialist of nervous diseases to make vulgar, jingoistic remarks. Musing that public opinion had been overcritical of the city of Paris, Janet went so far as to suggest openly and more than once that the sexual aetiology of neuroses could only have been developed in a city such as Vienna.[113] Jung, who attended the conference in Freud's stead, might not have been surprised at the remark, for after visiting Janet, under whom he had studied earlier, he had written to Freud that Janet was 'un plat causeur et le type de bourgeois mediocre'[114] ('a boring conversationalist, the very type of your mediocre bourgeois').

When Janet asked, two years before Freud's death, if they might meet, Freud refused. In a letter to Marie Bonaparte he rehearsed the principal insults Janet had directed his way over the years. Janet had never denied the rumour that after attending his lectures in Paris, Freud had appropriated Janet's ideas. Nor had Janet's comment about Freudian sexual aetiology being related to the city of Vienna ever been rescinded. Above all, Janet had said that the unconscious, on which Freud's entire psychoanalytic theory was based, existed merely as a 'une façon de parler'[115] ('a manner of speaking').

CHAPTER 2

Flaubert
Hysterical Duality, Hallucination and Writing

'The more a writer takes pains with his work to remove it from the personal and subjective', wrote Lionel Trilling, 'the more – and not the less – he will express his true unconscious.'[1] Based on such an advisory, critics should feel no qualms about exploring the ways the unconscious manifests itself in the writings of Gustave Flaubert, the great nineteenth-century apostle of the impersonal in literature. As he wrote *Madame Bovary*, communicating his problems and feelings almost daily to Louise Colet, his advice on style and form was multidirectional, often commentary for her, but always cautionary for himself. The legislation is repeated and peremptory: 'Nul lyrisme, pas de réflexions, personnalité de l'auteur absente';[2] ('No lyricism, no philosophical reflections, author's personality absent'); 'L'auteur, dans son œuvre, doit être comme Dieu dans l'univers, présent partout et visible nulle part' (Corr. 2, 177). ('The author, in his work, must be like God in the universe, present everywhere and visible nowhere.') At the same time as he banishes the self from *Bovary*, one observes a dramatic sense of loss for the self he has renounced:

> Il y a des moments où je crois même que j'ai tort de faire un livre raisonnable et de ne pas m'abandonner à tous les lyrismes, gueulades et excentricités philosophico-fantastiques qui me viendraient. Qui sait? Un jour j'accoucherais peut-être d'une œuvre qui serait mienne, au moins (Corr. 2, 11).
>
> There are moments when I even believe that I am wrong to create a rational work rather than to surrender to every kind of lyricism, to bellowing and to every philosophico-fantastic eccentricity that comes my way. Who knows? One day I might perhaps produce a work that would at least be mine.

Thus, works in the style of *Madame Bovary* are not 'his'; they represent an obliteration (or perhaps an occulting?) of the personal. And how would the writer recover the self that is lost? Not in a text offering present-day, realistic portraits of society but, as he suggests, in works that have both the mythic and the historical about them, an Oriental tale, an epic work, some subject involving vast vision and biblical times (Corr. 2, 416–17). And yet, although such narratives offer the grandeur and scope that appeal to Flaubert's lyrical bent, they too must follow the guidelines of outward impersonality. But the personal does get incorporated into the Flaubertian epic and the writer provides us with one avenue as to how this happens: 'Les choses que j'ai le mieux senties s'offrent à moi transposées dans d'autres pays et éprouvées par d'autres personnes. Je change ainsi les maisons, les costumes, le ciel, etc.' (Corr. 2, 416). ('Those things that I have felt most deeply come to me transposed into other countries and experienced by other persons. So I change the dwellings, the costumes, the sky, etc.') Subjectivity is invested in characters, of course, but as we will see it is also released into exotic geographic space ('d'autres pays') and the natural décor ('ciel'). The hidden presence of the subjective in the apparently impersonal is thus an important thread to follow in studying figures of the Flaubertian unconscious.

My approach in this chapter, initially, will be to focus on dual aspects of mental life in Flaubert, for such duality is not only a heritage of the Romantic tradition in which Flaubert participates, but a tangible product of medical and psychological research about the human psyche, investigations that were especially voluminous and productive across the nineteenth century. The rhetoric of Romanticism attributed traditional female characteristics to the male poet, 'compassion, intuition, sensitivity and emotivity', and acceptance of this feminization is readily visible, especially, for example, in the works of Hugo and Lamartine.[3] Not surprisingly, however, this feminization has drawn probing analyses from contemporary feminist critics whose points of view require attention. At the same time, and during the second half of the century in particular, writers were increasingly sensitized to medical research and psychological investigations, and, in turn, they became accustomed to the claim that psychic duality is the lot of the creative person. Genius, affirmed famously Dr Jacques-Joseph Moreau, was a neurosis.[4] Some, such as the Goncourt brothers, concluded that creative individuals likely possessed an aspect to their personality that could place them on the road to physical and mental breakdown. When Jules de Goncourt died prematurely in 1870, almost definitely of syphilis, Zola wrote consolingly to Edmond, 'L'art l'a tué.'[5] In his response, Edmond enlarged disingenuously on Zola's judgement: 'mon frère est mort du travail et surtout de l'élaboration de la forme, de la ciselure de la phrase, du travail du style'[6] ('my brother died because of the effort and especially the working out of form, the shaping of the sentence, the labour that is style'). In Edmond's view, both brothers were subject to a constitutional nervous weakness that they exacerbated by drawing on it in their fiction, to the point that writing became a pathological exercise:

> Songez enfin que toute notre oeuvre, et c'est peut-être son originalité durement payée, repose sur la maladie nerveuse, que ces peintures de la maladie, nous les avons tirées de nous-mêmes, et qu'à force de nous détailler, de nous étudier, de nous disséquer, nous sommes arrivés à une sensibilité supra-aigüe que blessaient les infiniment petits de la vie.[7]

> Just imagine that our complete œuvre, and this perhaps represents the heavy cost of its originality, rests upon nervous ailments, and that these depictions of sickness were drawn from ourselves, and as we described ourselves minutely, studied ourselves and dissected ourselves, we reached a level of super-acute sensitivity, so that even infinitely small things in life felt like wounds.

Flaubert died in 1880, a watershed year for the investigation of dual mental states such as hysteria. Experiments involving the hypnotism of hysterics by Jean-Martin Charcot's team at La Salpêtrière hospital had begun in 1878 (the young physician Charles Richet had written about his own experiments with hypnotism even earlier[8]) and the public performances of itinerant non-medical hypnotists like Pickmann and the celebrated Belgian Donato were ever more successful in France, Italy and Switzerland. If Flaubert, the self-diagnosed hysteric, had lived just a few years longer, would he have been drawn to or felt contemptuous of these experiments that seemed to demonstrate how individuals could, through suggestion, exhibit a second personality? For many doctors and psychologists, this second state seemed to indicate the existence, in all of us, of what was then thought to be the unconscious.

The question of Flaubertian duality or, more precisely, dualities, thus seems a mandatory entry point for any discussion of the man and his work. The prime and most intensely felt division in Flaubert is his sense of himself as creatively conflicted. He is half unbridled rhapsodist, half proficient documentalist, and although he tends to identify the rhapsodist as his true 'moi', it is clear, given his constant rule-making about the need for impersonality in literature, that the 'moi' needs to be constrained. His true self is caught somewhere in the mysterious bind between those two tendencies, and it is this division of self that I intend to explore.

This chapter will then reexamine in some detail the critical viewpoints that have been applied to Flaubert's hysteria, and the potential meanings of his statement to George Sand that he was an aging hysteric. A review of the notes Flaubert recorded while reading a famous primer on hysteria may help to contextualize Flaubert's claim. A subset of this theme is, of course, the question of bi-genderedness in Flaubert, a subject that immediately attracted the pen of Charles Baudelaire in his famous article on *Madame Bovary*, but which has been questioned and not infrequently considered a sore point by feminist critics.

Before addressing the final subject of the chapter, that is, the position from which Flaubert writes, his writing stance, I will trace how, over the years, various critics have interpreted Flaubert's dualism. What I will argue, in conclusion, is that in the moment of writing, and in the production of the written text, Flaubert is prone to a kind of absorption in his subject very much akin to a hallucinatory state, and that this mental state can be read as a repositioning of the crises Flaubert suffered during his epileptic attacks.

2.1 The Divided Writer

Perhaps the most famous expression of Flaubert's dual selves is the following text:

> Il y a en moi, littérairement parlant, deux bonshommes distincts: un qui est épris de *gueulades*, de lyrisme, de grands vols d'aigle, de toutes les sonorités de la phrase et des sommets de l'idée; un autre qui fouille et creuse le vrai tant qu'il peut, qui aime à accuser le petit fait aussi puissamment que le grand, qui voudrait vous faire sentir presque *matériellement* les choses qu'il reproduit (Corr. 2, 30).
>
> Literarily speaking, there are two quite distinct fellows inside me: one in love with bellowing, with lyricism, with grand flights of the eagle, with all the sonorities of the phrase and of the highest summit of ideas; the other fellow roots about and digs into truth as much as he can, likes to highlight the tiny fact as intensely as the major one, and would like to make you feel almost *in a material way* the things he depicts.

Immediately following the above comment to Louise Colet, Flaubert reports that he tried to marry these two conflicting tendencies when he wrote the first version of *Éducation sentimentale*, but that the experiment failed. The two tendencies, he felt, must be kept separate, in books with different styles; and of course with works as different as *Madame Bovary* and *Salammbô*, or *Éducation sentimentale* and *La Tentation de saint Antoine*, Flaubert appeared to stick to this approach. And yet the other capital guideline announced repeatedly by Flaubert was that of impersonality. That is, even in his epic works like *Salammbô* and *La Tentation*, his taste for high lyricism had to find an outlet beyond the first person or authorial presence. How this happens is a question I hope to answer later in this chapter.

Paul Bourget seems to be doing no more than parroting his subject's words when he professes to see in Flaubert 'deux personnages antagonistes, un poète romantique et un savant'[9] ('two antagonistic characters, a Romantic poet and a scientist'), but in commenting on Flaubert's style – perhaps Bourget was thinking here particularly of *Éducation sentimentale* – he points to quite a different aspect of the writer, a subconscious, forward-driving impulse in his texts, 'la notation continue et involontaire de notre parole intérieure' (ibid., 117) ('the continuous, involuntary notation of our interior speech'). Most probably, it is Flaubert's massive use of free indirect speech, that interiorization of thought and speech which has caught Bourget's attention here. Yet it is surprising to see Flaubert's prose style characterized as 'involuntary', given his often expressed, painstaking efforts to find appropriate language to express his ideas. Although Bourget pointed to the role of the unconscious in Flaubert's writing, he was somewhat skittish about developing the idea in more detail: 'Certes, chez [Flaubert] comme chez tout artiste puissant, il y a une grande part d'inconscience qu'il serait chimérique de prétendre déterminer' (ibid.,102). (Certainly, for [Flaubert] as for any powerful artist, the unconscious occupies such an important space that it would be frivolous to claim to quantify it.')

2.2 Flaubert Bi-Gendered

Flaubert's bi-gendered nature, which he accepted much like Hugo and Lamartine, has been explored from many perspectives. He was a hysteric, as diagnosed by Baudelaire, but also as self-diagnosed in Flaubert's exchanges with George Sand. Or he was an androgyne, like his character Emma. Indeed, perhaps he was a 'male lesbian', as feminist criticism has sometimes classified him. Let us investigate each of these positions, some of which overlap, and decide whether a reader might locate in these classifications a deeper understanding of what writerly duality meant for the man and his literature.

With his famous self-designation as a hysteric in a letter to Sand, Flaubert is one of a series of individuals who inaugurates a half-century of questioning about the psychic and sexual bivalence of the creative writer and of his or her characters. The lines he wrote to Sand in January 1867 have been studied *ad infinitum*:

> J'ai des battements de cœur pour rien. Chose compréhensible, du reste, dans un vieil hystérique, comme moi. – Car je maintiens que les hommes sont hystériques comme les femmes et que j'en suis un. Quand j'ai fait *Salammbô*[10] j'ai lu sur cette matière-là 'les meilleurs auteurs' et j'ai reconnu tous les symptômes. J'ai la boule, et le clou, à l'occiput. (Corr. 3, 591–92)

> My heart beats violently for no reason. Understandable, indeed, in an aging hysteric like myself. – For I maintain that men can be hysterics just like women and that I am one. When I was writing *Salammbô* I read 'the best authors' on the subject and I recognized the symptoms. I have the ball in the throat and the feeling of the nail in the back of the head.

Frequently mentioned, of course, are Baudelaire's article on *Madame Bovary*, his judgement about the novel's author, and Flaubert's reaction to the article. Baudelaire praises his colleague for his deliberate choice of the most banal literary subject available, adultery. He notes that the heroine, full of energy, ambition and the capacity to dream, is nonetheless of limited deep intelligence, and in some sense an anti-heroine. But the crucial comment in Baudelaire's article targets the heroine's gender and, almost as directly, that of her literary creator: she is half woman, half man: 'Comme la Pallas armée, sortie du cerveau de Zeus, ce bizarre androgyne a gardé toutes les séductions d'une âme virile dans un charmant corps féminin.'[11] (Like an armed Pallas Athena, straight out of Zeus' brain, this strange androgyne has retained all the attractiveness of a virile soul in a charming female body.') Flaubert has created a heroine who is a hysteric, and by conflation/juxtaposition Flaubert becomes, in Baudelaire's terms, 'le poète hystérique', suffering from a masculine hysteria 'qui se traduit chez les hommes nerveux par toutes les impuissances et aussi par l'aptitude à tous les excès'[12] ('which is seen in nervous men as every kind of impotence and as an aptitude for every type of excess').

Flaubert's letter of response to Baudelaire reads in part, 'Vous êtes entré dans les arcanes de l'oeuvre, comme si ma cervelle était la vôtre' (Corr. 2, 772). ('You have entered the arcane aspects of the work as if my brain were yours.') His satisfaction at being understood gives a foretaste of that moment when Proust, irritated at being accused of authoring a work of random autobiographical episodes, thanked Jacques Rivière effusively for intuiting that *À la recherche* was a 'dogmatic' work, that is, carefully constructed to make a point.

Whether Baudelaire had read the same 'best authors' as Flaubert on the subject of hysteria is a moot point; it is true that Baudelaire was tutored as a youth by Charles Lasègue, who was destined to become one of the great hysteria specialists of the late century alongside Legrand du Saulle and Charcot. But Lasègue does not seem to have had any impact on Baudelaire's medical ideas. What is more relevant is that in his essay on *Madame Bovary*, Baudelaire broaches the subject of *male* hysteria. The three major hysteria specialists of the pre-Charcot half-century, Hector Landouzy, Jean-Louis Brachet and Pierre Briquet, had all discussed male hysteria, though as a limited phenomenon.[13] There was therefore a documented medical category under which Flaubert could classify himself.[14] But is it fair to say that Flaubert's claim of personal hysteria (Baudelaire had made the same claim) was simply a reflex gesture to which male writers were prone?

Certain readers, most but not all female, have framed Flaubert's self-designation as a hysteric as simply part of a late-Romantic commonplace regarding creativity: the male who writes must obligatorily have a sensitive feminine side. Flaubert is said to participate in this canonic literary bi-genderism, 'an androgyny experienced as the two sides of the same personality, a necessary condition for artistic creativity'.[15] The other writers in the canon, according to this view, would be Baudelaire, Huysmans, Barbey d'Aurevilly and the Goncourts. Elaine Showalter has called this syndrome 'critical cross-dressing': the male writer always proudly retains his masculinity as his trump card and sees himself as 'a better woman than any biological female'.[16] Thaïs Morgan concurs with this view in discussing Baudelaire's self-definition as a hysteric. In spite of their claims to feminine subjectivities, 'both Baudelaire and Courbet remain primarily heterosexually oriented men who engage in cross-gendered play but who do not break out of a patriarchy that guarantees their masculinity'.[17]

There is, obviously enough, some truth in these observations, and some of Flaubert's statements about women support Showalter's trump card idea. To one of his macho correspondents, Ernest Feydeau, he wrote, for example:

> Il ne faut pas se fier aux femmes (en fait de littérature), que pour les choses de délicatesse et de nervosité, mais tout ce qui est vraiment élevé et haut leur échappe. La condescendance que nous avons pour elles est une des causes de l'abaissement moral où nous gisons aplatis. (Corr. 3, 4)
>
> One should count on women (as regards literature) only for questions of delicacy and nerves, but everything that is truly lofty and elevated escapes them. The accommodation we show them is one of the causes of the moral debasement we find ourselves in.

And in a broader, non-literary sense, he writes, 'On traite les femmes comme nous traitons le public, avec beaucoup de déférence extérieure, et un souverain mépris en dedans' (Corr. 2, 71). ('We treat women as we treat the public, with much exterior deference, and sovereign scorn on the inside.')

Later in the century, some observers would also dismiss hysteria claims as a screen hiding an overblown writerly ego. Supposedly defending the intellect and intelligence, Charles Maurras condemned the nineteenth-century hysteria of literary figures as inauthentic and egocentric:

> De 1825 à 1857, c'est-à-dire de Sainte-Beuve et de Vigny à Baudelaire, et de 1857 à 1895, c'est-à-dire de Baudelaire à M. Huysmans et à Mallarmé, d'importants sous-groupes de lettrés se détachent du monde qui achète et qui lit et se dévouent dans l'ombre à la culture de ce qu'ils ont fini par appeler *leur hystérie.*[18]

> From 1825 to 1857, that is to say from Sainte-Beuve and Vigny to Baudelaire, and from 1857 to 1895, that is, from Baudelaire to M. Huysmans and to Mallarmé, important sub-groups of writers severed themselves off from the world that buys and reads, devoting themselves, far from prying eyes, to the cultivation of what they labelled in the end *their hysteria.*

It was, in fact, as Martine Reid has pointed out, a commonplace to treat artistic creativity as a talent that required or presupposed a sense of gender duality, and one sees writers such as the dandyish Maurice Barrès saluting the cliché (perhaps with a hint of self-absorption) in a comment about the works and personality of Leonardo da Vinci: 'Tout vrai génie étant à la fois mâle et femelle se féconde elle-même.'[19] ('Given that very authentic genius is both male and female, the genius is able to find inspiration himself.') Hence, one must not dismiss the fact that Flaubert's and Baudelaire's self-diagnosis as hysterics is in part the sign of a certain narcissism, a feeling of congenial fit with their neuroses. But is there not also in Flaubert's and Baudelaire's claims an attentiveness to personal dislocation, even real malady, and to the explosion of medical research on nervous diseases, hysteria and mental alienation? Already in the 1840s and 1850s, close to a third of French medical theses were being devoted to hysteria;[20] it has been calculated that, in all, ninety-seven theses on the subject were defended between 1800 and 1854.[21] And in 1845, the Paris Académie royale de médecine recognized the popularity of hysteria by proposing a writing competition for the Civrieux prize under the theme, 'On the seat and nature of hysteria'. The two winners, *ex aequo*, were Hector Landouzy, whose study Flaubert would read in detail, and Jean-Louis Brachet.[22] At mid-century, the creative writer thus finds himself at a moment of powerful influence of medicine on literature, a moment when the Goncourts, in a work that they dedicated to Flaubert, *Idées et sensations*, observed that the public did not appreciate that the neurosis of the genius was a scientific and psychological reality.[23]

Part of the reason that feminist criticism scoffs at Flaubert's claim to the female malady and the female gender is the aversion he evinces for the very feminine self he claims to possess. He writes that he would have liked to make of Louise Colet a hermaphrodite. Why? 'Tu m'encombres et me troubles et t'abîmes avec l'élément femelle' (Corr. 2, 548). ('You clutter up my life and upset me and damage yourself with the female element.') As we have seen, he insists to Ernest Feydeau that everything that is high and exalted in life escapes women completely. The problem, he writes jovially on another occasion, is female genitalia:

> Tout cela vient de leur organe. Où l'homme a une Éminence elles ont un Trou! Cette éminence-là c'est la Raison, l'Ordre, la Science, le Phallus-Soleil, et le trou, c'est la nuit, l'humide, le trouble. (Corr. 3, 57)[24]
>
> It all comes from their organ. Where a man has a Rise, they have a Hole! That rise represents Reason, Order, Science, the Sun-Phallus, and the hole is darkness, moisture, troubles.

There are, however, opposing views in the discussions about Flaubert's hysteria. The historian of medicine Jan Goldstein has questioned the claim that Flaubert's hysteria is a facile commonplace of the times. She reminds us, for example, that the designation 'hysteric' normally had a stigmatizing, repressive impact in Flaubert's time. If the term pointed to a dysfunction of the procreative function in women, what did it mean for a man to self-designate as a hysteric? Was it just an offhand claim to canonic bi-genderedness? Was it a comment on his mental or physical state, or indeed on his own sexuality? Was it, for Flaubert, some sort of half-understood reference to a link between his creativity and sexuality? Mark Micale has noted that, 'From Graeco-Roman medicine to psychoanalytic theory, hysteria was linked in one way or another to inadequate or excessive or impaired sexuality',[25] and in a certain sense an attentive reader of Flaubert's correspondence might well conclude that his creativity, though finally productive, was in some sense impaired.

In an interesting reflection, Goldstein, in 'The Uses of Male Hysteria' (143), also sees a potential link between the classic hysterical symptom of the rising ball in the esophagus, the accompanying sensation of suffocation, and Flaubert's difficulties at self-expression. Just as, in the hysterical female, the ball chokes speech and leads to inarticulate cries or screams, it can be seen as producing Flaubert's well-documented defective speech and his cries, grunts and bellowing as he attempts to express himself.

Marie-Christine Desmaret is another critic wary of categorizing Flaubert's hysteria as a cliché adopted by other male writers. On hysteria in men, she notes that the hysteria specialist Briquet felt that male hysteria upset social law. More important, she reminds us, is that hysteria was, according to Charcot, the lot of the marginalized, the dispossessed, beggars, vagabonds, criminals, the *déclassés*.[26] It thus carried a more lurid and negative connotation than the self-valorizing that some critics mention; as Goldstein remarks

(135), applied by a man to himself, the category 'hysteria' hints at radical possibilities.

If not a true hysteric or an androgyne, was Flaubert a 'male lesbian' as the essay by Thaïs Morgan suggests? Naomi Schor has contended that Flaubert could be so classified.[27] Borrowing from Sartre, she argued that sexually Flaubert was essentially passive. His desire was to be caressed and it mattered little which gender did the stroking. He would thus take on the traditional attitude of the heterosexual female in love, apparent passivity. A liaison with an older, assertive and somewhat masculine woman like Louise Colet could thus be defined as a woman-on-woman, lesbian relationship, as could Gustave's masturbatory relationship with himself, his slightly more active self-manipulating side.

Not unexpectedly, perhaps, French feminist critics tend to accept that Flaubert came to his feminine side and his hysteria honestly, that is, familially. Rehearsing Sartre's discussion of Flaubert's family configuration, Hélène Cixous notes that Flaubert was the unwanted son of a mother yearning for a daughter and thus his family status was that of an outsider, a girl/boy: 'He was in a position of exclusion and thus necessarily in a female position.'[28] Catherine Clément sees an authentic femininity in Flaubert, not only because he was able to actually slip into the mind and imagination and sexuality of a woman such as Emma, although Clément sees this as important, but because like hysterics he suffered from attacks in which his reason foundered, whether those attacks were epileptic or hysterical.[29]

2.3 Hector Landouzy, *Salammbô* and Hysteria

Although most assessments of Flaubert's nervous condition agree that he was an epileptic,[30] he never apparently used the term 'epilepsy' in connection with his nervous attacks, as he called them, and it is not unlikely that he felt he was suffering from some other ailment.[31] To understand better his claim that he was a hysteric and to give some concrete context to what he meant by that, it is important to consult one of the principal 'best authors' on hysteria read by Flaubert in preparation for his novel *Salammbô*. In 1846 Hector Landouzy published his *Traité complet de l'hystérie*,[32] and the notes Flaubert took from that treatise can help us to assess in what ways he interacts with the medical text.

One fact that is evident is that we quickly notice a dual purpose in his reading of Landouzy. There are of course numerous notations that are lifted from the *Traité* to serve directly as aspects of the heroine Salammbô's hysterical nature. But Flaubert notes down just as many if not more of Landouzy's remarks that comment on his own hysterical characteristics. Landouzy serves on the one hand as a kind of arm's-length medical reference, a typical 'source', but Flaubert also has a personal investment in the *Traité*, for it provides potential evidence that his nervous attacks might be hysterical rather than epileptic. The following commentary, it should be noted, is based on two pages of notes Flaubert took from his reading of Landouzy, notes that have been discussed, as far as I have been able to ascertain, only once by Flaubert critics, in this case by Jan Goldstein.[33]

The hysterical symptoms recycled into *Salammbô* from Landouzy include the famous 'boule' rising in the throat. But Flaubert lends these borrowings a mystico-erotic aura that sees his heroine succumb, in one capital passage, to a kind of delicious, semi-erotic swoon. Salammbô herself describes the moment in this way:

> Des voix m'appellent, un globe de feu roule et monte dans ma poitrine, il m'étouffe, je vais mourir; et puis, quelque chose de suave, coulant de mon front jusqu'à mes pieds, passe dans ma chair... C'est une caresse qui m'enveloppe, et je me sens écrasée comme si un dieu s'étendait sur moi. (103)
>
> Voices call to me, a fiery globe rolls and ascends in my chest, it chokes me, I am going to die; but then something smooth and soft, running from my forehead to my feet, penetrates my flesh . . . It is a caress that envelopes me, and I feel crushed as though a god lay on me.

The ball becomes a foretaste of desire, a juxtaposition that is not to be found in Landouzy. Flaubert is rehearsing for us here the classical erotic nature of the hysteric, but the description as a whole also has the elements of a moment of rapture, with the sensation of soft envelopment, the irresistibility of a momentary ecstasy that comes over the subject. The mystical theme will continue as an irresistible sense, largely internal but partly attributable to the priest Schahabarim, who tells Salammbô that in retrieving the stolen veil, the *zaïmph*, she must not resist the advances of Mâtho, the Libyan leader who has stolen the veil but who loves her.

In another, transposed appearance of the 'boule', Flaubert was attracted by a Landouzy case study in which the hysterical attacks of a fifty-six-year-old woman included the sensation of a worm rising in her esophagus to strangle her.[34] Staring at her sacred serpent, Salammbô is overcome with a similar sensation, the worm becoming a snake: 'elle finissait par sentir dans son coeur comme une spirale, comme un autre serpent qui peu à peu lui montait à la gorge et l'étranglait' (*Salammbô*, 268) ('she finally felt a kind of spiral in her heart, as though another serpent were slowly rising in her throat and strangling her').

Salammbô shares notable characteristics with her author: she is a hysteric *à la Flaubert*. Her sense of fusion with the external world transposes onto a mystical plane what is a central characteristic of Flaubert's writing stance, his physical merging of self both with character and nature. Salammbô echoes Flaubert and anticipates saint Antoine when she cries: 'Je voudrais me perdre dans la brume des nuits, dans le flot des fontaines, dans la sève des arbres, sortir de mon corps, n'être qu'un souffle, qu'un rayon, et glisser, monter jusqu'à toi, ô Mère' (103). ('I would like to lose myself in the night mists, in the flow of fountains, in the sap of trees, leave my body, be a breath only, a ray, and slip away and ascend toward you, oh Mother.') It is her hope that the mystical absorption of prayer can fully spiritualize her: 'Je voudrais m'y [= dans les prières] dissoudre comme une fleur dans du vin' (102). ('I would like to dissolve [in prayer] like a flower in wine.') In the final section of this chapter, I will return to the question of Flaubertian quasi-mystical absorption into the external world and its relationship to Flaubert's writing posture and style.

Let us turn now to a closer inspection of those of Flaubert's notes from Landouzy that appear to be self-directed rather than direct fodder for his novel. At the same time as they set the stage for the novel he is researching, the notes underscore Flaubert's focus on understanding what he sees as his own nervous attacks. The symptoms he isolates while reading Landouzy confirm the impression that he did self-identify as a hysteric and that this was part of a very serious, attentive questioning of his own nerve problems. As he wrote to Mlle Leroyer de Chantepie, 'je suis revenu incidemment à ces études psycho-médicales qui m'avaient tant charmé il y a dix ans, lorsque j'écrivais mon *Saint-Antoine*. À propos de ma *Salammbô*, je me suis occupé d'hystérie et d'aliénation mentale.'[35] ('I have returned, incidentally, to those psycho-medical studies that charmed me so much ten years ago, while I was writing *Saint-Antoine*. For *Salammbô*, I investigated hysteria and mental alienation.')

The sounds a hysteric makes, a variety of cries or sometimes a single word repeated, are phenomenona that attract Flaubert's attention. He copies the following passage from Landouzy: 'Dans certains cas, ce sont, au lieu de cris variés des vociférations uniformes, ou *la répétition continuelle d'un seul mot*' (Landouzy, 47; author's emphasis). ('In certain cases, instead of a variety of cries, we observe uniform vociferations, or *the continual repetition of a single word*.') This same word repetition is recycled twice in *Salammbô* to characterize moments of trance-like semi-consciousness that replicate aspects of Flaubert's own attacks. At one point, the heroine suffers an inexplicable emotional crisis and becomes, like Flaubert in such moments, semi-comatose: 'Soudain elle éclatait en sanglots, et elle restait étendue sur le grand lit fait de courroies de boeuf, sans remuer, en répétant un mot, toujours le même, les yeux ouverts, pâle comme une morte, insensible, froide' (269).[36] ('Suddenly she began to sob, and she remained prone on the great bed made of ox harness, motionless, repeating one word, always the same, her eyes open, pale as a corpse, unconscious, cold.')

Perhaps more important, within those sounds that hysterics make, it is also Landouzy's reference to animal cries that attracts Flaubert's eye, those bellowing sounds that we have come to associate with the biographical Flaubert. Reading the *Traité*, he extracts and copies the following passage, which functions more as a confirmation to himself than a note to be employed in *Salammbô*: 'Ces cris simulent l'aboiement, les hurlemens, les rugissemens, le glapissement, jusqu'aux grognemens du cochon.' (These cries simulate barks, shouts, roars, yelping, even the grunts of pigs.')

The initial passage in Landouzy that interests Flaubert concerns the precursor symptoms of a hysterical attack, and much of the text seems a comment on Flaubert's tremors, shaking and ringing in the ears. He copies these lines:

> Tantôt c'est un frémissement, un fourmillement particulier, une chaleur vive ou un froid glacial qui s'irradient du bas ventre, ou de l'épigastre au cou ... en même temps surviennent des bouffées de chaleur au visage, ... des tintemens d'oreille ... etc. (Landouzy, 27)
>
> Sometimes it's a shudder, a special tingling, an intense heat or a glacial cold that spreads out from the lower groin, or from the upper abdomen to the throat ... at the same time there are waves of heat in the face ... a ringing in the ears ... etc.

A series of references to Landouzy then point to the sparks, kaleidoscopes, brilliant colours and fireworks-like visual effects that accompany Flaubert's convulsions. From a section titled *Convulsions* Flaubert copies this text: 'Dans tous les cas [de convulsions] les yeux fatigués et enflammés par ces contractions répétées, supportent difficilement la lumière' (52). (In every case [of convulsions] the eyes, fatigued and inflamed by these repeated contractions, have difficulty tolerating light.') He also notes down these lines: 'Une dame hystérique laissait au moindre contact dégager des étincelles électriques (observ. de Louyer Villermay).'[37] (At the least touch, a hysterical lady gave off electrical sparks (observation of Louyer Villermay).')

Discussing his own hallucinations with Taine, Flaubert mentions such 'étincelles' and 'un grand feu flambant'. Fiery images drain the body:

> On sent les images s'échapper de vous comme des flots de sang. Il vous semble que tout ce qu'on a dans la tête éclate à la fois comme les mille pièces d'un feu d'artifice, et on n'a pas le temps de regarder ces images internes qui défilent avec furie.[38]

> You feel these images escape from your body like blood coursing. You have the impression that the contents of your head are exploding all at once like a thousand rockets in a firework's display, and you don't have time to contemplate these internal images which roar by you.

Landouzy also evokes and Flaubert records the physical jolts of the hysteric, the cracking of his joints, 'Soubresauts, craquemens dans les articulations' ('bodily starts, cracking sounds in the joints') and the digestive and eating disorders that may accompany the condition: 'Paresseux de l'estomac. Jeûnes excessifs.' ('Lazy digestion. Excessive fasting.')

Flaubert's apparent unwillingness to allow a diagnosis of his condition as epilepsy may well reflect his connection of his own symptoms with the symptoms of hysteria laid out by Landouzy. Not unimportant, in this regard, is Landouzy's comparison of hysterical and epileptic attacks, in a section of his study titled 'Perte de connaissance. Syncopes' ('Losing consciousness. Fainting'). Here he maintains that the hysterical attack can provoke loss of consciousness just like an epileptic seizure.[39] Flaubert might thus classify himself, based on a competent medical source, as someone less afflicted than he was in reality.

2.4 The Critics and Flaubert's Divided Self

Sartre's analysis of the rift in Flaubert's early attitude towards language underlines the duality theme we have been following. He imagines the Flaubert of 1842 returning to the manuscript of *Novembre* and becoming a different person. That is to say, not only does Flaubert chasten his style as he resumes work on the manuscript, he modifies the voice of his narrator, his own voice:

> Flaubert a repris son manuscrit dans l'intention de le terminer au moment où il s'est aperçu qu'il ne pouvait plus parler de lui-même à la première personne. C'est la rupture de l'adhésion au vécu, cette brusque distanciation dans la relation intime de soi à soi-même.[40]

> Flaubert took up his manuscript intending to finish it at a moment when he realized that he could no longer speak of himself in the first person. This is

the rupture of his relationship to his life, this brutal distancing in the intimate relation of self with self.

Although we can sense Sartre stretching here to include Flaubert in the ambit of those who have had an unprogrammed realization of the Absurd, there is certainly something in what he says. A Flaubert Two has replaced a Flaubert One, and the latecomer judges the initial personage harshly:

> Le manuscrit s'arrête ici, mais j'en ai connu l'auteur, et si quelqu'un, ayant passé, pour arriver jusqu'à cette page, à travers toutes les métaphores, hyperboles et autres figures qui remplissent les précédentes, désire trouver une fin, qu'il continue; nous allons la lui donner.[41]

> The manuscript ends here, but I knew the author, and if someone who, to reach this page, has got through all the metaphors, hyperbole and other figures that fill the preceding pages and still desires to know how it ends, let him continue; we will give him what he wants.

Without employing the outlawed first person, however, the writer of *Salammbô* cannot resist the kind of style he condemns in *Novembre*, a style dotted with endless metaphors and comparisons, many of them flat and conventional. Proust, the great metaphorist, agreed with Flaubert Two: there was probably not, he maintained, in all of Flaubert's production a single beautiful metaphor.[42]

Did any of Flaubert's contemporaries understand his writing in a way we would find satisfying today? Bourget's view of him as part Romantic and part realist served as one of the canonic judgements of the man's style until well into the twentieth century. It is interesting that, as we have seen, Bourget felt obliged to mention the important role of the unconscious in Flaubert's writing but also chose to shy away from the topic. Of course, and as shown in Chapter 1, when Bourget wrote his essays in the early to mid-1880s, the nature – even the very existence – of the unconscious was a controversial subject that, as a literary critic, he was likely to approach with some care.[43]

To read Flaubert's letters and to consult the passages in the Goncourt *Journal* where the brothers describe time spent with him, it is almost impossible not to feel discomfited by his incessant complaints about the time and labour involved in writing. Everyone knows his cry, 'Ah! les aurai-je connus, les affres du style!' (Corr. 2, 551) ('Ah! did I know them, the torments of style!') Flaubert's storied difficulty in locating the exact wording that would translate his thought was but one perceived weakness. Friends like the Goncourts were aware of the long list of works he consulted for his novel of Carthage, *Salammbô*, and the detailed defence and illustration of his sources that he prepared *before* that novel was published. It could therefore be tempting, perhaps especially for the Goncourts, so proud of their 'style artiste', to perceive Flaubert as a deficient stylist whose true calling was the factual and the historical.

But there is even a further polarity in Flaubert that annoyed the Goncourt brothers and weighed on their judgement of his literature. Flaubert the country bumpkin, wearing last year's fashions and the wrong shoes, blustery, crudely sexual, laughing uproariously at the broadest farce – this is the image we derive from a sampling of the Goncourt *Journal* entries. Edmond, notoriously suspicious if not jealous of his fellow luminaries, was more and more convinced of Flaubert's plodding nature as the latter's career advanced while that of the brothers marked time. The view he began to articulate, derived in part from Flaubert's own insistence that fiction be impersonal, was that Flaubert was no more than a writer who made judicious use of his sources: 'En un mot, il n'y a pas d'invention personnelle, mais une appropriation intelligente, réfléchie.'[44] ('In a word, there is no personal creativity, rather an intelligent, reasoned borrowing.') À propos of the first *Tentation de Saint-Antoine*, Flaubert had written that the work was composed with his whole soul,[45] while Edmond notes, after reading the 1874 version, 'Lu *La Tentation de Saint-Antoine*. De l'imagination faite avec des notes.'[46] ('I've finished *La Tentation de Saint-Antoine*. Imagination based on notes.') In his growing distaste for Flaubert (or for Flaubert's prestige), Edmond went further, spinning out a theory of the importance of the artist's social self that evokes Sainte-Beuve and seems shallow almost beyond belief. He described what Flaubert lacked in the following way:

> je ne parle pas ici seulement de l'originalité des idées et des concepts, je parle de l'originalité des actes, des goûts de la vie; je parle d'une originalité particulière, qui est toujours le cachet d'un homme supérieur.[47]
>
> I am speaking here not only of the originality of ideas and concepts, I am speaking of the originality of acts, of tastes in life; I am speaking of a special originality, which is always the stamp of a superior man.

If Flaubert had had a collection of *japonaiseries* to rival that of the brothers Goncourt, would his potential for superiority have been more evident? Fair or not, aspects of this essentially external, aliterary view of Flaubert's *oeuvre* adhere to the writer's persona and reputation right into the next century.

In the *Mercure de France* of 1912 Jules de Gaultier authored an extensive essay, 'Le Génie de Flaubert',[48] in which he placed emphasis on the duality of all of Flaubert's characters, in the special sense that, like Emma, they were unable to see themselves as they were. From this arises their discord with reality, their unattainable hopes and desires, which nonetheless demand an eternal search. Gaultier characterized this essentially Flaubertian mindset as 'cette démence métaphysique et transcendante, selon laquelle l'homme plongé dans le monde de la représentation phénoménale s'efforce d'atteindre un absolu projeté dans le vide par la seule hystérie de son désir'[49] ('that metaphysical and transcendent madness, in which a man immersed in the world of phenomenal representation attempts to reach an absolute that is projected into the void by the simple hysteria of his desire'). This judgement accords well with a broad definition of hysteria that George Sand had offered to Flaubert. Asking why such a malady should be attributed to one sex and not the other, she wrote, 'N'est-ce pas un malaise, une angoisse, causés par le désir d'un impossible *quelconque*?'[50] ('Isn't it a malaise, an anguish caused by the desire to attain *almost any type* of impossibility?')

The critic Jules Lemaître imagined, behind the smokescreen of Flaubert's writing anguish, yet another kind of duality. As a young man, he was introduced to Flaubert and visited Croisset three times in 1879–80. He found the writer affable and unpretentious, and, writing a year before his own death, Lemaître is largely laudatory about Flaubert and his literature. And yet he is puzzled and skeptical about Flaubert's writing difficulties. How can it be that one morning he composes long letters to his friends, 'letters of twenty pages in quite an advanced style', and yet spends an entire week agonizing over the completion of two pages of a novel? And so he presents the reader with his own image of Flaubert: probably, given his penchant for idle strolling, pipe smoking and resting on his couch, Flaubert was very likely a lazy person who spent a lot of time daydreaming, 'in a vague pursuit of ideas'.[51] Perhaps here Lemaître was echoing parts of Maxime Du Camp's testament to Flaubert's weaknesses. Du Camp noted that Flaubert often spent time deep in reverie: 'Les notions de la vie réelle lui échappaient et il semblait flotter dans un songe permanent dont il ne sortait qu'avec effort.'[52] ('The awareness of real life escaped him and he seemed to float along in a permanent dream state which he found difficult to come out of.') Witnessing Flaubert lost in thought seems to have derailed, in these two production-oriented journalists, any understanding of the workings of the creative imagination.

The outwardly amicable squabble over Flaubert's style between Albert Thibaudet and Marcel Proust qualifies, in spite of its twentieth-century date – 1919–20 – as a kind of coda to the nineteenth-century debate about the author. When Thibaudet wrote his 1919 article on Flaubert's style,[53] he was participating in a discussion that involved a healthy contingent of critics either dubious about or frankly hostile to the notion of Flaubert as a great writer. His grammatical and syntactical weaknesses and improprieties had always been in the forefront of the mind of critics steeped in the prestige of French classicism. Thibaudet mentions the critique of Jules Lemaître, the skepticism of university critics such as Brunetière and Faguet (the latter's study on Flaubert includes a set of the writer's stylistic 'inadvertances') and a recently published essay by Proust's friend Louis de Robert in which the latter had said baldly that Flaubert didn't know how to write. Thibaudet leans in the same direction when he observes, 'Flaubert n'est pas un grand écrivain de race et . . . la pleine maîtrise verbale ne lui était pas donnée dans sa nature même' (943). ('Flaubert was not born a great writer and . . . a full mastery of language was not something granted him by nature.') Unimpressed by Flaubert's *gueuloir* Thibaudet insisted that his grammatical and literary ear was not very acute (945). Two additional ideas that qualify as Proustian *bêtes noires* followed: Flaubert is touted as a first-class intellect, and the high point of his intellectual activity is to be found in his correspondence: 'Le Flaubert d'intelligence et d'idées', wrote Thibaudet, 'c'est Flaubert parlant du coeur humain et surtout parlant de l'art, le Flaubert de ces admirables lettres à Louise Colet.'[54] ('The intelligent Flaubert, the Flaubert of ideas, is the Flaubert discussing the human heart and especially speaking of art, the Flaubert of those admirable letters to Louise Colet.')

Proust's response to Thibaudet would maintain that Flaubert was a man of no great intellect, nor did he have to be, for in what would become Proust's theory of creativity, the intelligence was in any case never the source of artistic originality. Intuition and evocative impressions came first, followed by the strenuous task of giving linguistic voice to rich but obscure sensations and memories. Only after interventions from the unconscious did the intellect play what Proust would label its ordering and administrative role.

Proust countered the attacks of linguistic purists by declaring Flaubert a grammatical genius whose innovations changed all of French nineteenth-century writing. It is, however, a further observation that begins to address how the unconscious manifests itself in Flaubert's technique. Lauding Flaubert's clear concepts and drive, Thibaudet's commentary does not seem to dip beneath the surface. Proust insisted that a creative vision begins below the level of consciousness and must be teased out in endless efforts: 'que d'application ne fallait-il pas [à Flaubert] pour bien fixer cette vision, pour la faire passer de l'inconscient dans le conscient, pour l'incorporer enfin aux diverses parties du discours' (*Contre Sainte-Beuve* [CSB], 592).

('What perseverance it took [on Flaubert's part] to define that vision, to move it from the unconscious to the conscious, and finally to incorporate it into the various parts of discourse.')

This last comment is obviously somewhat enigmatic. Certainly, the remark functions as self-reference since *À la recherche du temps perdu* is the expression, in one sense, of a combative aesthetic thesis touting instinct, intuition and the unconscious riches of the mind over the rational, the intellectual, and flat, unidimensional everyday reality. Episodes such as eating the *madeleine* demonstrate the difficult iterative process the writer must engage in so as to coax the meaning of these flashes from the unconscious into the full light of consciousness.

But Proust's remark about the difficulty of gradually wringing one's vision from the unconscious and attaching it to the various aspects of writerly discourse is explained more fully in his preface to the writer-diplomat Paul Morand's *Tendres Stocks*.[55] Flaubert, he says, is the example of a radical change in distance between writer and the object/scene to be expressed. In the past, writes Proust, there was an interval of reflection, an intellectual distance one could sense between author and narrative. But now the interval has all but disappeared. How? Flaubert's impersonality translates into his art as a merging of his subjectivity with the object: 'l'intelligence ... cherche à se faire trépidation d'un bateau à vapeur, couleur des mousses, îlot dans une baie' ('the intelligence ... tries to transpose itself into the shimmering of a steamer, the colour of mosses, an island in a bay'). As Flaubert becomes increasingly Flaubert, the reader is no longer conscious of the presence of an authorial mind at work; the intelligence has meshed with the movements of the object it contemplates: 'Cette ondulation-là, c'est de l'intelligence transformée, qui s'est incorporée à la matière. Elle arrive aussi à pénétrer les bruyères, les hêtres, le silence et la lumière des sous-bois' (CSB, 612). ('That undulation is intelligence transformed, incorporated into matter. It is also capable of penetrating heather, beech trees, the silence and light of the underbrush.') Flaubert's meshing with external phenomena anticipates Proust's own technique, as in the famous exploration of the hawthorn's charm in *Du côté de chez Swann* in which the Narrator attempts to 'mime, deep down in himself, the gesture of their flowering'. Flaubert, according to Proust, marries this outward pulsing of the mind with all creation, human beings included: 'dans cette vision continue, homogène, [les hommes] ne sont pas plus que les choses, mais pas moins, 'une illusion à décrire' (CSB, 589) ('in this homogeneous, continuous vision, [men] are no more than things, but no less, they are an illusion to be described.')

It is Proust's analysis that leads to the final section of this chapter, which examines a central element of Flaubert's writing stance. I posit here that the transfer of agency in his writing, via an incorporation of intelligence and subjectivity into external décor, derives from a rehearsal, only slightly conscious, of some of the hallucinatory aspects of his hystero-epileptic attacks and the mind states they create.[56]

2.5 Absorption, Hallucination, Writing Stance

> Le coeur m'a longtemps battu et il m'a fallu un quart d'heure pour me remettre. Voilà de mes absorptions, quand je travaille. (Corr. 2, 211)
>
> (My heart beat wildly for a long time and it took me fifteen minutes to recover. That's how absorbed I am when I work.)

Like Flaubert, many a writer, interrupted unexpectedly late at night by a visitor, might be startled and spend a few minutes before his heart stopped racing. That measure of absorption is well distributed among us all. But there is a further level of absorption in Flaubert that seems to bridge the gap between a concentrated intake of impression and a more active reaching outward of the mind to inhabit and vivify objects and impressions. This type of absorption is akin to hallucination. As a child, according to what he revealed to the Goncourts, Flaubert would become so immersed in books he was reading that, biting his tongue and twisting a lock of his hair, he would lose consciousness and fall to the floor.[57] Were these fainting spells simply harbingers of his later epileptic attacks? Possibly, but the fact that they were triggered by reading and by the absorptional potency of the book is significant. On another occasion, although the phrasing here may seem somewhat overworked, Flaubert speaks of the inspirational effect of his rummaging through childhood drawings and texts. His mind interconnects the text and images he sees there with other experiences and the result is a release into the hallucinatory: 'Mes voyages, mes souvenirs d'enfant, tout se colore l'un de l'autre, se met bout à bout, danse avec de prodigieux flamboiements et monte en spirale.'[58] ('My travels, my childhood memories, everything melts together, attaches in a continuous line, dances about with prodigious flames and rises in a spiral.') The term 'spirale' thickens the plot here for it was, of course, to be the title of a mystical novel that Flaubert never completed, 'un roman métaphysique, fantastique et gueulard' ('a metaphysical, fantastic and bawling novel'), as he wrote to Louise Colet.[59] The flames and sparks of Flaubert's epileptic attacks are here, without the fright that accompanied them, kindling a vision that again identifies reading as one of the imagination's significant triggers. The hallucinatory context, and the mention of a spiral, remind us, as did one of Salammbô's hysteria-like episodes quoted earlier in this chapter (*Salammbô*, 268), of Flaubert's comment, once again to Louise Colet, that he would employ aspects of his nervous attacks in his works.[60]

The Flaubert workspace itself focuses and intensifies attention; emotion is magnified to the point of delirium, but one senses that it is the delirium of a writer transfixed by his text: 'Je passe mes après-midi avec les volets fermés, les rideaux tirés, et sans chemise, en costume de charpentier. Je gueule! Je sue! C'est superbe! Il y a des moments où décidément, c'est plus que du délire.'[61] ('I spend my afternoons with the shutters closed, curtains drawn, no shirt on, dressed like a carpenter. I howl! I sweat! It's fabulous! There are moments when it's definitely more than delirium.') In appreciating the work of others, especially his favourite, Shakespeare, what is important for Flaubert is the evocative power of a text, its ability to trigger the dream state: 'Ce qui me semble, à moi, le plus haut dans l'Art (et le plus difficile), c'est ... d'agir à la façon de la nature, c'est-à-dire de *faire rêver*.'[62] ('What seems to me most elevated in Art (and most difficult) is ... to act as nature does, that is, to make us dream.') Working on his own texts or reading those of others, therefore, Flaubert draws energy and joy from their capacity to shift him into a second state.

One of the significant parallels between Flaubert and Proust, and one of the central reasons that Proust defends Flaubert against those who belittle his writing abilities, is that the two writers share ideas about the psychical absorption we experience in reading. Adam Watt writes of 'le délire de la lecture' in Proust, that is, at one level, his Narrator's tendency to give in to 'desire driven error' in 'reading' the world around him, for example his misapprehensions about the reality of scenes perceived, letters read, the true nature of people met.[63] As Watt argues, reading alerts Proust's Narrator to the permeability of the boundary between fiction and reality. Similarly, Flaubert's delirious recording of historical sources is a half-step on the road to the fantasy of creativity. *À la recherche* opens with a semi-somnolent Narrator who dreams that he is a church or a string quartet. The deep parallel between Flaubert and Proust is this melting into décor, those moments of compositional delirium in which authorial life is extended into external phenomena.

The congenitally jealous Goncourt brothers refused, as we have seen, to recognize any creative effort in Flaubert: they pictured him as an obsessive fact chaser and planner: 'Tout, chez lui, part d'un système, rien de l'inspiration.'[64] ('Everything in his work is system-based, there is no inspiration.') Flaubert was indeed a rabid documentalist. In letters to various correspondents during the spring and summer of 1857, for example, he mentions 57, then 93, then 100 volumes, plus the 18 volumes of the translation of the Jewish Bible by Samuel Cahen, that he has read as background for his novel *Salammbô*. And yet the Goncourts had ample opportunities to visualize the effects that 'documents' had on Flaubert. Here, in an apparently positive tone, is how they recounted the Sundays they spent chatting with him as he was finishing *Salammbô*:

> Ce sont des causeries qui sautent de sommet en sommet, remontent aux origines du paganisme, aux sources des dieux, fouillent les religions, vont des idées aux hommes, des légendes orientales au lyrisme de Hugo, de Bouddha à Goethe ... On se perd dans les horizons du passé ... on rêve aux choses ensevelies, on retrouve et on tire de la mémoire des citations, des fragments, des morceaux de poètes pareils à des membres de dieux![65]

> Our conversations fly from height to height, they return to the origins of paganism, to the sources of the gods, they rummage around in religions, transition from ideas to human beings, from Oriental legends to Hugo's lyricism, from Buddha to Goethe ... We lose our way in the horizons of the past ... we dream of things buried, we fix upon and draw from memory quotations, fragments, excerpts from poets that are the equal of the limbs of the gods!

Their description of these moments confirms that, in spite of being thrilled themselves by this 'buried history', they could be completely blind to the almost hallucinatory power such far-off times exercised on the psyche of their longtime friend Flaubert.

Without attempting to make of Flaubert a mystic, one wonders about the relationship between his drive to breathe life into historical characters and their physical surroundings and his belief, albeit hesitant, that he had lived previously at various moments in that history. The scattered statements he made on the subject always seem to maintain a whiff of skepticism, beginning with this profession of faith: 'Je suis mystique au fond et je ne crois à rien' (Corr. 2, 88). ('I am basically a mystic and I don't believe in anything.') But he would return to the theme of previous lives more than once. Regretting that he never lived under Louis XIV, or Nero, or Pericles, he wrote that under the Roman empire he had been a theatre director, a professor, a pimp and an artist (Corr. 2, 152). Fourteen years later in a letter to George Sand he seems somewhat surer of his past:

> Il me semble ... que j'ai toujours existé! et je *possède* des Souvenirs qui remontent aux pharaons. Je me vois à différents âges de l'histoire très

> nettement, exerçant des métiers différents et dans des fortunes multiples. Mon individu actuel est le résultat de mes individualités disparues. – J'ai été batelier sur le Nil, *leno* à Rome du temps des guerres puniques, puis rhéteur grec dans Suburre, où j'ai été dévoré de punaises. – Je suis mort, pendant les Croisades, pour avoir mangé trop de raisins sur la plage de Syrie. J'ai été pirate et moine, saltimbanque et cocher. Peut-être empereur d'Orient, aussi? (Corr. 3, 536)

> It seems to me . . . that I have always existed! And I *possess* Memories that go back to the pharaohs. I see myself very clearly, at different historical times, exercising different professions with varying degrees of success. The individual I am now is the result of my previous individualities. – I was a boatman on the Nile, a *leno* in Rome during the Punic Wars, a Greek orator in Suburre where I was eaten alive by bedbugs. – I died during the Crusades from eating too many grapes on a beach in Syria. I was a pirate and a munk, a busker and a coach driver. Maybe I was an Oriental emperor, as well?

One senses an element of self-amusement in any Flaubertian statement of 'belief', but his ability to slip into the identity of other, in this case, historical individuals, has its parallel in his style, in his writing stance. It allows him to merge with the personages he creates, as when he describes the poisoning of Emma to Taine during which the taste of arsenic in his mouth was so clear that he vomited his dinner[66] or to enter bodily into phenomena in the natural world, according to his oft-quoted statement, 'À force quelquefois de regarder un caillou, un animal, un tableau, je me suis senti y entrer' (Corr. 2, 335). ('Sometimes, simply by staring at a pebble, an animal, a painting, I have felt myself enter them.')

One of the important aspects of Flaubert's hallucinatory attacks was his wavering over the 'loss of self' the attack produced. I view that idea as important because in his writing and in his attitude towards his writing, there is a rehearsal of that loss of self, but in a different register, transposed to the positive. I will return to this aspect of the question shortly, but first let us review some of the characteristics of his nervous attacks.

During his first epileptic attack, in January 1844, his doctor brother was present to confirm that Flaubert lost consciousness for about ten minutes. Flaubert describes the experience as the equivalent of a stroke, a fiery one: 'je me suis senti emporté tout à coup dans un torrent de flammes . . .'[67] ('I felt myself suddenly carried away in a torrent of flames . . .') There is some imprecision in his statements about his attacks: at times, he may be referring simply to 'loss of consciousness', but one senses that his experience goes beyond that, to a terrifying ripping away of one's inner being. In a letter from 1857 in which he pronounces himself cured, he writes, 'C'était dans ma pauvre cervelle un tourbillon d'idées et d'images où il me semblait que ma conscience, que mon *moi* sombrait comme un vaisseau sous la tempête' (Corr. 2, 716). ('In my poor brain there was a whirlwind of ideas and images in which it seemed to me that my consciousness, my *self* was sinking like a vessel in a storm.') Some years earlier, he had suffered an attack while in the company of Louise Colet, in which he clearly lost consciousness. She describes the incident as follows:

> Sa crise à l'hôtel, mon effroi. Il me supplie de n'appeler personne; ses efforts, son râle, l'écume sort de sa bouche, mon bras meurtri par ses ongles crispés. Dans à peu près dix minutes il revient à lui, vomissements. Je l'assure que son mal n'a duré que quelques secondes et que sa bouche n'a pas écumé.[68]
>
> His attack in the hotel, my fright. He begs me to call no one; his efforts, the rattle in his throat, the foam at his mouth, my arm bruised by his fingernails squeezing me. In about ten minutes he revives, vomiting. I assure him that his attack lasted only a few seconds and that he did not foam at the mouth.

In another text from 1852, he again recalls the kaleidoscope of visual images, and here admits that he loses consciousness: 'mes attaques de nerfs . . . ne sont que des déclivités involontaires d'idées, d'images. L'élément psychique alors saute par-dessus moi, et la conscience disparaît avec le sentiment de la vie'[69] ('my nervous attacks . . . are simply an involuntary slipping past me of ideas and images. The psychic element leapfrogs over me and my consciousness disappears along with the feeling of being alive'). But this question of retained or lost consciousness is deeply important to him. In another substantial text from a few months later, he appears to remain convinced that he is always present even in the worst attacks:

> Chaque attaque était comme une sorte d'hémorragie de l'innervation. C'était des pertes séminales de la faculté pittoresque du cerveau, cent mille images sautant à la fois, en feux artifices. Il y avait un arrachement de l'âme d'avec le corps, atroce (j'ai eu la conviction d'être mort plusieurs fois). Mais ce qui constitue la personnalité, l'être-raison, allait jusqu'au bout.[70]
>
> Every attack was a sort of hemorrhage of my nervous resources. They were like seminal losses of the pictorial faculty of the brain, a hundred thousand images leaping all together, like fireworks. My soul was ripped from my body, it was awful (I felt certain I was dead several times). But the constituent elements of personality, the rational being, were present right until the end.

The fact that these attacks were painful is proof, he argues, that he was always conscious during them, even when unable to speak.

However, whether consciousness is lost completely or remains, what stands out in Flaubert's descriptions of these attacks is their inconclusiveness, the sense of wavering between aspects of one's being, of a dual sense of plunging out of psychic control and, at the same time, of observing the plunge. In a similar movement, Flaubert operates as both observer and participant in the imaginative scenes the writer sees before himself. And when he includes, within an observation about melding with the fictional world he has created, a reference to his self-identification as both female and male, the line reads not as a reflex appeal to an external canon dear to patriarchy but as a natural coda to a larger psychic movement of identification and fusion with all that is external:

> Aujourd'hui par exemple, *homme et femme tout ensemble, amant et maîtresse à la fois*, je me suis promené à cheval dans une forêt, par un après-midi d'automne, sous des feuilles jaunes, et j'étais les chevaux, les feuilles, le vent, les paroles qu'ils se disaient et le soleil qui faisait s'entre-fermer leurs paupières noyées d'amour. (Corr. 2, 483–84; emphasis added).
>
> Today for example, *man and woman together, at once lover and mistress*, I rode on horseback in a forest on an autumn afternoon, beneath the yellow leaves, and I was the horses, the leaves, the wind, the words they spoke and the sun that caused their eyelids, drowning with love, to close.

This freeing of self represents one of the important psychic movements in Flaubert, a joyous absorption into character and décor.[71]

In another well-known illustration of this identification process, we see Flaubert on the edge of hallucination as he senses Emma Bovary's nervous tension so viscerally that his body becomes hers, and, bellowing out his own suffering, he wavers on the edge of a nervous crisis himself:

> Voilà une des rares journées de ma vie que j'ai passée dans l'Illusion, complètement, et depuis un bout jusqu'à l'autre. Tantôt, à six heures, au moment où j'écrivais le mot *attaque de nerfs*, j'étais si emporté, je gueulais si fort, et sentais si profondément ce que ma petite femme éprouvait, que j'ai eu peur moi-même d'en avoir une.[72]
>
> This has been one of those rare days in my life that I have spent in complete Illusion, from beginning to end. A while ago, at six o'clock, in the instant that I wrote *nervous attack*, I was so carried away, I was bellowing so loudly, and was sensing so deeply what my dear little woman was feeling, that I was afraid I was going to have an attack myself.

From a somewhat different perspective, describing the phenomenology of perception and imagining the relationship between taking in a scene visually and the pre-language that goes with that gesture, Maurice Merleau-Ponty also evokes this classic Flaubertian phenomenon, the split of the individual who is entangled as both witness and participant in the scene he perceives. Merleau-Ponty writes:

> Le spectacle m'invite à en devenir spectateur adéquat, comme si un autre esprit que le mien venait soudain habiter mon corps, ou plutôt comme si mon esprit était attiré là-bas et émigrait dans le spectacle qu'il était en train de se donner. Je suis happé par un second moi-même hors de moi, je perçois autrui . . . Quand je parle ou quand je comprends, j'expérimente la présence d'autrui en moi ou de moi en autrui, la présence du représenté.[73]

> The spectacle invites me to become an adequate spectator, as though a mind other than my own had suddenly inhabited my body, or rather as if my mind was drawn away and emigrated into the spectacle that it was putting on. I am seized by a second self outside myself, I see someone else . . . When I speak or when I understand, I experiment with the presence of someone else in me or of myself in someone else, the presence of the represented.

What is characteristic about what Flaubert might have called his feminine sensitivity, is that inherent in it is a movement towards a type of hallucination that might better be called creative rapture. This effusion/transfusion and the ecstatic state it creates are central to Flaubert's sense of the writing experience: 'C'est une délicieuse chose que d'écrire! que de ne plus être *soi*, mais de circuler dans toute la création dont on parle'.[74] ('What a delightful thing it is to write! to no longer be oneself but to circulate in the whole of the creation one is describing.') Hence this writing state of mind is another approach, this one quasi-voluntary, for losing one's *moi*, but not as it had been forcibly removed from him in his epileptic attacks. Here the floating sensation, the out-of-body feeling that is accompanied by a cutting of ties, is rapturous, not appalling. Maxime Du Camp saw Flaubert's epilepsy as a pathological state that handicapped the writer and held him back from greatness, whereas nowadays a critic such as Pierre-Marc de Biasi considers those attacks as a key factor in Flaubert's self-discovery as a creative writer.[75]

Flaubert thus recovers the self of which he had been deprived during his attacks, and he accomplishes this along the same path of hallucination that caused the loss. It is not precisely that he is able to control his attacks, but in his relationship as writer to the natural world, those attacks can be rehearsed, reconfigured and rechannelled. His capacity to merge with what is exterior to the self becomes, if I may repeat an important statement already mentioned, a generalized hallucinatory ability to both observe (regarder) and to enter (y entrer): 'À force quelquefois de regarder un caillou, un animal, un tableau, je me suis senti y entrer' (Corr. 2, 335). ('Sometimes, simply by staring at a pebble, an animal, a painting, I have felt myself enter them.') In a very important sense, this aging hysteric is less a 'critical cross-dresser' than a creative individual increasingly attuned to the unconscious origin of his second states and to the refashioning of them into art.

In Catherine Clément's study on syncope and rapture,[76] she shows that the nineteenth-century medicalization of femininity culpabilized ecstasies. Whether perceived historically as religious raptures (Saint Teresa) or demonic possessions (the Ursuline nuns of Loudun), or studied as nervous attacks at La Salpêtrière hospital, these states of mind were all diagnosed as simple hysteria by the hysteria experts of the day, Lasègue, Charcot, Legrand du Saulle, Paul Richer and Charles Richet. Ecstasies became forbidden for women in the nineteenth century.

It is perhaps an overstatement to speak of 'epiphanies' in regard to Flaubert, as we might of Proust or Joyce. Yet there is indeed a connection between hysteria, creativity and a type of rapture in Flaubert. It is possible that Proust came closest to finding an expression for the way Flaubert 'converts' his hystero-epileptic attacks; that is, he brings a kind of trance into style. Viewed from Flaubert's perspective, the closing of distance between writer and object that Proust described is pictured perfectly in the love scene in the forest between Rodolphe and Emma: the interval between writer and his creations is so reduced that the author inhabits every element in the love-making tableau.

In a work like *Salammbô* where description becomes a central aspect of the narrative – Gérard Genette called the novel a story crushed by its own décor[77] – what surfaces somewhat obtrusively, if we are mindful of Trilling's admonition about the effort to avoid the personal, is the Flaubertian unconscious. That is, phenomena in the natural landscape express authorial mood and vision; the energy invested means that objects in the décor are infused with deflected authorial agency. One comes upon passages such as the following where the landscape moves and evolves of itself:

> Sur la gauche, à l'extrémité du golfe, des tas de sable *semblaient* de grandes vagues blondes arrêtées, tandis que la mer, plate comme un dallage de lapis-lazuli, *montait* insensiblement jusqu'au bord du ciel. La verdure de la campagne *disparaissait* par endroits sous de longues plaques jaunes; des caroubes *brillaient* comme des boutons de corail; des pampres *retombaient* du sommet des sycomores; on entendait le murmure de l'eau; des alouettes huppées *sautaient*, et les derniers feux du soleil *doraient* la carapace des tortues, *sortant* des joncs pour *aspirer* la brise. (163–64 ; emphasis added).
>
> On the left, at the outer edge of the gulf, piles of sand *seemed to be* great blond arrested waves, while the sea, flat like a pavement of lapis-lazuli,

> *ascended* bit by bit onto the edge of the sky. The green of the countryside *disappeared* here and there under long yellow plates; carobs *shone* like bits of coral; vine branches *fell* from the tops of sycamores; one could hear the lapping water; crested larks *hopped about*, and the last rays of the sun *gilded* the shells of the tortoises *emerging* from the reeds to *take* the breeze.

These moments of connection and fusion with the décor seem the reposeful counterweight to the violence that characterizes other passages.

Flaubert's borrowing from his hallucinatory symptoms has, of course, been a subject of fascination for a number of critics, and there are two recent readings that are of particular interest for this study, those of Chiara Pasetti and Marie-Christine Desmaret.[78] Pasetti is especially attentive to the fictional use of the brilliant, fiery incursions of Flaubert's nervous attacks, and what I would note in her commentary is that these moments or sensations usually retain their connection to the menace of loss, invasion of self or apprehended death that was part of the original attack. Among several examples that fit this pattern she cites from *Madame Bovary* is a passage that follows Rodolphe's refusal to give Emma the money she needs. I reproduce the text in part:

> Tout ce qu'il y avait dans sa tête de réminiscences, d'idées, s'échappait à la fois, d'un seul bond, comme les mille pièces d'un feu d'artifice [. . . Elle] sentait son âme l'abandonner par ce souvenir [d'amour], comme les blessés, en agonisant, sentent l'existence qui s'en va par leur plaie qui saigne.[79]
>
> All the memories and ideas in her mind slipped away in a single stroke, like the thousand pieces of a fireworks display [. . . She] felt her soul abandon her because of this memory [of love], just as the wounded, dying, feel their life slip away through their bleeding wound.

The fireworks are present, but also, in the image of the seeping wound, the sense of self slipping away. *Salammbô* has similar passages where stupor appears to portend death:

> [Salammbô] s'affaissa sur l'escabeau d'ébène; elle restait les bras allongés entre ses genoux, avec un frisson de tous ses membres, comme une victime au pied de l'autel quand elle attend le coup de massue. Ses tempes bourdonnaient, elle voyait tourner des cercles de feu, et, dans sa stupeur, ne comprenait plus qu'une chose: c'est que certainement elle allait bientôt mourir.[80]
>
> [Salammbô] collapsed on the ebony stool; she sat, her arms stretched out between her knees, all her limbs shivering like a victim at the foot of an altar waiting for the club to fall. Her temples were buzzing, she saw circles of fire turning before her, and, in her dazed state, she understood but one thing: she was certainly going to die soon.

Desmaret's approach is somewhat different from that of Pasetti. In the carnage and bloodletting, especially of battle scenes in *Salammbô*, she sees the unconscious at work. She argues convincingly that these moments represent the conversion and redirecting of the fear, violence and suffering of the writer's epileptic crises.[81] Flaubert's flight into a geographical and temporal elsewhere, into an exotic or biblical landscape, opens the space for the repressed, enraged side of Flaubert's polarity to emerge. She points to the myriad figures of attack and assault in *Salammbô* that can be seen to rehearse the struggles of the epileptic attack, and the moments of paroxysm and convulsion in the chapter 'Le Défilé de la hache' as the trapped warriors starve: 'Il leur semblait parfois qu'on leur arrachait l'estomac avec des tenailles. Alors, ils se roulaient saisis de convulsions, jetaient dans leur bouche des poignées de terre, se mordaient les bras et éclataient en rires frénétiques.'[82] ('They felt at times that their stomach was being ripped out with pincers. They rolled about, seized by convulsions, stuffed handfuls of earth in their mouths, gnawed at their arms and broke into frenetic laughter.') At other moments, one senses the pain and terror of someone who, like Flaubert, was a passive captive of disease. When the army of Carthage returns home with 2000 captives, the latter are tied up in a public space to be slowly tortured and killed by the population. Women and children turn out to help. Paralyzed citizens are brought on stretchers to watch. Enterprising individuals rent out bows and arrows and the crucified cadavers are left standing until they begin to smell too badly (251). As Desmaret puts it,

> Placé sous le signe de l'hystérie masculine, mal étrange lié à l'imagination, l'oeuvre permet d'extérioriser les hallucinations qui assaillent Flaubert pendant la maladie, de leur fournir un exutoire, en les exorcisant et les sublimant dans l'art, en un mouvement menant de la possession à l'exorcisme. (Desmarets, 14)

> Under the sign of male hysteria, a strange ailment linked to the imagination, the work allows the externalization of the hallucinations that assailed Flaubert during his condition, it provides them with an outlet, exorcising them and sublimating them in art, in a movement away from possession toward exorcism.

Desmaret's logic about the venting of Flaubert's rage is irresistible. But her focus on the violence in Flaubert's text, and Pasetti's attention to loss, invasion of self and death mean that another aspect of hallucination in Flaubert, the ecstatic side of his relationship to the material world and, by extension, to the writing act, is left outside the equation. When one totals up the number and intensity of Flaubert's expressions of rapturous oneness with the external world, it is impossible not to realize that here is another, indeed equally interesting, aspect of an unconscious use of the hallucinatory model. Ecstatic moments of merging with nature abound in the works of Flaubert's youth. Gérard Genette points to passages in *Novembre* and to this episode from *Par les champs et par les grèves* where the narrator is transfixed by the beauty of nature:

> À force de nous en pénétrer, d'y entrer, nous devenions nature aussi, nous nous diffusions en elle, elle nous reprenait, nous sentions qu'elle gagnait sur nous et nous en avions une joie démesurée; nous aurions voulu nous y perdre, être pris par elle ou l'emporter en nous.[83]

> Penetrated by nature and entering it we became nature also, we became diffuse in her, she took us up, we felt that she was taking us over and our joy was unbounded; we would have wished to lose ourselves in her, to be taken by her or to carry her off in us.

Flaubert's wish is to 'circuler dans toute la création'. I would therefore put the emphasis on openness to movement in Flaubert rather than on stasis or passivity, which Sartre describes as Flaubert's dream to become part of earth and water, to join up with matter in the form of the mineral.[84] It seems to me that Flaubert's attraction is not to the mineral, to immovable stone, but is rather an *active* desire to inhabit many objects, bodies and elements at once, a joy at the sense of spreading the self out among external phenomena and experiencing their particular life. This melting into nature, with its mystical overtones, is a movement we see in the mystic Salammbô (*Salammbô*, 103). This process is the reversal, the half-conscious but partly controlled reworking, wreathed in joy, of the horrific feeling of being forcibly drained of one's self. It rehearses the sensation of having the self torn from one, and now the aim, and the deep pleasure, is the voluntary melting of self into life. Flaubert confirms this relationship in his discussions of the nature of hallucination with Taine, to whom he writes:

> Dans l'hallucination proprement dite, il y a toujours terreur, on sent que votre personnalité vous échappe, on croit qu'on va mourir. Dans la vision poétique, au contraire, il y a joie. C'est quelque chose qui entre en vous. (Corr. 3, 562–63)

> In a real hallucination, one is always terrified, you feel your personality slipping away, you're going to die. In poetic vision, on the contrary, there is joy. It's something that has entered you.

But, this something that enters Flaubert the artist, filling him with happiness, seeps outward in such moments to inhabit décor and character.

In Flaubert's mature writing posture, and in his statements about it, we find all of the dualities of the man. His writing takes place within a dual movement of interrelated hallucinations. During his nervous attacks, he is overcome by a thousand fast-moving images accompanied by brilliant light flashes. These attacks are deeply frightening, even though he feels over time that he can begin to control or shape them. He wavers, hopefully, for example, around the question of consciousness: does he not sometimes remain conscious in these moments of crisis? Perhaps he is actually present during them, and this is an important emotional factor. Writing will be the medium through which he regains effective control, but it will involve, perhaps surprisingly, countering the irresistible hallucination by fashioning or adapting from it a personally triggered trance in which the self can be dispatched to the once terrifying outside world and be invested in it by merging with character and natural phenomena.

Strictly medical views of Flaubert's nerve ailments often conclude that, luckily, his condition had little negative impact on his writing.[85] But such judgements ignore the creative impact of the malady. Flaubert's attacks gave him the key, no doubt only partially consciously, to a very personal artistic vision and writing technique. The fact that Flaubert was 'carried away bodily' out of normal consciousness in his hystero-epileptic attacks led him to a cultivation of rapturous, visionary moments, to what we might call a position of writing from hallucination.

CHAPTER 3

Maupassant, Charcot and the Paranormal

When one considers what form the unconscious takes in Maupassant's writing, one is inevitably drawn to reflection on his famous story *Le Horla*. Is *Le Horla* meant as the personal journal of an individual slipping into insanity? Is the Horla figure itself, as some have suggested, meant to represent the unconscious? Is there perhaps an unconscious, malevolent force in us all that has the potential to take over our waking self? The question is an intriguing one, especially regarding an author whose fiction and other writings dealt extensively with unusual and troubled mind states.

Much critical writing attaches *Le Horla* and Maupassant's thinking on the unconscious to his relationship with Jean-Martin Charcot and the research on hypnotism and hysteria at the La Salpêtrière hospital. As others have at times suggested, I believe it is wrong to picture Maupassant as seeing in Charcot a master figure.[1] There is rather a need to reposition that relationship, to view it as but a part of the mid-1880s society-wide focus on the paranormal, on things psychic and on the meaning of the unconscious. There are important examples of medico-psychological experiments with suggestion, suggested crimes and apparent telepathy that are not related to La Salpêtrière, to which Maupassant would have been exposed and that are reflected in *Le Horla*. His interest in itinerant hypnotists, the 'magnétiseurs' of the 1880s, especially the Belgian clairvoyant Pickmann, is also worthy of investigation, as are Maupassant's experiences with autoscopia, that is, seeing oneself disembodied outside one's own physical body. While exploring ambient literature on psychic phenomena, and with a number of Maupassant's stories in mind, I will attempt to analyze, with the help of numerous critics who have looked at the question, the figure of the unconscious one can construct from Guy de Maupassant's writing.

3.1 Charcot, *Le Horla* and Ambient Psychic Research

The historian of psychiatry Élisabeth Roudinesco draws a number of unexpected conclusions from the bare details we know of Maupassant's relationship with La Salpêtrière and Charcot.[2] She asserts that the hallucinatory current in Maupassant's short stories was triggered when he realized that psychic research at La Salpêtrière could demonstrate that hysteria was not an illness in the classical sense but a neurosis from which anyone might suffer. In this way, she suggests, Maupassant was ahead of the psychiatric thinking of his time and, in fact, was anticipating Freud. This conclusion is based on a statement in Maupassant's article 'Une Femme' to which she assigns great importance:

> Nous sommes tous des hystériques depuis que le docteur Charcot, ce grand prêtre de l'hystérie, cet éleveur d'hystériques en chambre, entretient à grands frais dans son établissement modèle de la Salpêtrière un peuple de femmes nerveuses auxquelles il inocule la folie, et dont il fait, en peu de temps, des démoniaques.[3]
>
> We are all hysterics since Dr Charcot, that grand priest of hysteria, that breeder of hysteria within four walls, has supported a population of nervous women in grand style in La Salpêtrière, his model establishment. There he infects them with madness and in short order makes of them the demonically possessed.

In spite of the mocking tone of Maupassant's text, Roudinesco interprets these lines as his discovery of a fundamental truth about the human mind: we are all split between apparent normalcy and the risk of being 'inoculated with madness'. Yet in the mid-1880s the lament that 'we are all hysterics' was a journalistic cliché. Alexandre Hepp is one newspaper journalist who wrote extensively at the time about society's maladies, especially hysteria, in terms that echo Maupassant's exactly. In a collected volume of his articles, *Paris-Patraque*,[4] Hepp titles one of his texts 'Tous des hystériques'. Is he making the same discovery about human duality as Maupassant, or simply rehearsing and ridiculing a conventional truth of the moment?

Moreover, Maupassant's comment on Charcot contains a hefty dose of irony and of resentment towards the doctors who had become famous because of their hysteria research and who were seeking to control discourse about it. Maupassant's belligerence was already on record. Charcot's pretention to shape the debate on hypnotism via the famous paper he delivered to the Académie des sciences on 13 February 1882 had been followed, barely two months later, by Maupassant's story 'Magnétisme',[5] which skewers the famous doctor as someone wandering aimlessly in the midst of nervous conditions he does not understand.

Reading a bit further in 'Une Femme', one would have to say that the text surrounding the passage Roudinesco cites can be read to mean the exact opposite of what she argues, given that the author expresses open contempt for Charcot's claim for the universality of Salpêtrière-style neuroses. If you are a faithful wife, writes Maupassant, doctors say you are a chaste hysteric; if you are unfaithful, you are a sensual hysteric; if you are a woman at all, in fact, you are a hysteric; all great men of history were hysterics; talent is a type of hysteria resulting from a lesion on the brain. 'Nous voilà bien renseignés' ('We're not much further ahead, are we') is the writer's disdainful conclusion. Maupassant's claim in 'Une Femme' that Charcot is a 'breeder' of hysterics is probably the most subversive of his assertions, and on this point he was not alone. Increasingly, as the decade progressed, La Salpêtrière was accused of exacerbating patient suffering by inducing hysterical symptoms via hypnotism, rather than treating the condition that had brought the women to the hospital.

A Maupassantian level of contempt seems to underlie Hepp's view of hysteria and of its medical guru, for in another column, titled 'Le Clou et la boule',[6] he labels hysteria 'the great, bizarre, unique malady of the century, which earns Dr Charcot an annual income of three hundred thousand francs' (175). The cover image of his collection *Paris-Patraque* captures the fixation of the moment: it shows an attractive, elegantly coiffed and dressed young woman tugging at the bell cord of a door marked 'Charcot' as an endless queue of patients await their turn behind her. Hepp gives almost equal value to other societal contagions of the moment, claiming that 'all women are anemic today' (61), while another story titled 'Tout à la morphine' (119–25) deals with morphine addiction as well as the problem of rampant syphilis. Jean Lorrain makes a similar, if typically more exaggerated observation, while assessing the audience at the Concerts Colonne: 'toutes les clientes du joli docteur [sont là]; toutes morphinées, cautérisées, dosées, droguées, médicamentées, anémiées, poitrinaires, hystériques'[7] ('all the patients of the handsome doctor [are there]: all on morphine, cauterized, dosed, drugged, medicated, anemic, tubercular, hysterical').

What do we actually know of Maupassant's attendance at Charcot's demonstrations at La Salpêtrière? A number of commentators have expressed surprise at the confidence with which critics have assigned Maupassant's attendance at Charcot's Tuesday demonstrations to the

1884–86 period.[8] One source often referred to is Léon Daudet, but his memoirs confirm only that Maupassant frequently queried doctors about psychological questions, not that he met and questioned Charcot.[9] The principal 'source' for the Maupassant/Salpêtrière relationship thus remains the Swedish doctor Axel Munthe's book of memoirs, *The Story of San Michele*. He recounts there his meeting Maupassant at La Salpêtrière:

> It was during one of [Charcot's Tuesday lectures] that I became acquainted with Guy de Maupassant then already famous for his *Boule de Suif* and his unforgettable *Maison Tellier*. We used to have endless talks on hypnotism and all sorts of mental troubles. He never tired of trying to draw from me what little I knew on these subjects. He also wanted to know everything about insanity. He was collecting just then materials for his terrible *Le Horla*, a faithful picture of his own tragic future. He even accompanied me once on a visit to Professor Bernheim's clinic in Nancy which opened my eyes to the fallacies of the Salpêtrière school in regard to hypnotism.[10]

Yet Munthe mentions no date for Maupassant's attendance at La Salpêtrière and admits at the same time that parts of his memoir are fanciful. All we do know, in fact, is that Maupassant consulted Charcot about his eye problems in April 1886.[11]

It would seem that the focus on doctors, possession and then hypnosis in the two versions of *Le Horla*, published in 1886 and 1887, has provided critics with a convenient but unverifiable temporal endpoint in the guessing game of when Maupassant stopped frequenting the Salpêtrière. One or another guess may be correct, but what seems potentially quite misleading about the supposed Charcot episode is that it can compress and funnel our understanding of Maupassant's interaction with the mind doctors of the 1880s into a kind of formulaic Maupassantian 'debt to Charcot', a formula summed up by Élisabeth Roudinesco when she calls *Le Horla*, '[cette] vampire accouchée par La Salpêtrière'[12] ('[that] vampire brought forth by La Salpêtrière'). The encounter with Charcot does merit full consideration, but as we will see, the debate needs to be widened so as to assess Maupassant's exposure to the plethora of French research, writing and fiction on the psyche in the mid-1880s period. There is far more to his interest in the apparently paranormal, abnormal psychology and the unconscious than can be derived from a focus on his relationship to La Salpêtrière.

Is the definitive version of *Le Horla* (1887) 'a child of La Salpêtrière', a product of Maupassant's reflection on Charcot's technique and practices? I would contend, along with Marlo Johnston, that *Le Horla* represents, on the contrary, a reorientation away from Salpêtrière teachings and, instead, an opening both to theories and practices emanating from the Nancy school and to other aspects of the ambient percolation of ideas on hypnotism. Johnston emphasizes a remark by Maupassant's character Dr Parent, who lauds Bernheim's successes: '[Parent] nous raconta longtemps les résultats prodigieux obtenus par des savants anglais et par les médecins de l'école de Nancy.'[13] ('[Parent] described at length the prodigious results obtained by English scientists and by the doctors of the Nancy school.') If Maupassant did accompany the unreliable Munthe to Nancy, perhaps he was impressed by some of the case studies going on there.

To add to Johnston's argument, one might also underline a phrase that immediately precedes the quotation above: Parent marvels at the extraordinary discoveries made via 'les expériences sur l'hypnotisme et la suggestion' (ibid., 272). This remark may seem anodyne enough, but it recalls Bernheim's contention that it was suggestion, not neuroses or pathology as Charcot insisted, that was at the heart of hysterical behaviour. A number of Nancy publications from the mid-1880s drove home ever more explicitly the view that the structured, three-stage hysteria attack seen at La Salpêtrière was absolutely not universal, but rather the result of suggestion, whether conscious or not, coming from the medical team under Charcot.[14] Charcotian hysteria was 'cultivated'.

Moreover, another focus of the Nancy school was, as we will see in detail in Chapter 5, the range of actions, from eccentric to criminal, that one could suggest to the hypnotized, to be carried out posthypnotically. The Nancy group was still very active in research on this topic,[15] and the fact that Maupassant inserts such an episode (that involving the hypnotism of Mme Sablé) into *Le Horla* again supports the idea that he was now less preoccupied with Charcot and La Salpêtrière. And what of the reference Dr Parent makes to English researchers? This is surely not an allusion to the Scottish physician James Braid, who, some decades previously, had coined the term 'hypnosis'.[16] It is far more likely that the reference is to members of the English Society for Psychical Research, some of whom were active participants in 1885–86 in the well-publicized experiments with telepathy involving Dr Pierre Janet at Le Havre. An article by Sandra Janssen, mentioned earlier, 'L'Inquiétante étrangeté', also downplays severely the importance of Charcot's work to Maupassant, arguing rather for a significant debt the writer owes to Taine and Théodule Ribot. We will return to Janssen's essay in a concluding discussion of the nature of the unconscious in Maupassant.

French society as a whole in the 1880s was permeated and riveted by articles, editorials, novels, stories, medical case studies, and personal testimonials about possession and mind control, not to speak of the extremely popular salon demonstrations of hypnotism, on the one hand, and of the channelling powers of 'possessed' mediums, on the other. Prominent journalists such as Jules Claretie were writing lengthy columns about the strange behaviours of hysterics under hypnosis (not only imperviousness to pain, sudden catalepsies or induced paralyses, but openness to a range of eccentric suggested behaviours) as early as 1881.[17]

Two of the most widely read journals that featured stories on hypnotism and exploration of the unconscious mind were the *Revue Scientifique* and the *Revue Philosophique*, the first directed by Dr Charles Richet, and the second by the psychologist Théodule Ribot. In the mid-1880s Ribot's publication especially overflowed with essays, articles and book reviews on these topics. Richet was known (and sometimes criticized) for his capacity to approach paranormal questions with an open mind. Following a show by the magnetizer Donato, an observer noted Richet's presence, his role as director of the *Revue Scientifique* and the way Richet had praised Donato's powerful hypnotic talents.[18]

Another journal launched in 1887 was the *Revue de l'Hypnotisme Expérimental et Thérapeutique*. If Maupassant had read its initial issue he would have noted an unusual act committed under posthypnotic suggestion that is structured in the same way as the episode involving the narrator's cousin in *Le Horla*, also published in 1887. A pharmacist, Focachon, intrigued by hypnotism, joins forces with Drs Bernheim and Beaunis of the Nancy school to try to replicate in real life the type of posthypnotic crime the public read about in Claretie's novel *Jean Mornas*. As in the novel, a particularly suggestible female subject is hypnotized and instructed to sneak into Focachon's home the following day and steal a bracelet located in a certain armoire. They watch her commit the offense, then order her to deny that she stole the bracelet. She does so in a letter to an examining magistrate in which she blames an innocent man for the robbery.[19] The interplay between 'real' hypnosis and the fictionalization of hypnotic scenarios caught the attention of the *Revue*'s editor, and other novels were reviewed in its pages, with references to Dumas, Balzac and contemporary writers such as Claretie and Adolphe Belot.[20] The journal also acknowledged the extension of fascination with hypnotism to the other arts, publishing a review of Brouillet's famous painting *Une Leçon clinique à la Salpêtrière* and a canvas of a hypnotized woman titled *Une Suggestion* by the Swedish painter Richard Bergh, both displayed at the Salon of 1887.[21]

Richet, who would later win a Nobel Prize for physiology, had a deep interest in hypnotism and had authored an important, early paper on the subject that predated the publications of the Charcot group.[22] As a fiction writer publishing under the pseudonym Charles Epheyre, he also wrote several works featuring not only hypnotism but all manner of paranormal ideas, and all his fiction was published by one of Maupassant's regular publishers, Ollendorff.[23] Richet's novel *Possession* appeared in late 1886 after the first and before the second version of *Le Horla*. Was Maupassant aware of this tale? There is the potential Ollendorff connection, but perhaps more important, the book was reviewed in November 1886 in the newspaper *Gil Blas* by its regular literary critic Paul Ginisty, who knew Maupassant well because the latter was a frequent contributor to the newspaper and had reviewed some of Ginisty's own fiction.[24]

Early on in *Possession*, Richet defines his subject as follows: 'An incarnation, or a possession, takes place when a dead person returns for a few days or hours to inhabit the body of a living being.'[25] In far off, spirit-washed Russia, two women, Marie-Anne and Sacha, compete for the love of Stéphane. It is Sacha who wins the prize, even though Marie-Anne has warned Sacha that she will never renounce her affection: her soul will always accompany the man she loves. Indeed, during the Stéphane/Sacha honeymoon, the spirit of Marie-Anne appears (she is now deceased) and occupies the sleeping (or hypnotized?) body of Sacha, in order to 'make use of her body and her voice' (243). Each night that voice accuses Sacha of treacherous acts and, obsessed by these insistent suggestions, Stéphane shoots his bride. In a stroke, the apparition disappears, and, finally understanding that he has murdered his wife, he commits suicide.

Could Richet's novel have influenced Maupassant in some way? The notion of possession is not the same in *Le Horla* as in Richet's work, although it is interesting to reflect that each story ends with a crime brought on by evil suggestions (a murder in the case of Richet; Maupassant's protagonist setting fire to his house and incinerating his servants) and a suicide (carried out in *Possession*, promised in *Le Horla*). In any case, however, this instance is but one of many that provide an evocative context for Maupassant's famous story. Perhaps even more important than homegrown writings on the topic was Dostoyevsky's *The Possessed*, sometimes titled *The Devils* or *The Demons*, which appeared in a French translation as *Les Possédés* in 1886.[26]

One of the obsessive societal themes in France of the 1880s was indeed possession. The medical perspective on the question, in line with the anticlericalism of the times, was one of denial: scores of medical publications appeared arguing that any religious interpretation of what had been called demonic possession was unfounded. The historical possessions of nuns, for example, that of the Ursuline nuns of Loudun in the early 1700s, were simply instances of group hysteria. Already in 1885 the novelist Camille Lemonnier had updated the historical narrative of nuns and priests in *L'Hystérique*,[27] in which a Beguine nun is seduced and possessed both physically and in spirit by the unprincipled abbé Orléa. The text compares the priest's actions to those of Urbain Grandier, the priest who was accused of witchcraft in 1632 by those Ursulines and who was burned at the stake two years later.

An important publicist for the Loudun episode was Dr Gabriel Légué, who authored three versions of the story. In late 1886, again before Maupassant had completed the second version of *Le Horla*, Légué joined with Charcot's assistant Georges Gilles de la Tourette to publish another work on Loudun, this time focusing on the mother superior of the Ursuline convent, sister Jeanne des Anges. To the confessional manuscript of the nun, they added a lurid title, 'Autobiography of a Possessed Hysteric', which at least had the virtue of announcing their biased approach.[28]

Maupassant was certainly aware of such publications, for he pictures Charcot ironically as a priest changing neurotic subjects into 'démoniaques', women possessed by the devil. It may be, he suggests, that Charcot is too caught up in ecclesiastical explanations of psychological mysteries. Was Maupassant familiar with the various descriptions of Jeanne's contacts with demons? She experiences a number of nighttime visitations that resemble the nightmarish moments in *Le Horla*. One controlling demon takes the form of a lion that presses on her chest: 'il se rua sur moi, mit sa patte sur ma poitrine, m'envisagea avec des yeux terribles, demeura quelque tems [*sic*] en cette posture' (*Sœur Jeanne des Anges*, 119) ('it launched itself onto me, put its paw on my chest, stared at me with terrifying eyes and remained in that position for some time').

Charles Richet experienced a dream similar to that of the narrator in *Le Horla*, and his description of it alludes to the historical background of this type of nightmare:

> Une seule fois, un de mes rêves s'est continué pendant la veille. C'est intéressant parce que c'est la forme typique du *cauchemar* des vieux auteurs. Je me suis réveillé ayant la sensation d'un chat ou d'un animal à fourrure, pressant ma poitrine et me tenant à la gorge. J'ai passé la main, étant réveillé, sur son dos fourré, étendu sur ma poitrine, et je me suis aperçu que c'était un rêve parce que la fourrure de la bête se prolongeait de manière à être plus longue que celle d'une bête ordinaire. Peu à peu cela s'est dissipé. (Chabaneix, 43)

> Just once, one of my dreams continued while I was awake. It is interesting because it took the typical form of the nightmare discussed by ancient authors. I woke up with the sensation of a cat or a furry animal pressing down on my chest and holding me by the throat. Awakening, I slid my hand onto its furry back stretched out on my chest, and realized that it was a dream because the animal's fur became much longer than that of an ordinary animal. Little by little the dream faded away.

Lisa Downing has summarized the history of this type of nightmare, which goes back at least to ancient times. It is also studied nowadays under the heading of sleep paralysis. She describes the phenomenon in a way that suggests Maupassant would have been familiar with its history:

> The Greeks wrote of a kind of nocturnal phenomenon in which a dreamer becomes aware of a feeling of physical weight, as if something or someone, often figured in pictorial arts as a demonic or monstrous entity, or an animal, were pressing on the dreamer's chest and causing a sensation of asphyxia.[29]

Cauchemar, demonic possession, sleep paralysis, the episode in which the Horla almost throttles the narrator borrow from a number of traditions of the nightmare.

In the first version of *Le Horla* the presence of hypnotism is minimal: it is mentioned in a single sentence as a phenomenon far inferior to the truly supernatural. The narrator says to an audience of doctors and scientists:

> Et tout ce que vous faites vous-mêmes, messieurs, depuis quelques ans, ce que vous appelez l'hypnotisme, la suggestion, le magnétisme – c'est lui [le Horla] que vous annoncez, que vous prophétisez! (*Le Horla*, Bury, 248)

> And everything you have been doing yourselves for the last few years, gentlemen, what you call hypnotism, suggestion, magnetism – it is he [the Horla] that you are setting the stage for, that you are prophesizing!

In comparison, the hypnosis episode in the second *Horla*, involving the narrator, his cousin Mme Sablé and Dr Parent, occupies seven pages.

The increased emphasis on hypnotism testifies to Maupassant's developing fascination with the subject. From late 1885 until 1887, there were a number of sensational, well-publicized events in hypnotism research, suggestion and mental telepathy that preoccupied medico-psychological attention. Some of these mirror episodes in *Le Horla.*

Experiments carried out in Le Havre by Dr Joseph Gibert and his soon-to-be famous colleague Pierre Janet (the latter not yet in possession of either his philosophy doctorate or his medical degree) demonstrated the uncanny abilities of certain neurotic or hysterical patients. Not only could they receive and act upon suggestions at a distance, they also seemed to have clairvoyant gifts, an ability Maupassant would bestow on Mme Sablé in *Le Horla*.

Pierre Janet's first paper on his Le Havre research was read in 1885 by his uncle Paul to the Société de psychologie physiologique. Within a short time, Janet received a delegation of psychological researchers: Charles Richet; Julian Ochorowicz, a Polish psychologist working in Paris; Frederic Myers of the Cambridge Society for Psychical Research; and Janet's psychopathologist brother Jules. The paper was published a year later under the title 'Notes sur quelques phénomènes de somnambulisme' in the widely read *Revue Philosophique* where it created quite a stir. Aspects of these experiments involving Janet's subject Léonie foreshadow two episodes of hypnosis-based suggestion that Maupassant inserts in *Le Horla*. Here is Janet's description of one experiment:

> Je voulais faire décrire par Mme B . . . [=Léonie] des photographies qu'elle ne voyait pas mais que j'avais entre les mains. Je m'aperçus qu'elle les décrivait aussi bien quand je ne les connaissais pas que lorsque je les connaissais. Sept fois de suite elle me désigna exactement quel était le portrait touché par moi avant que personne ne l'eût regardé.[30]
>
> I wanted Mme B . . . [= Léonie] to describe photos she could not see but which I was holding in my hands. I realized that she described them just as well when I wasn't familiar with them as when I was. Seven times she indicated exactly which photo I had touched before anyone else had seen it.

The narrator of *Le Horla* is involved in an equally unexpected and unsettling experience with photographs that intimidates members of a small dinner party who beg for the demonstrations to stop. Dr Parent hypnotizes the narrator's cousin Mme Sablé and asks the narrator to stand behind her. Handing the woman a business card, the doctor says it is a mirror and asks her to report on what is happening behind her:

> – Je vois mon cousin.
>
> – Que fait-il?
>
> – Il se tord la moustache.
>
> – Et maintenant?
>
> – Il tire de sa poche une photographie.
>
> – Quelle est cette photographie?
>
> – La sienne . . .
>
> – Comment est-il sur ce portrait?
>
> – Il se tient debout avec son chapeau à la main. (*Le Horla*, Bury, 274)

– I see my cousin.
– What is he doing?
– He's twisting his moustache.
– And now?
– He's taking a photo out of his pocket.
– A photo of what?
– Himself . . .
– What does he look like in the photo?
– He's standing with his hat in his hand.

Thus, like Mme B., Mme Sablé can correctly identify scenes and objects that she cannot physically see, including a photo she has never been exposed to, for the narrator has just received it from the photographer that morning.

One of the psychologists present in Le Havre, Ochorowicz, recounts a second experiment that seems to closely parallel the episode of post-hypnotic suggestion that serves to unnerve the narrator of *Le Horla*:

> Il s'agissait de commander mentalement une action qui ne devait être exécutée que le lendemain matin. À onze heures sonnées (cet ordre a été indiqué par M. F. Myers par écrit) Mme B . . . devait passer au salon, prendre un album de photographies qui se trouvait sur la table, et l'ouvrir en examinant les portraits.[31]

> The point was to ask mentally for an action that was to take place only the next morning. At eleven o'clock precisely (the order was put in writing by M. F. Myers) Mme B . . . was to enter the salon, pick up a photo album that was on a table, open it and examine the portraits.

Léonie carries out the instructions to the letter, even though she has received them only mentally and at a distance. As we know, directly following the photograph episode in Maupassant's story, Dr Parent, in similar fashion, directs the hypnotized Mme Sablé to carry out a series of actions the next day. She is to wake up at eight o'clock, proceed to the narrator's home and ask him for 5000 francs supposedly needed by her husband. The next morning she arrives as instructed and asks for the money. Later, she has no memory whatsoever of being told to carry out her mission. For his part, the narrator is perplexed and deeply troubled, for here is another example of a kind of possession, the control of one's mind from outside.

There is a further medico-psychological text of which Maupassant must surely have been aware as he revised *Le Horla*. His story 'L'Auberge' (later to appear in the 1887 collection *Le Horla*) was published in the September

1886 issue of the review *Les Lettres et les Arts*. In the immediately preceding, August issue, a doctor J. Renaut had contributed an article on hypnotism that once again anticipates themes and episodes that would be reiterated in Maupassant's story.[32] Renaut's text immediately evokes, for example, the figure of hypnotism as an avatar of demonic possession:

> L'hypnotisme est de nos jours tout ce qui reste de la sorcellerie . . . Le fait fondamental en quoi il consiste évoque en effet la notion étrange de la possession . . . Dans de certaines conditions un homme acquiert sur un autre homme un pouvoir absolu, tel qu'à son gré il le plonge dans un sommeil semblable à la mort. Il l'en tire ensuite à sa volonté, soit pour le rendre immobile comme une statue, soit pour en faire un automate obéissant à tous ses caprices . . . Le patient devient alors un véritable possédé . . . (160)

> These days hypnotism is all that is left of sorcery . . . In fact, the basic element it consists of is the strange notion of possession . . . In certain situations a man acquires absolute power over another man, such that he can plunge him at will into a death-like sleep. He then wakes him from it as he wishes, whether to make him motionless like a statue, or to make him into an automaton who will obey his every whim . . . The subject then becomes truly possessed . . .

Renaut then speaks of the kind of disturbing hallucinatory dreams that leave the dreamer, like the narrator of *Le Horla*, 'cloué en place avec des membres de plomb' (167) ('frozen in place, his limbs feeling like lead'). And just as in Janet's texts from Le Havre, posthypnotic suggestion, even if involving only an eccentric or illogical act rather than a criminal one, is a significant and alarming feature of hypnotic reality. Thus, when the subject is asleep, asserts Renaut, 'on peut aussi lui suggérer des actes, des besoins, des illusions pour une heure donnée de l'état de veille qui suivra . . . Il n'aura aucun souvenir de cette suggestion' (174) ('one can suggest actions to him, things he will need and illusions to be carried out at a given time in his following waking hours . . . He will have no memory of this suggestion'). Mme Sablé's 'need' for 5000 francs and her amnesia regarding the suggestion made to her are foreshadowed here.

3.2 '*Les Magnétiseurs*': Pickmann versus Donato

Maupassant's mixed reaction to the two itinerant hypnotists above – approval of Pickmann, disparagement of Donato – is another illustration of the attraction/repulsion we observe in his texts where mind control is concerned. The 1880s were the decade not only of the hospital-based, hysteria-focused 'medical' hypnotism of doctors such as Charcot, Jules Luys and Amédée Dumontpallier, but the heyday of a baker's dozen of itinerant *magnétiseurs*, almost always characterized as sideshow magnetizers ('magnétiseurs de foire') by the doctors who were often employing identical hypnotic techniques and who, in some cases, had actually learned those techniques by observing one of their non-medical rivals.[33] The Belgian *magnétiseur* Donato (Alfred d'Hont) was by far the most prominent of the lay hypnotists. We have seen that certain doctors, the prominent Charles Richet, for example, admired his abilities and said so. Dr Léon Tétard attended a public demonstration of Donato's skills in 1887 on behalf of the *Revue de L'Hypnotisme* and was impressed by both the man's skills and his modesty. Hypnotism was neither paranormal nor fluidic, Donato explained to his audience; controlled behaviour under hypnosis was achieved by suggestion, especially verbal or by gesture.[34]

Maupassant's dual reaction where the paranormal is concerned shows up in his attitude towards these two men. Donato is always presented as the perpetrator of hoaxes, while Pickmann, encountered later, apparently in 1887, is not ridiculed but rather celebrated for his mind-reading ability. Maupassant's 1882 story 'Magnétisme' consigns the *magnétiseur* Donato and the eminent hypnotist Charcot to the same dubious category. Donato is a kind of shady prestidigitator, 'un très malin faiseur de tours', while Charcot is pictured as wandering almost blindly among misunderstood nervous conditions: 'Il a constaté des phénomènes nerveux inexpliqués et encore inexplicables, il marche dans cet inconnu qu'on explore chaque jour, et ne [peut] toujours comprendre ce qu'il voit.'[35] ('He has observed nervous phenomena that are unexplained and inexplicable, he circulates in this world of the unknown which is being explored daily, but [is unable] to understand what he sees.') These judgements no doubt relate in part to the public success Donato and Charcot were enjoying. It was in 1882 that Charcot was being elevated to the Chair of Nervous Diseases at La Salpêtrière, and it was in February of that year that he read his famous paper retrieving hypnotism from its magnetic past and rebranding it as an artificially induced neurosis akin to hysteria. If anything, Donato was even more in the public eye, performing to acclaim at prestigious venues such as the Jockey Club and the salon of Napoléon's niece, Princesse Mathilde.

Donato clearly went far out of his way to produce showy effects. A Marseille correspondent reported that after inviting various young men onstage, he hypnotized them as a group and had them act out 'tableaux vivants', for example, 'les naufragés de la Méduse', the drama of the survivors of a French marine disaster who cannibalized their fellows in order to survive. Maupassant mocked Donato's galvanic, anaesthetizing gaze, and indeed, one of Donato's classic numbers was to put Lucille, his favourite subject, into a trance in which she was insensitive to pinches and pinpricks. He would then have her lie rigid between two chairs, only head and feet supported, and in that position her body would withstand almost any amount of weight.

In his article 'Aux bains de mer', Maupassant provides a neat synopsis of those aspects of hypnosis that were making headlines in 1887, including the possible criminal use of posthypnotic suggestion in the then-current case of a triple murderer, Henri Pranzini. But it is here as well that Maupassant speaks of his fascination with the apparent psychic gifts of the *magnétiseur* Pickmann.[36] Although the latter had also been known for 'experimental crimes' (he had employed suggestion to have a young man from a reputable family steal a watch from a jewellery store),[37] it was Pickmann's mind-reading capabilities that made an impact on Maupassant.

The writer Jean Lorrain, a childhood playmate of Maupassant's brother Hervé (the two enjoyed games with Guy, the latter dressed up as a ghost in bedsheets), recalled Guy's attachment to the *magnétiseur* Pickmann, describing the Belgian as one of the most famous mind-readers of the period whom Maupassant had introduced to society two years previously.[38] 'Two years ago' places Guy's fascination in 1887, and it was indeed in the late summer and early fall of that year that he and Pickmann became acquainted. Some contemporaries felt that Pickmann's gifts might have influenced the writing of *Le Horla*. A journalist for *Gil Blas* wrote:

> La fréquentation de cet homme curieux [= Pickmann] devait avoir une influence singulière. [Maupassant] eut la crainte de l'invisible, et je ne serais pas étonné que de ces conversations avec Pickman [*sic*] fût née l'idée première du *Horla*.[39]
>
> Spending time with this curious man [= Pickmann] must have had a powerful influence. [Maupassant] feared the invisible and I would not be surprised that the idea for *Le Horla* was born out of conversations with Pickman [*sic*].

It is of course not impossible that Maupassant was aware of Pickmann and his abilities before he composed the final version of *Le Horla*. On the other hand, Mme Sablé's clairvoyant powers could have other sources, such as Pierre Janet's experiments with Léonie.

Marlo Johnston has shed increased light on the Pickmann episode by revealing certain letters relevant to it. It was apparently Pickmann, performing on the Norman coast in August 1887, who contacted Maupassant proposing that he demonstrate his gifts personally to the novelist. At the conclusion of a letter to Marie Kahn, Maupassant noted:

> Dans cette solitude je recevrai demain soir la visite d'un magnétiseur célèbre, nommé Pickman [*sic*], qu'on dit être le plus remarquable de tous, et qui m'a demandé la permission de venir me convaincre par des expériences extraordinaires et décisives – J'ai permis – J'attends.

> In this solitude I will receive tomorrow evening the visit of a famous *magnétiseur* named Pickman [*sic*], said to be the most remarkable of them all. He asked my permission to come and convince me using extraordinary, decisive experiments. I said yes – I am waiting.

The letter then concludes with an interrupted half-sentence that might have revealed something more of Maupassant's attitude, or concerns: 'S'il me dit que je suis violemment . . .'[40] Pickmann's speciality was the location of objects, supposedly by thought transfer. Before entering one auditorium, Pickmann is told by attendants that a murder has taken place and an object related to it is hidden somewhere in the room. He returns to the space blindfolded, takes the hand of an assistant and orders him to think forcefully about the just committed crime and the location of an object related to it. After some feverish movements and false starts, which add drama to the event, Pickmann locates the object mentally and fetches it for the audience.

It seems that the experiment with Pickmann described in 'Aux bains de mer' and which took place at Maupassant's residence, La Guillette, was a version of this. Maupassant was instructed to focus his thoughts on a particular object that Pickmann searched for, eventually located in a second-story room and brought back to the writer. Maupassant was very impressed and his judgement in 'Aux bains de mer' reads:

> Il m'a paru posséder à un degré plus étonnant que ses confrères ce bizarre flair nerveux que nous a révélé M. Cumberland et que possède aussi très étrangement, paraît-il, M. Garnier, l'architecte de l'Opéra.[41]

> He seemed to me to possess, to a more surprising degree than his fellows, that bizarre nervous flair revealed by M. Cumberland and that, strangely enough, it seems, the architect of the Opera, M. Garnier, also possesses.

Other luminaries, such as the famous anthropologist Cesare Lombroso, tested Pickmann's card-reading abilities. Blindfolded and ears plugged, Pickmann could guess nine out of ten cards Lombroso touched.[42] An article from 1901 quotes Lombroso as saying that no modern scientist could any longer deny the existence of such powers.[43] This kind of mind-reading was of interest to Maupassant for his character Mme Sablé, as we have seen. However, some wondered at Maupassant's gullibility in favouring Pickmann's tricks over those of Donato. A doctor who had read 'Aux bains de mer' and who had apparently studied both Donato and Pickmann wrote to Maupassant in the following terms:

> Il n'est pas permis à un homme de votre mérite d'écrire des choses aussi contraires à la science, et de confondre l'hypnotisme avec le magnétisme et le magnétisme avec le cumberlandisme, le mentivisme et la double-vue. M. Pickmann n'est qu'un vulgaire farceur, je l'ai vu à l'oeuvre. Il a dû dissimuler son truc à votre perspicacité.
>
> A man of your worth is not allowed to write things so opposed to science, and to confuse hypnotism with magnetism and magnetism with Cumberlandism, mentalism and second sight. M. Pickmann is no more than a vulgar charlatan, I've seen him at work. He must have hidden his tricks from you.

He advised Maupassant to clear up his misunderstanding by contacting Bernheim and the Nancy school or Donato, described as the most sincere and most competent hypnotist extant.[44]

There remains, as one can sense, a kind of contradiction in Maupassant's reactions to the paranormal. The attitude is not unlike that of the writer Rachilde, who, as a woman raised by a family of spiritualists, would vehemently deny the claims of spiritualism while highlighting in her works curious coincidences that beg for a paranormal explanation. Maupassant is unusually attracted to apparently paranormal phenomena but is very diligent, in personal and often in fictional writing, in showing them to be normal happenings. A story Paul Bourget recounted about Maupassant is a good example. Bourget described a frighteningly detailed nightmare he had had about the sickness and death of a mutual journalist friend, Léon Chapron. Did Bourget not know that Chapron was quite sick and had died? asked Maupassant. Bourget did not know. Maupassant insisted that there must be a logical explanation for this dream, and after reflection, he proposed it: a couple of weeks previously Bourget had received a letter from Chapron and had deduced, probably unconsciously, because of the shaky handwriting, that the man was ill.[45]

In the much-discussed story 'Magnétisme', the main character rationalizes a supposed instance of telepathy, while at the same time the conclusion of the story provides an example of its possible existence. The children of sailors lost at sea do not intuit the moment of their father's death, comments Maupassant; they merely reiterate in their dreams the constant community-wide fear of such loss. But as that story ends and the hero dreams of possessing a woman heretofore imagined as unappealing, when he approaches her in the flesh and finds her almost anticipating his desire, the reader is teased with the suggestion that telepathy exists. He reinforces this idea of erotic telepathy in 'Aux bains de mer', arguing that a persistent stare at the object of one's desire will always arouse a desire in her and force her to return the look.

In this instance, as in others mentioned below, Maupassant professes to see nothing paranormal. He insists instead that humans simply do not fully understand the workings of their own faculties: 'Je laisse à d'autres le soin d'expliquer ces phénomènes qui ne m'étonnent aucunement, tant nous ignorons encore les propriétés et les puissances de nos organes.'[46] ('I will leave to others the task of explaining these phenomena which do not astound me in the least so little do we know at this time of the properties and powers of our organs.') A focus on these missing organs of perception becomes a mini-obsession in Maupassant's stories. More than once we find his first-person narrators grappling with the relationship between a powerful psychic impression and missing physical abilities.

A passage in 'Un fou?' underlines how deeply this theme of organic deficiency is ingrained in the Maupassantian psyche: 'Nous sommes entourés de choses que nous ne soupçonnerons jamais, parce que les organes nous manquent qui nous les révéleraient. Le magnétisme est de celles-là peut-être' (*Le Horla*, Bury, 180). ('We are surrounded by things whose existence we will never suspect because the organs that would reveal them are missing. Perhaps magnetism is one of these.') We encounter the same focus on insufficiently acute organs in both versions of *Le Horla*: in the first the narrator laments the limited capabilities of the human eye (247), and in the second version he says that having additional organs would enable us to discover countless hidden miracles (262).

These stories underline the obsessional longing in Maupassant's texts for physical explanations of the immaterial, and in this Maupassant is a faithful creature of his age, for in this same period a broad swath of spiritualists and some scientists were trying to imagine psychic phenomena as poorly understood extensions of the physical. The astronomer Camille Flammarion interpreted wave phenomena and electricity as pathways leading to the occult. He wrote,

> Astronomie physique, analyse spectrale de la lumière, vapeur, télégraphe électrique, téléphone, et tant d'autres merveilles nous offr[ent] en ce moment, dans l'étude du magnétisme, de l'hypnotisme, du spiritisme, des rameaux d'avenir, des espérances nouvelles . . . En fait, dans la nature, il n'y a rien d'occulte, de surnaturel: Il y a *l'inconnu*.[47]

> Physical astronomy, spectral analysis of light, steam, electric telegraph, telephone and so many other marvelous things, offer us at this moment, in the study of magnetism, hypnotism and spiritualism, bits of the future,

> new hopes ... In fact, there is nothing occult or supernatural in nature: there is only *the unknown.*

Similarly, Joris-Karl Huysmans' hero Durtal equates electricity with the fluid of a magnetizer who can instruct a distant subject to join him in another part of Paris.[48] Maupassant, who knew Flammarion and had accompanied him on a visit to the Paris Observatoire,[49] made fun of the man's science in his story 'L'Homme de Mars' where Flammarion appears as an unbearably garrulous visitor who lectures the narrator on the planets, especially Mars where the lower gravity would enable residents to fly like spirits.[50]

It was not only nominal defenders of spiritualist beliefs that sensed such a convergence of paranormal and scientific. In 1904, Émile Duclaux, a member of the Académie des sciences and Director of the Pasteur Institute, gave a speech to an international psychological body in which he maintained that given so many new inventions that allowed communication at a distance, telepathic communication was easily imaginable.[51] Charles Richet, with Janet's experiments at Le Havre in mind, confidently predicted the scientific explanation of telepathy, which, he wrote, would seem something quite obvious 'in a few years'.[52]

What are we to make of Maupassant's contention that the paranormal has a physical explanation, that is, that an organ or organs are missing, untapped or unactivated? Is the missing organ itself a mysterious avatar of the unconscious, in that it screens off the ability to see through to a deeper level? What does seem clear is that Maupassant has interiorized the mechanistic, reflex lessons of his generation and that this material explanation of the supernatural or psychic helps the author to drain fraught situations of what is troubling in them. For his or her part, the reader, faced with nothing but repeated, unsatisfying assertions, feels increasing diffidence about the author's self-knowledge. Of course, overshadowing this denial of the paranormal and psychic are a sequence of duality-based moments and phenomena, attested in Maupassant's life and represented in various ways in his fiction, that appear to reveal the unconscious as a power of dispossession, best represented as the occupation of the rational, conscious mind by a malevolent other consciousness.

3.3 Dualities and Doubles

It can be instructive to observe what qualities attract Maupassant in other writers of fiction. An ability to bring the unconscious to life is certainly one of these as we see in his discussion of Paul Bourget's novella *L'Irréparable*, published in 1884, and the idea of dissociative states explored there. Maupassant's enthusiasm relates to Bourget's ability to lay bare a basic human duality, the self-destructive nature of two warring instincts in the same person, this under the general heading of the unpredictability of our unconscious. Bourget gives this disharmony medical and psychological validity via a reference to a conversation with the great (though fictitious) metaphysician Adrien Sixte, author of the imposing tome *De la dissociation des idées*, 'où il a étudié les maladies de la volonté consécutives à celles de l'intelligence'[53] ('in which he studied diseases of the will linked to those of the intelligence'), a phrase that neatly juxtaposes the titles of two works that are the principal negative keys to Sixte's character, *De l'intelligence* by Hippolyte Taine and *Les Maladies de la volonté*, the latter published by Théodule Ribot a year before *L'Irréparable*, in 1883.

As we know, Maupassant's mental state worsened as the 1880s progressed, but in this article on Bourget from 1884, his analysis seems serene and unruffled:

> Aujourd'hui, ce sont surtout les romanciers observateurs qui s'efforcent de pénétrer et d'expliquer l'obscur travail des volontés, le profond mystère des réflexions inconscientes, les déterminants tantôt plus instinctifs que raisonnés, et tantôt plus raisonnés qu'instinctifs; d'indiquer la limite insaisissable où le vouloir réfléchi se mêle, pour ainsi dire, à une sorte de vouloir matériel sensuel, à un vouloir animal; de noter les actions de l'un sur l'autre, etc.[54]
>
> These days it is above all the novelists of observation who attempt to penetrate and explain the obscure workings of the will, the profound mystery of unconscious thoughts, the factors that determine these things, sometimes more instinctive than rational, and at other times more rational than instinctive; to indicate the elusive limit where conscious willpower, so to speak, meets and mixes with a material, sensual willpower, an animal willpower; to the actions of the one upon the other.

The mention of the novelist as observer recalls the opening pages of Zola's *Le Roman experimental* (1881) in which he discusses observation and experimentation as the two keys to novelistic writing. Presumably as well, Maupassant's remark is self-inclusive, recalling that he is also a member of the naturalist *groupe de Médan*. But does Zola's central idea, an emphasis on science with a focus on physical life, lead, as he writes, to 'an understanding of both the life of the passions and of the intellect'?

In any case, though poised, this text shows Maupassant angling away from the scientific and the experimental. He becomes, here, an early forecaster of his own psychic itinerary. He sets writers of fiction a difficult task: how to sense and represent the elusive, even indiscernible contact point – or slippage point – where rational desire butts up against and is overtaken by unconscious drives. The language chosen for unconscious desires and impulses is important: the latter represent a material, sensual, animalistic willpower.

A reader may well draw the impression that Maupassant is still mulling over the idea of the unconscious from a slightly distanced, even philosophical point of view, but three years later another passage on dissociation translates a more intimidating sense of what can happen to the mind:

> Combien de fois n'avons-nous pas senti obscurément travailler en nous ce double cerveau dont un désaccord fonctionnel presque insensible peut expliquer tant de phénomènes de double volonté, de double croyance, de double jugement, et tant de contradictions dans notre être pensant et raisonnable.[55]
>
> How often we have felt in ourselves the obscure actions of that double brain with its almost undetectable functional imbalance that can explain so many instances of dual willpower, of dual belief, of dual judgement, and so many contradictions of our thinking, rational being.

This minor functional imbalance in the brain seems to be accepted dispassionately, as though such problems were common and perhaps widely shared. But a further, dramatic dissociation would reveal a deep-seated anxiety in Maupassant's makeup. The phenomenon of autoscopia, the fact that Maupassant at times saw a double of himself, is a spectacular illustration of the particular nature of the unconscious in his world. Paul Bourget, among others, was privy to Maupassant's insistence that his writing was at times interrupted by the appearance of a double of himself, and if Bourget's memory is correct, Maupassant was having these hallucinations as early as 1884, at the time their mutual acquaintance Léon Chapron died.[56] As we have seen, Bourget first recounts a horribly portentous dream he has had about Chapron's declining health. He is informed that Chapron has in fact died, but Maupassant finds a way of rationalizing the dream: it was not an uncanny prediction of Chapron's death. Then he speaks of his own problems:

> Que serait-ce, si vous subissiez ce que je subis? Une fois sur deux, en rentrant chez moi, je vois mon double . . . J'ouvre ma porte, et je me vois assis sur mon fauteuil. Je sais que c'est une hallucination, au moment même où je l'ai. Est-ce sérieux? Et si on n'avait pas de jugeotte, aurait-on peur?[57]
>
> How would you feel if you felt the things I feel? On half of the occasions I go home, I see my double . . . I open my door and I see myself seated in

> my armchair. I know it's a hallucination even as it happens. Is it serious? And if one had no common sense, would one be afraid?

In a study from 1903, Dr Paul Sollier, who later would host Proust in his nerve clinic, cited what he called the positive and negative autoscopic experiences of Maupassant. These had been recounted to him, he said, by one of the writer's close friends (Bourget again?), and the autoscopia had happened beginning in 1889.[58] Working at his desk, Maupassant heard the door open and saw a figure that was himself sit down opposite, put his head in his hands and begin to dictate what Maupassant himself was writing.[59] Axel Munthe was another who claimed to have been privy to Maupassant's autoscopic episodes, although his text sounds close enough to Sollier's that Munthe was either the mysterious friend or read Sollier's text and appropriated part of it:

> One day he told me that while he was sitting at his writing-table hard at work on his new novel he had been greatly surprised to see a stranger enter his study notwithstanding the severe vigilance of his valet. The stranger had sat down opposite him at the writing-table and began to dictate to him what he was about to write. He was just going to ring for François to have him turned out when he saw to his horror that the stranger was himself.[60]

Maupassant's lover Gisèle d'Estoc – if her *Cahier d'amour* can be accepted as an authentic document written by her – refers to several episodes of autoscopia. On one occasion, Maupassant supposedly told her that his double had visited him three times and had rifled through his papers and manuscripts, and that he had finally understood the double's attitude on the last visit: 'Il est furieux de ma presence, il me hait, il me méprise . . . parce qu'il pretend que *lui seul est l'auteur de mes livres. Et il m'accuse de le voler!*'.[61] ('He is furious at my presence, he hates me, has contempt for me . . . because he claims that *he alone is the author of my books. And he accuses me of robbing him!*')

Autoscopia became a minor literary phenomenon in the 1880s, and it is possible that Léon Hennique's use of it in his novel *Un Caractère*[62] owes something to the notoriety of Maupassant's problems. In Hennique's work, the emotional yearning of Agénor, marquis de Cluses, for a lost love leaves him open to all manner of hallucination and paranormal phenomena, although he experiences the latter, including autoscopia, as an expansion of self, minus therefore the fright that troubled Maupassant. In Léo Trézenik's novel *La Confession d'un fou*, the first-person narrator suffers a bout of negative autoscopia accompanied by the feeling that he has become another person: he cannot recognize himself in a mirror. Here, however, we sense that title, plot and the incident with mirror are all borrowed from Maupassant.

3.4 Figuring the Maupassantian Unconscious

Let us now examine some focused discussions of what the unconscious might be, or at least of how it might operate, for Maupassant. Jean-Louis Cabanès argues straightforwardly that the Maupassantian obsession is with 'dépossession'. The connection between poking holes in magnetism in the story of that name and the narrator's anxiety about hypnotism in *Le Horla* is Maupassant's obsession about the power to alienate a subject's will, to occupy his psyche, just as in a possession, demonic or otherwise. 'Dispossession' could also mean that the psyche is splittable and that the other unconscious half may rise to consciousness, replace it and occupy its space.[63]

Sandra Janssen sees this dispossession as a gnawing mental parasitism, quoting aptly *Le Horla* itself where the narrator's cousin suffers just this sort of incursion: 'Elle subissait un vouloir étranger entré en elle, comme une autre âme, comme une autre âme parasite et dominatrice.'[64] ('She sensed that a foreign willpower had entered her, like a second soul, like another parasitic, domineering soul.') Janssen quotes a discussion by Maupassant about the way our intellect is limited by our dependence on the five senses, and she underlines, as we have done, Maupassant's supposition that the human problem is an organic weakness: 'La valeur de la pensée dépend donc évidemment d'une façon directe de la valeur des organes, et son étendue est limitée par leur nombre. M. Taine d'ailleurs a magistralement traité et développé cette idée.'[65] ('The value of thought thus obviously depends directly on the quality of our organs, and its reach is limited by their number. M. Taine has in fact treated this question and elaborated on it in a masterful fashion.') She then traces Théodule Ribot's thinking on the idea of mental parasitism in *Les Maladies de la mémoire* and *Les Maladies de la personnalité*, connecting it with Taine's idea that there can exist two moral persons in the same individual. That is, mentally we are made up of a temporary harmony between often opposing views, but in Maupassant's stories, the balance is disturbed. Noting the strong interest in hallucination in this period, Janssen wonders if the ideas of Taine and Ribot on the subject may have come together in Maupassant's mind. For Taine, reality was a hallucination that was true, and for Ribot, hallucinations could become concrete. They were 'états de conscience que le moi ne considère pas comme siens, qu'il objective, qu'il place en dehors de lui et à qui il finit par attribuer une existence propre, mais indépendante de la sienne'[66] ('states of mind that the self considers foreign to it, that it objectifies and situates outside the self and, in the end, to which it attributes an actual existence, but independent of its own'). If one opts to read Maupassant with Taine and Ribot in mind, concludes Janssen, what Maupassant fears is to be cut off, alienated from his own thought.

Pierre Bayard, who enjoys imagining that Maupassant and Freud may have met and exchanged ideas while attending Charcot's demonstrations in 1885–86, proposes dropping the term 'inconscient' (too loaded since Freud) in discussing Maupassant and replacing it with 'étrangeté psychique' ('psychic strangeness').[67] His purpose is to identify what he feels Freudian analysis misses, an obsession for searching in Maupassant, a difficulty of naming what obsesses him, so that the real psychical problem is undecidability. Bayard traces this theme of irresolution in many stories and at many levels, some unexpected. Meetings in Maupassant's fiction have a certain undecidability about them, and not only the encounters with doubles of oneself. In 'Rencontre' the baron d'Étrailles meets for a second time a beautiful woman who resembles his separated wife, only realizing gradually that she is in fact his wife. Bayard notes the presence of adulterous women in a number of stories, arguing that the theme shows a fear of unresolved duality. 'Denis' features the faithful servant who stabs his master, then nurses him back to health. Stories about illegitimate children pose the question, 'Is he/she like me?' but can be read as 'Who am I?' Bayard demonstrates, with persuasive examples from every type of short story and novel, that Maupassant's mind is haunted by an undecidability that is person-related and which reflects back on his narrators, protagonists and himself: which one is I, which one is he? The anguish of many of his works stems from an inability to be sure of identity. Undecidability and duality are thus the unconscious embedded in the writer's style:

> Le double, chez Maupassant, n'est pas qu'un thème: il intervient au plus près des mécanismes d'écrire et c'est en cela qu'il correspond à une véritable manière, non théorisée, mais effectuée par écrit, de penser le monde physique.[68]
>
> The double in Maupassant is not just a theme: it intervenes in the very midst of his writing function and in this it corresponds to a true manner, not theorized, but effected in writing, of imagining the physical world.

I have attempted to parse some of the oversimplifications that are attached to Maupassant criticism, one being that the figure of the Horla is itself the representation of the unconscious. That statement may be almost true, but analyses of parasitic depossession in his works, and the concomitant inability of his characters to be certain about identity, seem separate, richer veins to explore. At the same time, it is important to understand that the Horla figure is not, in some straightforward sense, 'a vampire fathered by La Salpêtrière',[69] but rather that aspects of that story show to what extent Maupassant was attuned to the many apparently paranormal phenomena that inundated French society in the 1880s, including experiments in telepathy, apparent mind control via hynotism and the powers of suggestion publicized by the Nancy school of hysteria studies led by Dr Hippolyte Bernheim. Although *Le Horla* is clearly the jewel in the crown of Maupassant's stories of identity anguish, it needs to be seen in the context of a plethora of other tales that demonstrate in sometimes deflected ways the semi-understood anxiety at the centre of his writing stance.

CHAPTER 4

The Unconscious Female/The Female Unconscious

> Les qualités plus particulières de l'intelligence féminine revêtent presque toutes une forme automatique frappante.[1]
>
> (Almost all the qualities unique to female intelligence have a strikingly automatic form about them.)
>
> The fear of the masses in this age of declining liberalism is always also a fear of woman, a fear of nature out of control, a fear of the unconscious, of sexuality, of the loss of identity and stable ego boundaries in the mass.[2]

Although the idea may not have been phrased in exactly this form, the female herself became one of the figures of the unconscious in the late nineteenth century. To warrant this categorization, she had, according to numerous 'scientific' treatises, everything going for her. Psychologically, men did not understand her; they imagined that her behaviour was the result of inner, invisible drives. Her bodily functions, which were seen to control her, also made of her an unreflective being. Criticism has shown how Zola, the Goncourts, Henry Céard, and to some extent Huysmans and Maupassant, focused inordinately on those bodily functions, female maladies, menstruation, metritis and giving birth. As one critic has put it, 'Unable to understand the enigma of femininity, novelists convert women into a machine governed by humours.'[3] Involuntary vapours and liquid reduce the female to an elemental level, 'the abomination of pure nature'.[4] In its most condemnatory sense, this is what is meant by the frequent fin-de-siècle references to woman's 'naturalness'.[5]

Mireille Dottin-Orsini, among others, has discussed in some detail the great range of 'replacement females' one finds in fin-de-siècle fiction, those inanimate, easily approachable stand-ins for a living woman, the anatomical Venus, wax replicas, machines, automatons, and Villiers de l'Isle-Adam's 'andréide', his artificial future Eve. Nor were the twentieth- or the twenty-first centuries the inventors of the blow-up doll. In an

1891 novel by Henri Nizet, the oversexed main character wonders if he might enjoy 'une de ces Galathées de caoutchouc que certaines orthopédistes vendent dicrètement aux célibataires forcés'[6] ('one of those rubber Galateas that certain orthopedists sell on the quiet to men facing enforced celibacy'). All of these substitutes retain the female form but are dispossessed of their female psyche. These male creations reflect the fact that the male has no access to nor can he face either the physical reality of a live female or interaction with her mind and personality. In discussing these replicas Dottin-Orsini notes that as dolls or automatons, they are frequently destroyed or 'die'.[7]

Jacques Noiray delineates in Zola a movement from consideration of the female as a beautifully complex machine to the view that because she is overdelicate of constitution, she risks imbalance, even becoming unhinged.[8] Hélène de Rieu is the admirable automaton in *Madeleine Férat*, a 'petite machine singulièrement curieuse', while in *Son Excellence Eugène Rougon*, Clorine is the 'machine la plus compliquée qu'on pût imaginer'. But there are far more 'femmes détraquées' in Zola's works, machines that become unbalanced because of their sex itself, like the perverted Renée in *La Curée*, an 'adorable et étonnante machine qui se cassait'. In later works, as Noiray remarks, possibly because of Zola's encounter with Jeanne Rozerot, a new, positive, happily child-bearing heroine appears in his novels. However, like Marianne in *Fécondité*, her positive qualities are required as foils to sexual machines like the character Sérafine in the same novel who, when her multiorgasmic career is cancelled by an ill-considered operation to remove her ovaries, literally becomes insane with frustration and must be institutionalized.

My central interest in this chapter is to explore those arguments, articulated by many nineteenth-century researchers, psychiatrists and doctors, concerning the inferior nature of the female mind. I wish to show, in addition, that as women debated this medical dogma about themselves, there were those activist or potentially activist females who, in spite of themselves, found the male arguments convincing and appeared to promote them in their writing. But there was inner conflict as well as they tried to resist or somehow rationalize the overwhelming pull of 'scientific' theory related to female cerebral inferiority. It seems even more intriguing that these women were still confronting these demons in the very last years of the nineteenth century. Three novelists will be discussed: Rachilde (Marguerite Eymery), the androgynous antifeminist, her older colleague and Périgord countrywoman Georges de Peyrebrune, and Daniel Lesueur, pseudonym of Jeanne Lapauze (née Loiseau). A fourth figure, the female doctor Georgette Déga, came to some curious conclusions regarding the female mind in her medical thesis, *Essai sur la cure préventive de l'hystérie féminine par l'éducation* (1898). I will reserve my discussion of Rachilde until the end of the chapter because she surely represents a special case, that of a woman who reflected, sometimes fearfully, at times with more assurance, on the powerful role the unconscious played in her personal life and in her ability to create fictional narratives.

4.1 Fictions of Female Physiology

Much intriguing research continues to focus on nineteenth-century medical theory regarding male/female differences, theory that, as Pierre Bourdieu put it, frequently attempted to attribute the justification for the inferior social status accorded to women to the physical characteristics of the female. An American medical historian has noted that, particularly with regard to women, a number of nineteenth-century theories of disease 'masqueraded rhetorically as objective, empirical science while in fact serving functions of social control'.[9] An 1885 study on women by Dr Henri Thulié, to which we will return later, argues more or less directly that the female's natural functions determine her status and condition in society.[10] Bourdieu noted as well that traditional oppositions such as interior/exterior, sensibility/rationality and passivity/activity were invoked to 'put women in their place'.[11] For the philosopher Pierre-Joseph Proudhon, female passivity emanates from her bodily 'softness', but his corporeal reasoning targets in fact the female intellect:

> Partout éclate la passivité de la femme, sacrifiée, pour ainsi dire, à la fonction maternelle; délicatesse du corps, tendresse des chairs, ampleur des mamelles, des hanches, du bassin; en revanche, étroitesse et compression du cerveau. En elle-même, je parle toujours du physique, la femme n'a pas de raison d'être.[12]
>
> The passivity of women is on view everywhere, sacrificed as she is, so to speak, to the maternal function; the delicate body, the tender flesh, the ample breasts, hips and pelvis; on the other hand, the narrowness and compressed size of the brain. In her own right, I am still speaking of the physical, a woman has no reason to exist.

In this view, 'her self' does not include a brain, a statement that appears to hark back to the notion of a *donna matrice*, the 'womb woman' of antiquity who is reduced to being a uterus.[13]

Increasingly, as the century advanced, it was indeed the female brain that was the key to the discussion for the male medical investigator, and that investigation was two-pronged. Dr Paul Broca embedded in nineteenth-century anthropological theory the idea that female intellectual inferiority was evident given her smaller brain size. Antifeminists were still offering this view well after the turn of the century and stressing the 'discovery' that women's frontal lobes – a measure of degree of civilization in all humans – were not as developed as those of a man.[14] Other researchers, especially hysteria specialists and *aliénistes* of the first half of the century, as we will see, focused more on the supposedly anomalous, quasi-reflex functioning of the female brain that left it vulnerable to nervous exhaustion and to potential breakdown. It is especially this second line of medical thinking that will interest me here. Of course, there was opposition to these theories, and I will highlight briefly a few of the authors who questioned them or dismissed them as groundless.

This doctrine of female mental debility presents itself as a medical one, prominently developed in the 1840s and 1850s by hysteria specialists, but it is revealing to compare with this scientific doxa some of the less scientific writings about her that appeared as the century began. Sylvain Maréchal's *Projet d'une loi portant défense d'apprendre à lire aux femmes*[15] is one such document, a bogus draft law that men likely read as a clever put-down of female attempts to be intellectual. But in many of its clauses, it represents a savage indictment of the female as a permanently inferior being, and probably constitutes a frustrated salvo in a debate about female equality and women's education that had been going on since at least the beginning of the eighteenth century.[16] What strikes one, in Maréchal's numbered list, is that in 1801 (and no doubt many years before that), the layman's view of female inferiority already included most of the clichés that would be mobilized and parroted as scientific gospel by eminent medical men such as Pierre Briquet and Jean-Louis Brachet. What are some of these commonplaces?

One of those cited by Maréchal is borrowed from a compendium dated 1695 and looks forward to a theory about the defective nature of women's brain function:

> la fluidité du sang et l'agilité des esprits animaux rendent les femmes incapables d'apporter une attention sérieuse à tout ce qui est un peu abstrait, et le dégoût qu'elles sentent pour tout raisonnement suivi prouve la délicatesse de leur imagination qui n'a plus la force de soutenir cet effort.[17]

> the fluidity of their blood and agility of their animal spirits render women incapable of focusing any serious attention on anything the least bit abstract, and the disgust they evince for any extended reasoning demonstrates the delicacy of their imaginative powers: the latter do not have the strength to sustain such an effort.

Maréchal has a particular dislike of the female writer, for by her writing she de-sexes herself, a cliché that is taken up with a vengeance at the fin de siècle. A comeuppance awaits the *femme auteur*. Women authors risk mental troubles or physical degeneration because their effort to understand abstractions is too much for their limited intelligence. And these women's fertility is compromised. His Clause 89 reads in part: 'Il est prouvé que les femmes auteurs sont moins fécondes que les autres.' ('It is a proven fact that female authors are less fertile than other women.') Many of the other admonitions point to the dangers of studying. One after another, traditional subjects are condemned. Curiously, for instance, girls who study languages and other sciences are subject to premature death (Clause 39). Female weakness is abetted, not prevented, by studying the humanities (Clause 36). And in other clauses, it is suggested that geography, history, botany and chemistry are inappropriate or debilitating given limited female mental capacities. Later in this chapter, and almost exactly 100 years later, we will see that such limitations on the 'female curriculum' are still in vogue.

Evelyne Ender, in *Sexing the Mind*, has provided a lively documentation on how, in the first half of the nineteenth century, doctors/physiologists asserted radical differences between the male and the female in every domain: the emotional system, sexual response, the brain, the very tissue in our bodies. Ender points in particular to four especially authoritative medical spokesmen for these differentiations, each of whom seemed to focus on one aspect of the female emotional makeup that appeared excessive: François Voisin (a surfeit of passion), Jean-Louis Brachet (high excitability) and Pierre Briquet (excessive impressionability).[18] Brachet and Briquet, two of the best known hysteria researchers, merit special attention, while the fourth doctor, Julien-Joseph Virey (extreme sensibility), wrote a tome on physiology to which we will return momentarily.

If the dictionary definition of hysteria had infamously become, by the 1880s, femininity exaggerated,[19] it was already viewed not that differently earlier in the century. Briquet had written, for example, 'La femme est faite pour sentir, et sentir c'est presque de l'hystérie.'[20] ('A woman is made to feel, and to feel is almost hysteria.') This hyper-emphasis on female sensitivity was a porous cliché into which self-interested scientific analysis could fit many a non-scientific conclusion. Even before the Revolution, as two medical and scientific commissions were assigned to assess the validity of Anton Mesmer's hypnotic healing, a negative, confidential report went to Louis XVI using female physical hypersensitivity as a reason for discrediting Mesmer. The report alleged that Mesmer's habit of placing his hands on his patients could lead to sex, although the reason given was not

Mesmer's seductiveness: 'En ... touchant [les femmes] dans une partie quelconque, on pourrait dire qu'on les touche à la fois partout.'[21] ('One might say that ... to touch any part of [a woman] is, at the same time, to touch her everywhere.')

This obsessional male attachment to the supposedly different sensibility of the female has important consequences for fin-de-siècle battles over female intellectual equality and for the feminist movement itself. Brachet contends that, given her high-pitched impressionability, the centre in a woman's brain responsible for sensitivity is constantly in action, and almost instantaneous in its response to stimuli. There are two main results. First, her entire mental life is unreflective: 'sa vie, en un mot, se traduit presque tout entière en sensations, ... c'est une véritable vie de sensations'.[22] Second, her presumedly delicate nervous system is at risk from nervous exhaustion consequent to this non-stop activity. This idea of stimulus/response would fit comfortably into the very conservative conception of the unconscious, that is, that what characterized unconscious activity was limited, reflex, automatic brain function versus the high-level, rational reflection of (male) consciousness. Were women, then, walking, talking examples of the unconscious gone awry?

4.2 The Late-Century Female Brain and Education

In the 1890s, as the first generation of lycée- and normal school–educated females reached their twenties, as the French birth rate sputtered (French deaths outstripped live births in 1890, 1891, 1892, 1895 and 1900[23]) and as the feminist movement flowered, arguments about the female role in society became more truculent and the question of women's educability and cerebral capacity resurfaced in texts prescribing normative femininity. The study of medical doctor and politician Henri Thulié, *La Femme*, was a typical product of the time, and the word 'typical' extends to its subtitle, *Essai de sociologie physiologique*.

Although this work argues for female equality and improved and expanded rights of women within marriage, their principal role remains maternity, and the life focus of women should be centred on this fact. Certain life choices, especially political involvement, are not only out of bounds morally for women, they have health implications. Thulié writes tersely, 'Les devoirs politiques sont incompatibles avec les devoirs de la maternité; la femme-citoyen est fatalement stérile' (236) ('Political responsibilities are incompatible with the responsibilities of motherhood; the female citizen is fatally sterile.') In other words, women must not try to right wrongs through political action. Participating in politics, voting – these erase female fertility. Thulié actually goes as far as to say that politically involved women will see their breast milk dry up, and the breasts of such females will eventually disappear (ibid.). (Late-century feminists ought therefore to have understood that there was no need to harp on the theme 'la grève des ventres' (uteruses on strike); their political involvement alone would protect them from unwanted pregnancies.) A medically trained politician such as Henri Thulié could not resist equating feminist political involvement and lesbianism. Writers of fiction would add a medical element to the constellation, interpreting female desire to limit or avoid pregnancy via a new operation for the removal of ovaries as an unspoken lesbian instinct.[24]

Another area of feminist involvement where female intellectual ability was called into question was that of the debate over vivisection. As they struggled to obtain their own rights, women saw around them a male medical community torturing helpless animals with impunity and trumpeting to the skies the advantages of the experimental method of vivisectionist Claude Bernard. The preface of an 1882 vivisection manual begins as follows:

> Nous ne sommes plus à une époque où pour tout homme intelligent, il soit nécessaire de démontrer l'utilité de la physiologie expérimentale et partant des *vivisections*. L'expérimentation s'est imposée comme une nécessité à la marche toujours en avant des sciences biologiques.[25]
>
> We are no longer in a time when, for any intelligent man, it is necessary to demonstrate the usefulness of experimental physiology and therefore of *vivisection*. Experimentation has become a necessity for the forward advancement of the biological sciences.

Respected, eminent physicians such as Charles Richet could write that non-experts had no business trying to question vivisection. It did not matter one way or the other whether they agreed with it or even understood it: for the non-initiated – and thus women by definition – science was an untouchable, sacred vessel.[26]

Dr Anna Kingsford, an English antivivisectionist who had received her doctorate in medicine in Paris and was therefore well informed about a variety of unsavoury vivisection-related practices, returned to the continent in the early 1880s to build support for government legislation to limit or control vivisection, as had been done in England. Her visit to Switzerland led to a publication that sets out, in uncomplicated fashion, how, in spite of a woman's medical specialty, gender can negate her arguments. In employing science to prove her points, writes Henri Kleffler, 'elle sort de son rôle naturel'.[27] In defining that role, Kleffler lays down the basic rules of nineteenth-century male and female nature: 'la femme, dans le type normal qui caractérise sa nature, est intellectuellement passive et moralement active, tandis que l'homme est au contraire intellectuellement actif et moralement passif' (ibid., 10) ('a woman, in the normal type characterized by her nature, is intellectually passive and morally active, whereas a man is, on the contrary, intellectually active and morally passive'). If this makes men seem morally deficient, Kleffler's companion dictum is that 'la morale' is not just subservient to science, it is already included in it. Yet what clearly irritates Kleffler as unnatural is the activism that is at the heart of the antivivisectionist philosophy: here are women trying to change the laws of Switzerland when it is men who represent action and activity and women 'la sensation passive' (ibid., 79)!

Jean-Marie Guyau's posthumous 1889 volume *Éducation et hérédité*[28] is a key compendium of male reflections on the female education question. It contains a chapter titled enticingly 'L'Éducation des filles et l'hérédité' that provides a long list of reasons why women should not be subjected to an education that is mentally strenuous. From what is subtitled 'a sociological study', we might expect statistics, population and education reports, etc. This is not the tack taken; Guyau's analysis (193–95) is rooted rather in references to human biology and medicine that take us back forty years to Brachet's and Briquet's conjectures about the frailty of the female brain. The central points in Guyau's argument seem to be the following: women are weaker than men – they do not have the reserves required for intense cerebral work; physiologists say that the reproductive function and the cerebral function are antagonistic. Given the physical demands of reproduction on the female, she risks imbalance if she tries to combine maternity and brain work; educated women, generally of well-off background (called by Guyau 'les filles au sein plat qui survivent à une éducation à haute pression' (194) ('the flat-chested girls who survive a high pressure education')) offer perfect examples of these poor reproductive results – an inability to breastfeed, reduced fertility, sometimes sterility. The cause 'has to be' intense intellectual efforts. All this points not to the past, but to *future hereditary problems*: a few generations of the fatigue caused by higher education and women will no longer be capable of motherhood.

To which physiologists is Guyau referring? In fact, many popular texts such as that of Dr J.-P. Dartigues, published in 1887, argued that intellectual fertility in the female leads to procreative infertility.[29] And there was always Cesare Lombroso to fall back on. He had remarked that the development of brain life was in inverse proportion to the development of sexual life.[30] Geneviève Fraisse notes that this doctrine developed much earlier in the works of Julien-Joseph Virey, especially in his *De la physiologie dans ses rapports avec la philosophie*. According to Virey, a pharmacist who became a doctor but touted himself as a 'médecin philosophe', the sexual organs and the brain are the two extremities of a chain of nerves, and the chain is subject to tensions. As the female is not oriented naturally to intellectual pursuits, any overemphasis on her part on the brain end of the chain creates an imbalance and weakens the organs of sexuality and reproduction. Fraisse observes that for Dartigues and Lombroso, the fertility of the mind always occasions physical sterility, and vice versa.[31]

One might tend to attribute the late-century resurgence of these misogynistic theories to a specifically French mindset, stoked by those omnipresent concerns about a failing birth rate and the rise of an educated, increasingly demanding modern woman. This is not the case. Similar views were being expressed at Harvard University by the professor of medicine Edward H. Clarke, who in the early 1870s found New England girls pale, weak and sickly and attributed their delicate constitutions to the way they were educated.[32] (He had particular ill-feelings about Vassar College.) Given the strain female bodies were under between the ages of twelve and twenty, with the reproductive system maturing and the menses starting to occur, the stress and anxieties of advanced brain work, particularly at the college level, could cause problems of all types, especially menorrhagia (excessive menstrual bleeding), but also incomplete development of the ovaries. Such stress could, he said, produce 'excellent scholars' but leave the women sterile in their marriages (29). One way or the other, higher education for females led, in his view, to a slow suicide.

It is, of course, not unlikely that women who completed a college education produced fewer children, since they probably started families later than the average. And it may well be that the better educated female practised birth control in her marriage, with the result that she could appear less fertile than her less educated sisters. These two factors might be seen to provide a type of muted support for Professor Clarke's radical theses. But the social activist and poet Julia Ward Howe responded to Clarke's work by editing a volume of replies, these coming from men and women, regretting the insufficient data on which his work was based (five case studies), the untruths Clarke had printed about education at Vassar College, and the polemical rather than scientific tenor of Clarke's argument.[33]

Guyau's and Clarke's theories about women's intellectual capacity were shared by many at the turn of the century. In England, Darwin's agreement with other writers – for example, the craniologist Carl Vogt and Herbert Spencer – that, partly because of brain size, the human female seemed to be an intermediate form between the child and the mature male, meant that women's evolution had been stunted. Arguments similar to those in France were heard regarding the exhaustion of the female brain and the impact on her reproductive abilities if she were pushed into too energetic an education.[34] Spencer's early belief in female equality turned to a view that women were inferior, lacked reflective ability and should never be given the vote.[35] In Germany, Paul Möbius authored an essay entitled *Über den physiologischen Schwachsinn des Weibes* (On the Physiological Feeble-Mindedness of the Female) in 1901 and accused the Viennese Otto Weininger of plagiarism when the latter wrote an equally damning attack on women. In *Geschlecht und Charakter* (Sex and Character), Weininger focused on what he argued was the female inability to conceptualize:

> Man has the same psychic contents as woman, in a more articulated form; while she thinks, more or less, in henids [an unclarified, sub-conscious 'feeling'; a proto-thought; Weininger invented the term], he thinks in clear, distinct concepts linked to definite feelings which can always be removed from their objects. In W 'thinking' and 'feeling' are one, undivided, for M they can be separated. That is, W still experiences many things in henid form, when in M clarification has long taken place.[36]

His conclusion was that men live consciously, women unconsciously.

In all of these arguments against female overeducation, the relationship between female physiology and psychology is a vicious circle of mutual and deleterious influences. Another typical document is an 1893 essay on the psychology of the sexes from the influential *Revue des Deux Mondes*, written by the distinguished philosopher and columnist Alfred Fouillée, in which female overeducation is the nominal topic. Again, there are references to unnamed physiologists who straightforwardly equate inferior female muscle strength with inferior brain power: 'le système nerveux de la femme est . . . moins développé dans les centres qui président plus spécialement au travail musculaire et au travail cérébral'[37] ('the nervous system of women is . . . less well developed in those centres that have specific control over muscular work and cerebral work'). The reference is again to female hypersensitivity with the added nuance that her emotions are, unlike those of men, part of the basic reflex system, thus more intense and efficient in draining female energy (410). The underlying proposition is that female mental life is more that of an unconscious automaton than of a thinking person.

Significantly, Fouillée's article ends with a glance at the French job market, where he sees the signs of bitter, impending female-male struggles for professional positions, and here, finally, one understands that the real subtext of the article is a longing to establish agreement on enduring, consoling values that differentiate gender roles. The appearance of females in the professions in the 1880s and 1890s was a shock, but their progress was not as rapid as many men feared. Jeanne Chauvin, the first woman to defend a law dissertation in 1892, was refused admission to the bar, and even after a 1900 law allowed female lawyers to practise, male resistance kept numbers low. Although the first woman to graduate in medicine did so in 1870, between 1882 and 1903 the number of female doctors in France increased from seven to only ninety-five. Coveted internships in Paris hospitals almost always went to men. The American Augusta Klumpke became the first female intern in 1886, though not without first failing the oral exam.[38] But the reception accorded females was very rough. When Klumpke's colleague Caroline Schultze was defending her thesis, 'La Femme médecin au XIXe siècle', jury president Charcot criticized her for wanting to practise 'aristocratic medicine' (i.e., in Paris), lectured her on the female's duty to take care in dress and appearance, unlike certain Anglo-Saxon women, he added, who neglect themselves (Caroline was Polish), and he expressed the view that female doctors should specialize in care for women and children. How could a female physician, for example, even contemplate operating on the hip of a man?[39]

The Loi Falloux of 1850 had mandated the creation of primary schools for girls in villages with more than 800 inhabitants.[40] The Loi Duruy of 1867 applied this same requirement to villages with a population of more than 500.[41] However, the creation of a national network of secondary schools for women began only after the Camille See law was passed in 1880. (By 1900, there were forty-one *lycées* and twenty-nine *collèges* for girls.[42]) The question of female intellectual and educational equality was very much in the air from the 1860s forward. In an 1870 lecture aimed at Barbey d'Aurevilly, the journalist Olympe Audouard made the very straightforward argument that if women were to study Greek and Latin like men, and have a window on the sciences, in one or two generations the public would see what the female intellect was made of. She spoke of the inequalities of education, boys from seven to eighteen being schooled while women vegetate, even though instinctively, she contends, they have higher ideals than boys:

> Dans ce moment, malgré tous les préjugés contraires, l'esprit féminin se réveille, la femme commence à comprendre l'insuffisance de son éducation, elle désire en sortir, ayant dans sa nature, plus que l'homme encore, l'instinct de ce qui est élevé. Elle réagit contre l'abaissement de son niveau intellectuel, et aspire à sa part d'influence.[43]

> At this time, in spite of all the opposing prejudice, the female mind is awakening, women are beginning to understand the insufficiency of their education, they want to leave that behind, for they have in their nature even more than men an instinctive feeling for what is elevated. They are reacting against the debasement of their intellectual level and they aspire after their own share of influence.

It was not that her intellectual level was inferior, but that men belittled it.

The journalist and feminist Camille Delaville liked to take a humorous tack in confronting the education question, suggesting that educating the female would not destroy the Republic:

> Quant à celles qui n'espèrent pas se marier, vaut mieux, n'est-ce pas, qu'elles soient bonnes à quelque chose de sérieux, que de devenir ... ce que vous savez.
>
> As for those women who do not expect to marry, it would be better, would it not, that they have some serious occupation rather than to become ... well, you know.

> Il faut que l'espèce masculine en prenne son parti, la femme marche depuis vingt ans, sinon vers l'émancipation, au moins vers l'égalité.
>
> The masculine species needs to realize what is happening, women have been on the march for twenty years, if not toward emancipation, at least toward equality.

> La pratique des principes de la Révolution française les a amenées là, et un jour viendra où elles seront ce qu'elles auraient toujours dû être: la moitié du genre humain. Elles n'en seront ni moins belles, ni moins bonnes, ni moins douces.[44]
>
> Practising the principles of the French Revolution has brought them this far, and the day will come when they will be what they always should have been: half of the human race. They won't be any less beautiful, or less good, or less sweet-natured.

It was, however, extremely difficult for a female gaining an education in what were the male disciplines to defend the idea of female equality. It took the trained anthropologist Madeleine Pelletier years to decide to oppose Paul Broca's anthropological paradigm that the smaller female brain and smaller skull size were a measure of female intellectual inferiority. This bias, as Charles Sowerwine has argued, became an embedded feature of Republican thought. Even the normally humanistic Émile Durkheim would approve the racist Gustave Le Bon's formula regarding the advantages of male skull size, this as late as 1893.[45] It was not until the feminist Pelletier began to abandon anthropology for psychiatry that she was able to voice her true opinion. In 1904 she authored an ironic article aimed at Broca's comparative study of the brains of humans and primates. 'La Prétendue Infériorité psycho-physiologique des femmes' argued that the male skull had a more ape-like morphology than that of the female.[46] A few years later she abandoned anthropology completely and became, along with her colleague Constance Pascal, one of the first females in France to qualify as a psychiatrist (aliéniste).[47]

There were also, of course, emerging views among men who opposed directly the ideas of Guyau and Fouillée. In his study *La Femme devant la science contemporaine*, Jacques Lourbet argued, much like Olympe Audouard decades previously, that any observed inferiority in the female was simply a result of the way she was trained and educated. He wrote sympathetically, and prophetically, 'la femme [du dix-neuvième siècle] est le produit artificiel d'un milieu qui doit changer' (119). But reviewing Lourbet's study, the sociologist Gaston Richard contends that Lourbet has forgotten to take into account 'the law of regression', that is, the fact that women retrograde mentally during menstruation and pregnancy, sometimes to the point of mental imbalance, so that being a mother cuts the female off from advanced intellectual activity. Moreover, he is disturbed by the idea of ill-defined freedom for women: emancipation for them can turn out to be an abdication.[48] Even when a male writes in support of women, old clichés about the brain are hard to jettison. Marcel Prévost writes that *both* historical prejudice and the structure of her brain explain the state of female intelligence in 1910.[49]

4.3 Four Female Writers on the Female Brain

Let us turn now to four women who exhibited in their writings, sometimes purposefully, at other times unconsciously, the troubled, conflicted mind states of women impressed with nineteenth-century male theory about their own intellectual inferiority.

The female brain is at the epicentre of *Une Décadente*,[50] a novella by the female novelist Georges de Peyrebrune, an older literary acquaintance of the novelist Rachilde (Marguerite Eymery) who played a kind of mothering role for her from time to time and was a very successful writer of the 1880s and 1890s, publishing more than thirty-five novels.[51] Certain letters written by Rachilde's friend Camille Delaville to Peyrebrune confirm that the two older women were concerned, at one point, for Rachilde's mental health.[52] Peyrebrune chose to employ, in *Une Décadente*, a transparent *roman à clef* as a way of warning Rachilde that her lifestyle was potentially a danger to herself and very troubling for her friends. The heroine, Hélione, is a would-be writer who recalls Rachilde in almost every detail, 'une jeune fille . . . qui prêche le renversement des rôles et des sexes, s'habille au masculin, ligote ses formes délicates dans des vestons et des gilets, salue du cou, secoue les poignets d'un *shake hand* brutal, tire l'épée, chasse, fume la cigarette' (55) ('a young woman . . . who preaches the reversals of roles and of sexes, dresses as a man, binding up her delicate body in jackets and waistcoats; she says hello with a toss of the neck, shakes your wrists with a brutal handshake, fences, hunts, smokes cigarettes'). Two doctors in the text, one of whom is Marcus, who is in love with the heroine Hélione, act as ventriloquists for the scientific view that roles outside the maternal, such as writing or seeking an education, are traps for the female that can unsettle her nervous system and lead to a full breakdown. As Marcus puts it, science is a very heavy burden for the delicate female brain (73–74).

This reference to the brain is not just a throwaway line. Marcus decries Hélione's abandonment of the maternal for 'philosophical speculations' and 'artistic delirium', predicting that she will become unbalanced or insane: 'En annihilant en vous ces précieux et féminins dons, vous développez outre mesure des facultés latentes *qui rompent votre équilibre cérébral* et feront de vous une malade ou une folle, une malheureuse toujours' (24–25; emphasis added) ('By annihilating in yourself these precious female gifts, you overdevelop latent faculties *that destroy your mental balance* and will make of you a sick or a deranged person, and in any case an unhappy woman.') There is a point in the text where Hélione senses how unhealthy her choices are, realizing that she has been attempting to alter her natural female brain functions. She says, 'il est possible, en effet, que dans la transformation cérébrale que j'ai tenté d'accomplir en moi, j'aie détraqué jusqu'à un certain point mes facultés natives' (72) ('it is in fact possible that in the brain transformation I was trying to trigger in myself, I upset my native faculties to a certain degree'). Hélione's conversion drips with unintended irony: the author of this fable, Peyrebrune, is a female and arguably a feminist novelist herself, at least in other works such as *Le Roman d'un bas bleu* and *Les Femmes qui tombent* that depict the single woman's dilemma in a man's world. Peyrebrune's great regret was not to have had children, and in that sense, she may have felt that she missed her true calling, but she was a successful female writer all the same, her head and fiction, like those of Rachilde, full of 'philosophical speculation' and 'artistic delirium'.

At least one of Peyrebrune's attempts to stretch the conventions of female-authored, love-centred fiction foundered because she ran up against the unexpected conformism of the potentially feminist Juliette Adam, since 1879 director of *La Nouvelle Revue*. Charles Sowerwine has wondered why so few of the prominent women we might think of as late-century feminists, Adam being a good example, fought for political rights for women.[53] He feels that many of them accepted the biological model of gender roles. Historian of psychiatry Élisabeth Roudinesco agrees. Writing of the late nineteenth century, she sees the same mindset undermining the efficacy of French feminist movements: 'Il n'y a pas de mouvement féministe de masse, car la France est dominée par l'influence occulte des bourgeoises au foyer, conscientes de la puissance de leur règne sur les traditions familiales.'[54] ('There is no mass feminist movement, for France is governed by the hidden influence of stay-at-home bourgeois women who are conscious of the power they wield over traditional families.') Prominent female figures like Adam who avoided feminist conflicts were not that rare. In spite of her career as a poet and art critic and her participation in the efforts to create the Prix Femina, Julia Allard, alias Madame Alphonse Daudet, espoused a view of normative femininity. In the short work she dedicated to her granddaughter Odile, she invited the child to reflect on a woman's life: it was composed of first communion, marriage, widowhood and religious pilgrimages. She added that she knew Odile would love novels just like any adult woman, 'tout comme la femme, que tu seras plus tard, cherche dans le livre qui l'émeut, ou dans la suite des feuilletons journaliers, la péripétie, les circonstances ou aventures de ses héros'[55] ('just like the woman you will be later, who seeks, in a book that moves her or in serial novels, the drama, the circumstances or adventures of the hero'). It seems anomalous and highly ironic to encounter this clichéd image of the exquisitely sensitive female, anxious like a prehysteric Emma Bovary to read the next instalment of a romantic serial novel, under the pen of a fully affranchised female author.

In 1881, Peyrebrune wrote to Adam, hoping to publish a novel in her journal. In her response, Adam agreed that the text was well written and would certainly be a success, but she labelled the work 'odious' because the heroine's excessive chastity created unhappiness for all the other characters. The judgement is curious: it seems to mean 'unpublishable because the convention of the happy ending is absent'. The fictional heroine must give in to nature and to 'normal' human attraction or she will outrage her audience.[56] Peyrebrune's severe novels shared a feature of those written by her decadent colleague Rachilde, whose stories – outrageous for their time – also disallowed standard sex.

Speaking in her own voice, Peyrebrune authored a strange pamphlet in 1876, *Les Vierges de feu*, nominally a contribution to a depopulation debate, but readable as a defence and illustration of her own sexual reticence. What is interesting about the text, among other things, is the resort to a medico-neurological argument to explain absent female libido. In an epoch when much research focused on the topography of cerebral function, her theory centres on the cerebellum, thought to be the site of sexual desire. She calls it 'la source de toute sensibilité' (25).

Peyrebrune begins with the portrait of the typical adolescent girl caught up in religious fervour, her brain excited by the efforts required to conceive of the miraculous and the supernatural (24). During this period, the imaginative portion of her brain is force fed, as it were, becomes overdeveloped and robs the cerebellum of needed sustenance. Because the latter, she argues, is the seat of intercostal nerves connected to the lumbar region, when it atrophies and its vivifying fluid dries up, the overly imaginative young woman can end up impotent, if not sterile. To support this explanation, she observes that anatomy has proven that an enlarged cerebellum is a feature of the overlibidinous hysteric. And in a comparison she makes of cerebellum misfunction to troubled digestion, it is not difficult to see a sexual allusion: 'lorsqu'il [l'estomac] est, ensuite, véritablement sollicité d'agir, ses parois inertes, privées de leur mucosité stimulante, refusent de fonctionner' (23) ('when it [the stomach] is then truly called upon to act, its inert walls, deprived of their stimulating mucus, refuse to function').

It is not clear from what sources Peyrebrune developed her theory of female 'impotence', although, as we saw in Chapter 1, situating the sexual instinct in the cerebellum was one of the teachings of Franz Josef Gall, among others. What is characteristic of the period is that a (male-developed) medical model involving the female brain and female sexual apparatus was once again seen as a touchstone explaining female nature.

The novelist Daniel Lesueur, *nom de plume* of Jeanne Lapauze, née Loiseau, was a recipient of the Légion d'honneur and is generally regarded as a moderately conservative author who disliked the term 'feminist' but did publish a report demanding marriage reform and equal pay for equal work for females.[57] It is a fact that all of her writing is women-centred, but less clear, as one critic has proposed, that all of her texts are 'contestatory of the narrow scope of female lives under patriarchy'.[58] In 1890, one year after Jean-Marie Guyau's text on female education appeared, Lesueur published her novel on the same subject, *Névrosée*,[59] in which the young heroine, after a lycée education and attending lectures at the Collège de France, follows the exact itinerary that Guyau imagined for the overeducated girl who returns home to an intellectual void. Without any outlet now for her percolating ideas and experiencing early imbalance because of a nervous system depleted by mental effort, she has only the options of flirting, the female coquetry of salon time and the exchange of rumors and *potins* that are the social lot of every marriageable young woman of the upper classes.

The pall that lies on the future of Étiennette d'Épeuilles is dual: first, she carries the accumulated nerve weaknesses of an aristocratic family, and second, she makes the hot-headed decision to opt for an intellectual education that will trigger her breakdown. At age twelve she insists on attending the newly established first *lycée* for girls in Paris, but her mind demands more and she later frequents the lectures of the strapping young Maxime Delaure, who has just been awarded a chair of biology at the Collège de France.

Maxime himself is a quasi-medical figure, and a creature of his time, for as a biologist he admits his interests are veering towards experimental psychology (26). Where the psychology of women is concerned, physiology seems always involved, at least in 1900, if we reflect back on the title and content of Thulié's *La Femme, essai de sociologie physiologique* and Fouillée's *Revue des Deux Mondes* article, 'La Psychologie des sexes et ses fondements physiologiques'. Delaure is incensed that women attend his lectures because, as he says, 'La femme est absolument incapable de raisonnement' (64). But Étiennette's education serves her, for he realizes that she understands his lectures, and in a private session he is ecstatic that she even comprehends Fechner's law, the concept that the magnitude of a subjective sensation increases proportionally to the logarithm of the stimulus intensity (66). Such female brilliance dazzles Maxime, but the author intervenes later to put female education in its place. In the past the normal outlet for girlish exuberance would have been dressing for society balls, or perhaps religious devotion, but nowadays education takes their place, even though abstractions can never satisfy the female makeup, aspects of which Lesueur depicts as inattention, indifference, apathy and frivolity (122). Conflicted and fickle, Maxime marries Étiennette. When later she develops emotional problems, he becomes the stiff, unempathetic male, blocking out his young wife's emotional tirades by locking himself up in his office.

The more mainstream doctor figure, Berger-Ricard, is at base good-hearted, but censorious because he sees the follies of the female. He is a proponent of fin-de-siècle *hygiène*, that is, fresh air, exercise and bicycling, and an enemy of 'l'instruction exagérée des femmes' (219). In a kind of extended lecture in the penultimate chapter, Berger-Ricard voices uncritically another aspect of late-century anthropological theory, which was that 'Caucasic', Western European individuals exhibited more advanced intellectual functions than other racial groups, and for non-Europeans, racial and cerebral perfectibility were limited.[60] Given her basic intellectual inferiority, the French female was in the same position as the non-European and faced the same limitations. Berger-Ricard describes her brain as about as developed as that of a Polynesian woman; the Frenchwoman could advance only so far because her hereditary constitution could assimilate only a certain amount (304).

When Étiennette has a fifth-month miscarriage, an authorial voice attributes it to the pressures laid on a strained reproductive system when she was an adolescent. For Guyau and Harvard professor Clarke, precocious cerebral efforts could make a woman sterile. Here, under Lesueur's pen, they interrupt a pregnancy: 'Ce qui fait vivre le penseur tue la femme, l'enfant ... L'excès de civilisation amène ces désordres' (294). ('What enlivens the thinker kills the female, and the child ... It is the excesses of civilization that create these disorders.') Étiennette's life follows the usual fin-de-siècle downward spiral: she wastes away of nerve weakness and dies of a drug overdose.

Lesueur's put-down of overeducation for the female is surprising even in an incomplete feminist, but it does demonstrate the antagonistic forces at work within views of female psychology at the turn of the century. Her novel earned her a mention in a friendly review of Lombroso's *La Femme criminelle et la prostituée*, as though her views dovetailed with that of the eccentric anthropologist. The reviewer, Raymond de Ryckère, noted, 'La femme, dit Daniel Lesueur, dans *Névrosée*, échappe à la logique, au raisonnement, à la démonstration géométrique, qui n'ont pas de prise sur sa petite cervelle.'[61] ('Women, says Daniel Lesueur in *Névrosée*, are incapable of logic, of reason, of geometric demonstrations, which have no impact on her tiny brain.') Quoting Spencer and Max Nordau in support of Lombroso, the same reviewer observes that the special nature of female intelligence is indeed to be automatic in form, that is, reactive and unreflective.

Perhaps unwittingly, Lesueur's worldview seems to dovetail broadly with some of the most sordid pre-1900 misogynistic writing, such as the novels of Albert Cim, *Fille de lettres*, *Demoiselles à marier*, *Émancipées* and especially *Bas-bleus*. Educated girls, and more particularly women with pretentions to be writers, were all headed for a tripartite end: the insane asylum, the morgue or streetwalking. All these pretentious females, writes Cim, turning the tables on author Lesueur by using the title of her own novel, are 'névrosées, détraquées'.[62] In response to Jules Huret's *Enquête* of 1891, Anatole France had already downgraded novel writing by saying that only women read fiction nowadays. Female writers, as Lesueur should have remembered, were a special category, a group of women who seemed to have forfeited their gender.[63] And in the end, what did it matter if they wrote fiction? Compared with men, suggested the critic Émile Faguet, the female's lack of any intellectual gifts made her perfect for novel writing.

Georgette Déga was not the first French woman to write a thesis on hysteria. That honour went to Hélène Goldspiegel, who defended her work in 1888 before a jury headed by Charcot and whose analysis was apparently very much in line with Charcot's doctrine.[64] Ten years later, Déga addressed the question of hysteria and the young in her medical thesis, *Essai sur la cure préventive de l'hystérie féminine par l'éducation*.

We know very little about Georgette Déga. Her dissertation, which seems to have been her only publication, was completed at the Faculty of Medicine in Bordeaux in 1898 where she worked under Dr Albert Pitres, who had been a student of and had co-published with Charcot. Déga's title might suggest that her views were just the opposite of those expressed in *Névrosée*[65] and that the female might escape, via education, the *névrose* that threatened the female half of France's population. In fact, Déga's approach is novel, in that, contrary to so many men, she *does* believe in strenuous mental efforts on the part of women. But those efforts are necessary because, left in its 'natural', unfocused state, at least in Déga's view, the female mind is prone to emotional breakdown.

The education she refers to is strictly the early family precepts and teachings that are crucial because of the female child's relative intellectual debility. Déga's text observes, for example, that when one speaks to a young woman, she hears not the objective facts of what is said, only the emotional content of the words; girls must therefore be taught to focus, to increase their attention span. Already oversensitive by nature, they should never be encouraged in the direction of increased empathy. Discipline should be firm and balanced and difficulties should not be smoothed over for young women, these young 'novices de l'hystérie' (10). Finally, and this is important for the synthesis of the girl's self and personality, her tendency to tell stories, to embroider, to pretend, to act a role, must be repressed because the very nature of the hysteric she might become is to have a dual personality.

At the very end of her essay, Déga focuses on what might be the academic curriculum of women's education, a curriculum that surprises because almost every discipline would be excluded from it. Philosophy is arid for girls, the natural sciences too concrete. Although literature and foreign languages fit into female capabilities, 'elles ne cultivent pas en particulier ce don d'attention si nécessaire à l'être psychique' (77)[66] ('specifically, they do not cultivate that gift of attentiveness so necessary to the psychic self'). In other words, they allow for too many imaginative flights and too much lateral thinking. Similarly, history and geography do not force uninterrupted attentiveness.

Interest in the opera with its exaggerated theatrical element must be discouraged because it causes female nervous overload. Concerts and recitals may be all right, but the fact remains that playing or listening to music does not address the intelligence (91), and that while music may be thought to be an antidote to sadness, it may in fact exacerbate or prolong it in girls (93). What is left, one may ask? Surprisingly, it is mathematics! Maths, and especially geometry (*pace* Lesueur and de Ryckère), are excellent for the female because they provide multiple opportunities for intense mental effort and concentration (76). Was it maths that saved Déga's own medical career? The reader is left to wonder how she managed her own education and how she might have explained her career success.

What underlies the principles of this educational regime is a mechanistic view of the female mind. Déga makes liberal use of images from Dr Maurice de Fleury's *Introduction à la médecine de l'esprit* [67] to picture humans acting as machines (Déga, 21). They respond to stimuli no differently from 'piles électriques' (25) ('electric batteries'), and the problem is at its worst with girls and women.[68] Déga writes, 'chez la femme, l'émotion n'arrive pas à un degré de cérébration suffisante' (27) ('in women, emotion is not accompanied by a sufficient level of brain effort'). Very often women act even before thought has truly instructed the proper organs to do so; the female operates, she contends, in a 'demi-conscience' (22).

At the same time as Déga's effortful analyses attempt to find a middle road between female intellectual 'debility' and her educability, male chauvinism, as we have seen, was rampant. An especially truculent example will close this section. In Remy de Gourmont's novel *Sixtine* the main character Hubert Entragues passes by a girls' school as the students are exiting and notes their pallor, ugly creased dresses and ink-stained fingers. Their chests appear caved in from too much bending over their desks studying, of all things, spelling! What should their curriculum be, asks the thoughtful Entragues:

> Ni de la grammaire, ni de la géographie, ni de la répugnante histoire chronologique; ni presque rien d'usité ne convenait aux femmes, mais seulement l'Ancien et le Nouveau Testament, la Vie des saints, de solides lectures mystiques, puis les poètes, les romanciers du rêve, tout ce qui peut

> aux heures noires, refleurir dans l'âme, à l'appel des harpes sacrées, à la sommation des baisers d'amour, sous des caresses d'enfant.[69]
>
> Neither grammar, nor geography, nor that disgusting chronological history; nor did almost anything usual seem appropriate for women. Instead the Old and New Testaments, the lives of the saints, solid mystical readings, then the poets and novelists that make us dream, everything, when life seems hopeless, that flowers in the soul, answering the call of sacred harps to love's kisses and the caresses of a child.

Is there perhaps a semi-jocular tone, or even confusion, in this passage? After all, a convent education with its cloudy mysticism followed by endless exposure to love novels with ideal endings – this is what made of Emma Bovary the hysteric that she became. In any case, we see here an unusually unapologetic plea for a sensuous female education, in order to prepare girls for their rightful role as romantic partner and mother.

The fourth woman author in our quartet is the novelist and critic Rachilde. Her attraction to brain function and malfunction was intense and lifelong. Part of her interest was generated within her family, by the fact that her table-rapping grandparents and mother believed in the spirits and felt certain that the non-conformist Marguerite was inhabited by one. Rachilde had concerns about her own genetic heritage, especially as her mother was confined for a time in the mental hospital at Charenton. There are indications in some of Rachilde's letters that she worried about becoming unbalanced herself.

References to the brain are everywhere in her fiction, especially, though not exclusively, in her earlier works. As a child, one of her heroines is so troubled by her 'overheated brain' that she would prefer to revert to an animal state: 'Être l'oiseau, la souris . . . le petit loup, la créature sans la contrainte cérébrale.[70] ('Oh, to be a bird, or a mouse . . . a little wolf, a creature without cerebral constraints.') Thus, Rachilde's lifelong attraction to animals and especially her fictional use of the wolf figure derive in part from a need to escape ratiocination, to revert to animality. The idea recalls Flaubert's famously expressed wish: 'être la matière'.

Rachilde pictures a serious nervous attack she suffered in her twenties as a 'transport au cerveau' ('a brain seizure').[71] Maurice, her hero in the novel *Le Mordu* (she describes the fellow as one of her own numerous fictional avatars[72]), ascribes his own erratic behaviour to a possible lesion on the brain. He also posits that his paranormally inclined family members – they are labelled as 'cérébraux',[73] which seems here to be a synonym of 'unbalanced' – are tainted in the same way. Rachilde will later be influenced by medical theory of the period according to which injury to the brain may be at the root of altered sexual behaviour:

> On a connu des malades, doués d'une imagination trop vive, qui, frappés par une violente commotion cérébrale, ne concevaient plus l'acte d'amour que sous l'empire de l'idée fixe de voir couler du sang et devenaient des *sadiques*, malgré leur propension à la plus romanesque des pudeurs.[74]

> We have observed sick people, equipped with an extremely vivid imagination who, suffering from a violent brain concussion, no longer thought of lovemaking except via the *idée fixe* of seeing blood flow; they became *sadists* in spite of their propensity to exhibit ultra-Romantic modesty.

There was in fact research in the 1880s, including an article by the well-known hysteria specialist Dr Charles Lasègue, who had treated Rachilde, that came to similar conclusions regarding the effect of physical trauma on the brain.[75] Is Rachilde not perhaps describing herself in this passage? She had incurred the brain trauma mentioned here, and her heroines in *Monsieur Vénus* and *La Marquise de Sade* practise a sadism centred on blood. She was possessed of an extremely vivid imagination, and yet in spite of the sadistic overtones in her fiction she wrote allusively and ungraphically about sex itself, priding herself on the fact that her novels never ended with a couple in bed.

Rachilde's women control their own sexuality and sap male power in every possible way. It is men who are the victims and who bleed (that female weakness) at the hands of women in *Monsieur Vénus* and *La Marquise de Sade.* Yet in spite of this empowering of the female, Rachilde demonstrates in several ways that she has reservations about female intelligence and mental powers. Her stated intention, in a novel like *Monsieur Vénus*, was 'to react against the hypocrisy that relegates women to the lowest level of humanity'.[76] And yet creative abilities are attached, in both her correspondence and her fiction, to the masculine principle. In a letter from 1885, as she increases her production of novels to two or three annually, she writes that she has become more of a man than ever from the simple viewpoint of ideas.[77] One of her stories written in the same period presents an artist heroine who exercises her craft not with hesitant brush strokes but with virile surehandedness: 'Elle avait le dessin ferme d'une main d'homme énergique'.[78] ('She sketched firmly as though with the hand of an energetic man.')

Even many years after the 1890s debates on female educability that we have examined, writing in her *Pourquoi je ne suis pas féministe* of 1928, Rachilde's tendency is still to see female analytical abilities as compromised by her physical 'deficiencies'.[79] She appears to be saying that because monthly hormonal changes are emotionally and intellectually disruptive, women do not reason cogently at any time. Any man, by contrast, even the least intelligent, retains his capacity for logical thinking. Cerebral frailty in women also means ideological susceptibility. Intellectually, a woman lacks balance, and Rachilde feels that she tends too easily to all-consuming involvements. And this is why feminism can be bad for a woman, monopolizing her faculties: 'Je continue à regarder comme un danger tout accaparement cérébral de la femme parce que son cerveau est peut-être moins solide que celui de l'homme' (ibid., 21). ('I continue to see any assumed cerebral control of women as dangerous because their brain is perhaps less solid than that of a man.') Rachilde also seems to have formed an unpleasant image of the educated woman: in her novel *Le Dessous*, her heroine Marguerite is an ironic construct of an unintimidating, middle-of-the-road young woman, 'une variété juste milieu . . ., rien du lycée, mais rien du couvent'[80] ('a variety occupying the juste milieu . . . no lycée overtones, but no reminders of convents either').

Rachilde was one of the authors who, in 1897, responded enthusiastically to the survey of Paul Chabaneix, querying artists, scientists and writers about the role of the subconscious in the creative process. The study, mentioned earlier, was the medical thesis of a naval doctor whose supervisor at the Faculty in Bordeaux, Emmanuel Régis, was a colleague of Charcot and who would later, along with his student Angelo Hesnard, begin the introduction of Freudian ideas in France. The preface to the Chabaneix work, contributed by Régis, has distinct overtones of the Pierre Janet school, especially his use of the term 'automatique' to describe the subconscious cerebral function that Chabaneix is about to study. The very use of the word 'subconscient' bows to Janet's insistence that this term, not 'inconscient', was the correct one, because in Janet's view the subconscious was not separate from consciousness, simply a lower level of it. The bulk of the study, however, demonstrates that the workings of the unconscious in creative people have nothing of the low-level automatic functions listed by Janet, but rather often facilitate novel constructions in the mind. The unconscious does not regurgitate; Chabaneix presents it as a free-floating place where ideas spontaneously graft onto and combine with one another to produce novelty, and sometimes answers to issues that have proved insoluble in waking life.

Rachilde was adamant that the creative trigger that launched each of her works was not part of intelligent reflection. In 1896, in response to a separate questionnaire, she had written, 'Je conçois une œuvre dans l'ignorance absolue de tout acte raisonné. Si le mot possession pouvait être appliqué à mon cas cérébral, il faudrait le prononcer sans crainte . . . de m'humilier.'[81] (I imagine a work in the absolute absence of any reasoned act. If the word possession could be applied to my cerebral case, people should use the word without fear . . . of humiliating me.') The fictional subject invades and possesses the writer, as the spirit of the Horla had possessed Maupassant's narrator. And such subjects could be equally terrifying to the adolescent Rachilde.

As a young girl she suffered from violent, hallucinatory dreams, including one involving a pale, malformed cadaver that rose nightly out of the pond in front of her home, gesturing and telling her never to speak about their encounters. Such dreams persisted into the waking state so intensely that she felt she had two selves, a living, waking personality and a dreaming personality, and at times, even in the waking state, she was not sure which was dream and which reality. But those dreams gradually became less frightening, and she took to playing with their endings, like a writer: 'souvent le rêve achevé, je le terminais moi-même tout éveillée, ce qui m'a donné ainsi l'habitude de me raconter des histoires, de composer des romans'[82] ('often, the dream completed, I would give it an ending in a full waking state. This gave me the habit of telling myself stories, of composing novels'). Perhaps the most telling remark she makes about this personal creative process involves her sense that there is a dual texture in her own finished writing. Most of her basic narratives, she notes, emerge first from a dream, but then the intelligence must frame and give them structure. She is not convinced, however, that the intellectual portion of her stories has improved them. She writes, instead, 'très souvent quand j'ajoute des chapitres *de ma propre autorité*, ce n'est pas ce qu'il y a de mieux dans l'oeuvre' (ibid., 57) ('very often when I add chapters *on my own authority*, it's not the best part of the work').

With Rachilde, more than any other writer we have studied except perhaps Maupassant, the unconscious is inordinately present, a moving pool of images and narratives pulsating outward in dreams that barely fade in the light of day. The brain remains a locus of peril in Rachilde's world. Her diffidence about her own brain, about the 'cerebral case-study' she considers herself to be, and probably about the female brain in general, stems from a totally different quarter than the same sentiments in the other women we have studied. Her supposed acceptance and interiorization, as an adult, of the threat of unbidden images rising from the unconscious still leaves her with qualms about the control the female really has over her thoughts.

4.4 Femme Fatale, Femme Inconsciente

The resurgence, in the 1880 to 1900 period, of constructions of the female as a mentally diminished male, had an immediate social explanation, as we have seen: the anxiety about procreation related to unsustainably low birth rates and to concerns that female emancipation could lead to competition for jobs, to spinsterhood and to frighteningly altered family configurations. But within these theories, references to the half-conscious female, the female who reacts mechanistically to stimuli like an electric battery, who is not naturally capable of reflection and ratiocination and produces 'henids' in their stead, relate more specifically to the late-century, pre-Freudian, medico-psychological debate over the nature and role of the unconscious.

In his widely admired philosophy thesis, *L'Automatisme psychologique*, published in 1889 in the full flow of this resurgence of female inferiority theory, Pierre Janet appeared to argue that the operation of the unconscious, devoid of creative or imaginative capacity, was purely reflex-based and automatic. The patients upon whom he based his theories were, of course, usually women, and chosen because of their hysterical tendencies. They were frequently hypnotized and their hypnotized behaviour was indeed distinctly reflex. In the general favour that the theory of automaticism took on in the 1890s, it was to some extent forgotten that in using the term 'subconscient' to describe the thought processes of his case studies in *L'Automatisme psychologique*, Janet was speaking about mentally ill individuals. There is no doubt that his view of women of abnormal, 'automatic' psychology spilled over to some extent and was coopted into the theories of other writers regarding the deficiencies of female cerebral function.

In a way, it is not difficult to comprehend the directions taken in the works of the four women studied. In discussing them, I have emphasized the hegemony of male medical and psychological theory regarding the female and the more or less conscious acceptance of its accuracy by these women themselves. Pierre Bourdieu has theorized that the female – and his theory is all the more applicable to the nineteenth-century woman – is inescapably inhabited by an androcentric unconscious. That is, women produce an unwitting bow to male theory, what Bourdieu has called an 'adhésion doxique', an unrealized, symbolic adherence to a theory that the female helps to construct by being conditioned to its premises. The doxa represents the symbolic violence of which the beliefs are a product. Bourdieu stresses that in using the term 'symbolic' he is not attempting to posit an anodyne type of violence that would minimize and contrast with actual physical violence, beatings, rape, etc. It is in a sense a self-inflicted violence in that, unconsciously, by a process of imperceptible familiarization with the structures of male dominance, the female comes to experience those structures as natural. It is this domination itself that is violence, nor can it be reasoned or willed away because it becomes anchored in the body in the form of what Bourdieu calls 'corporal dispositions', or in the intellect of women like Lesueur or Déga in the form of mental dispositions.[83]

Bourdieu's late twentieth-century perspective will read to some as maddening, since it appears to inhibit any sense of female autonomy and intellectual freedom. On the other hand, it may also read as persuasive and as a useful prod for both women and men struggling with the problem of gender-based bias. As for the late nineteenth century, the contiguity and eventual interweaving of two sets of theories influenced societal views of women. The medical doctrine regarding female conceptual limitations based on the inferior performance of the female brain, and Janet's theory of automatism whereby the (mostly female) hysteric was judged to have a limited field of consciousness and to act in a reflex manner, meant that the fin-de-siècle 'femme fatale' took on yet another personification. Quite aside from her mysterious, dangerous sexuality, she became the embodiment of a fear of the unconscious, an anxiety that the unpredictable, uncontrollable unconscious might be lurking in the shadows, ready to pounce on the male and displace him from his fortress of reason and willpower.

CHAPTER 5

Hypnotism, Dual Personalities and the Popular Novel

In making of the 1880s the decade of hysteria not only in France, but more widely in Europe and North America, French doctors and psychologists also brought into the public domain the practice of hypnotism and, with it, a broad societal reflection on the phenomenon of second personality and beyond that, on the nature of the unconscious. In fin-de-siècle literature, as one critic has written, hypnotism came to constitute not simply another anecdotal theme, it was a practice that forced one to question what reality, and especially mental reality, was.[1] Hypnotism could produce unexpected, eccentric, even sometimes deviant behaviour in its subjects: was this not proof that all of us possessed a second personality, just waiting to be released? The fact that the hypnotized subject forgot what his activities had been while under hypnosis was further proof that there existed a level of the psyche that was off-limits to conscious willpower. Because of its access to the unconscious mind, and because hypnotists could create thoughts, feelings, and willed actions in their subjects, hypnotism appeared to some researchers as an extraordinary mechanism for exploration of the psyche. As medicine was now resolutely experimental because of the prestige of Claude Bernard's experimental medicine, doctors and researchers spoke of an emerging experimental psychology with hypnotism as its favoured tool. Borrowing from Bernard, they averred that hypnotism was 'a procedure for moral and intellectual vivisection';[2] it would be for the philosopher what vivisection was for the physiologist;[3] or, as Dr Charles Richet, later a Nobel Prize winner, was quoted as saying: hypnotism was an admirable tool for psychological vivisection.[4] The expression moved into fiction as well: Paul Bourget's character Greslou in *Le Disciple* is engaged in the 'sentimental vivisection' of the young woman he is planning to seduce. Encountering such language in doctors' texts, potential hysteria patients, most of them of course women, certainly knew where they stood in the medical value system.[5]

Hysteria and hypnosis were an exciting new mystery for the medical community, the press and novelists. There was so much to observe: hypnotized hysterics pierced by pins or burned but feeling no pain, contorted faces, smiling on one side, grimacing on the other, young women convulsed in an *arc de cercle*. Paris and, to a lesser extent, Nancy, where Professor Hippolyte Bernheim and his team vied with Charcot for notoriety in the hypnotism field, became compulsory waystations for those studying hysteria. Parisian doctors and researchers such as Jules Luys at La Charité hospital and Amédée Dumontpallier at La Pitié followed Charcot's example at La Salpêtrière and invited students, foreign visitors, the press, writers and fellow medical men to attend public demonstrations of hypnotized behaviour. The painting *Une Leçon clinique à la Salpêtrière* (1887) shows a typical group of spectators observing a Charcot demonstration; in addition to medical personnel, present are the writer Paul Arène, writer and journalist Jules Claretie, and the psychologist and editor of the *Revue Philosophique*, Théodule Ribot. Freud began his visit to La Salpêtrière in the fall of 1885; he would later interview Professor Bernheim in Nancy. In 1885 as well, the Belgian psychologist and philosopher Joseph Delboeuf was allowed personal access to some of La Salpêtrière's star hysterical patients. Axel Munthe maintains in *The Story of San Michele*, as we have seen, that he met Maupassant while attending Charcot's lectures and that he later accompanied the writer in a visit to Bernheim's clinic in Nancy.

Two of the most revealing accounts of the hypnotism craze in Parisian medical institutions are that by Delboeuf and a later article by the then-famous Russian mathematician Sofia Kovalevskaya, who was visiting Paris in 1888 to receive the French Prix Bordin for mathematics.[6] Delboeuf was amazed and thrilled by what he saw, perhaps especially because, along with Dr Charles Féré and Alfred Binet, he was allowed to experiment with various hypnotized behaviours on the voluptuous Blanche Whitmann, Charcot's favourite subject. Kovalevskaya's impressions were the exact opposite. Accompanied by a journalist from the newspaper *Justice*, she remarked that Jules Luys' interactions with his hypnotized patients were full of methodological flaws: photos of grimacing, cataleptic or ecstatic patients lined the walls of one demonstration room where patients were to perform. Luys also gave away orally what behaviour he desired, maintaining that a hypnotized patient couldn't hear him unless he addressed him or her directly.

On her visit to La Salpêtrière, Kovalevskaya was accompanied by Dr Edgar Bérillon, editor of *La Revue de l'Hypnotisme*. Both were shocked and depressed by Charcot's brutal, unhelpful treatment of his patients, and

Bérillon, the French host, was particularly distressed and embarrassed. The novelist Paul Bonnetain must have attended a similar session at La Salpêtrière: in his novel *Charlot s'amuse* Charcot reserves equally boorish treatment for the hero's aging alcoholic mother.

Of course, hypnosis was hardly a medical phenomenon alone. As we observed in Chapter 3, non-medical hypnotists, known as 'magnétiseurs' or 'fascinateurs', attracted large crowds all over France, Belgium, Switzerland and Italy.[7] Pickmann, whose apparent mind-reading abilities so fascinated Maupassant, was one of these, but the most renowned of all was the great Belgian hypnotist Donato (Alfred Édouard D'Hont), whose popularity surpassed even that of Charcot in the early 1880s when he performed at Parisian venues like the exclusive Jockey Club.

On many fronts, hypnotism was moving very much into the public eye. It was said, for example, that a well-conducted hypnotic evening in a Parisian salon could earn a practitioner 500 francs.[8] But it was one spectacular phenomenon, the 'experimental crime', widely publicized by medical men, that caught the public's attention. The crime was experimental in the sense that it was the result of posthypnotic suggestion but conducted 'experimentally'; that is, no real crime was allowed to take place.

In the pages that follow, I trace the history and itinerary of the 'crime expérimental' or 'crime suggéré', beginning with the medical laboratory and demonstration room, where it was first practised. I then move into French courtrooms where certain real crimes began to be scrutinized as potentially caused by posthypnotic suggestion, by external control over the accused's unconscious or, on some occasions, by a subject's second personality taking over his waking self. However, as we saw in Chapter 3 on Maupassant, the richest repository for the theme of posthypnotic suggestion and the idea of dual personality in general was fiction. The final section of this chapter will explore some of the many novels and stories that focused on hypnotism and dual personality with an eye to weighing the messages writers were sending to the public regarding medical mastery over the mind.

5.1 Experimental Crimes, Real Crimes

We have seen in a previous chapter the plethora of experiments with posthypnotic suggestion that took place during the mid-1880s. Many of them, such as the suggestion, planted in a young woman's mind in *Le Horla*, that she approach her cousin for a large loan, were aimed at producing surprise, not offensive or criminal results. One of the most arresting of these, because of the time lapse involved, was the suggestion made by Henri Beaunis to a subject in Nancy. On 14 July 1884 he hypnotized her and told her that on 1 January 1885 he would arrive at her home, wish her Happy New Year and then leave. A half-year later the woman explains to friends, including Dr Liébeault of the Nancy group, that on 1 January Beaunis had appeared at her apartment, wished her Happy New Year, and disappeared. He was wearing a summer suit, she reported. In fact, however, Beaunis had never left Paris.[9]

In 1882, when Charcot delivered his paper to the Académie des sciences in which he recuperated magnetism from its quasi-occult past – renaming it hypnotism – he argued that the phenomenon must be studied medically as an artificially induced pathological state of mind similar to hysteria. Lay hypnotists were to be discouraged and if possible banned by law. However, when novelists began to connect the words 'hypnotism' and 'pathological', a new world of fictional plots opened up.

The fact that hypnotized individuals lost control of their willpower was important. Actions not initiated and directed by one's conscious willpower were potentially the acts of the insane. The exercise of the will was a clear sign of rationality for psychiatrists trained in the psychiatrist Esquirol's tradition or for followers of Victor Cousin's theories, whereas 'l'involontaire, l'inscient, l'automatique, [avaient] partie liée avec l'aliénation'[10] ('the involuntary, the unconscious, the automatic [were] closely linked to mental alienation'). Not only could evil impulses arise from the unwilled, that is, the unconscious, but lack of controlled, willed thought was itself a springboard to madness.

One of the most widely publicized early experimental crimes was described in a spring 1881 column in the newspaper *Le Temps*.[11] The novelist, journalist and later director of the Comédie Française Jules Claretie promoted his novel *Les Amours d'un interne* by describing a visit to La Salpêtrière where the new hysteria experiments were taking place. For his part, Claretie was probably the first non-doctor to broach in France the issue of crimes, even murder, that could be committed under such suggestion. In the following passage Claretie quotes an unnamed doctor working at La Salpêtrière:

> On peut . . . dire à une hystérique à l'état de sommeil:
>
> – Dans deux heures, à telle heure, tu iras à tel endroit et tu feras telle ou telle chose!
>
> – Tu frapperas quelqu'un, par exemple!
>
> J'ai fait de la sorte . . . assassiner quelqu'un (en pensée) par cette petite blonde que vous voyez là-bas![12]

> One can . . . say to a hysteric in a sleeping state:
>
> – In two hours, at such and such a time, you will go to a certain place and will do this or that!
>
> – You will strike someone, for example!
>
> In this way . . . I had someone murdered (fictionally) by that short blonde woman you see over there!

Young doctors in the novel *Les Amours d'un interne* chortle over this type of power over patients, without exercising it for underhanded purposes, but such scenarios could obviously involve doctors gone bad, and this became one of the themes of 1880s fiction.

The abilities of both lay and medical hypnotists to access a second, apparently compliant, level of human personality enhanced popular belief that there was such a thing as an evil unconscious, the potential for monstrous two-sidedness in us all. Given the play this subject received in the central medium of the day, the newspaper, the fiction that hypnotism launched or abetted becomes a reflection of a modern, societal questioning about the nature of the unconscious. In 1884 Jules Claretie would again enthusiastically promote a forthcoming novel, *Jean Mornas*, the classic French study of posthypnotic crime, with a long, alarming column in *Le Temps* inviting readers to imagine the dangers of living unsuspectingly next door to an automaton-like individual programmed to commit a crime.[13] He also discussed admiringly a paper delivered to the Académie des Sciences Morales et Politiques by a member of the Nancy school, the lawyer Jules Liégeois, that described a wide variety of experimental crimes, both petty and serious, carried out by hypnotized patients in Nancy.[14] Liégeois suggests to one patient that she has overheard a confession of arson, and she reports the arsonist, who has done nothing, to the police. Other patients willingly sign false documents. A young woman is hypnotized and advised to shoot her own mother; she takes a pistol and does so without compunction (the pistol is not loaded). Liégeois also finds that he can hypnotize and control individuals by telephone.[15]

Claretie's 1884 article also relates in detail how Charcot's colleague Gilles de la Tourette successfully instructs the famous hysteric Blanche Wittmann, under hypnosis, to 'poison' Claretie as retribution for Claretie's having supposedly murdered an intern. We will return to Gilles de la Tourette's role in suggested crimes momentarily when we discuss his comments about a real murder trial, that of Gabrielle Bompard and Michel Eyraud.

Although the phenomenon took hold much earlier in the decade, experimental crimes were still a showpiece for doctors in 1888. Our Russian visitor, Sofia Kovalevskaya, was treated by Dr Luys to such an episode. He instructs a hypnotized patient to strangle one of his assistants because the man is 'a crook'. Apparently returned to a normal waking state but still under the influence of the suggestion, the patient notices the assistant and lunges at him. He is prevented from throttling the man 'just in time', writes Kovalevskaya skeptically.[16]

A vogue for crime stories was even more 'natural' than usual during the 1880s and 1890s, a period of anthropological and medical research focused on degeneration and criminal types, material that appeared in publications such as Alexandre Lacassagne's *Archives de l'anthropologie criminelle*, founded in 1886, and in the French translations of Cesare Lombroso's studies *L'Homme criminel* (1887) and *La Femme criminelle et la prostituée* (1896). Marc Renneville, among others, has examined the question of how the nineteenth century linked mental alienation, degeneration and crime.[17]

The public interest in the phenomenon of the murderer had an underside: what particular form of unrealized, unutterable deviance was the impetus behind a killing? Periodicals and newspapers were especially fond of playing with the notion of strange dualities in these murderers. In spite of the gruesome fact that the man had killed three women, the journalist Maurice Barrès finds that Jules Pel, a watchmaker from the Parisian suburbs, has an attractive, contemporary style about him. He is a dandy: 'Sa tenue distinguée, sa réserve, sa parfaite urbanité, jusqu'à cette note de pédantisme, tout en lui est de cette époque scientifique et audacieuse.'[18] ('His distinguished bearing, his reserve, his perfectly urbane air, even that note of pedantry, everything about him speaks of this scientific, audacious age.') Front-page newspaper columns by Anatole France and Barrès made of Henri Chambige, the student turned author of an 1888 suicide pact in which he killed his married lover, Madame Grille, but only succeeded in shooting himself in the jaw, what they called 'a literary assassin' because of his humanities education and the aesthetic quality of texts about his life and literary interests that had begun to circulate.[19] Both emphasize Chambige's rare sensitivity, sharpened by his study of contemporary decadent and symbolist literature, and his corresponding lack of a sense of practicalities. It is of some interest for the hypnosis-related fiction we are about to study that in order to preserve the family honour, Mme Grille's husband and mother maintained that she had been the victim of a rape under hypnotic suggestion. The fact that both the Charcot and Bernheim schools believed such rape was possible seemed to validate one avenue of approach for the defence.

A subsequent article by the social psychologist and magistrate Gabriel Tarde lays much more emphasis on the unconscious forces at work in the case.[20] He speaks of Chambige's dual apprehension of love, 'l'acuïté d'une passion qui trouve le moyen d'être sincère et littéraire à la fois et de s'exalter en s'analysant'[21] ('the acuteness of a passion that can be both sincere and literary at the same time and become exalted as it analyzes itself'). The suicide pact is the fruit of a struggle between the morbid self and the healthy self and is linked to 'la dualité psychique essentielle à la passion folle' (101). The text supports this idea of psychic disorder by noting that Chambige's nervous disposition had landed him in a Bordeaux medical facility for three months. Tarde intimates as well, citing the testimony of two former schoolmates of Chambige, that part of an adolescent crisis he underwent may have involved an idealized attraction to another male. Chambige had described the episode ambiguously as '*presque uniquement* intellectuelle' (emphasis added).

Journalists and newspapers were particularly attracted to the phenomenon of the mass murderer, and the crimes of Jean-Baptiste Troppmann were chronicled in great detail. In 1869 and at the age of nineteen, he had slaughtered eight members of the same family.[22] The *Petit Journal* is said to have tripled its print run during the affair to over 500,000 copies daily, a measure of national interest in the case. Troppmann's particular duality was physical and psychological. One focus of public and journalistic attention was an apparently deformed hand: the thumb was overly long and there was an overlarge gap between thumb and index, which gave it the appearance, wrote one observer, of 'une pince de homard' (a lobster's pincer); another viewed the hand as a set of vulture's claws.[23] Troppmann was, in addition, a not unattractive young man who, like the dandy-cum-assassin Pel described by Barrès, took careful care of his dress and presentation. Some saw in this an apparent effeminacy perhaps a sign of sexual difference, especially as there was no record of his having any particular interest in women.

Another serial killer, Joseph Vacher, was born in the same year Troppmann committed his crimes. This 'French Ripper' was brought to justice in 1898, convicted of killing, eviscerating and sexually abusing twelve people of both sexes. He does seem to have suffered from mental deficiencies, especially after one of his suicide attempts in which a bullet entered part of his brain.[24] An assessment of the perpetrator's mental stability was almost always carried out, but in the 1880 case of Louis Menesclou, who was apprehended with the two forearms of the four-year-old girl he had killed in his pockets, the assessment came too late: a post-guillotine autopsy revealed that he suffered from softening of the brain.

The question of whether a hypnotized individual could be persuaded to commit an actual crime – a query fiction writers would answer with a resounding yes – became a matter of increasingly bitter debate between the two main hysteria factions, the Nancy school under Bernheim and the Charcot group in Paris. This debate operated in parallel to a related campaign about suggestion, that is, Bernheim's increasingly vigorous and insistent promotion of his belief that the unvarying, supposedly universal multistage hysteria attacks seen at La Salpêtrière were produced by unconscious suggestion if not outright coaching by the doctors involved. Bernheim would lose the very public debate over suggested crimes in a court case, as we will see, but he returned to the attack and delivered the *coup de grâce* in the affair of suggestion and coaching with an article in *Le Temps* of 29 January 1891. It was here that Bernheim repudiated Charcot's core teaching. The hysteria attacks at La Salpêtrière he called 'une hystérie de culture', a hysteria that had been cultivated.[25] That is, whether or not they understood it, the doctors in their naiveté had shown their patients what they required of them and the patients had delivered. The expression 'hystérie de culture' created its own scandal and still has an impact today.

One important court case involving real crime merits consideration as we contemplate the fin-de-siècle juxtaposition of hypnotism, the unconscious and potential crime. In 1890 Gabrielle Bompard went on trial with her lover Michel Eyraud for the murder of the bailiff Augustin Gouffé. She was accused of having lured Gouffé to a romantic rendezvous where he was garrotted by her accomplice. She then helped Eyraud dispose of the body, sending it off in a railway trunk.

The case, like that of Troppmann, became a sensation. The medical establishment was immediately involved as the court appointed a trio of renowned doctors, Paul Brouardel, Dean of the Paris Faculté de médecine, Gilbert Ballet and Auguste Motet, to assess the medico-legal responsibility of Gabrielle Bompard, who had demonstrated strange, possibly unbalanced behaviours. One of the issues they had to decide was whether she had been under the hypnotic control of her companion Eyraud. What strikes a twentieth-first-century reader are the multiple, shifting incongruities that surrounded the case. Charcot himself, for example, took the occasion to ridicule Bernheim's Nancy group for believing that hypnotized subjects could actually commit real crimes, as did his lieutenant Georges Gilles de la Tourette, who spoke of 'fictitious' crimes that never happened outside the laboratory.[26] Yet in the same year, 1890, another of Charcot's prime collaborators at the Salpêtrière, Charles Féré, reissued a major study on hypnotism that noted that such crimes, including murder, were perfectly plausible. He wrote, 'Il est possible, dans l'état de somnambulisme provoqué, de suggérer des idées fixes, des impulsions irrésistibles auxquelles l'hypnotique réveillé obéira avec une précision mathématique.'[27] ('It is possible, in a state of induced somnambulism, to suggest *idées fixes*, irresistible impulses that once awake the hypnotized patient will obey with mathematical precision.') Perhaps Bompard had acted out of such an irresistible impulse, planted in her mind by her criminal associate.

Bompard had been a known hypnotic subject in the previous decade. Her family physician, Dr Sacreste, had hypnotized her at one point to try to temper her wild behaviour, and she admitted to him that other men, including a Lille businessman, had hypnotized her as well. It was in fact under hypnosis that she had admitted her crime to a Mr Garanger who had accompanied her back to Paris.[28] The hypothesis that Bompard could have murdered in a hypnotic trance was defended by the Nancy school representative Jules Liégeois (Hippolyte Bernheim had a broken leg and could not attend). For her part, Bompard maintained that she had been dominated by Eyraud, had at times been beaten by him and had run away, only to be brought back. One of her letters to another lover, Jules, mentioned that Eyraud had almost killed her on learning of her infidelity.[29] But one has to assume that the syndrome of the battered partner was not identified as a key factor by the court; the court judged that the relationship did not involve psychological damage or any degree of pathological dependency.

There were other known court cases in which the hypnotic or somnambulistic state of the accused had led to a verdict of not guilty. One of these was a case mentioned in Chapter 1, that of a dentist-in-training, Ulysse, who was discovered taking items of furniture from an antique store opposite his apartment building and calmly stacking them in the courtyard of his own building. A doctor demonstrated that Ulysse suffered from 'absences' and that when he was hypnotized, his own personality gave way to a second self that acted independently. His acts were realized via 'automatisme inconscient' and when he committed his crimes, these were simply '[des] scènes d'automatisme et de cérébration inconsciente'.[30]

More telling, given what the three doctors' verdict would be, were other cases that had involved them. One dated from 1881 in which the same Dr Motet demonstrated to the court that an exhibitionist was not responsible for his actions by hypnotizing him before the judges, showing that he was without willpower in that state, and having the court hear all the details of his crime as he recounted them. He was acquitted. The doctor who reported this, Paul-Émile Garnier, head physician at the special infirmary for the insane at the Préfecture de police in Paris, wrote that opinion on this question of acts under somnambulism was unanimous: such persons were not responsible.[31] A later case, discussed by Marcel Proust's father Adrien, concerned an Émile X. . . who also suffered from bouts of second personality in which he committed acts of petty theft. When Motet and Ballet informed the court of his mental absences, he too was found not guilty.[32]

The three-doctor panel actually tested the posthypnotic suggestion scenario on Gabrielle Bompard, and she performed as many a hypnotic patient had:

> Nous avons ensuite provoqué chez l'inculpée la suggestion de divers actes que nous lui avons ordonné d'exécuter après son réveil, et ces actes ont été exactement réalisés au moment voulu.[33]
>
> We then induced in the accused the suggestion of various acts that we ordered her to carry out after she awoke, and these acts were executed at the precise time prescribed.

It is interesting that they thus followed, at least halfway, the proposed approach of Charles Féré and Alfred Binet. That is, if an accused person invoked hypnotism as a cause of a criminal act, doctors were obliged to confirm that he or she was hypnotizable.[34] They also had the evidence of Dr Jules Voisin, who hypnotized Gabrielle several times while she was in prison. The panelists were thus able to confirm that Bompard could be hypnotized, but this did not alter their guilty verdict.[35] In the end, the doctors' report concluded that a hypnotized person would not commit a major crime.[36]

Bompard was amoral and incapable of remorse, they said, and she was a hysteric. They also maintained (without explanation or apparent justification) that neither hypnosis nor suggestion had played a role in her criminal acts. It is likely they were simply closing ranks around Charcot. An article by Gilles de la Tourette trumpeted the news: the court victory was 'le triomphe des idées de nos deux maîtres, MM. les professeurs Charcot et Brouardel'.[37]

But not everyone sensed that the trial result covered all the bases needed. What was true, overall, was that it was impossible to prove that Bompard had been hypnotized and was thus not responsible for her actions. Dr Émile Laurent, the translator of Krafft-Ebing, took a middle position in the debate, arguing that at least in some cases, a hypnotized person would in fact carry out a serious crime under posthypnotic suggestion. In the case of Bompard, however, he saw a different sort of loss of control, an individual lacking conscience and driven by unconscious instincts, something like a thinking automaton, a puppet capable of thought (40). Had this view prevailed with Drs Motet and Ballet, the result of the trial for Gabrielle Bompard might have been quite different.

How does crime itself connect to the question of the unconscious? In a general way, the late nineteenth century perceived that rationality was not necessarily the governing principle in our lives. Zola's *La Bête humaine* is often cited as an example of the negative unconscious gone awry, but it is only one example among many. The last thirty or so years of the century saw an especially rich wave of crime novels in France. That flowering included, at a minimum, *La Bête humaine*, Rachilde's *La Sanglante Ironie*, Camille Lemonnier's *L'Homme qui tuait des femmes*, various short stories by Marcel Schwob, 'Madame Herbaud' by Jean Lorrain and *Contes pour les assassins* by Maurice Beaubourg.[38] Numerous other titles could be added to these, for example, Hector Malot's 1888 bestseller *Conscience*, the story of a medical doctor turned assassin, Rachilde's murderous *La Marquise de Sade* and Paul Bourget's *Le Disciple*, with which we will end this chapter.

5.2 Dual Personality, Hypnotism and the French Fin-de-Siècle Novel

The popular novel of the 1880s and 1890s became the natural vehicle for exploring the most spectacular characteristics of the hypnotism and dual personality craze that dominated thinking about the unconscious in France during those decades.[39] There are several families of popular works that stand out in this regard, for example, the fiction that embraced the bad doctor or bad hypnotist figure, seen as charlatan/mystic/magician, who had the available science and techniques to create great damage and no moral imperatives to stop him. Many of these works tinkered affectionately with a new genus of crime, an experimental, posthypnotic felony committed by a hypnotized subject. However, and perhaps unexpectedly, we will also discuss a pair of novels in which hypnotism is employed to thwart the criminal mind. Novels involving spiritualism were another symptom of the clamoring for an explanation of the human psyche, and for some, it was the unconscious mind that was the vehicle of communication with the spirits. As the 1890s advanced, the hypnotism obsession began to wane, but the final section of this chapter will show, via a sampling of fin-de-siècle novels of psychological analysis by Paul Bourget and Marcel Prévost, that interest in the duality of the psyche had become a powerful fictional theme. However, while these works represent a serious attempt to explore the duality of the human psyche, the result is not infrequently awkward and self-conscious.

Edmond de Goncourt made his own study of mental duality before the hypnosis obsession took hold. His novel *La Faustin* is the story of an actress aware of how her role-playing life of illusion differs from her off-stage existence. Gradually, as she practises and interiorizes her part, the role takes possession of one part of her, it begins, in an unconscious operation, to *inhabit* her: 'Je suis deux', she says, 'C'est tout le secret de mon travail.'[40] The Goncourt authorial voice, ever attuned to the nerves and the medical, diagnoses her case as that of a 'somnambuliste lucide', a 'voyante' (55). But this type of duality, natural to the acting profession, quickly gave way in fiction to artificial dual states induced by the hypnotism.[41]

Novels of malevolent hypnotism such as *Jean Mornas* and a copy-cat work by Adolphe Belot, *Alphonsine*,[42] are part and parcel of the wave of crime fiction that surged over France in the 1880s and 1890s. But Claretie's and Belot's narratives are highly medicalized and closely focused on the potentially criminal unconscious. Both employ evil hypnotists who coach unwitting women into crime or sexually compromising situations. In Claretie's story a neurotic woman is hypnotized by a Salpêtrière-trained doctor too mediocre to establish a practice in Paris. When she executes a robbery under suggestion she inadvertently frightens an elderly man, who collapses and dies at the scene. But in both novels, the evil doctor or hypnotist is ultimately defeated by a good doctor or a 'bon génie' who credits real-life physicians for his own hypnotic expertise. Thus in *Alphonsine*, the more pandering of the two works, there are references to a spate of doctors deeply involved in hypnotic practice and theorizing: Alexandre Cullerre, Paul-Louis Ladame, Jules Luys and an individual named Barillot who edits the *Journal de l'Hypnotisme* and sounds suspiciously like Dr Edgar Bérillon, who was the editor of the *Revue de l'Hypnotisme.*

In 1885, the year *Jean Mornas* was published, there were many articles in the press marvelling at the mind-control powers of hypnotists. Two pieces from *Le Rappel* (11 June and 18 September 1885) and one from the *Journal des Débats* (11 June 1885) demonstrated how, once hypnotized, a young woman's muscular and joint pains could be cured by the placement of false vesicatories on the painful spot, with the result the next day that the complaint would be gone but the fake application would have left a large red blister. These were examples of the therapeutic potential of hypnotic suggestion, but it was the criminal potential that created more of a stir. In November, the lawyer Charles Foureaux recounted in a legal journal, *La Loi*, how he had tested the plot line of *Jean Mornas* in real time. He hypnotizes a young woman and instructs her to return the next day at a certain hour and go to a certain room, steal a bracelet from an *armoire* and bring it to him. She accomplishes the task, remembers nothing of it in a waking state, and so must be rehypnotized and placed under the greatest duress before she admits that she was the thief. 'Voilà toute la thèse de M. Claretie justifiée', writes Foureaux.[43]

Posthypnotic crimes become so topical that scientific journals begin to review the fiction they encouraged. When Belot's *Alphonsine* appeared, Paul Copin penned an extensive critique summarizing the plot in detail and expressing a preference for it over *Jean Mornas*, because it read more like a detective novel, with many more hypnosis-related peripeteias than Claretie's book.[44] He also found that the inclusion in the novel of semi-disguised names keyed to real doctors, instead of trivializing the work, leant it a sober and scientific tone that made it more realistic.

The theme of dual personality continued to fascinate Jules Claretie. In 1909 he published a novel, *L'Obsession (Moi et l'autre)*,[45] in which the main character, André Fortis, is split between two selves, a gentle, loving husband and a cruel, dark, ironic individual. The dramatic heightener in the tale is that the cruel personality takes over in the midst of André's wedding, the ceremony having just taken place. Surprised by his beautiful bride Cécile, who is dressed for bed, André 2 greets her with the exclamation, 'Pourquoi suis-je ici? Pourquoi êtes-vous ici?' (58, 62). Informed that they are married, he responds that he likes his freedom and will never marry. Cécile's confusion and travails begin, especially as she has some knowledge of asylums and a great fear of the insane. Both Andrés are painters: André 1 paints serene landscapes, while André 2 creates works that are bloody and violent, even apocalyptic (82).

The narrative is chock-a-block with references to the paranormal, the unconscious and the eccentric in art and science, to Schumann's 'satanic choruses' in *Manfred*, to Musset's 'insanity', to Schopenhauer's and Mozart's puzzlement that they were mentally absent when certain of their works were written. Reference is made to the famous Félida, treated by Dr Azam for her multiple personalities. Claretie's protagonist Fortis appears to resemble closely a real patient with split personality, Louis V. . ., studied by Henri Bourru and Ferdinand Burot. The research of these two doctors is mentioned in the text (236–37).[46] Like André 1, Louis has a gentle, open, sympathetic nature, but his second personality is combative, impolite and arrogant. For example, his first self has no interest in wine, while his second steals his fellow inmates' portions (21–23).

The novel testifies to the ongoing interest in dual personality as a manifestation of the unconscious well after 1900. One of the novel's chapters, titled 'Inconscient' (235–44), sums up contemporary research on dual personalities and ends with the decision that the alter ego, André 2, must be 'killed off'. André Fortis is hypnotized and told that his alter ego is now André David. Later, a death notice for David is produced and Fortis is thus cured. Interestingly, the cure borrows from Pierre Janet's psychotherapeutic practice in that the therapist plants incorrect but restorative information in the hypnotized patient's mind in order to neutralize neurotic and obsessional thoughts. But let us return to the 1880s.

The medical and legal communities were fully aware of the issues and concerns that surrounded posthypnotic crime. Newspapers and bestseller fiction like *Jean Mornas* made the general public aware of, and no doubt somewhat apprehensive about, the unpredictable and largely inexplicable behaviours induced by hypnotism. But there was a category of novel that captured the sensationalism of the posthypnotic debate while at the same time challenging medical authority by unmasking the confused state of scientific and medical thinking about the unconscious mind. Journalists such as Alexandre Hepp had already reported on the staged theatricality of Charcot's public lessons, and Maupassant had voiced his own skepticism about the doctor's understanding of hysteria, but Simon Boubée's novel *Main-de-cire* (The Wax Hand), published in 1888, set a new record for dissent.[47] The motif of the assassin's hand was widespread in French crime fiction – and not absent from French crime – in the last half of the nineteenth century, as we have seen in the case of Jean-Baptiste Troppmann.[48] In *Main-de-cire* the assassin's hand returns in the form of the unworldly, waxy whiteness of the young Sarah's hands, hands that tremble slightly because, as we learn later, they have plunged knives between the shoulder blades of a series of men. Freud would draw attention many years later, in *The Uncanny* (1919), to the frightening phenomenon of the inanimate that threatens to become human – wax figures, dolls, automatons – all these sensed as representations of an intimidating duality. For sheer attunement to the fascination and fears of the paranormal and unconscious that permeated French society in the 1880s, it would be hard to improve on *Main-de-cire*, a tale of posthypnotic murders, dual and triple personality, mind control, ESP, incest, parricide, death and redemption.

The story revolves entirely around medicine, good and bad, but at another level, it speaks to the confusion and even the alarm felt broadly in society about unusual manipulations of the psyche. The agent of evil in the narrative is 'Doctor' Martory (real name, Marius Fabre), who has completed certain medical studies but never obtained the legal status of doctor. He has become a sideshow hypnotist, a *magnétiseur*. Like other, real-life *magnétiseurs* of the period, say, Hansen or Donato, what the text underlines in Martory is that he is more a foreigner than native French: he became famous for his powers in Germany, the homeland of an equally criminal hypnotist in Frédéric Soulié's bestseller *Le Magnétiseur*[49] and, of course, of E.T.A. Hoffmann. It is Martory who has made of Sarah a killer through a kind of permanent mind control that seems to allow mental manipulation even at a distance.

Although Boubée's text presents Martory almost as a conjurer or sorcerer, it also assures the reader, somewhat disturbingly, but in accordance with what many observers felt at the time, that it was not the medical hypnotists who invented their own techniques. Martory simply employed the techniques of hypnosis before the doctors learned of them: he had anticipated Charcot (65). What we see confirmed throughout the narrative is that the medical establishment is no further advanced in the use and understanding of hypnosis than amateur practitioners. The author also underscores the fact that official medical hypnotism, personified by Charcot, is at a loss to interpret its own experiments:

> Les savants expérimentateurs actuels sont atterrés des résultats qu'ils obtiennent dans le vaste champ des études psychiques … Ils formulent de leur mieux les causes qu'ils prêtent à ces effets incroyables *a priori*. Mais, interrogez-les en particulier, ils conviendront qu'il y a encore là pour eux un grand inconnu. (65)
>
> The current crop of expert experimenters is appalled at the results they obtain in the vast field of psychic studies … They formulate as best they can the causes they attach to these astounding effects. However, when you ask them in private, they will agree that they still understand very little about the field.

The character who utters these last judgements is a sympathetic medical man, Dr Triquier. His comments underscore the fact that medical hypnotists have released unknown, potentially malevolent powers without knowing their origin or their potential dangers. This is reinforced by Dr Blanchemain (his name likely a bow to the real-life psychiatrist Dr Émile Blanche), who has studied Sarah in his clinic. Blanchemain predicts that men of science will never get to the bottom of her nervous affliction (184). These views of medical ignorance and therapeutic impotence were echoed, in the same year *Main-de-cire* was published, by Dr Edgar Bérillon, who, after witnessing the great Charcot's inability to help patients with nervous afflictions and his brutish dismissal of their questions, went so far as to condemn all of his medical colleagues. Their collective ignorance about the mind made them all charlatans.[50]

The novel does have one moment of lighter, piquant interest, as the novelist reaches for his *dénouement.* Canadian and Québécois readers will smile (some will frown) as Blanchemain suggests that Sarah, the owner of the nervous hands, be allowed to live out her days in 'a bright and lively' country. The choice turns out to be Canada and the city, Montréal, where, it is noted, 'de très bonnes gens ... parlent le patois normand ou vendéen ... Il paraît que c'est le vrai français' (259) ('very good-hearted people ... speak in a patois from Normandy or Vendée ... It appears that this is the true French').

A novel published a year earlier, in 1887, attacks a familiar sore point for doctors: were they as skilled in their hypnotic techniques as an experienced *magnétiseur*? The author, identified only as E... T..., includes a substantial, favourable analysis of the powers of Donato compared with those of Charcot, Dumontpallier, Cullere and Beaunis,[51] and, as in *Main-de-cire*, he makes the pointed suggestion that in experimenting with hypnotism the medical establishment is fumbling around in dangerous territory. The book also includes the story of a criminal hypnotist, a military lieutenant who hypnotizes a young woman into believing that they are married. She also commits a suggested crime, taking funds from her father that he was responsible for administering. Slipping in and out of hypnotic states, when she realizes what she has done, she commits suicide.

Under the pseudonym of Charles Epheyre, as we have seen in the chapter on Maupassant, Dr Charles Richet wrote numerous works of fiction that played with the dramatic potentialities of dual personality. In 1879, before he was thirty, and two years after he wrote his medical thesis, Richet published a collection of stories with paranormal themes, *À la recherché du bonheur.*[52] One of them, 'L'Expérience du professeur Rothbein', is framed by a phrase drawn from a found Brahman manuscript that reads, in part, 'L'homme est double ... chaque individu contient deux êtres, l'un qui est bon et l'autre qui est mauvais' (53). ('Mankind is split in two ... each individual contains two beings, one who is good and the other who is evil.') The text is a demonstration of this maxim, featuring Lucius, the professor's student, a sage young man sincerely in love with the professor's daughter and tasked with completing a volume titled *La Dualité de l'homme.* Unfortunately he has an alter ego named Lucien, who behaves like a rich decadent with few morals, gambling, fornicating and mocking life itself.

In Richet's novella *Soeur Marthe* the young doctor hero Laurent Verdine is a believer in hypnotism and maintains that, when hypnotized, individuals have a series of personalities within themselves. He becomes fascinated with a novice nun, sister Marthe, and when he plays Gounod's Ave Maria for her, she 'becomes' Angèle de Mérande, a more aggressive woman who predicts that Marthe will die. When begged, Angèle promises to ensure that Marthe lives, but this means that Angèle must 'die'. Laurent has lost both loves, because Marthe remains a nun. He is deeply troubled with this brush with the paranormal and admits that this love for a dual personality has destroyed his inner tranquillity.

If the unconscious seemed a natural reservoir for criminal themes, the posthypnotic state was a place of compulsory obedience. Some writers saw the practice of hypnotism as a device not for effecting crime but for solving it. *La Magnétisée* by Joséphine (alias Georges) Maldague[53] is an awkward narrative involving numerous sub-plots in which two doctors, Pertin and his son-in-law Groussier, the elder one calling himself a disciple of Drs Braid, Azam and Broca (240), hypnotize Aurélie Pierson, a woman suspected of criminal arson. The equipment they employ may not be up to tip-top Parisian standards, but it is functional. They first use a crystal bottle-stopper to focus the woman's attention, then later a special, battery-operated lamp brought from the capital. Their efforts pay off and when Aurélie reveals the truth, the doctors have her write and sign a confession while she is still hypnotized. Later, she challenges the authenticity of the document, but a deaf mute, Hubert Ricout, the only person to have actually witnessed the crime, has educated himself sufficiently to be able now to write down what he saw and confirm her guilt. The doctors stress that if there is any question about his testimony, physicians will be able to hypnotize him and confirm what he has written. Aurélie, subject to local justice, is thrown in the river and drowns.

Sometimes a physical object can become a metaphor for the unconscious, as in a novella by Gilbert Augustin-Thierry, *Marfa*.[54] Here, posthypnotic suggestion functions as a vehicle for dispensing justice. The story has both its homegrown French and exotic sides. The eccentric Russian Prince Volkine, an *amateur* of magnetism and ancient manuscripts and the owner of a palimpsest manuscript holding a potentially supernatural message, dies, and his wife Marfa is scheduled to remarry the French diplomat Lucien de Hurecourt. The latter has in fact assassinated the Prince, in order to marry his wife, but before he expires Volkine plants a posthypnotic suggestion in Hurecourt's mind and, unable to resist the hypnotizer's command and in a sort of trance, Hurecourt admits his crime publicly just before his marriage. He and his partner/accomplice commit suicide. The palimpsest itself, for which both Volkine and Hurecourt have felt a maniacal attraction, becomes the symbol of the hidden, unconscious power of the mind, which is the true core of the story.

Augustin-Thierry's story shares certain features of *Possession* by Charles Richet, discussed earlier, and may have been influenced by it as Richet's work preceded *Marfa* by a few months.[55] Both tales are exotic, taking place in spirit-prone Russia (journalist Jules Claretie had called Russia the most hysteria-prone country on earth and pictured the Russian female as 'cette Orientale conservée dans de la glace'[56] ('that Oriental woman preserved in ice')). Both tales involve murder, suicide and appeals to the quasi-occult, but then diverge as Richet explores the notion of spirit possession and Augustin-Thierry that of the irresistible power of posthypnotic suggestion.

The paranormal and psychical may seem an unexpected preoccupation for a writer such as Paul Bonnetain, author of the resolutely naturalistic novel *Charlot s'amuse*, the tragic history of a serial masturbator. But his friend Gustave Guiches knew better: 'Bonnetain s'intéresse, de préférence, à l'étude des phénomènes de la suggestion', he wrote in 1891.[57] Moreover, in Bonnetain's life, the curve of which seems to have been continually downward, his attempts to leave behind everyday reality already included the use of opium and ether. Between 1889 and 1891 he worked on a novel to be called *L'Endormie* (Hypnotized) but was forced to abandon it after losing his preparatory notes. Still, a number of his short pieces hint strongly at his interest in suggestion and the paranormal.[58]

Among these texts, 'Maternité'[59] is one that might have earned the title *L'Endormie*. It also demonstrates that hypnotism can create a second self that may in the end be happier than the first. Mme Falquet has survived six years of torture in a hellish marriage but unexpectedly becomes pregnant and gives birth to a son, Georges, henceforth the joy and obsessional focus of her existence. Her life is one of great happiness until Georges is called to do his military service. Awaiting her son's first day of leave in the provincial town to which he has reported, she is instead visited by an officer who informs her that Georges has been injured in a fall from his horse: he has in fact died in the accident.

In her grief, Mme Falquet almost succumbs to suicidal thoughts. However, after listening to a doctor friend discuss Bernheim, Charcot, and experiments with hypnotism he has himself seen, she hires a medical student to hypnotize her. He suggests that she dream of Georges as he was in their happy moments and she proceeds to have gloriously happy visions of their life together, without the pain of knowing Georges is gone. The treatment goes on for some weeks, but Mme Falquet becomes more obsessed, now wanting to plan a 'future' with her son: 'Faites-le-moi revoir encore, je vous en supplie, mais que je dorme toute la nuit et que nous vivions non plus le passé, mais une existence nouvelle que j'arrangerai . . .' ('Please let me see him once more, but let me sleep through the night and let us live not in the past, but in an existence that I will arrange . . .') Friends move her to the calm of the countryside where, one morning, her servant finds her sitting upright, stone cold, her hands joined in a beseeching attitude as though she were staring towards some vision known only to her. Bonnetain's tale seems to combine two themes. Dissimulated beneath the dominant late 1880s idea that posthypnotic suggestion can create a new and separate reality is the theme of reconnecting with the spirits of the dead and the intense need and desire that accompany this wish.

We have noted more than once that observers cited the automatic writing capacity of female mediums as a proof that an unconscious mind might exist alongside consciousness.[60] That is, the medium might engage in a normal conversation with those around her, while at the same time her hands copied messages from another level of her psyche. This alternate level of consciousness was compared by many to the second state into which hypnotism plunged the hypnotized. How was one, asked spiritualists, to define the special state of mind in which we were capable of communicating with the dead? Was it somehow an extension or a twin of this mysterious second state one experienced under hypnosis? Sylvie Thorel-Cailleteau has looked at this issue and noted that there was a scientific, positivistic impetus behind this late nineteenth-century desire to interrogate the paranormal and the occult: '[Il faut] . . . y voir moins une pure réaction spiritualiste à l'empire du positivisme, que l'exploration d'une zone définie, et déterminée par le positivisme lui-même.'[61] ('[We should] see here less a pure spiritualist reaction to the domination of positivism as the exploration of a defined area, determined by positivism itself.') In other words, the spirit of investigation of experimental science that was part of the positivistic mindset meant that for the scientist the apparently paranormal might well reveal behind its doubtful exterior a concrete, technical truth that should be explored. The scientific interest in paranormal phenomena was confirmed by the involvement of persons such as Dr Charles Richet, the men at Cambridge who formed the Society for Psychical Research in 1882, Dr Jules Luys and even, for a time, as we have seen, Pierre Janet. Thus the investigation of and interest in telepathy, mediums and conversations with the absent was to a not insignificant extent the product of psychological and medical research, most of it centred around hypnosis and hysteria.

Two examples of fin-de-siècle novels on spiritualism show the deep gulf between believers and non-believers, and both texts provide peripheral hints of the interaction between spiritualist thought and discoveries about mental dualism and the unconscious. In André Godard's *L'Agence spirite*[62] the painter René de Mordanes suffers from a deep melancholy, a 'mal du passé': he was to marry his beloved cousin Henriette, but she died in her teens, and, obsessed by memories of her bright spirit and the need to communicate with her, he has been in an emotional morass ever since. In an attempt to return René to a more rational state, his skeptical friend, Maurice Clavier, introduces him to the Agence spirite, a for-profit venture whose specialty is connecting gullible clients with the 'spirits' of their dead loved ones. After the Agence is raided by the police, the owner's daughter Eva, a convinced spiritualist, remains and René is torn between memories of his beloved fiancée, attraction to Eva and the reality of filial duties to an aging and sick father. A final passage shows the similar desire of spiritualist and conventional believer to communicate with the deceased, and suggests that faith in a Christian-style afterlife is the true option:

> Au fond, [Eva et René] partageaient le même espoir, phénomène de bicorporéité, pour elle, mystique présence des âmes, selon lui. René sentait toutefois combien son idéalisme était plus consolant que le spiritisme d'Eva, puisqu'il substituait l'immortalité vraie au dogme des réincarnations futures. (292)
>
> At bottom, [Eva and René] shared the same hope, a phenomenon of bicorporality for her, the mystical presence of souls for him. René could feel, however, how much more consoling his idealism was than Eva's spiritualism, because it substituted true immortality for the dogma of future reincarnation.

Eva's hopes are lodged in a belief involving a duality not of the psyche but of the body. At one level the spiritualist, while living, believes she can communicate with the dead, that is, with their partly material perispirit. At a second, material level, in the future she will be reborn in a different physical envelope. René's belief in the immortal soul is made of more ethereal stuff.

Paul Guiraud's quirky novel *La Conversion de Gaston Ferney. Roman spirite*[63] takes a position opposite to that of André Godard. His preface expresses irritation at those fin-de-siècle men of science who deny out of hand any appeal to the supernatural. His hero Gaston has married the adorable Lucienne, a young woman presented as a 'living enigma' largely because of her belief in spirits; Gaston, on the other hand, is a non-believer. Before they have even consummated their love, however, she mysteriously dies. Yet without transition, a new chapter finds Lucienne and Gaston enjoying a delicious summer idyll on the Mediterranean near Monaco. Is she not dead, is this a dream sequence?

The final pages inform us that Mr. and Mrs. Gaston Ferney have announced the birth of their son Lucien-Gaston on 10 September 1890, one year to the day Lucienne died. Some of Gaston's friends suggest that he must have remarried quickly, but the reader is left with the idea that perhaps the 'remarriage' was a union with the transmigrated soul of the first Lucienne.

What might explain the appearance, much later, in 1930, of a third novel of spiritualism, J.-H. Rosny aîné's *L'Initiation de Diane. Roman spirite*?[64] Was it nostalgic testimony to the vogue of paranormal beliefs at the fin de siècle, or was there a renewal of interest in these questions in the 1930s? Spiritualist ideas including mental telepathy and clairvoyance are explored, while at the same time the narrative adheres to contemporary reality via frequent references to automobile and airplane travel, telephone and radio use, comparisons of spiritualist communication to the buzz of an induction coil, Hertzian waves and radioactive emissions, and even an allusion to the American tennis great Bill Tilden, finalist in the French Open of 1930.

The student spiritualist Diane is advised to start with a little automatic writing, in which one is the docile instrument either 'of the subconscious or of the Beyond' (37). She attends séances, then on her own learns to call up the spirits of her family. The dramatic moment of the story sees a telepathic, clairvoyant character predicting that Diane will receive a telegram about someone boarding a ship, and a voice later whispers to her that the ship will sink. Indeed, a same-day telegram announces that her father is arriving from Australia, and yes, his ship sinks, but all ends well: he is rescued.

Rosny's text alludes, hesitantly, to how the unconscious might intervene in spirit communication. His view dovetails with that of the astronomer and spiritualist spokesman Camille Flammarion. For the latter, the concentrated focus of the group involved in a séance creates a new psychic personality that subsumes them all, and, he theorizes, it is our subconscious subliminal self that acts as the trigger mechanism for this outward projection of this joint thought: 'C'est notre être subconscient, notre moi subliminal qui paraît agir, un peu comme dans le rêve, mais en se projetant, pour ainsi dire.'[65] ('It is our subconscious self, our subliminal self that seems to act, somewhat like in a dream, but projecting itself forward so to speak.') Fused together, this concentrated psychic force is directed like a beam to the medium who calls up the apparitions requested.

5.3 Sex, Hypnotism and the Unconscious

Perhaps the most sensational and extreme of the fin-de-siècle novels constructed around hypnotic powers was *Suggestion* by the Belgian writer

Henri Nizet. Though he begins with hypnotism, the hero of the story, Paul Lebarrois, becomes involved in telepathy, spiritualism, esoteric practices and black magic. Stressing the way these movements are explored in a systematic way, critics have seen the novel fitting into a kind of expanded naturalism, along the thematic lines of *L'Hystérique* or *Le Possédé* by Camille Lemonnier.[66] But the early emphasis on Nizet's scientific approach may well have been an attempt to protect the author from a charge of obscenity: *Suggestion* is surely one of the most sexually graphic novels of its time to have been published by a reputable press.[67] My own reading is that it is primarily a novel of masculine phantasms in which hypnosis and telepathy become the ideal mechanisms of domination of the female, of sexual control and of the realization of sexual obsessions of every type.

The story begins with a train trip. The Parisian Paul Lebarrois is travelling to Galicia, to the town of Tchernowitz where he has business, when he becomes enthralled by the beauty of a young woman seated in the same compartment. With some knowledge of hypnotism, he uses the power of a fixed gaze to bring her under his control, kissing her brutally on the mouth and teeth. The woman is Séphorah Benedek, twenty-two years old, recently divorced and the daughter of the factory manager that Paul is slated to do business with. Once arrived at his destination, Paul is billeted in the father's house. From the train ride forward, Paul has but one thought: 'il rêve à la lubricité des juives d'Orient' (76) ('he dreams of the lasciviousness of Jewish women from the East').

Séphorah has a secret that explains her divorce: her vaginal passage is blocked and apparently she has no uterus.[68] Although she is referred to as 'l'insexuelle', after Paul's repeated hypnotic suggestions she becomes a totally eroticized being, setting aside completely all her inhibitions and compliantly allowing Paul to entertain his own salacious fantasies (67). There is a lot of sex in the novel: a huge, battering-ram of a phallus that appears in a dream; fellation; masturbation; sodomy. There is male-female oral-genital contact, sometimes phrased awkwardly, sometimes more poetically:

> [Paul] mont[ait] des pieds dont il rougissait de suçons la peau fine jusqu'à l'ombre aphrodisiaque et parfumée des cuisses où ses lèvres trouvaient comme des contacts de fruits inconnus. Il la goûtait toute suave jusqu'à ce que le spasme enlevât l'esprit de l'almée dans la félicité décisive (253).

> [Paul] be[gan] at the feet, whose fine skin he reddened with little suckings, rising up to the aphrodisiacal, perfumed shadow in the thighs where his lips found the contact of unknown fruits. He tasted the shadow, its suavity, until orgasm bore off the spirit of his exotic partner in a final felicity.

In spite of the visibility of the female orgasm in this text, I cannot agree with some who see this as an early novel of female sexual liberation. I do not disagree that, freed from any concern about pregnancy and from inhibitions, Séphorah experiences orgasms daily. But I would argue that the novel is much more about the nature of desire, and of a certain genus of male sexual desire. In an important moment in the text, where Paul is contemplating the naked body of the hypnotized Séphorah, he realizes that her seductive physical features are a veil behind which lies something more abstract. Her hips, thighs and breasts 'mettaient dans le cerveau de Paul ces idées qui prennent aux moëlles et font désespérer de jamais trouver dans la sensation l'équivalence du désir' (84) ('put the kind of ideas in Paul's mind that shake you to the core and make you despair of ever finding in a sensation the equivalent of your desire'). We sense, and Paul senses, that desire is indefinable, perhaps immense, incommensurable with any erotic act or acts.

And I would argue as well that the text places not only control but sadism at the heart of a certain masculine desire. Early in their relationship Paul imagines he is a doctor preparing to dissect Séphorah's nude body, or a gravedigger who might rape it, or even a version of Sergeant Bertrand, the real-life disinterrer and abuser of putrid bodies (82–83). What he likes, in sex he has paid for, is absolute immobility on the part of the woman, robotic assent. What he has created, in hypnotizing Séphorah, is, in his words, 'une sorte de beau mannequin, vide de pensée, – le meilleur avatar de la femme' (82). Later in the story, sexually beyond himself, Paul actually acts on these fantasies, lacerating, piercing and biting her body (255).

The dénouement of *Suggestion* has certain elements of a typical fin-de-siècle pathography, with Paul inching steadily towards madness and Séphorah slipping into ever-more-serious hysterical attacks. But for both of them the text emphasizes that it is their unconscious, their dark second self that is taking over, in his case 'la seconde personnalité de Paul' (138). For her, there was initially a 'sentimentalité positive', but now it is dominated by an insatiable alter ego: she is 'la messaline impossible à assouvir' (280) ('the Messalina, impossible to satisfy'). Paul's 'second self' is one of pure compulsion and *idées fixes*: he pronounces the same words over and over, cannot choose between alternatives, begins to suffer from agoraphobia. The text appears to assume that this is moral and medical retribution for the couple's erotic excesses; their logical mind has become dominated by inexplicable, reflex desires.

Part of the plot is the idea of counter-suggestion. That is, Paul has been inoculated in return with the same erotic suggestibility that he transmitted to Séphorah: he is 'sexuellement suggestionné lui aussi' (58). Giving in once again to fellation, Paul worries about 'le gâtisme final, l'ataxie, le cortège des misères dont la nature punit' (281) ('the final senility, ataxia, those attendant miseries that nature punishes us with'). As the story ends, therefore, he rids himself of the instrument of his degeneration, Séphorah, leaving her in their apartment in a hypnotic sleep to die from gas inhalation, while he heads off cheerfully to attend a meeting of his newfound paranormal colleagues at the esoteric lodge Aleph.[69]

5.4 A More Sophisticated Unconscious?

Heralded in a sense by Paul Bourget's volumes *Essais de psychologie contemporaine* (1883) and *Nouveaux essais de psychologie contemporaine* (1885), and by the undermining of the reigning naturalist school by the appearance of Huysmans' *À rebours* and the confrontational stance of the writers who signed the anti-Zola *Manifeste des Cinq*, there was a growing movement among French novelists from the late 1880s forward to prefer over the *roman de moeurs* and the *document humain* fiction highlighting human psychology. Bourget famously lauds Maurice Barrès' first novel *Sous l'œil des barbares* (1888) as a sterling example of a new fictional form, the novel of psychological analysis.[70]

Two of the most successful popular novelists of the late nineteenth century were Paul Bourget and Marcel Prévost. Although Prévost was at times mocked as 'le Bourget du pauvre' by certain of his contemporaries,[71] probably because he was prone to publishing sensationalist and suggestive works such as *Les Demi-Vierges* (1895), whereas Bourget seemed more intellectual, he also authored a text, *L'Automne d'une femme*, that has been touted as perhaps the finest novel of hysteria of its generation.[72] It would attract the attention of Henri Ellenberger in his *History of the Unconscious*.[73]

The central character is Julie Surgère, a forty-something woman in guilty love with Maurice Artoy, a failed artist of nervous disposition half her age, who has suffered a major emotional shock after the death of his mother and the suicide of his banker father. The story presents him as morbidly emotional, eternally indecisive. Daumier, the medical doctor of the piece, diagnoses his malady as an unstructured, licentious lifestyle (176) and offers advice canonically dispensed to nerve-prone young women: 'mariez-vous', he says.

Julie's husband Antoine Surgère treated her disgracefully on their wedding day, deflowering her brutally on the first couch at hand so that subsequently his advances have disgusted her. Now in her forties and emotionally deprived (her husband is by this time impotent and unable to walk), she is showing classic hysterical symptoms, saying of herself, 'j'ai un poids sur le coeur, une sorte de boule très lourde qui l'écrase, pèse sur lui et se soulève alternativement' (12) ('I feel a weight on my heart, a kind of heavy ball that crushes it, weighs down on it then rises up'). She is presented as having a puerile, maternal heart, preferring to think of her lover Maurice as a child. At this point the text, somewhat sententiously, explains the autumnal crisis that awaits childless women: Julie is 'possessed to the core by that false sense of motherhood that awaits childless women in their autumnal years' (76–77).

All of this might suggest that Julie is the hysteric of the tale. But Ellenberger's eye was drawn to something else, to the obscure malady of Claire Esquier, who is wasting away out of unspoken love for Maurice, and to the approach Dr Daumier employs in treating her. As Ellenberger suggested, Daumier is very likely modelled on Pierre Janet: both are from Lorraine and both are head of experimental laboratories at La Salpêtrière, Daumier in biology, Janet in experimental psychology. Moreover, Daumier's therapeutic techniques include a version of Janet's talking cure. Explaining how he has relieved the languor of an earlier young female patient, Daumier says that instead of using drugs, he probed and discovered how to solve her problem: 'j'ai confessé la malade', he says (268). The girl's secret was her love for a young army officer, an emotion that she kept entirely to herself until the therapist brought it forth. Informed of her love, in short order the officer asks for her hand and the girl's difficulties are at an end.

For Ellenberger, this is Janet's technique of uncovering the 'pathogenic secret' that is at the heart of hysterical neuroses,[74] or in a more modern sense, of psychosomatic illness. It is clear we are in the realm of the unconscious, for when Claire suffers a hemorrhage and it is obvious she is declining, Daumier diagnoses her condition in then-contemporary psychiatric terms: she is being eaten up inside 'under the influence of an unconscious cerebration' (294). Writing to Maurice, the doctor says that Claire is dying because she is unable to say that she is in love and whom she loves (314). Daumier will manoeuver Maurice into declaring his love for Claire and, as he did with his other female patient, Daumier enables Claire to bare her heart by admitting her infatuation.

Prévost continued to tinker with the idea of subconscious ideas in his novel *Le Jardin secret*,[75] whose central character, Marthe (Madame Jean Lecoudrier), left on her own one night after thirteen years of marriage, experiences a resurrection of her submerged, premarital self. The story evokes a series of psychological phenomena that would have served as mechanisms for a novel of crime and hypnotism a decade earlier. She is drawn to and investigates the documents and letters in a drawer her husband left unlocked, and a whole world of heretofore untold secrets, including infidelities, opens up. That drawer, its keys left in the lock, becomes a figure of a pathway to the unconscious in the novel, a symbol of Marthe's quest to uncover 'la Marthe d'autrefois, qui avait eu cette autre conscience dont je retrouvais inopinément la clef' (113) ('the Marthe of another time, who was of another mind to which I unexpectedly found the key').

Hypnotism is in the air, but now only as an undercurrent, for Marthe's mental state has been achieved not through the gestures of a charlatanesque magnetizer, but through self-suggestion when she saw a bright, luminous object. The question of dual personality is posed, but the text humanizes and normalizes the response. Perhaps in all of us there are off-limit mental regions, secret doorways deliberately sealed (142). A measure of Prévost's attunement to ambient psychological research is the fact that some of Marthe's memories come to her in moments of déjà vu, an expression mentioned at least twice in the text and, in fact, a genus of involuntary memory that was being researched at the time:

> Des pensées que j'avais eues *un certain jour*, ressuscitèrent dans mon cerveau et j'entendis des paroles qui avaient été dites autour de mes oreilles, et je vis des choses déjà vues, et mon cœur se serra de l'ancienne angoisse. (271)
>
> Thoughts I had had *on a certain day* were reborn in my mind and I heard words that had been said in my hearing, and I saw things that I had seen before, and my heart cringed with its old anxiety.

A year before the appearance of *Le Jardin secret*, the psychologist Théodule Ribot had published *La Psychologie des sentiments*, in which he addresses involuntary memory – or 'mémoire affective', as it was called.[76] As Prévost's story ends, Marthe realizes that both she and her husband have had secrets, in a sense second personalities, but as a good bourgeois wife she accepts that their relationship is functional and can continue. As if in an exercise of auto-psychoanalysis, she has explored the deepest level of herself, her consciousness and what had remained unconscious, and has retraced her steps back to equilibrium.

As a prominent literary critic and prolific creative personality, but also as a technician of fictional plots, Paul Bourget had a multifaceted interest in the nature and potential of the unconscious. Anticipating – and quite likely influencing – Proust's argument about the intellectual versus the instinctive, Bourget wrote that the creations felt nominally to be of the intellect are probably shot through with the emanations of the unconscious:

> Il est probable que toute création intellectuelle comporte une part énorme d'inconscience. La psychologie moderne nous démontre que nous vivons à la surface de notre être; toute une végétation cachée de pensées obscures, de sentiments ignorés, d'émotions inexprimables, s'agite dans les ténèbres de notre personnalité instinctive. Peut-être la même loi gouverne-t-elle ces êtres, issus de notre être, qui sont nos livres.[77]

> It is likely that every intellectual creation contains a huge portion of the unconscious. Modern psychology shows us that we live on the surface of our being; a hidden vegetation of obscure thoughts, feelings ignored and inexplicable emotions tosses about in the shadows of our instinctive personality. Perhaps the same law governs those beings produced by our being that are our books.

There may be a tinge of wistfulness in these lines, as though no conscious effort could succeed in penetrating these depths.

When it came, as it were, to 'demonstrating' the unconscious in fictional characters, Bourget's efforts were conventional and disappointing. Scrutinizing the research of the 1880s and 1890s on dual personality, he suggested that we are all perhaps possessors of two selves, the one that we know and another that might be its opposite, perhaps menacingly so: 'une créature [qui est] ... précisément le contraire de la créature que nous croyons être'.[78] His early novella *L'Irréparable* (1884) focuses on the self-destructive nature of two warring instincts in the same person, a kind of split in the psyche, this under the general heading of the unpredictability of our unconscious. References are made to the great (fictitious) metaphysicien Adrien Sixte, author of the imposing tome *De la dissociation des idées*, 'où il a étudié les maladies de la volonté consécutives à celles de l'intelligence' (4)[79] ('in which he studied the diseases of the will related to those of the intelligence'). As we will see in discussing Bourget's novel *Le Disciple*, the philosopher figures that Bourget targets in Sixte are Hippolyte Taine and, to a lesser extent, Théodule Ribot, each of whom investigated in his own way human psychic duality. We might also add Pierre Janet as a model for Sixte, given that the idea of 'dissociation' came to be seen as Janet's discovery. Théodule Ribot's *Les Maladies de la volonté* appeared in 1883, just a year before *L'Irréparable*, and in spite of its title, the work encourages the view that there are two types of willpower. Ribot equates the efforts of conscious, intellectualized willpower with artificiality compared with the intensity of spontaneous attention that originates in the deeper levels of the mind.[80] Bourget was quick to latch onto the expression 'maladie de la volonté', for in his *Essais de psychologie contemporaine*, as we have seen, he assigns this diagnosis, among others, to the Goncourts, Zola, Guizot, Amiel and Maxime Du Camp.

What is lame in the depiction of human duality in *L'Irréparable* is the proposition that for most women, a second self is released when they are made aware of the physiological facts that accompany their first lovemaking. (Men somehow escape this phenomenon.) This 'fact' explains the unexpected turns taken by many marriages: a girl who disliked her fiancé discovers she loves him, or the opposite. This is 'la multiplicité du moi' (6). However, in the narrative itself, the psychological dice have been loaded against the main protagonist, Noémie Durtel, for she is no simple disappointed or enthusiastic bride. Her initial sexual experience has been a rape: she naively allowed an unwanted suitor to enter her bedroom. That event has indeed altered her personality, all the more so as it has been impossible to tell her mother about it since Noémie discovered about the same time that her mother was having an affair with a twenty-year-old man.

When her mother mentions a possible marriage to the impeccable Sir Richard Wadham, the idealist painter, Noémie's remorse is triggered. She considers her rape to be 'son inexpiable, son ineffaçable souillure' (101) ('her unforgiveable, indelible stain'). The act has made her unmarriageable, for she could never tell Richard about it, and she is concerned that in the midst of their embraces she might recall those of her rapist. She escapes Richard's love and her own feelings for him by accepting a marriage offer from M. de la Roche d'Ayrac, an older man she doesn't love. But the painful image of the rape returns and, unable to face the prospect of actually playing her conjugal role, she commits suicide.

In Bourget's bestseller *Le Disciple* (1889), a narrative based largely on the abortive suicide pact, mentioned earlier in this chapter, between Henri Chambige and his lover, Magdeleine Grille, the novelist has mixed results creating modern characters. His portrait of the philosopher Adrien Sixte is so one-sided as to be caricatural.[81] Sixte's student, Greslou, is more complex, but the fact that the work is a transparent *roman à thèse* has undermined its readability and the immediacy of its characters. However, what is particularly relevant to our investigation, and somewhat fascinating, because it seems like a kind of throwback to hypnosis-based pulp fiction, is that the text frames the idea of duality and exploring duality as dangerous if not criminal. The object of this criticism is Hippolyte Taine and especially his *De l'intelligence* (1870),[82] in which the early pages speak of 'cette pluralité foncière du moi', that is, 'deux personnes morales juxtaposées dans le même cerveau' in what is therefore a 'dédoublement du moi' (16–17). The word 'dédoublement' ('splitting') is used repeatedly by Greslou in *Le Disciple* (125, 159, 174, 182, 190) to explain his ability to think abstractly and at the same time to revel in a passionate, impulsive nature. His dream, as he puts it, is to have both a feverish and a lucid makeup so that he can be both the subject and object of his analysis (129). The problem is that Greslou has no sense of right and wrong nor of social responsibility to accompany his acute analytical talents; instead, he adopts the impassiveness one sees in the natural world that teaches the individual '[une] indifférence absolue au bien et au mal' (243). He has inherited this lopsided values system from Taine's famous introductory formula to *Histoire de la littérature anglaise*, 'Le vice et la vertu sont des produits comme le vitriol et le sucre.'

Straightforward, amoral mind control techniques are thus the obvious vehicle for seducing Charlotte, the young daughter of the Jussat-Randon family for which Greslou is a tutor. He has had experience with hypnotism and tries out suggestions on her (207), so that when she gives herself to him it is with 'une passivité d'hypnotisée' (274). His success in dominating her is at one point attributed to his ability to read her mind (he enjoys 'la double vue'): it is transparent to him that she loves him passionately. In the feverish state of mind that accompanies his thoughts of a double suicide, he says he hypnotizes himself via auto-suggestion so that when he actually goes to purchase the required poison – one wonders if this may be an effort at self-exculpation – it is as a somnambulist, an automaton (270).

The apparent grudge against hypnotism and the paranormal we see here is part of the text's objection to scientific experimentation with the psyche. In 1889, the Charcot decade was ending and the penchant at La Salpêtrière for experimenting with patients to the detriment of curing them was a complaint one heard from many quarters. Greslou himself, as we saw earlier in the chapter, parrots the cold-blooded mind doctors who compare their research to a vivisection of the soul (see 203–4; 224). But Gargantua's maxim overlays the story. He warned his son Pantagruel: 'Science sans conscience n'est que ruine de l'âme'. As Antoine Compagnon would have it, this is the indictment of the novel that reads as 'le procès de l'homme de science comme celui d'un monstre d'aveuglement moral et d'inconscience sociale' (29) ('the trial of the man of science as a monster of moral blindness and of absent social conscience').

Chapter 6, the next, and last, chapter, addresses Marcel Proust's thinking about the unconscious and, with it, his analysis of the subordinate role the intellect and the intellectual should play in artistic creation. Are

Bourget and Proust therefore allies? Do we see Bourget, the critic of overemphasis on narrow science and dry intelligence, as a Proust-like partisan of instinct and intuition rather than logic and reason? This image does not cohere with what we know of him. However, it has been argued by Michel Mansuy that Bourget was part of an anti-intellectual movement that took shape in the mid-1880s,[83] even though it is clear that his opposition did not target the intellectual broadly, but rather ivory-tower scientism. In many ways, for example, in the burgeoning interest in mysticism, in the paranormal and the spirits, the purely logical and reasonable came to be challenged at the fin de siècle. In my final chapter, I will explore this theme of questioning the intelligence in favour of the unconscious mainly in Proust but also as it comes to the fore in writers such as Remy de Gourmont, psychologists such as Théodule Ribot and medical doctors such as Paul Chabaneix. I will not forget to interrogate Antoine Compagnon's comment, which he wrote about Bourget, that 'l'intellectuel serait une invention de l'affaire Dreyfus' (*Disciple*, 29) ('the intellectual is apparently an invention of the Dreyfus Affair'). I will also be careful to assess the shift in meaning of the term 'intellectual' as the century turned. One measure of its mobility is a text from *Le Disciple*. In the preface of the 1889 edition, dedicated to 'a young man', Bourget wrote that 'le beau nom de dilettantisme ... dissimule la férocité froide, la sécheresse affreuse' ('the fine term dilettantism ... hides the cold ferocity and terrible dryness') of a certain type of intelligent, but immoral, sensual youth. When he finalized the text of the novel in 1901, Bourget changed his wording and spoke, instead, of 'le beau nom d'intellectualisme'.[84] Was an intellectual thus automatically a dilettante in 1900? Bourget's altered terminology is a valuable indicator of a shift and a dispute in French thinking about the rational, which we will now explore in the chapter on Proust.

CHAPTER 6

Proust, the Intellect and the Unconscious

> Je ne crois même pas l'intelligence première en nous . . . Je pose avant elle l'inconscient qu'elle est destinée à clarifier. (Corr. 18, 388)[1]
>
> (I don't even believe that intelligence comes first in us . . . I would give precedence to the unconscious, which it is meant to clarify.)
>
> Ste-Beuve paraît plus intelligent que Flaubert. Débuter par méfiance d'intelligence.[2]
>
> (Sainte-Beuve appears more intelligent than Flaubert. Begin with mistrust of the intelligence.)
>
> L'intellectualité c'est l'art d'éviter la difficulté.[3]
>
> (Intellectuality is the art of avoiding difficulties.)

Proust and the unconscious: the question has intrigued many of his readers, especially as Proust's dates mesh evocatively with major publications by Sigmund Freud. One critic has identified four approaches to examination of the unconscious in Proust: psychoanalytical readings of *À la recherche*, comparative aspects of Proust and Freud, historical investigations of Proust's thought in the context of nineteenth-century thinking about the unconscious, and studies on dreams, spoken language and wordplay in *À la recherche*.[4]

This chapter can be most closely related to the third category, as it examines Proust's position in the ongoing late nineteenth- and early twentieth-century debate involving two views of the mind, the conviction that it was dominated by reason and willpower, and the view that the unconscious generated many of our actions and that it was a wellspring of potentially inventive and creative thoughts. If I resist the quasi-magnetic draw of Proust/Freud comparisons, it is of course because my focus is thinking about the unconscious before Freud, but also, as I have argued in detail to close Chapter 1, because Freud's works were not translated and his theories were virtually unknown in France or, when known, frequently discredited, until after Proust's death in 1922. Yes, Marcel had studied

German, but as his friend Jacques Rivière commented in 1923, Proust knew nothing more of Freud than his name. Moreover, Proust's most reliable biographer, Jean-Yves Tadié, argues convincingly that Proust had no knowledge of Freud whatsoever.[5] How significant are anecdotes such as the diary entry of the famous society confessor Abbé Mugnier, who wrote on 23 April 1917 that over dinner at the Ritz Proust's acquaintance Princess Soutzo mentioned to Mugnier the existence of a Jewish doctor from Vienna named Freud who had a theory about working out conflicts in dreams?[6] Some propose that this exchange proves Proust had knowledge of Freud,[7] but could it not be used just as persuasively to suggest that he knew nothing about the Viennese doctor?[8]

Disagreements about Proust's possible knowledge of Freudian theory continue, but it is time now to move on to the principal subject of this chapter, the resistance of a great intellectual, Marcel Proust, to intellectualism, and his attachment instead to certain types of emanations from what he called his unconscious, and the way these two opposing positions collide in early twentieth-century debates about the mind.

6.1 Trials of the Intellect

Proust was, of course, a very serious intellectual, in the sense that he was deeply interested in ideas. After all, unsure of the nature of the work that would become *À la recherche*, he was at one early point drawn as much to the idea of a philosophical essay as to that of fiction: 'Faut-il en faire un roman, une étude philosophique?'[9] As he tinkered with the structure of *Contre Sainte-Beuve*, he contemplated either a classical essay in the style of Taine or an essay on aesthetics that would transition into a conversation with his mother.

Part of Proust's hesitation about fiction has to do with the status of the novel at the turn of the century. With figures like Pasteur, Charcot and his school and the *méthode expérimentale* of Claude Bernard, science is at an unimagined apogee. By contrast, literary prestige is on the wane. The naturalist novel is moribund and has been since *À rebours* and the *Manifeste des Cinq* of 1887. Other movements, both active or already stillborn, are fighting for space in fiction and poetry: *le décadentisme*, mysticism, symbolism, remnants of *le Parnasse*. There is a movement towards a more intellectualized and ideological literature. In Jules Huret's 1891 *Enquête sur l'évolution littéraire* a number of writers maintain that in the future literature will be socialist. Paul Bonnetain exclaims, 'la littérature de demain, après tout, serait purement socialiste que je n'en serais pas surpris'[10] ('I would not be surprised if the literature of the future were, after all, wholly socialist'). Octave Mirbeau agrees.[11] Jean Ajalbert sees J.-H. Rosny's works as having moved the novel towards science and socialism.[12] For his part, in his essay *La Littérature de tout à l'heure*,[13] Charles Morice predicts the end of the Romantic analysis of feelings and the naturalist analysis of sensations. Instead, he sees the conjunction of the religious sense and the scientific sense in a new aesthetic arrangement. Proust captures these tendencies in *Le Temps retrouvé*, writing, 'Aussi la meilleure partie de la jeunesse . . . n'aimait plus en littérature que les œuvres ayant une haute portée morale et sociologique, même religieuse' (IV, 471). ('The best part of the younger generation . . . admired nothing but works with a lofty moral and sociological, and even religious, significance' (6, 295).) The mature Proust underscores the fact that such values do not equate to fine literature. But in the early years of the twentieth century, these values and the kinds of novel they spawned held more sway and appear to have conditioned Proust's early struggle with fictional form.

Learning that a subscription has been started to finance a statue of Sainte-Beuve in the Luxembourg gardens, one medical observer of the literary scene proposes that this is the age of the writer-critic, or perhaps the writer-essayist. The writers worthy of admiration at the moment, he asserts, are Bourget, Anatole France, Jules Lemaître and Maurice Barrès, the latter lauded as the greatest intellect of them all. Why these gentlemen in particular? They exhibit a critical sense and a penchant for general ideas: 'Ils philosophent chemin faisant.'[14] ('They philosophize as they go.') Indeed, after the eccentricities and improprieties of decadent writers such as Jean Lorrain and Rachilde, after Zola's pseudo-science and his 'filth', a heavy burden of responsibility is henceforth placed on the novel. In a text specifically directed at women writers but revelatory in other ways, the critic Émile Faguet insists that the novel must have a 'high' purpose:

> Partant de ce point de vue que le roman – sauf, bien entendu de haute portée sociale ou de très large thèse philosophique – est indigne de l'homme que son intelligence réserve à d'autres travaux, je trouve logique et bon que les femmes s'y adonnent.[15]
>
> Based on this point of view that the novel – except, of course, the novel of elevated social scope or very broad philosophical thesis – is unworthy of men whose intelligence prepares them for other work, I see it as logical and good that women get involved in writing them.

As if he had read Faguet's specifications about fiction, Proust reveals in his 1908 *Carnet* that he is torn between generic approaches: 'La paresse ou le doute ou l'impuissance se réfugiant dans l'incertitude sur la forme d'art.'[16] ('Laziness or doubt or inadequacy hidden behind uncertainty over the art form.') Thus the early hesitations of Proust's Narrator regarding literary form and content seem to rehearse the uncertainties of Proust himself, a would-be novelist surrounded by literature characterized by essayistic and intellectualist tendencies and moral imperatives. *À la recherche* captures these tensions neatly. In his search for a literary vocation, the adolescent Narrator makes the dilemma of the would-be novelist almost unmanageable: he seeks a subject with 'une signification philosophique infinie' (I, 170). Later, in a typical Proustian reversal, the mature Narrator says of literary subjects, 'la matière est indifférente' (IV, 489).

Proust questioned the high value placed on intellectual activities that derived purely from the reasonable and the logical. In this, he was part of another sub-group within his generation that exhibited a multifaceted, turn-of-the-century anti-intellectualism that some traditional thinkers in France considered un-French. It has been suggested that since Schopenhauer's assertions about willpower and intuition the nineteenth century as a whole tended increasingly to discount the importance of the rational intelligence.[17] But another way of measuring the strength of this growing interest in the non-rational – in the paranormal, the esoteric and mystical, the instinctive, the intuitive and the unconscious – is to contemplate the degraded meaning of the term 'intellectual' itself around 1900.

As we have seen, in 1919 it was the frequency of references to a proper unconscious in discussions of the workings of the psyche that led the philosopher Dominique Parodi to worry that reason and thinking themselves were losing their importance. Pierre Citti has noted that the contamination of things 'intellectual' happened much earlier, in the 1890s and as the century turned. He quotes an entry in André Lalande's *Vocabulaire technique et critique de la philosophie*[18] on 'intellectualism' that is instructive. The pejorative sense of the term is

> apparenté à l'usage qui a été fait aussi du mot *intellectuel* dans les discussions politiques. L'un et l'autre impliquent d'ordinaire: 1° le reproche de penser les choses d'une façon verbale et superficielle, en imposant à la réalité des cadres artificiels et rigides, qui la déforment en prétendant la représenter; 2° le reproche de sacrifier 'la vie', c'est-à-dire la prudence naturelle et la fécondité de l'instinct, aux satisfactions de la pensée critique, qui est une force d'arrêt, de destruction, et d'inhibition.[19]
>
> linked to the use made of the word *intellectual* in political discussions. Both terms imply normally: (1) a reproach about thinking of things in a verbal, superficial way while imposing on reality artificial, rigid frameworks which

deform it even as they claim to represent it; (2) the reproach of sacrificing 'life', that is, the natural prudence and the fertility of instinct to the pleasures of critical thinking, which is a force for inertia, destruction and inhibition.

We have observed in the previous chapter a concrete illustration of the degraded sense of 'intellectuel' in the way Paul Bourget gave equal weight to 'dilettantisme' and 'intellectualisme' in his novel *Le Disciple*.[20] There is certainly some equally negative flavour in Proust's assigning of the intellect to a subordinate role in the creative process and in his characterization of literary criticism, along with other types of non-imaginative writing, as derivative.

One must not forget, however, that the term 'intellectual' attracted derision from a very specific quarter as the century turned, and this is likely what is meant by Lalande's reference to its use in politics. In the midst of the Dreyfus Affair supporters of Dreyfus who had recorded their approval of Zola's article *J'accuse* were attacked as 'intellectuals'. The campaign was championed in spectacularly aggressive style by Maurice Barrès with a front-page article in *Le Journal* of 1 February 1898. The 'intellectual' aspect of the anti-Dreyfusard argument developed by Barrès and later by Ferdinand Brunetière was that men of necessarily narrow erudition – intellectuals – could not pretend to understand patriotism, honour, the nation's defence and the army. The involvement of the intellectual in questions such as these was interference, an illegitimate use of a personal claim to science and knowledge.[21] Of course, the definition of 'intellectual' included all those who did not blindly agree that Dreyfus was guilty, and for Barrès, the group was composed in particular of Protestants, foreigners, Jews, a few good-hearted but naïve Frenchmen like Anatole France, and learned boobies ('nigauds'). Zola himself was a perfect example of the Dreyfusard: he was of foreign, not French stock (his family came from Venice). The historian Eugen Weber has provided a piquant illustration of this Dreyfus-era dissension. He describes a family rift that came before the French courts in 1901. Enraged by his mother-in-law, who aggressively defended Dreyfus, her anti-Dreyfusard son-in-law slapped her and called her an 'intellectuelle'. Lawsuits were set in motion, but once in court the parties were reconciled.[22]

In 1900 Remy de Gourmont published an essay, 'La Dissociation des idées', in which he subjects aspects of the Dreyfus affair to linguistic and logical analysis and plays tangentially with the idea of the intellectual. The psychological notions of 'association of ideas' and Janet's term 'dissociation' are very much in the air, and, with mischief in mind, Gourmont applies them to the Affair. When and how, he wonders, did the ideas of honour and the military become associated? What has happened recently is that the army and dishonour are the new pairing. Many truths are composed of two ideas, he suggests, and one does not have to be an 'intellectual' to observe that at times these two terms become unglued, dissociated: 'une vérité est morte lorsqu'on a constaté que les rapports qui lient ses éléments sont des rapports d'habitude et non de nécessité'[23] ('a truth dies when one observes that the relationships that connect its elements are habitual relationships, not necessary ones'). Linguistic dissociation, evident to someone not necessarily of intellectual bent, is the result of the Affair.

Pierre Citti scrambles somewhat to articulate the social and political reasons that might explain the negativity attached to intellectualism and the attack on the intelligence. Not surprisingly, it is less in the sociopolitical sphere and more in the arts and writing that there is resistance to the kind of inhibitions that an overly intellectualized approach might occasion. Citti finds that major turn-of-the-century writers valued, over the intellectual, a kind of meaning that was more profound: '[Cette réalité] est naturelle, c'est-à-dire plutôt "authentique" dans le sens que Valéry, Proust, Gide donneront à ce mot opposé à "artificial". Elle est par conséquent dynamique, le fond en est bien un élan vital, largement inconscient.'[24] ('[That reality] is natural, that is, "authentic" in the sense that Valéry, Proust and Gide will lend to the term in opposition to "artificial". It is, consequently, dynamic, its basis is a vital impetus, largely unconscious.') Of course the exaggerated belief in the positive, in the ability of science with its experimental methods to locate and demonstrate 'reality', is surely one of the main factors explaining the disdain for the intellect.

Moving forward momentarily to the end of the Great War, we see members of the French intelligentsia on the left and right attempting to assert a leadership role in the postwar recovery. But there is also another type of 'recovery' in their minds: their involvement no doubt signals an attempt to recover the prestige that the term 'intellectuel' had lost during the Dreyfus Affair. Romain Rolland launched an appeal to intellectuals on the left in *L'Humanité* of 26 June 1919 titled 'Un appel: fière déclaration d'intellectuels' ('An appeal: a proud declaration of intellectuals'). Knowing of Proust's low opinion of the author of *Jean-Christophe*, we are not surprised that there seems to be no recorded reaction to the column on Proust's part. This was not the case, however, for a separate manifesto, 'Pour un parti de l'intelligence', that appeared in *Le Figaro* about a month later.

Along with Paul Bourget, Binet-Valmer, Henri Ghéon, Maurras, Henri Massis and Francis Jammes, Proust's friend Daniel Halévy had signed it.

What principles, ask the authors, should guide postwar reconstruction of society? 'Où les trouver, sinon dans les lois de la pensée qui sont la condition même de notre progrès individuel et du progrès de l'espèce?' ('Where is one to find them, unless it be in the laws of thought, which are the very condition of individual progress and the progress of the species?') The signatories speak of wanting to organize the defence of French intelligence as part of safeguarding the spiritual future not only of France but of all civilization.

Edward Hughes has pointed out the central issue in the manifesto that irked Proust: its tone of cultural triumphalism, not to speak of hints of jingoism.[25] Hughes explores the interesting shift in Proust's mindset, from the politically idealistic hero of *Jean Santeuil* to a different character, the Narrator of *À la recherche*, who turns away from such idealism, as embodied in the value system of Combray, in order to find his own autonomy.

The expression 'cultural triumphalism' is well chosen, but beneath its general sweep one can see in the manifesto a number of specific references that collide jarringly with Proust's principles of literary creativity. First of all, there is the question of national, or nationalistic, literature. The document asks, 'Mais n'est-ce pas en se nationalisant qu'une littérature prend une signification plus universelle?' ('But is it not in becoming national that a literature takes on a more universal meaning?') Proust writes Halévy to say that equating the intellectual with nationalism reduces the meaning of each: 'je désapprouve ton manifeste du *Figaro* [. . . N]'est-ce pas une vérité . . . qu'on ôte sa valeur générale et même nationale à une œuvre en cherchant à la nationaliser?' ('I disapprove of your manifesto in *Le Figaro* [. . . Is it not] true . . . that you remove general significance and even national significance from a work by attempting to render it national?') If a principle other than the search for aesthetic perfection or scientific truth drives a project, contends Proust, its purpose and truth are falsified.

More annoying for Proust may have been two other specific points in the manifesto. These are the lines in the document that castigate 'le soulèvement de l'instinct' ('the stirring up of instinct') and laud 'une méthode intellectuelle qui hiérarchise and qui classe' ('an intellectual approach that establishes hierarchies and classifies'). The impotence of an intellectual approach to literature, abundantly demonstrated across *À la recherche* – 'chaque jour j'attache moins de prix à l'intelligence' – resided for Proust in the fact that the intellect had no creative potential: it was, precisely, capable only of classifying and organizing. And as for instinct, in the Proustian thesaurus it was the creative antonym of the word 'intellect'.[26]

6.2 The Unconscious and Creativity: 1900

With its title that suggests a kind of fin-de-siècle split personality in Proust, Edward Bizub's study *Proust et le moi divisé* brings into tight focus the image of Proust's novel as a kind of experimental laboratory, where mental processes and phenomena – association of ideas, dual personality, voluntary and involuntary memory, unconscious phenomena – are bubbling along in a rich stew that will feed into Proust's budding novel. Especially interesting is Bizub's discussion of Dr Paul Sollier, the physician of nervous afflictions who persuaded Proust to take a rest cure in his clinic after Proust's mother had died. Though Marcel's stay there was brief – from late December 1905 to 25 January 1906 – the patient had ample time to read some of the doctor's publications, especially *Le Problème de la mémoire* (1900), and to enjoy informative exchanges with a well-respected psychologist.

Bizub's study includes useful readings of Taine's *De l'intelligence* (which Proust much admired) and its statements about the duality of the human mind. Bizub also explores the research on split personality in Alfred Binet's *Les Altérations de la personnalité* as a support for his own somewhat problematic argument that Proust's Narrator is constructed as a kind of extension of the nineteenth-century dual personality via the split between 'moi social' and 'moi profond'.

My focus here, however, is that in and around the year 1900, a number of studies from quite different fields began a serious exploration of the links between creativity and the unconscious. I have chosen to sample the views on this question of a psychologist, a medical doctor, a writer of fiction and essayist, and a renowned mathematician. Each in his own way might be seen as confirming Proust's theoretical pathway as his thinking moved towards an aesthetic of the unconscious.

It is not at all certain that Proust read important works by the psychologist Théodule Ribot, *La Psychologie des sentiments* or his *Essai sur l'imagination créatrice*, although he was, as we will see, an admirer of Ribot's *Les Maladies de la volonté*. Dr Paul Chabaneix's *Le Subconscient chez les artistes, les savants et les écrivains*, which we discussed briefly in Chapter 1, is an unusual medical thesis that probes the links between the unconscious and creativity via a questionnaire that received positive responses from musicians such as Vincent d'Indy, writers such as Paul Adam, Sully Prudhomme and Rachilde, and doctors such as Charles Richet. (Perhaps not surprisingly, six of the eight doctors who answered the questionnaire reported no experiences relating unconscious phenomena to creative activity.) I have seen no reference in Proust to Remy de Gourmont's volume *La Culture des idées*, with its essay 'La Création subconsciente', although there are scattered references to Gourmont in Proust's correspondence, and, according to the editor of the Pléiade *Sodome et Gomorrhe*, Antoine Compagnon, Proust was aware of Gourmont's articles on homosexuality in the *Mercure de France*. Finally, it is two works from a very non-literary position that confirm the convergence, sometimes from the apparent periphery, of a scientific mindset and thinking about the creative power of the unconscious. Those studies are *La Valeur de la science* and *Science et méthode*[27] by the mathematician Henri Poincaré.

Given his own problems with what he considered his willpower deficit, it is not surprising that Proust was enthusiastic about Ribot's 1883 work *Les Maladies de la volonté*, which, although it did speak of ailments of the will, attested somewhat surprisingly to the superiority of spontaneous ideas that arise from deep portions of the mind over the effortful activities of conscious willpower.[28] Perhaps Ribot was not quite comfortable in ascribing inspiration to an autonomous unconscious: 'Ce que les poètes appellent l'inspiration, n'est-ce pas un travail cérébral, involontaire, presque inconscient, ou qui, du moins, n'arrive à la conscience que sous forme de résultats?'[29] ('What poets call inspiration, is it not cerebral work, involuntary, almost unconscious, or which, at least, only becomes conscious in the form of results?') But his most important contributions to what would be Proust's mature aesthetic were his discussion of 'mémoire affective', or involuntary memory, and his insistence that the intelligence does not intervene in the creative experience.[30] He devotes a chapter to 'mémoire affective' in *La Psychologie des sentiments* and defines such memory as follows:

> La mémoire affective, vraie ou concrète, consiste dans la reproduction *actuelle* d'un état affectif antérieur avec tous ses caractères . . . Ici, le souvenir ne consiste pas seulement dans la représentation des conditions, circonstances, bref des états intellectuels; mais dans la reviviscence de l'état affectif lui-même, comme tel, c'est-à-dire *ressenti*. (161)

> True or concrete affective memory consists in the reproduction *in the present* of an earlier affective state with all its characteristics . . . In this case, memory does not consist solely in the representation of conditions and circumstances, that is, in intellectual states; but in the reliving of the affective state itself, as such, that is, as it was *experienced*.

His examples of instances of affective memory are striking; they sometimes look forward to Proust. One instance he cites is that of Émile Littré, whose sister died when he was ten years old. He felt little emotion at the time, but much later in life experienced a crisis of regret, much like Proust's Narrator in relation to the death of his grandmother. Ribot quotes Littré as follows: 'Tout à coup, sans le vouloir ni le chercher, par un phénomène d'automnésie affective, ce même événement s'est reproduit avec une peine non moindre, certes, que celle que j'éprouvai au moment même et qui alla jusqu'à mouiller mes yeux de larmes.'[31] ('Suddenly, without wishing it or trying to remember it, by a phenomenon of affective automemory, this same event happened again with no less pain than I felt when it happened initially, and my eyes filled with tears.')

Compared with Ribot's 1883 view, his later understanding of creativity is much firmer: 'la création n'est pas fille de la volonté, mais de cette poussée inconsciente qu'on appelle l'inspiration'[32] ('creativity is not a product of the will but of that unconscious pulsing that we call inspiration'). He also notes that contemporary psychology has devoted little attention to creativity, and he sets out to fill this gap in *L'Imagination créatrice*,[33] especially in chapter 3. Inspiration arrives like an encrypted dispatch: the responsibility of the receiving consciousness is, as Proust had also imagined it, that of a translator (48). Nor does it help to strive for creative thoughts: inspiration (like long forgotten memory in Proust) is not at the beck and call of the individual (43), and it often appears suddenly, when thinking is focused elsewhere. The unconscious imagination is spontaneous and true, the conscious imagination artificial, simulated; the latter is 'un appareil de perfection' (48), that is, an after-the-fact organizing agent.

Still, Ribot reflects the diffidence of his age regarding the unconscious. He has not fully escaped from the physiological view and he feels obliged to cite its definition: 'l'activité inconsciente est purement cérébrale; c'est une "cérébration inconsciente"; le facteur psychique ... est absent' (284) ('unconscious activity is purely cerebral; it is "unconscious cerebration"; the psychic factor ... is absent'). Thus the subconscious is a diminished consciousness 'no longer attached to the self' (45). In spite of this, however, in what seems a flagrantly self-contradictory observation, he insists that the unconscious takes two forms, one static, the other dynamic. The static unconscious is that of Janet, 'comprenant des habitudes, la mémoire et en général tout ce qui est savoir organisé'. But the dynamic unconscious is powerful and unpredictable; it is a latent state of activity, of elaboration, of incubation (283).

Although Paul Chabaneix's title page is framed by the heading 'Physiologie cérébrale' (a gesture that would have pleased his preface writer and thesis director, Emmanuel Régis, as it appears to announce another orthodox study of automatic, reflex mental activity), his text veers rapidly away from Pierre Janet's schema of the subconscious in *L'Automatisme psychologique*.

The subconscious is not, he asserts, a simple locus of psychological automatisms that fit with Pierre Janet's subtitle, 'les formes inférieures d'activité mentale' (10). One of those inferior forms was identified by Janet as 'abstraction', absent-mindedness. Chabaneix writes, 'L'abstraction constitue une existence séparée indépendante, une nouvelle vie qui donne à son possesseur une double personnalité' (93). ('Distraction constitutes a separate, independent existence, a new life which provides its possessor with a dual personality.') The lack of focused attention in absent-mindedness, according to Janet, was a potential marker of a divided, disintegrating personality. On the contrary, the expression 'unconscious cerebration' is used consistently in the Chabaneix text in the sense of a mental activity that, like a dream, is dynamic, combinatory and creative (41). Other doctors who were also writers were just as keen to relativize the superiority that had always been accorded to reason and willpower. Arguing that the unconscious and spontaneity were creators of aesthetic beauty, Charles Richet suggested, anticipating Proust, that a balanced, reasonable nature was not a creative one: 'l'homme bien équilibré et de santé morale parfaite est le plus souvent incapable d'invention et d'originalité'[34] ('the well-balanced individual, exhibiting perfect moral health, is in most cases incapable of invention and originality').

Chabaneix also focuses on memory, noting that the subconscious proper holds a reservoir of memories that we cannot access in a normal waking state (11). He has read *La Psychologie des sentiments* and supports enthusiastically Ribot's idea that involuntary memory is a key trigger for creativity: 'La reviviscence affective est une source inépuisable d'oeuvres' (14). ('Affective reliving of experience is a limitless source of artistic works.')

For Henri Poincaré, scientists and mathematicians are on the wrong track if they think that reasoned analysis rather than intuition is the key factor in their work: 'La logique toute pure ne nous mènerait jamais qu'à des tautologies; elle ne pourrait créer du nouveau; ce n'est pas d'elle toute seule qu'aucune science peut sortir.'[35] ('The purest logic would never lead us beyond tautologies; it could not create anything new; no true science can proceed from logic alone.') The ability to invent, to be creative, he links to intuition and the unconscious. In a text comparing Poincaré and Proust, Nicola Luckhurst cites a striking example of convergence of their thinking and writing about the unconscious.[36] Poincaré tells the story of a discovery. He worked very hard one evening to identify a particular 'analogous function'. Upon awakening, he realizes that the problem has been solved during sleep, the unconscious part of the mind having continued to examine the issue, and he has but to write up the results. But that is not all. Luckhurst quotes the following related passage. As Poincaré arrives in Coutances, he climbs into an omnibus:

> Au moment où je mettais le pied sur le marche-pied, l'idée me vint, sans que rien dans mes pensées antérieures parût m'y avoir préparé, que les transformations dont j'avais fait usage pour définir les fonctions fuchsiennes étaient identiques à celles de la géométrie non-euclidienne.[37]

> In the second I put my foot on the step, I had the idea, without anything in my previous thoughts having alerted me, that the transformations I had used to define Fuchsian functions were identical to those in non-Euclidean geometry.

Poincaré cites several comparable moments of epiphany that lift him out of a negative mood, for they are all accompanied by 'les mêmes caractères de brièveté, de soudaineté et de certitude immédiate' (52) ('the same characteristics of brevity, suddenness and immediate certitude'). The emotion and structure of these moments recall unmistakably the moment of imbalance on the uneven paving stones of the discouraged Proustian Narrator:

> Mais au moment où, me remettant d'aplomb, je posai mon pied sur un pave qui était un peu moins élevé que le précédent, tout mon découragement s'évanouit . . . Comme au moment où je goûtais la madeleine toute inquiétude sur l'avenir, tout doute intellectuel étaient dissipés. (IV, 445)

> And at the moment when, recovering my balance, I put my foot on a stone which was slightly lower than its neighbor, all my discouragement vanished . . . Just as, at the moment when I tasted the madeleine, all anxiety about the future, all intellectual doubts had disappeared. (6, 255)

The scene in Proust is, of course, an instance of involuntary memory: the Narrator reexperiences the full sensuous atmosphere of Venice and Saint Mark's church and a strategic moment in his life is resuscitated, not to be lost again, via a kinetic sensation. The solutions to Poincaré's mathematical problems arrive unbidden from the same unconscious place, but in his case he feels that preliminary conscious work on the question at hand is crucial. These efforts set in motion an unconscious machine (54).

All the authors I have cited in this section focused closely on the relationship between creativity/discovery and the unconscious, and all of them, with perhaps the exception of Poincaré, see such creativity as occurring freely and spontaneously. For Proust, one point of emphasis is distinctly different: access to creativity and the unconscious is too easily perturbed not only by the simple preoccupations of everyday life, but also by the improper value assigned to the products of our critical and intellectual faculties. His list of the trivial and the unimportant is long; he speaks ruefully of

> le refuge dans toutes choses qui ne demandent pas de génie, les excuses trouvées dans l'affaire Dreyfus, les affaires de famille, une passion qui a troublé sans inspirer, la critique littéraire, la notation de choses justes qui apparaissent telles à l'intelligence mais dépourvues de cet enivrement qui est le seul signe des choses remarquables par quoi nous puissions les distinguer au moment où elles nous viennent. De là l'effort perpétuel qui finit par faire pénétrer notre préoccupation esthétique jusque dans le domaine inconscient de la pensée.[38]
>
> the taking refuge in everything for which no genius is required, the excuses found during the Dreyfus affair, family concerns, a passion that disturbs without inspiring, literary criticism, the notation of things that are right or appear so to the intellect yet lack the excitement which is the one sign by which we can recognize remarkable things the instant they come to us. Hence the perpetual struggle which leads our aesthetic preoccupation finally to penetrate even into the unconscious domain of the mind. (ASB, 144–45)

For those of us who are impressed by the ubiquity of the involuntary in Proust, there is a tendency to forget the importance of effort, concentration and willpower in his text. But what does his final sentence here mean? How can aesthetic preoccupations, which by definition would appear to be conscious desiderata or concerns, come to condition and mesh with the workings of an active unconscious mind? Some training of the unconscious would seem to be in order, and Proust did feel, as I will argue, that he had developed a writerly ability to get beneath everyday reality and language. We will explore, momentarily, the perspectives on the unconscious developed in *À la recherche du temps perdu* itself, this 'series of novels of the unconscious', as Proust described it in a newspaper interview. But before that, let us focus on the rather special connection between nature and the unconscious in Proust's unfinished novel *Jean Santeuil* and the debt, also related to nature and the unconscious, which he owes to the Belgian writer and essayist Maurice Maeterlinck. I will not discuss here Proust's fascination with the symbolist dramas of Maeterlinck, a subject to which the critic Elena Lozinsky has recently devoted a detailed chapter.[39]

6.3 The 'Natural' Unconscious: Proust and Maeterlinck

In the half-finished preface to his novel *Jean Santeuil*, thought to have been abandoned about 1901–2, Proust speaks of two contrasting attitudes: the chilling effect of involvement in an active social life and the uplifting release afforded by 'la vue de la nature' (JS, 181). The desire for social recognition presents the greatest danger for the creative individual, argues Proust; it is 'le plus grand stérilisant de l'inspiration, le plus grand amortisseur de l'originalité'[40] ('the greatest sterilizer of inspiration, the greatest dampener of originality'). Proust's hero Jean, as we will see, has an almost mystical reverence for nature. The Narrator of *À la recherche* retains some of this quasi-mystical attraction to natural beauty – in the hawthorn sequence, for example – but as an older man, reflecting on his youthful enthusiasms, he concludes wistfully that nature has abandoned him: 'Peut-être dans la nouvelle partie de ma vie, si desséchée, qui s'ouvre, les hommes pourraient-ils m'inspirer ce que ne me dit plus la nature' (IV, 433–34). ('Perhaps in the new, the so dessicated part of my life which is about to begin, human beings may yet inspire in me what nature can no longer say' (6, 238).)

One of the major differences between *Jean Santeuil* and *À la recherche* is in fact the singular role of nature in the earlier work: in the form of the wind, flowers, natural scenes and moments bathed in sun, nature provides both the décor and trigger of involuntary memory and thus creative inspiration. In an uncomplicated sense, nature is a reservoir of unconscious memories that can be revived, of flowers, sunlit moments, seaside scenes once experienced that are 'naturally' relived because nature is cyclical, reproducing its wonders each year, and therefore it has a permanence, an immutability. Encounters with flowers repeat an initial encounter; spring rays of sunlight fall in the same way even years later; Lake Geneva can replicate a seaside visit. Tributes to nature are everywhere in *Jean Santeuil*:

> La nature sait où est ce que nous avons à exprimer et nous y conduit à coup sûr . . . Et elle le sait seule. Seule, en nous faisant sentir ce que nous avons senti une fois, elle nous mène droit à quelque point de ce monde fabuleux de nos souvenirs qui est devenu le monde de la vérité. (JS, 396–97)
>
> Nature knows the whereabouts of what we must express and it leads us there with a sure hand . . . And nature alone knows it. Alone, by making us feel what we once felt, it leads us straight to a point in the fabulous world of our memories which has become the world of truth.

> Ce n'est guère que la nature qui nous dicte par moments des révélations dont nous sentons qu'il est essentiel de les écrire. (JS, 447)
>
> It is really only nature that at times dictates revelations which we sense must be written down.

> [Le contact avec la nature] nous [enivre] du charme de notre passé et de la substance même de notre vie. (JS, 497)
>
> [Contact with nature] makes us [drunk] with the charm of our past and the very substance of our life.

The contemplation of natural phenomena is thus a series of uninterrupted bursts from the unconscious for Jean, affording feelings similar to the more developed moments in the mature novel and the same sentiment of certainty and happiness that is evident there and in the texts we have seen by Poincaré. The Proust of *Jean Santeuil* writes: 'À ces moments il n'avait plus de *doute*, plus *d'inquiétudes*, plus de tristesse' (JS, 392). In a text already cited, almost identical terms express the Narrator's certitude as he teeters on the uneven paving stones: 'Comme au moment où je goûtais la madeleine, toute *inquiétude* sur l'avenir, tout *doute* intellectuel étaient dissipés' (IV, 445; emphasis added).

The innate growth instincts of trees and plants exhibit a form of the unconscious, the development of a native structure that is their unconscious externalized. A description of a double cherry tree ('cérisier double') in full bloom in a short text possibly contemporary with the writing of *Jean Santeuil* highlights the word 'unconscious' in a revealing way. The text recalls the elation triggered by the hawthorns and the madeleine in that, contemplating the tree, a poet figure experiences a mysterious impression that is difficult to explore further:

> Mais il ne semble pas naturel qu'un poète reste une heure devant cet arbre à regarder comment cette *inconsciente* et sûre pensée architecturale qui s'appelle l'espèce cerisier double a disposé, le printemps venant, ces innombrables petites [boules] blanches ... Le poète regarde et semble regarder à la fois en lui-même et dans le cerisier double. (CSB, 418; emphasis added)

> But it does not seem natural that a poet should remain for an hour before this tree, gazing at how, the spring being imminent, the sure yet *unconscious* architectural thought known as the double cherry tree genus has arranged these innumerable small white balls ... The poet gazes and seems to be gazing both into himself and into the double cherry tree. (ASB, 147)

Here, in the plant, is an inborn creativity, an instinctive, inner notion of shape and colour, a singular identity whose silent drive finds articulation in form, not speech. This fragment is related in important ways to Proust's attraction to some of Maeterlinck's works and the way the innate intelligence of plants appealed to Proust as a demonstration of a natural unconscious abroad in all living things.

The essays published by Maeterlinck in the years leading up to the drafting of *Contre Sainte-Beuve* and *À la recherche* had a powerful impact on Proust, especially *Le Temple enseveli* (1902), *Le Double Jardin* (1904) and *L'Intelligence des fleurs* (1907), although he also read other works including *La Vie des abeilles* (1901).[41] In these early years of the twentieth century, Proust had turned thirty and both his father (1903) and his mother (1905) would soon die. What was happening during this time to his own literary activity? Instead of penning creative works, he was involved in the translating and critical annotation of *The Bible of Amiens* and *Sesame and Lilies* by John Ruskin, and had half committed to translating other volumes. His self-confidence was on the wane, and, as he wrote to Maurice Barrès, he wondered seriously whether he might ever write his own creative literature: 'J'ai encore deux Ruskin à faire et après j'essaierai de traduire ma pauvre âme à moi, si elle n'est pas morte dans l'intervalle' (Corr., IV, 93). ('I have two more Ruskins to do and after that I will try to translate my own poor soul, if it hasn't died in the interval.')

Largely because of his asthma, Proust's contact with nature had waned, as had his conviction that nature could provide inspiration. Maeterlinck's essays, with their intense focus on and affection for flowers, plants, landscape and the outdoors, allowed Proust to reserve a non-pessimistic corner of his mind for his ebbing belief in nature's restorative and inspirational powers. What enthused Maeterlinck in his observation of insects and plants was their native ingenuity, their intuitive ability to reach their objective, an objective that was always considered to be natural and healthy. The author of *Pelléas and Mélisande* wrote:

> Hors de nous, dans l'univers qui nous enveloppe, ... [ce] n'est plus la justice de la conscience qui préside; c'est la logique de la nature ignorante de notre morale. Il y a en nous un esprit qui ne pèse que les intentions; il y a hors de nous une puissance qui ne pèse que les faits. Nous nous persuadons qu'ils agissent de concert.[42]

> Outside, in the universe that enfolds us, . . . [it] is no longer the justice of conscience which presides; it is nature's logic, ignorant of our morality. Within us is a mind that weighs only intentions; external to us is a power that weighs only facts. We persuade ourselves that the two act together.

In a sense, Maeterlinck wished to explore in the natural world the same laws of the unconscious that Proust wished to lay bare in humankind, and we will see this in a discussion of *L'Intelligence des fleurs*. But nowhere is the Belgian writer's attraction to the non-rational more evident than in *Le Temple enseveli*, 'the buried temple', a figure that he used to signify 'the supreme refuge of our being' (*Temple*, 300), that is, the unconscious itself.

Even a cursory reading of *Le Temple enseveli* will perk up the ears of a reader of Proust, and certainly, some of the subjects Maeterlinck addresses must have given inspirational support to Proust at a time when he was bogged down in non-creative writing. Maeterlinck mentions the new translation of the *Arabian Nights* by Mardrus (*Temple*, 66), as does Proust, and the role of the *Nights* in *À la recherche* is a significant one. In one long section Maeterlinck argues that the past, even though sometimes hanging only by a thread of memory, is not lost, and that an unhappy past, if resuscitated, may be a source of joy:

> Notre passé, c'est notre secret promulgué par la bouche des années, c'est l'image la plus mystérieuse de notre être, surprise et gardée par le Temps. L'image n'est pas morte; un rien la dégrade ou la pare, elle peut encore s'éclairer ou s'assombrir. (222)

> Our past is our secret voiced by the mouth of years gone by, it is the most mysterious image of our being, overtaken and conserved by Time. The image has not died; any tiny thing may degrade it or interrupt it, it may still become brighter or turn dark.

It is in a chapter titled 'La Chance' (229–82) that Maeterlinck develops an intensely felt argument about the need to be more conscious of, less 'apathetic' about, our deep self. In a superficial, unexamined approach to living, we advance more or less unreflectively, as though the inner recesses of the mind were unapproachable, a prison. But beneath the conscious intellect and willed activities of our days lies something else:

> Il y a en nous, sous notre existence consciente, soumise à la raison et la volonté, une existence plus profonde, qui plonge, d'une part, dans un passé que l'histoire n'atteint pas, et de l'autre dans un avenir que des milliers d'années n'épuiseront jamais. (255–56)

> There is within us, beneath our conscious existence that is subject to reason and willpower, a deeper existence which, on the one hand, plunges into a past that is inaccessible to history, and on the other, into a future that thousands of years will never exhaust.

This passage is followed by a text that looks directly forward to *Contre Sainte-Beuve* and to the idea of deep self versus social self. Maeterlinck couples it with an attack on the priority of the intelligence and the will, an appendix to the two-self argument that of course resurfaces in such an important way in *Contre Sainte-Beuve* and again in *Le Temps retrouvé*. Maeterlinck writes, 'En nous se trouve un être qui est notre moi véritable, notre moi premier-né ... Cet être inconscient vit sur un autre plan et dans un autre monde que notre intelligence. Il ignore le Temps et l'Espace' (257). ('Within us is a being who is our true self, our first-born self ... That unconscious being lives on a different level and in a different world than our intelligence. It ignores Time and Space.')

The capitalization that Maeterlinck applies to the word 'Temps' (236, 257, 286, 301, 305, 306) is that which Proust adopts repeatedly in *Le Temps retrouvé*. Beyond that, however, Maeterlinck's idea that the unconscious is not subject to the normal rules of Time and Space becomes a subject of discussion in Proust's creative and aesthetic debate. A few pages before the end of *Le Temps retrouvé*, it is still the notion of space that is the Narrator's referent, as he attempts to evoke psychology's third dimension. The novelist must employ, 'par opposition à la psychologie plane dont on use d'ordinaire, d'une sorte de psychologie dans l'espace' (IV, 608) ('not the two-dimensional psychology which we normally use, but a kind of psychology in space' (5, 505)). However, in the final sentence of Proust's novel space finally gives way to time:

> Aussi ... ne manquerais-je pas d'abord d[e] décrire les hommes, cela dût-il les faire ressembler à des êtres monstrueux, comme occupant une place si considérable, à côté de celle si restreinte qui leur est réservée dans l'espace, une place au contraire prolongée sans mesure ... dans le Temps. (IV, 625)

> So ... I should not fail, even if the effect were to make them resemble monsters, to describe men as occupying so considerable a place, compared with the restricted place which is reserved for them in space, a place on the contrary prolonged past measure ... in Time. (6, 531–32)

Proust obtained a copy of *L'Intelligence des fleurs* signed by its author in a watershed year, 1907. Critics have shown that this work is probably the most important source of botanical images in Proust's novel.[43] The 'botanization' of the homosexual encounter between Jupien and Charlus in *À la recherche* owes much to Maeterlinck's botanical curiosity and enthusiasm and reflects his idea, cited earlier, that 'la logique de la nature [est] ignorante de notre morale'. Marcel Muller best elucidated the morally neutralizing effect of employing botanical comparisons to characterize human same-sex attraction.[44] As Proust's text draws connections between homosexuality and the sexuality of plants, his Narrator insists on viewing the coupling of the two men as 'empreint de beauté'. One finds the same admiration in *L'Intelligence des fleurs*, whose author views the blind, self-propagation effort of every plant as the vital expression of a distinct personality: 'l'énergie de son idée fixe qui monte des ténèbres de ses racines pour s'organiser et s'épanouir dans la lumière de sa fleur est un spectacle incomparable'[45] ('the energy of its idée fixe, which ascends from its dark roots to organize and spread out in the bloom of its flower, is an incomparable spectacle'). From Maeterlinck Proust also borrows several examples of flowers whose reproductive life is curious or fraught, for example, the *Sophora japonica*, or pagoda tree, and the foul-smelling lizard orchid ('le loroglosse à l'odeur de bouc'). Speaking of a water plant, the vallisneria, and the fact that the male plant dies as it reproduces, Maeterlinck says that nature placed in it 'une belle idée', 'un effort magnifique', underlining that it hurtles itself from its stem 'd'un incomparable élan' (22–24).

In his copious translator's notes to *Sésame et les lys*, Proust pays tribute not only to the beauty of Maeterlinck's style (admitting, candidly, that it resembles his own), but also to the irrational, that is, the role of the unconscious in that style. Proust quotes a long passage on the lily from a section titled 'Fleurs démodées' in *Le Double Jardin*, marvelling at how Maeterlinck's metaphors call up the dual majesty of the flower. Maeterlinck wrote:

> Dans une touffe de rayons, le grand Lys blanc, vieux seigneur des jardins, le seul prince parmi toute la roture sortie du potager . . . Le Lys immémorial dresse son sceptre antique inviolé, auguste, qui crée autour de lui une zône de chasteté, de silence, de lumière.[46]
>
> In a tuft of sun's rays, the great white Lily, noble, aged lord of the gardens, the sole prince among all the rabble that comes from the vegetable garden . . . The eternal Lily raises its venerable, inviolate scepter, creating all about it a zone of chastity, silence and light.

For Proust, these images capture a deepened reality: the figure of the scepter, for example, suggests both the lily's shape and its noble, heraldic past. Maeterlinck's language has a suggestiveness about it that is not simply logical: 'On sent très bien que ce n'est pas parce que le penseur s'est développé que l'écrivain a grandi. Conclusion: la beauté du style est au fond irrationnelle.'[47] ('One has the clear impression that the writer has grown, but not in the sense that he has made intellectual progress. Conclusion: the beauty of a style is essentially irrational.') What surfaces here is Proust's growing conviction that what counts for a writer is not the logical or the intelligent, but the unconscious. In his important 1908 notebook, Proust underlines his belief in similar language: 'les gens du monde trouveront bête précisément ce que j'ai voulu en ayant toujours de l'irrationnel comme objet'[48] ('society people will regard as stupid precisely what I have wanted to do by always considering the irrational as my subject').

In a finely judged article on Maeterlinck's influence on Proust, W. L. Hodson argues conclusively that the Belgian writer is a subconscious presence in Proust's work, an 'unrealized subliminal absorption' in the stylistic fabric of *À la recherche*.[49] But I believe that there exists as well at least one much more pointed, specific and important intertextual link related to nature and creativity between Maeterlinck's *L'Intelligence des fleurs* and Proust's novel.

One of Maeterlinck's nature descriptions provided Proust with a pivotal textual element he would use in his Narrator's search for creativity. In 1907, in a review of Anna de Noailles' poetry collection, *Les Éblouissements*, Proust quoted almost reverentially from a Maeterlinck description of trees that he found in *L'Intelligence des fleurs*. Proust calls the text one of the most beautiful pages of French prose written in the previous sixty years.[50] This is the passage he found so beautifully evocative:

> Sans évoquer la mer, la montagne, les ciels, la nuit, les crépuscules, que ne pourrait-on dire, par exemple, sur la beauté des arbres? . . . *Parmi ces impressions qui, sans que nous le sachions, forment le creux limpide et peut-être le tréfonds de bonheur et de calme de toute notre existence, qui de nous ne garde la mémoire de quelques beaux arbres? Quand on a dépassé le milieu de la vie, quand on arrive au bout de la période émerveillée, qu'on a épuisé à peu près tous les spectacles que peuvent offrir l'art, le génie et le luxe des siècles et des hommes, après avoir éprouvé et comparé bien des choses, on en revient à de très simples souvenirs. Ils dressent à l'horizon purifié, deux ou trois images innocentes, invariables et fraîches, qu'on voudrait emporter dans le dernier sommeil, s'il est vrai qu'une image puisse passer le seuil qui sépare nos deux mondes.*[51]
>
> Without evoking the sea, mountains, skies, night, dawns, what could one not say, for example, about the beauty of trees? . . . *Among the impressions which, without our knowing it, form the limpid base and perhaps the innermost place of happiness and calm of our whole existence, which of us does not have a memory of a few beautiful trees? When one has passed the midpoint of life, when one reaches the end of the period of wonderment, when one has exhausted almost all the spectacles offered by art, genius and the luxuries of the centuries and of man, after having tested and compared many things, one returns to very simple memories. On a pure horizon they present two or three innocent, unvarying and fresh images that one would wish to carry off in one's last sleep, if it is true that an image can cross the threshold that separates our two worlds.*

I would contend that an important text on trees, this one written by Proust, should be read as a response to this passage by Maeterlinck. As he struggled with the notion of form – would he write an essay, a novel, was he a novelist? – Proust recorded in his notebook of 1908 his feeling of despair at forfeiting the type of inspiration in nature that had moved him and clearly moved Maeterlinck. It was trees, Maeterlinck's trees, that symbolized that loss:

> Arbres vous n'avez plus rien à me dire, mon coeur refroidi ne vous entend plus, mon oeil constate froidement la ligne qui vous divise en partie d'ombre et de lumière, ce seront les hommes qui m'inspireront maintenant, l'autre partie de ma vie où je vous aurais chantés ne reviendra jamais.[52]

> Trees, you have nothing to say to me now, my hardened heart no longer understands you, my gaze observes impassively the line that divides you into shade and light, it will be people who will inspire me now, that other part of my life where I would have celebrated you will never return.

This text from a personal journal, retrieved and amplified, serves a key function in the final volume of *À la recherche* (IV, 433–34; 6, 238): it measures the Narrator's dejection at his inability to write, providing a dramatic emotional low point soon to be supplanted by the joy and certainty that involuntary memories evoke beginning in the courtyard of the Princesse de Guermantes. Both Maeterlinck's and Proust's passages are written in what we might call 'Proustian time'. That is, both speak of an existence that is in two parts: an individual has reached the middle of his life, and, having depleted what art, humanity and a social life have provided him, he now reconnects or attempts to reconnect with vivifying memories of nature.

In underlining his Narrator's dilemma, Proust adopts the terms used by Maeterlinck, but reorders their meaning to indicate despair. Maeterlinck proposes a recuperative return to nature '[quand] on a épuisé à peu près tous les spectacles que peuvent offrir *l'art, le génie et le luxe des siècles et des hommes*.'[53] Proust's Narrator, his access to nature's inspiration blocked, reverses Maeterlinck's itinerary, engaging in the false hope that humanity and the appreciation of art may serve as a replacement. The italics in the texts below are mine:

> ce seront *les hommes* qui m'inspireront maintenant. (*Carnet de 1908*, 52)
>
> it will be *people* who will inspire me now.

> Peut-être dans la nouvelle partie de ma vie, si desséchée, qui s'ouvre, *les hommes* pourraient-ils m'inspirer ce que ne me dit plus *la nature*. (IV, 433–34).
>
> Perhaps in the new, the so dessicated part of my life which is about to begin, *human beings* may yet inspire in me what *nature* can no longer say. (6, 238)

> Si quelque chose doit m'inspirer maintenant c'est *la pensée humaine et esthétique*. (IV, 802 – Esquisse XXIV).
>
> If something is to inspire me now, it is *human thought and aesthetics*.

Maeterlinck's text thus appears to offer up certain capital elements in the structure of the Narrator's intellectual search: a life divided into two parts; the awareness that authentic literary inspiration is a function of a remembered sentiment for nature; and the occluded symbolism of two or three trees that will haunt the Narrator's memory. Indeed, Maeterlinck's hallowed trees, 'deux ou trois images innocentes, invariables et fraîches', appear to provide the link to the Narrator's mysterious attraction to the three trees of Hudimesnil (II, 76–79; 2, 404–7) and, beyond that, to the youthful Narrator's prose text on the two or three church spires of Martinville[54] whose sunbathed steeples provide the inspired counterpoint that will contrast with the artistic inertia the Narrator experiences as he contemplates the half-illuminated trees during his train stop. Behind this network of Proustian texts that all rely on two or three arborescent images lies the memory of a primitive scene, very probably Maeterlinck's description of trees, if one judges by the powerful impression it made on Proust.

There are other writers, beyond Maeterlinck, who touched directly on Proustian themes such as involuntary memory and whose texts we may find strikingly prescient. Among those writers is Hippolyte Taine. He may personify, for some, the hard-headed positivist, but one should not forget that he trained as a literary scholar, completing a doctoral thesis on the *Fables* of Lafontaine. Although his star may have waned in Proust's later estimation, Marcel listed Taine as one of his favourite authors in an early letter to Daniel Halévy.[55] Not only, as we have seen in Chapter 1, did Taine insist on the important role of the unconscious, he authored texts in *De l'intelligence* that evoke the poetry of renascent, unanticipated memory. One such passage provides, almost unmistakably, an early scenario of Proust's Narrator's madeleine-triggered revisiting of Combray:

> Ce qui rend ces résurrections [de la mémoire] plus remarquables encore, c'est que souvent elles se font sans que jamais dans tout l'intervalle l'image ait reparu. Si, après plusieurs années d'absence, on rentre dans la maison paternelle ou dans le village natal, une multitude d'objets et d'événements oubliés reparaissent à l'improviste. *L'esprit, subitement peuplé de leur foule remuante, ressemble à une boîte de rotifères desséchés, inertes depuis dix ans, et qui, tout d'un coup, saupoudrés d'eau, recommencent à vivre et à fourmiller.*[56]

> What makes these resurrections [of memory] even more remarkable is that they often take place without the image having reappeared in the interval. If, after several years away you reenter your father's house or the village where you were born, a great number of forgotten objects and events appear unexpectedly. *Suddenly, the mind is teeming, resembling a box of dried rotifera, inert for the previous ten years, and which, suddenly, dampened with water, take on a new life and swarm about.*

The rotifera in this text, obscure, microscopic, 'wheel' animals that, after being dried, take on life and movement again if put in water, are a striking anticipation of the Japanese game in *À la recherche* in which bits of paper steeped in water stretch, twist and transmute into the people and the houses of Combray.

Such lyrical pieces based on sensation and memory could be generated in unexpected corners. Dr Jules Luys wrote of the poetry of memory, but his focus, as in the madeleine sequence, was squarely on the interaction between sensory triggers and resurrected memory. Proust's madeleine experience was set in motion by smell and taste: 'plus frêles mais plus vivaces, plus immatérielles, plus persistantes, plus fidèles, l'odeur et la saveur restent encore longtemps, comme des âmes, à se rappeler' (I, 46) ('more fragile but more enduring, more immaterial but more persistent, more faithful, smell and taste remain poised for a long time, like souls, remembering' (1, 63)). One text of Luys on recollection reads: 'On peut dire que tout le passé de notre sensibilité intime, tout ce que nous avons vu, entendu, odoré, goûté, senti ... tout cela survit en nous à l'état d'ébranlement posthume.'[57] ('One might say that the entire past of our intimate sensibility, everything we have heard, smelled, tasted, felt ... all of that survives in us as a kind of posthumous shock.') I would not suggest for a moment that Proust was aware of this text of Luys, which dates back to 1874. But it is but one example of the wide-ranging scientific interest in sensation, image, memory and the unconscious that carried Proust along into the early twentieth century.

6.4 Towards the Proustian Unconscious

In assessing the writing production of Sainte-Beuve, Proust contends that he prefers his poetry to his criticism, even though it is slight and somewhat severe. But even in his verse there is something missing: 'De [Sainte-Beuve], de lui inconscient, profond, personnel, il n'y a guère que la gaucherie' (CSB, 232). ('Of [Sainte-Beuve], of the deep, unconscious, personal self there is hardly more than the clumsiness' (ASB, 23).) For Proust, as it was for many in the nineteenth century, the unconscious was that part of the mind that is beyond conscious, voluntary reach. But it also had a structure, though certainly not a Freudian one. His eye on Stendhal's fiction, Proust identifies a certain shape to the unconscious there: 'Si l'on considère comme faisant partie du style cette grande ossature inconsciente que recouvre l'assemblage voulu des idées, elle existe chez Stendhal' (CSB, 611). ('But if the great unconscious bone-structure underlying the assemblage of deliberate ideas is seen as forming part of style, then there is style in Stendhal' (ASB, 280).) Part of style is underpinned by an unconscious foundation; in Stendhal's case, Proust identifies part of that latter sub-structure as his heroes' attachment to high and thus exalted places, for example, the prison in which Fabrice del Dongo is incarcerated. In a letter to Jacques Copeau, Proust claims to have read Thomas Hardy, Stendhal and Balzac for their deep intuitive themes. In Hardy, he identifies a habit of attraction to parallel structures, for example, rows of cemetery headstones, plus the theme of sculpted stone seen in all his novels.[58] Moreover, Proust contends that his ability to 'read' the unconscious lineaments of another personality opened his eyes to the essential characteristics of his own unconscious: 'De même en me lisant moi-même j'ai dégagé après coup des traits constitutifs de mon moi inconscient' (Corr., XII, 180). ('Reading myself in the same way I have uncovered after the fact the traits that constitute my unconscious self.')

The unconscious is a structure resident in aspects of a writer's style, just as, resident in the dual-flowered cherry tree, there is an intrinsic nature and shape, 'cette inconsciente et sûre pensée architecturale qui s'appelle l'espèce cerisier double', which we saw earlier. The remark about style in Stendhal, for its part, clarifies a somewhat opaque statement about the nature of Maeterlinck's style, which we also observed earlier. Maeterlinck's success in evoking the deeper reality of a flower, the lily, transcends the logical: the lily's purity translates in the words 'inviolé' and 'chasteté', and its royal, heraldic history and symbolism in the words 'prince', 'auguste' and 'sceptre antique'. Maeterlinck's language has a rich allusiveness to it that is a product not of reasoned thought but of an impression sensed intuitively, unconsciously.

There are thus a variety of contexts in which Proust evokes the idea of the unconscious, but there are three, in particular, that require more extended commentary. The most important of these is the imperative of interrogating and articulating what is unconscious. Proust's Narrator has an obsession: he is driven to discover by what mechanism or process one can interpret, explain and use these bursts of sensation/memory that flash unexpectedly into his mind. The efforts at elucidation of these phenomena are a focus of great intensity in *À la recherche*. A message from the unconscious left unelucidated seems to mean an aspect of the writer's reality abandoned. Still, we will see that Proust's writerly efforts at such elucidation are not always successful. Before we address this question, however, we will examine two other matters: the relationship of the involuntary to the unconscious and, separately, Proust's apparent contention that the unconscious has anticipatory powers.

6.4.1 Willpower and the Creative

In a press interview from November 1913, Proust described his novel as 'un essai d'une suite de "Romans de l'Inconscient"' (CSB, 558) ('an attempt at a sequence of "Novels of the Unconscious"' (ASB, 235)). But he is not quite certain whether what is unconscious in us is totally beyond our senses, for he says, as well, that his work will feature certain profound impressions that are 'almost unconscious'. Much of the text that follows immediately focuses on the difference, in the author's mind, between voluntary and involuntary memory, and the fact that only the latter provides a writer with the core, 'authentic' material for his work. As Proust's Narrator admits somewhat more generously in *Le Temps retrouvé*, such authentic material is not in large supply, and the intellect must expand, explain, connect and organize these precious bursts of personal impression.

Impressions and memories that arrive spontaneously and unbidden from some past memory or association are thus guarantees of how the unconscious functions, but is the involuntary itself, as the interview with Élie-Joseph Bois might suggest, 'the unconscious'? The answer can only be a partial yes. There are reasons both very personal to Proust and related to ambient medico-psychological debates that explain this heavy emphasis on the involuntary. For example, in 1896, as Proust was exploring involuntary memory in *Jean Santeuil*, Théodule Ribot was noting that most psychologists denied the existence of true affective memory. They contended that while we may recall the conditions and circumstances of an event of an affective character, we do not reexperience the affective state itself.[59] Ribot rejects this view vigorously, for there are individuals, he writes, who experience the affective state in its entirety. However, like the belief in the unconscious itself, French acceptance of the theories of Ribot and others on this subject was very slow to gather momentum. In 1914, a year after *Du côté de chez Swann* had been published, Ribot observed that there were still psychologists refusing to admit the existence of involuntary memory, or 'mémoire affective'.[60] Thus, one way to read Proust's powerful emphasis on the involuntary is as a salvo in a scientific, psychological debate: Proust is a militant in the turn-of-the-century campaign against intellectualism that we have discussed, and the importance of the spontaneous workings of the mind is crucial to him. He writes of 'la grossière tentation pour l'écrivain d'écrire des oeuvres intellectuelles' (IV, 460–61) ('the temptation for the writer to write intellectual works – a gross impropriety' (4, 278)). Intellectual reasoning about a subject is surface meandering without attention to obscure deep impressions: 'On raisonne, c'est-à-dire on vagabonde' (IV, 461). ('A writer reasons, that is to say he goes astray' (4, 278).)

I have argued elsewhere, as I have noted, that lack of willpower is one of the powerful themes that drives Proust's early novel *Jean Santeuil* and a number of the stories in *Les Plaisirs et les jours*, and what I stressed was that in reading Théodule Ribot's study *Les Maladies de la volonté*, Proust in fact found ample material to support the idea that the spontaneous ideas that emerge from the deep layers of the mind are less artificial, have more reality, than the ideas fashioned by conscious willpower and the intellect. I will requote here a typical text from Ribot, and two corresponding texts from Proust, that address the voluntary/involuntary divide. Ribot writes:

> l'attention volontaire est un état artificiel où, à l'aide de sentiments factices, nous maintenons à grand'peine certains états de conscience qui ne tendent qu'à s'évanouir (par exemple, quand nous poursuivons par politesse une conversation très ennuyeuse). Dans un cas [= l'attention spontanée], ce qui détermine cette spécialisation de la conscience, c'est tout notre individualité; dans le second, c'est une portion extrêmement faible et restreinte de notre individualité.[61]
>
> voluntary attention is an artificial state in which, with the aid of factitious feelings, we maintain with some difficulty certain conscious states that tend only to vanish (for example, when out of politeness we follow a very boring conversation). In one case [= spontaneous attention] what determines this specialization of the consciousness is our whole individuality; in the second [= voluntary attention], it is an extremely weak and limited portion of our individuality.

Thus our entire being is engaged in the spontaneous, the involuntary. Two brief texts from Proust show the continuity of his thought on this matter from *Jean Santeuil* to the mature work:

> au moment où je . . . vivais [les scènes de ma vie], c'est ma volonté qui les connaissait dans un but de plaisir ou de crainte, de vanité ou de méchanceté. Et leur essence intime m'échappait. J'y eusse fixé les yeux avec force qu'elle m'eût échappé de même. (JS, 490)
>
> in those moments when I . . . lived [these scenes of my life], it was my will that experienced them, searching for pleasure or out of fear, vanity or cruelty. And their intimate essence escaped me. Even if I had fixed a powerful gaze on it, it would have escaped me in the same way.

> Sur l'extrême différence qu'il y a entre l'impression vraie que nous avons eue d'une chose et l'impression factice que nous nous en donnons quand volontairement nous essayons de nous la représenter, je ne m'arrêtais pas. (IV, 448)
>
> The thought that there is a vast difference between the real impression which we have had of a thing and the artificial impression of it which we form for ourselves when we attempt by an act of will to imagine it did not long detain me. (6, 259)

Let us not forget, however, some important life reasons behind Proust's point of view on volition that have little to do with the turn-of-the-century debate over intellectualism. By about 1900 Proust had abandoned work on *Jean Santeuil*; his volume *Les Plaisirs et les jours* had appeared in 1896, but it was a heteroclite work greeted by many as a collection of preciosities. In most of the first decade of the twentieth century, Proust was not a creative writer but rather a dogged man of letters with many uncreative irons in the fire: he translates, prefaces and annotates two works of Ruskin, and ponders translating more; he composes a handful of salon chronicles focused on the major *salonnières* of the period and develops a reputation as a social columnist. He publishes numerous book reviews and a series of pastiches of major writers, the latter well received. Yet during these years both his father and mother die, without Marcel having produced the important work or works that, in his view, might have justified their love and support for him and his lifestyle. Proust had, essentially, since the beginning of his interest in Ruskin, devoted himself almost exclusively to writing derivative of others and in secondary, non-creative genres. His voluminous correspondence is perhaps further testimony to a life focused if not on the journalistic at least on the social. Proust's discovery that involuntary mechanisms could furnish the material of personal creativity allowed the author a joyous escape from the reasonable and intelligent writing that had occupied and preoccupied him for almost a decade.

6.4.2 Unconscious Anticipation

In a small handful of texts, Proust appears to bestow a very special though unexpected capacity on the unconscious. In the extreme version of what he argues, the creative personality has the gift of absorbing material and ideas from another writer not as texts that inspire him but as 'unconscious anticipations' of his own thoughts. The cynic in us may think immediately of a remark by the English Francophile Julian Barnes, who noted, in relation to the surrealists' designation of precursors, that 'posterity likes to see itself predicted'.[62] And one may of course also sense that in this manner, a writer such as Proust will be preserved from Harold Bloom's 'anxiety of influence' and can continue to believe that all the material he produces is authentically his own.[63]

At its simplest level, in a reference to Baudelaire, this Proustian faith in the predictive genius of our unconscious is both convincing and easy enough to understand. In discussing the poem 'La Mort des pauvres' and the line 'Et qui refait le lit des gens pauvres et nus' ('And which remakes the bed of the naked poor'), Proust argues that Baudelaire anticipates not only the fate of the poor, but the fate of Baudelaire himself. Proust writes: 'c'est une "anticipation" de son inconscient, un pressentiment du destin qui lui dicta un vers pareil' (CSB, 622) ('it was an "anticipation" of his unconscious, a presentiment of his destiny that dictated such a line' (ASB, 290)). So here a writer has a secret presentiment of what his future holds; it is embedded in his poetic line, but shielded from his consciousness.

We may extrapolate, based on Proust's reference to Valéry that follows immediately, that the presence of such unconscious elements is, for Proust, a necessary feature of authentic art. Whereas in *Eupalinos* Valéry, voicing Socrates, suggests that enlightened acts and enlightened art cause civilization to leap forward, Proust maintains his preference for writers like Dostoevsky and Baudelaire, whose suffering he compares to waves battering away endlessly to sculpt, unconsciously, the great granite rocks that are their lasting works.

Another discussion of the anticipatory capability of the unconscious is somewhat more disconcerting. In a text about the effect other writers have on him – Jammes, Maeterlinck, Emerson, Joubert – Proust refers to the ideas and sensations similar to his own encountered in these writers as 'réminiscences anticipées' of his own preoccupations. These similar thoughts are simply confirmations, with the word 'reminiscence' bringing them under the umbrella of a kind of involuntary memory once removed (CSB, 311; ASB, 101). One senses that Proust's theoretical framework is so focused on the importance of memory that the affinity of these writers' ideas with his own inescapably evokes the mechanism of recollection.

A final text that develops these ideas at length shows us once again a Proust somewhat awkwardly articulating his own theory of art and influence through a proxy, this time Schopenhauer.[64] Proust is impressed by the myriad quotations from other writers with which Schopenhauer illustrates his ideas. His diagnosis of this habit is intriguing because of its final words:

> Schopenhauer n'avance jamais une opinion sans l'appuyer aussitôt sur plusieurs citations, mais on sent que les textes cités ne sont pour lui que des exemples, des allusions inconscientes et anticipées où il aime à retrouver quelques traits de sa propre pensée, mais qui ne l'ont nullement inspirée. (CSB, 185)

> Schopenhauer never puts forward an opinion without at once supporting it by several quotations, but one has the feeling that for him the texts he cites are merely examples, unconscious or anticipatory allusions in which he likes to discover a few features of his own thought. (ASB, 217)

Is it not the observer, Proust, who sees an anticipated allusion to his own thought pattern and his own permeability to the thought of others in this habit of Schopenhauer? Proust may be right in one sense: the original thought may well be Schopenhauer's and the page of references that the philosopher lists may be simple illustrations of his own idea. But in extending the 'anticipatory' reach of the unconscious, one detects inevitably a defensiveness, a desire to cloak the receiving writer in the mantle of the unconscious in order to preserve the authentic, personal nature of one's work so that its originality and inspired nature will not be questioned.

To what extent was Proust a victim of anxiety of influence? A potentially aggressive remark about his philosophy professor Alphonse Darlu gives one answer: 'Aucun homme n'a jamais eu d'influence sur moi (que Darlu et je l'ai reconnue mauvaise).'[65] ('No man has ever had any influence on me (except Darlu and I have recognized that it was negative).') And his Narrator writes in the same vein, 'Aussi dans les livres que je sentais maintenant que je voulais écrire ne laisserais-je jamais quelque souvenir d'un autre écrivain.'[66] ('And so, in the works that I now felt I wanted to write, I would never leave a trace of another writer.') Critical readers of Proust do not agree with this last remark: they have argued for his being influenced by Schopenhauer,[67] by most of his professors from the mid-1890s (Jules Lachelier, Émile Boutroux, Albert Sorel, Paul Janet, Victor Egger[68]), by the aesthetician Gabriel Séailles[69] and by Henri Bergson,[70] to name but a few. And countless critics – not to speak of Proust himself – have pointed out what they feel are Proust's debts to Flaubert, Balzac, Nerval, Maeterlinck, Chateaubriand and many other writers. Like Baudelaire, Proust is subject to a kind of criticism by identification[71] in that at times he finds himself in the situation of a Flaubert, or the stylistic position of a Balzac. A good example is the text 'Senancour c'est moi' (CSB, 568–69), in which Proust both compares himself with and distances himself from a brother writer. Although there is a recognition on Proust's part of resemblances, there is also a powerful desire not to be tainted or muffled by the voice of the Other. Hence, the need to convert to his own what belongs to the Other, and the unexpected assigning of anticipatory powers to the unconscious.

6.4.3 Deep, behind, within: Articulating the Unconscious

'On appelle intuition cette espèce de *sympathie intellectuelle* par laquelle on se transporte à l'intérieur d'un objet pour coïncider avec ce qu'il a d'unique, et par conséquent, d'inexprimable.'[72] ('What we call intuition is that type of *intellectual sympathy* by which we transport ourselves inside an object so as to coincide with what is unique in it and, therefore, inexpressible.') The importance of intimate, intuitive union with objects and obscure sensorial impressions is a key to Proust's writing, and, as in Bergson's definition, these convergences do have a unique impact and are necessarily preverbal. But for Proust they are far from indecipherable. At first opaque, it is imperative that their meaning be identified and adequate expression found to articulate it. Inventing the language to explain these impressions and involuntary reminiscences that radiate from the unconscious requires assiduous effort:

> la recréation par la mémoire d'impressions qu'il fallait ensuite approfondir, éclairer, transformer en équivalents d'intelligence, n'était-elle pas une des conditions, presque l'essence même de l'œuvre d'art telle que je l'avais conçue? (IV, 621)

> was not the re-creation by the memory of impressions which had then to be deepened, illuminated, transformed into equivalents of understanding, was not this process one of the conditions, almost the very essence of the work of art as I had just now conceived it? (6, 525)

In a comment on Flaubert that we saw earlier, Proust confirms what he views as the crucial task of the writer: 'que d'application ne fallait-il pas pour bien fixer cette vision, pour la faire passer de l'inconscient dans le conscient, pour l'incorporer enfin aux diverses parties du discours!' (CSB, 592) ('what application did it not take fully to capture that vision, to translate it from the unconscious into the conscious, to incorporate it finally in the various parts of speech!' (ASB, 266)). Indeed, this plumbing of the unconscious is, as Proust sees it, his essential creative activity.

In some of Proust's sketches for his final work, the reader discovers that finding the language of 'intelligible equivalents' is not always successful. On a few occasions, speaking in his own name, Proust seems hesitant, at a loss for words: he reaches below, behind, beyond his impression, but cannot express precisely either how he extracts meaning or what his efforts have uncovered. Two passages from his manuscripts address nominally how his pastiches uncover the beauty of another writer's style, but they show Proust's attempt at explanation petering out, though in an evocative manner:

> Quand je montre *q* [*sic*] (sur le pont de Combray, mais mieux ailleurs) que pour moi la vraie réalité est q. q. chose qu'on aperçoit [*sic*] pas d'abord, qui est derrière ce qu'on croit voir ou entendre et qui est si confus, tandis qu'elle est claire (et le pastiche est au fond cette perception en littérature car là où un autre dit c'est délicieux je descends audessous [*sic*] et je prends connaissance du thème clair . . .

> When I show (on the Combray bridge, but better elsewhere) that for me true reality is something that one does not perceive immediately, which is behind what one thinks one sees or hears and which is so confused, whereas true reality is clear (and the pastiche is essentially this perception in literature, for where someone else would say that's lovely I dig underneath and I connect with the pure theme . . .

The pastiche is neither an intellectual explanation of the nature of another writer's prose, nor a meaningless exclamation such as 'How lovely!' Instead, it is a way of attuning oneself to the musical air of the Other's prose, to the clear theme that Proust calls the reality of that prose style and by which he appears to mean the basic unconscious substructure. Another passage related to Proust's pastiches trails off in a similar way:

> d'autres parlent de la jolie langue de France, je descends plus bas jusqu'aux choses qui s'enlacent au fond de sa prose il faudra ajouter (très important) que c'est à cause de cela, à cause de cette réalité immanente à nos impressions et plus durables [*sic*], que tout ce qui a trait à la 1ère couche ne m'intéresse pas . . . Quand Daniel Halévy dit: l'affaire Dreyfus qui nous a pris 2 ans de notre vie, toute notre vie peut'être, je ne peux pas comprendre ce que cela signifie, car toute ma vie quelque [*sic*] soit l'apparence de mes actions ou de mes sentiments est occupée à un travail dans des couches plus profondes . . .[73]

> others speak of France's pretty language, I descend to a lower level, to those things that are entwined deep down in his prose one would have to add (it's very important) that this is the reason, because of this reality that is immanent to our impressions and more lasting, that everything that has to do with the first layer doesn't interest me. When Daniel Halévy says: the Dreyfus affair took 2 years out of our life, our entire life perhaps, I can't understand what that means, for my whole life, whatever the appearance of my actions or my feelings, is engaged in a task at deeper levels . . .

Underneath, below the top layer of the everyday, lies a reality superior to it, and it is a reality that may be tangled ('les choses *qui s'enlacent*') and thus require patient disentangling. One last text, though once again it focuses on engineering a pastiche, underscores a key step in Proust's creative process, that is, a mimetic technique for elucidating the meaning of a moment of intuition:

> même les petits pastiches qu'on a lus de moi ne sont que la continuation de l'effort qui commence sur le pont-vieux, du côté de Méséglise, et au lieu de dire devant Renan ou Flaubert 'zut que c'est beau' de *tâcher à revivre exactement* ce que nous exprimons d'une façon si inadéquate et confuse. (I, 836; Esquisse LV, emphasis added)

> even the brief pastiches of mine that people have read are simply the continuation of the effort that begins on the Pont-Vieux, on the Méséglise way, and instead of exclaiming, reading Renan or Flaubert, 'gosh that's beautiful', *I attempt to relive exactly* what we express in such an inadequate and confused manner.

The writer must be wary of the words that spring to the lips immediately when he or she experiences a moment of potential insight. 'Reliving exactly' an impression means instead that the first level of creativity is not verbal, but imitative, simulative, an inner mirroring of the experience itself. Proust makes this clear in a text in which the writer/translator is invited to set the intellect aside. He must become 'une matière poreuse, ductile, se faisant elle-même l'impression qu'elle veut rendre, la mimant, la reproduisant, pour être sûr de ne rien altérer, de n'y rien ajouter' (IV, 811. Esquisse XXIV) ('a porous matter, ductile, making itself the impression it wishes to create, miming it, reproducing it, so as to be sure that nothing has been altered, or anything added'). This kinetic copying exercise does not in itself bring the impression to the surface of consciousness in the form of words. That step is demonstrated almost didactically in one of Proust's most famous descriptions, that of the hawthorn blossoms. And here we see reinforced the idea that this creative mime has a kinetic aspect, for the flower-covered altar vibrates with the perfume of the hawthorn, and the blossoming of the flower has a rhythm:

> en suivant, ... en essayant de mimer au fond de moi le geste de leur efflorescence, je l'imaginais comme si ç'avait été le mouvement de tête étourdi et rapide, au regard coquet, aux pupilles diminuées, d'une blanche jeune fille, distraite et vive. (I, 111)
>
> in following, in trying to mimic to myself the action of their efflorescence, I imagined it as a swift and thoughtless movement of the head, with a provocative glance from her contracted pupils, by a young girl in white, insouciant and vivacious. (1, 156)

Of course, this moment in the text is overdetermined as the *incipit* of the *filles-fleurs* theme: the coloured flecks on the hawthorn blossoms are immediately juxtaposed to the freckles of Vinteuil's daughter, who is sitting nearby. Fascination with and desire for flower and girl become one in what is henceforth a founding metaphor. Though the passage shows the birth of a thematics, equally if not more significant is that it lays out the building blocks, the manoeuvres that precede language, the mimesis that transforms a raw, semi-conscious impression into a preverbal equivalent. Why is this step so important for the Proustian text? Because it reveals how the artist is to retrieve precious materials from his unconscious. This imitative gesture is actually a creative one, 'the operation in which, by miming within oneself the external gesture of a tangible object, one imagines, one creates something'.[74]

In a sketch for the hawthorn passage the Narrator reveals the equivalent he is searching for. The text likely remained in Proust's manuscript drafts because it served up too straightforwardly the linguistic figure, the metaphor, that would form the basis of Proustian style. The manuscript speaks of:

> une de ces métaphores sans prix qui sont la formule révélatrice d'une vérité esthétique enfin conquise, et qui font des livres des grands poètes un résumé de découvertes, un trésor de certitudes d'un autre ordre que celui de la science et qui ne peut s'exposer d'une façon rationnelle, mais plus important encore et éclaircissant une réalité plus profonde, plus spirituelle que la réalité physique. (I, 862; Esquisse LXII)

> one of those priceless metaphors which are the revelatory formula of an aesthetic truth finally mastered, and which make of the works of great poets a compendium of discoveries, a treasure of certitudes of an order different from that of science and which cannot be explained in a rational way, but which are even more important, bringing light to a more profound reality, more spiritual than physical reality.

No doubt fittingly, in linking metaphor to the irrational, Proust appears to catch himself in one of those self-directed unconscious anticipations that he spoke of in relation to earlier nineteenth-century writers. One wonders: did he anticipate fully that he would be one of those great poetic figures whose aesthetic formula would make of him the literary glory of the twentieth and twenty-first centuries?

Postscript

The quarrel over the existence of the unconscious, and later over whether the unconscious had dynamic, creative capabilities, played out in parallel to a separate but related drama. What we have seen is that, as the nineteenth century progressed, psychology ascended from being a subset of philosophy to take on an autonomous status.[1] The professional psychologist was a late addition to the nomenclature. In 1845 the term 'psychologiste' was used by Jacques-Joseph Moreau to describe his colleague Louis-Francisque Lélut,[2] but the usage seems to have gone no further. Interestingly, the French term 'psychologue' ('psychologist') as a noun is recorded as entering the French language only in 1903: 'Psychologue. Personne qui exerce un des métiers de la psychologie appliquée'[3] ('A person who exercises one of the professions of applied psychology').

Philosophy not only was losing adepts to psychology, it also was in the process of divesting itself of the deity, particularly in post-Napoleonic France. The French reading of Eduard von Hartmann's study on the unconscious (translated as *La Philosophie de l'inconscient* in 1877) focused critically on its second volume, titled 'Metaphysics of the Unconscious'. Science had to have a physical, empirical grounding, and there was no longer room for a creator. Emblematic of this evolution is Pierre Janet, of whom we have spoken frequently and who remains for me a cornerstone figure. One can read in the titles of his academic credentials the fin-de-siècle movement in which he found himself. First came a philosophy thesis, *L'Automatisme psychologique* (1889), whose title would suggest that Janet was already a fugitive from philosophy. Next, after working under Charcot at La Salpêtrière, he wrote and defended a medical thesis, *Contribution à l'étude des accidents mentaux chez les hystériques* (1893), which was published as *L'État mental des hystériques*. This was the necessary medical qualification giving him credibility as a psychologist and medical analyst, and the subject chosen, hysteria, placed him at the centre of the great research subject of the day.

Before his two theses, Janet's publications had flirted with telepathy, but soon enough he would distance himself from such research and would miss no opportunity to highlight the credulous side of rival scientists such as Dr Charles Richet, intrepid explorer of most things supranormal and inventor of the French term 'métapsychique', soon to be supplanted in English and German by 'paranormal'. Janet's diffidence about the suprasensible extended to his skepticism about theories of the unconscious, notably Freud's. In his own way, Janet seems to have been rehearsing a core position of late nineteenth-century philosophy, mentioned earlier: 'everything psychic is a priori conscious and hence ... an unconscious mental process is an absurdity and a contradiction.'[4]

In the 1890s, partly in reaction to the increased scientification of knowledge, interest in the psychological, in instinct, intuition and the creative bases of literature, was both revealed and fuelled by Jules Huret's *Enquête sur l'évolution littéraire* and the sampling of artistic opinion about the unconscious that blossomed in *Le Subconscient chez les artistes, les savants et les écrivains*, the questionnaire/thesis of Dr Paul Chabaneix.

In literature, in particular by novelists and prose writers, the debate about the unconscious was taken up by each writer in his or her own personalized way, Flaubert transferring impressions of epileptic delirium into characters and external phenomena; Maupassant identifying a frightening undecidability, an in-betweenness, about psychic life; pulp novelists exploiting hypnotism to posit a dark, violent underside to the mind. Proust brings the literary examination of the unconscious into the twentieth century, but not via a debate with Freud. As I have attempted to show, Pierre Janet makes a much better opponent for Freud than Proust. But what of Proust and Janet, the former well-connected medically but a visible prophet of the unconscious, and the latter a respected and well-published non-believer? There was no open debate between the two, but Janet did have something to say about Proust.

As he read sections of *À l'ombre des jeunes filles en fleurs*, Janet recorded his reactions. With a few personal edits he quotes the following passage:[5] 'On ne trouve jamais aussi hauts qu'on avait espéré une cathédrale, une vague dans la tempête, le bond d'un danseur' (I, 518). ('One never finds a cathedral, a wave in a storm, a dancer's leap in the air quite as high as one has been expecting' (2, 137–38)). Janet then refers to a second passage where Proust's Narrator regrets that he is no longer looking forward to meeting the *jeunes filles* because meeting them is now inevitable (II, 211; 2, 594). Readers of Proust will recognize here his theory of the ambiguity of expectations; that is, desire is either kept alive through the imagination or becomes moribund if satisfied in real life. The two texts draw the following diagnosis from Janet: 'This variety of loss of happiness in the real world and its retention in one's imagination is very important and will allow us later to explain reverie and the maladies of reverie.'

Janet's judgement is to be found in a chapter titled 'States of morose inaction and fatigue'. Of course, Proust's analyses were sometimes gloomy; to many he was apparently inactive and his fatigues were all too frequent, but does the fact that his Narrator opts for the imaginative over day-to-day reality set him on a path to the 'illness' of daydreaming? In his quest for the pathological, it is indeed Janet who seems too close to normative everyday reality to realize that he was applying a medical assessment to one of the most persuasive and poetic treatments of psychology and the teachings of the unconscious to come out of the twentieth century.

Notes

Introduction

1 See, for example, Thomas Laycock, 'On the reflex function of the brain', *British and Foreign Medical Journal* 19 (1845): 298–311.
2 See in particular Marcel Gauchet, *L'Inconscent cérébral* (Paris: Éditions du Seuil, 1992).
3 Anne Harrington, *Medicine, Mind and the Double Brain: A Study in Nineteenth Century Thought* (Princeton: Princeton University Press, 1987), 17.
4 Mark Micale, 'Charcot and the Idea of Hysteria in the Male: Gender, Mental Science and Diagnosis in Late Nineteenth-Century France', *Medical History* 34, 4 (1990): 363–411; Jan Goldstein, 'The Uses of Male Hysteria: Medical and Literary Discourse in Nineteenth-Century France', *Representations* 34 (Spring 1991): 134–65; Benjamin Bart, 'Male Hysteria in *Salammbô*', *Nineteenth-Century French Studies* 12 (1984): 313–21.
5 An entire and very interesting issue of the following journal is devoted to Flaubert, dreams and hallucinations: *Revue Flaubert* 6 (2006), available at http://flaubert.univ-rouen.fr/revue/revue6/.
6 Adam Watt, *Reading in Proust's 'À la recherche': 'le délire de la lecture'* (Oxford: Oxford University Press, 2009).
7 Élisabeth Roudinesco, *Histoire de la psychanalyse en France 1885–1939*, vol. I (Paris: Fayard, 1994), 76–84. All references in all chapters are to volume I of this text.
8 Pierre Bayard, *Maupassant juste avant Freud* (Paris: Éditions de Minuit, 1994), 11.
9 Jean Thuillier, *Monsieur Charcot de la Salpêtrière* (Paris: Laffont, 1993), 239.
10 In this I concur with recent research by Marlo Johnston, who sees Maupassant's interest shifting from Charcot to the philosophy and practices of the Nancy school. See Johnston, *Guy de Maupassant* (Paris: Fayard, 2012).
11 Richet interacted with Léonie as well and reported in his *Souvenirs d'un psychologue* (Paris: Peyronnet, 1933) that while still in Normandy, she had 'seen' the fire that had destroyed his Paris laboratory.
12 Cabanès, *Le Corps et la maladie dans les récits réalistes (1856–1893)*, 2 vols. (Paris: Klincksieck, 1991); Bayard, *Maupassant*, 1994; Janssen, 'L'Inquiétante

étrangeté de la physiologie nerveuse. Parasitisme mental, illusionnisme et fantastique chez Maupassant', in *Paradigmes de l'âme. Littérature et aliénisme*, Jean-Louis Cabanès, Didier Philippot and Paolo Tortonese, eds. (Paris: Presses Sorbonne Nouvelle, 2012), 195–212.

13 In addition to Brachet and Briquet, Evelyne Ender discusses the works of Drs François Voisin and Julien-Joseph Virey. Her first chapter provides a striking account of how female physical weakness was projected onto her intellectual abilities. See Ender, *Sexing the Mind: Nineteenth-Century Fictions of Hysteria* (Ithaca: Cornell University Press, 1995), 25–65.

14 Deaths outstripped live births in France for several years in the 1890s.

15 Alfred Fouillée, 'La Psychologie des sexes et ses fondements physiologiques', *Revue des Deux Mondes* (15 September 1893): 397–429 (407); Jean-Marie Guyau, *Éducation et hérédité: étude sociologique* (Paris: Alcan, 1889), see especially the chapter 'L'Éducation des filles et l'hérédité'; Henri Marion, *Études de psychologie feminine. L'Éducation des jeunes filles* (Paris: Colin, 1902); Edward Hammond Clarke, *Sex in Education: A Fair Chance for Girls* (New York: Arno Press, 1972 [1873]); Henri Thulié, *La Femme, essai de sociologie physiologique* (Paris: Delahaye and Lecrosnier, 1885). See the critique of Thulié's volume in *Revue Philosophique* 10th year, 20 (November 1885): 538–40.

16 Georges de Peyrebrune, *Les Vierges de feu et la décroissance de la population* (Paris: En vente chez tous les libraires, 1876); Daniel Lesueur, *Névrosée* (Paris: Lemerre, 1890); Georgette Déga, *Essai sur la cure préventive de l'hystérie féminine par l'éducation* (Paris: Alcan, 1898). Rachilde, *Pourquoi je ne suis pas féministe* (Paris: Éditions de France, 1928). I also refer to Rachilde's answers to the survey discussed in Paul Chabaneix, *Le Subconscient chez les artistes, les savants et les écrivains* (Paris: Baillière, 1897).

17 See, for example, Jules Liégeois, *De la suggestion hypnotique dans ses rapports avec le droit civil et le droit criminel* (Paris: Alphonse Picard, 1884).

18 Pierre Citti, *La Mésintelligence. Essais d'histoire de l'intelligence française du symbolisme à 1914* (Saint-Etienne: Éditions des Cahiers Intempestifs, 2000).

19 See Remy de Gourmont, *La Culture des idées. Du style ou de l'écriture, la création subconsciente, la dissociation des idées* (Paris: Mercure de France, 1964 [1900]).

20 I owe a large part of my analysis of Poincaré to Nicola Luckhurst. See her *Science and Structure in Proust's 'À la recherché du temps perdu'* (Oxford: Oxford University Press, 2000), especially 226–35.

21 Proust, *Jean Santeuil* (Paris: Gallimard, 1971), 397.

22 See Maurice Maeterlinck, *Le Temple enseveli* (Paris: Fasquelle, 1902), 229–82.

1 Before Freud

1 Henri Ellenberger, *The Discovery of the Unconscious: The History and Evolution of Dynamic Psychiatry* (New York: Basic Books, 1970).

2 '*Swann* expliqué par Proust', interview of Proust by Élie-Joseph Bois, *Le Temps*, 13 November 1913, collected in Proust, *Contre Sainte-Beuve* (Paris: Gallimard [Pléiade], 1971), 558. Henceforth, CSB.

3 Isador Coriat, *Abnormal Psychology*, 2nd edn (London: Moffat, Yard and Co., 1917 [1910]), 10.
4 Jacqueline Carroy, *Hypnose, suggestion et psychologie. L'invention des sujets* (Paris: Presses Universitaires de France, 1991), 19–20.
5 See Lancelot Whyte, *The Unconscious before Freud*, 2nd edn (New York: St. Martin's, 1978), 156–57. French dictionaries of psychiatry date Amiel's use of the word 'inconscient' to the early 1860s. See Élisabeth Roudinesco and Michel Plon, *Dictionnaire de la psychanalyse* (Paris: Librairie Générale Française/ Fayard, 2011), 731. Amiel does not figure in Ellenberger's index.
6 Text of 28 April 1861. Amiel, *Fragments d'un journal intime*, 7th edn (Geneva: Georg, 1897), 157.
7 *Dictionnaire de l'Académie française*, 7th edn (Paris: F. Didot, 1878), vol. 2, 23.
8 Nicolas Rand, 'The Hidden Soul: The Growth of the Unconscious in Philosophy, Psychology, Medicine, and Literature, 1750–1900', *American Imago* 61, 3 (2004) 257–89 (261). Rand's article is a succinct and readable summary of thinking about the unconscious with a strong focus on German and to some extent English thinkers.
9 See *Thinking the Unconscious: Nineteenth-Century German Thought*, Angus Nicholls and Martin Liebscher, eds. (Cambridge: Cambridge University Press, 2010), 9.
10 Harrington, *Medicine, Mind*, 3.
11 *Nouvelles considérations sur le sommeil, les songes et le somnambulisme*, in *Maine de Biran. Oeuvres* (Paris: Vrin, 1984), V, 82–83. See also Rand, 'The Hidden', 269, and Anne Devarieux, *Maine de Biran: L'individualité persévérante* (Grenoble: Jérôme Millon, 2004), especially 381–89.
12 I am not thinking so much of reviving *La Querelle des anciens et des modernes* as of the title of Pierre-Henri Castel's wonderfully documented, incisive volume *La Querelle de l'hystérie* (Paris: Presses Universitaires de France, 1998).
13 Tony James discusses reflex response and unconscious cerebration briefly in *Dream, Creativity and Madness in Nineteen-Century France* (Oxford: Clarendon Press, 1995), 218–19.
14 Marshall Hall, 'On the Reflex Function of the Medulla Oblongata and Medulla Spinalis', *Philosophical Transactions of the Royal Society*, 130 (1833): 635–65; Johannes Müller, *Handbuch der Physiologie des Menschen für Vorlesungen*, 2 vols. (Koblenz: J. Hölscher, 1833–40).
15 The beginning of this section owes much to Marcel Gauchet's succinct but masterful work, *L'Inconscient cérébral*, especially his chapter 'Le Réflexe à l'assaut de l'esprit'.
16 Thomas Laycock, 'On the Reflex Function'.
17 *Dictionnaire encyclopédique des sciences médicales*, 26 (1882): 336. The first paragraph of this excerpt is quoted by Gauchet, 120.
18 Michael Foucault, *Les Anormaux. Cours au Collège de France. 1974–1975* (Paris: Gallimard/Seuil, 1999), 145–47.
19 *The Journal of Mental Science* 21 (January 1876): 477–98.

20 William Carpenter, *Principles of Mental Physiology*, 2nd edn (London: Henry S. King, 1875), 515–43.

21 Léon Dumont, 'L'Action réflexe cérébrale. MM. Laycock, Carpenter, Luys', *Revue Scientifique de la France et de l'Étranger*, 28 (8 January 1876): 25–33.

22 Coriat, *Abnormal Psychology*, 11. The reference is to the German-American psychologist Hugo Münsterberg, a Harvard professor.

23 Reported by Paul-Émile Garnier, *L'Automatisme somnambulique devant les tribunaux* (Paris: Baillière, 1887), 12.

24 Ibid., 18.

25 Marcel Prévost, *L'Automne d'une femme* (Paris: Lemerre, 1893).

26 Henri Nizet, *Suggestion* (Paris: Tresse and Stock, 1891).

27 *Encyclopedia of Occultism and Parapsychology*, 3rd edn, 2 vols., Leslie A. Shephard, ed. (Detroit: Gale, 1991), vol. 2, 1626.

28 See Arthur Pierce's 'Subliminal Self or Unconscious Cerebration?', *Proceedings of the Society for Psychical Research* 11 (1895): 317–25, and, as part II of the same article, the response of Frank Podmore, 325–32. Podmore was a colleague of Myers with whom he had co-authored *Phantasms of the Living*.

29 See Jeremy Stubbs, 'Between Medicine and Hermeticism: "The" Unconscious in *fin-de-siècle* France', in *Symbolism, Decadence and the Fin de Siècle: French and European Perspectives*, Patrick McGuinness, ed. (Exeter: University of Exeter Press, 2000), 144–72 (160), and Alain de Mijolla, *Freud et la France* (Paris: Presses Universitaires de France, 2010), 143.

30 Camille Flammarion, *Mémoires biographiques et philosophiques d'un astronome* (Paris: Flammarion, [1912]), 235.

31 Harrington, *Double Brain*, 17.

32 Jules Luys, *Études sur le dédoublement des opérations cérébrales et sur le rôle isolé de chaque hémisphère dans les phénomènes de la pathologie mentale* (Paris: Masson, 1879), 4.

33 Gabriel Descourtis, *Du fractionnement des opérations cérébrales et en particulier de leur dédoublement dans les psychopathies* (Paris: medical thesis 194, 1882).

34 Luys, *Études sur le dédoublement*, 35.

35 For a discussion of this point, see Ian Hacking, *Rewriting the Soul: Multiple Personality and the Sciences of Memory*, 2nd edn (Princeton: Princeton University Press, 1995), 169.

36 Castel, *La Querelle*, 240.

37 Jules Luys, *Études de physiologie et de pathologie cérébrales. Des actions réflexes du cerveau dans les conditions normales et pathologiques de leur fonctionnement* (Paris: Baillière, 1874), 1. Quoted by Gauchet, *Cérébration*, 113.

38 See Harrington, *Double Brain*, 191–93, and Edgar Bérillon's thesis, *Hypnotisme expérimental. La dualité cérébrale et l'indépendance fonctionnelle des deux hémisphères cérébraux* (Paris: Delahaye & Lecrosnier, 1884).

39 See a review of Alfred Vulpian's 1876 lecture on the excitability of the brain and its topography where he refers to Ferrier's work, *Revue Philosophique* 7–12 (1876): 649.

40 See Alan Beaton and Peter Mariën, 'Language, Cognition and the Cerebellum: Grappling with an Enigma', *Cortex* 46 (2010): 811–20.
41 Henri Beaunis, *Les Sensations internes* (Paris: Alcan, 1889), 50.
42 Joris-Karl Huysmans, *À rebours* (Paris: Garnier-Flammarion, 1978), 66.
43 Valentin Magnan, 'Des anomalies, des aberrations et des perversions sexuelles', in *Recherches sur les centres nerveux: alcoolisme, folie des héréditaires dégénérés, paralysie générale, médecine légale* (Paris: Masson, 1893), vol. 2, 151–73.
44 Ibid., vol. 2, 156.
45 For a discussion of these differing views on hallucination, see Juan Rigoli, *Lire le délire. Aliénisme, rhétorique et littérature en France au XIXe siècle* (Paris: Fayard, 2001), 328–29, note 1; James, *Dream*, 158–68; and Jean-Louis Cabanès, *Le Corps*, vol. I, 217–20.
46 Among the medical doctors who participated in these experiments were Brierre de Boismont, Esquirol, Ferrus, Cerise, Macario and Baillarger. See Rigoli, *Lire le délire*, 442.
47 Jacques Joseph Moreau, *Un Chapitre oublié de la pathologie mentale* (Paris: Masson, 1850), 4.
48 James Braid, *Neurypnology, or the Rationale of Nervous Sleep, considered in relation to Animal Magnetism* (London: John Churchill, 1843). There are those who, perhaps misled by this title, maintain that Braid never used the term 'hypnotism' itself: on the contrary, he uses it everywhere in this study, beginning with his preface.
49 See Jean Martin Charcot, 'Physiologie pathologique. Sur les divers états nerveux déterminés par l'hypnotisation chez les hystériques', *Comptes-rendus hebdomadaires de l'Académie des Sciences* 94 (1882): 403–5.
50 This was the view of Pierre Janet, cited by Anne Harrington, *The Cure Within: A History of Mind-Body Medicine* (New York: Norton, 2008), 55.
51 The edition of reference is Taine, *De l'intelligence*, 2 vols., 6th edn (Paris: Hachette, 1892 [1870]).
52 In addition to citing Taine, Jacqueline Carroy also points out that late eighteenth-century literary authors were addressing human duality. In works such as *Le Neveu de Rameau* (composed around 1770, first French edition 1821) and *Le Paradoxe sur le comédien* (composed slightly later, published in 1830), Diderot's heroes debate an alter ego, while in Xavier de Maistre's *Voyage autour de ma chambre* (1794) there is a dialogue between the author's 'soul' and the 'beast' in him, the 'other'. Carroy, *Les Personnalités doubles et multiples. Entre science et fiction* (Paris: Presses Universitaires de France, 1993), xi.
53 Dr Charles Richet's three articles on historical possessions and hysteria in the influential *Revue des Deux Mondes* (15 January, 1 and 15 February 1880) certainly had an impact, as did the three volumes devoted to the same subject by Dr Gabriel Légué, *Documents pour servir à l'histoire des possédées de Loudun, Urbain Grandier et les possédées de Loudun. Documents inédits de M. Charles Barbier*, and *Urbain Grandier et les possédées de Loudun. Nouvelle édition revue et augmentée.*
54 Guy de Maupassant, *Le Horla, et autres récits fantastiques*, Mariane Bury, ed. (Paris: Librairie Générale Française, Livre de Poche Classique, 2000), 49.

55 Jean-Martin Charcot and Paul Richer, *Les Démoniaques dans l'art* (Paris: Delahaye & Lecrosnier, 1887).
56 Élisabeth Roudinesco reports this anecdote, *Histoire*, 36.
57 Jules Héricourt, 'Psychologie. L'activité inconsciente de l'esprit', *Revue Scientifique* (31 August 1889): 257–68 (257–58).
58 Pierre Janet, *L'Automatisme psychologique: essai de psychologie expérimentale sur les formes inférieures de l'activité humaine* (Paris: Alcan, 1889). My references are to the second edition (1894), same pagination as the first.
59 Théodule Ribot, *Les Maladies de la personnalité* (Paris: Alcan, 1885).
60 Joseph Jastrow, *La Subconscience*, preface by Pierre Janet (Paris: Alcan, 1908).
61 Pierre Janet, *La Médecine psychologique* (Paris: Flammarion, 1980 [1923]), 17.
62 See Brunschvicg's review of Desdouit's work, *Revue de Métaphysique et de Morale* (1893): 406.
63 Lawrence Rainey, 'Shock Effects: Marinetti, Pathology, and Italian Avant-Garde Poetics', in *The Mind of Modernism: Medicine, Psychology, and the Cultural Arts in Europe and America 1880–1940*, Mark Micale ed. (Stanford: Stanford University Press, 2004), 205.
64 Jastrow, *La Subconscience*, vii.
65 Janet, *Automatisme psychologique*, 5.
66 Ellenberger, *The Discovery*, 338.
67 Pierre Janet, 'À propos de la Métapsychique', *Revue Philosophique* 96 (July–December 1923): 5–32 (27). This article is a review of Charles Richet's *Traité de métapsychique* (Paris: Alcan, 1922).
68 Micale, *The Mind of Modernism*, 5.
69 Micale, *Approaching Hysteria: Disease and Its Interpretations* (Princeton: Princeton University Press, 1995), 9.
70 See Ellenberger, *The Discovery*, 406, and his chapter 'Pierre Janet and Psychological Analysis', 331–417.
71 Hacking, *Rewriting*, chapter 13, 'Trauma'.
72 The word 'probably' probably suggests where Hacking's sympathies lie.
73 See Hacking, *Rewriting*, 44 and note 15.
74 Elisabeth Bronfen, *The Knotted Subject: Hysteria and Its Discontents* (Princeton: Princeton University Press, 1998), 279–89.
75 See Jacqueline Carroy and Régine Plas, 'La Volonté et l'involontaire: l'exemple de l'automatisme', in Jean-Louis Cabanès et al., eds., *Paradigmes*, 34.
76 See Janet, *L'Automatisme psychologique*, 406, and 'À propos de la Métapsychique', especially 25 and ff.
77 Richet, *Traité de métapsychique*, 50.
78 See Stubbs, 'Between Medicine and Hermeticism'.
79 Jean-Yves Tadié, *Marcel Proust: Biographie*, 2 vols. (Paris: Gallimard [Folio], 1996), vol. I, 152, 154.
80 Dominique Parodi, 'L'Inconscient dans la vie mentale', *Bulletin de la Société française de Philosophie*, 10th year, 2 (February 1910): 21–50 (47). Passage quoted by Stubbs.

81 Alfred Fouillée, *La Pensée et les nouvelles écoles anti-intellectualistes* (Paris: Alcan, 1911), 33, quoting Théodule Ribot, *Problèmes de psychologie affective* (Paris: Alcan, 1910), 9.
82 Dominique Parodi, *La Philosophie contemporaine en France* (Paris: Alcan, 1920 [1919]).
83 Ibid., 112.
84 Ibid., 17–18. See also 120.
85 Gustave Géley, *De l'inconscient au conscient* (Paris: Alcan, 1919), 111.
86 Géley eventually became the first president of the paranormalist Institut métapsychique international.
87 Gustave Le Bon, *La Psychologie des foules* (Paris: Alcan, 1895), 15.
88 See, in *Le Peintre de la vie moderne*, section III, 'L'Artiste, homme du monde, homme des foules et enfant' (*Œuvres complètes)*, vol. 2, 687–94, and, in *Le Spleen de Paris*, 'XII Les Foules', ibid., vol. 1, 291–92.
89 James, *Dream*, 262 note 2.
90 See Henri Beaunis, 'Comment fonctionne mon cerveau. Essai de psychologie introspective', *Revue Philosophique* 67 (January 1909): 29–40 (39). Jacqueline Carroy discusses this text in *Les Personnalités doubles*, 128–30.
91 Théodule Ribot, *Essai sur l'imagination créatrice* (Paris: Alcan, 1900).
92 Reported by Jules Huret, *Enquête sur l'évolution littéraire*, Daniel Grojnowski, ed. (Paris: José Corti, 1999), 166. Gourmont's essay on the unconscious is contained in *La Culture des idées.*
93 Christophe Prochasson, *Les Années électriques, 1880–1910* (Paris: Éditions de la Découverte, 1991), 225.
94 Parodi, *La Philosophie*, 88.
95 René Rousseau, 'Marcel Proust et l'esthétique de l'inconscient', *Mercure de France* (15 January 1922): 361–86.
96 Élisabeth Roudinesco develops the interesting if not entirely convincing argument that in the French mind there were two denominations of Jews, the 'Israélite' and the 'Juif', the former being measured and domesticated in his desires and integrated in his outlook, the latter the bad Jew, low, acquisitive and lustful. Freud's emphasis on sex made of him the second type. She writes, 'En d'autres termes, l'anti-pansexualisme qui prétend combattre la doctrine freudienne de la sexualité est toujours l'expression vive ou atténuée d'une psychologie de la race qui ne dit pas son nom.' ('In other words, the anti-pansexualism which claims to combat the Freudian doctrine of sexuality is always the expression, more or less intense, of a racial psychology which dare not speak its name.') *Histoire*, 191.
97 Ibid., 245.
98 Emmanuel Régis and Angelo Hesnard, *La Psychoanalyse des névroses et des psychoses: ses applications médicales et extra-médicales* (Paris: Alcan, 1914). Régis died in 1918 (not in 1928 as Roudinesco states, p. 278) and it was Hesnard who revised further editions of the study. It was particularly the third edition, in 1929, that contained major revisions by Hesnard, who became the guru of Freudian psychotherapy in France. Regarding the Janet–Freud relationship,

I have found the following especially useful: Ellenberger, *The Discovery*, 331–417; Roudinesco, *Histoire de la psychanalyse*, 242–66; Marcel Gauchet and Gladys Swain, *Le Vrai Charcot. Les chemins imprévus de l'inconscient* (Paris: Calmann-Lévy, 1997); and Mijolla, *Freud et la France*. Jacques Sédat has made a yeoman's effort to summarize the main points in Mijolla's 947 pages in 'La Réception de Freud en France durant la première moitié du XXe siècle. Le freudisme à l'épreuve de l'esprit latin', *Topique* 2, 115 (2011): 51–68. I have also consulted with profit a collection of essays by Ellenberger, *Beyond the Unconscious: Essays of Henri Ellenberger in the History of Psychiatry*, Mark Micale, ed. (Princeton: Princeton University Press, 1993); Serge Nicolas, *Histoire de la psychologie française. Naissance d'une nouvelle science* (Paris: Éditions In Press, 2002); and *Discovering the History of Psychiatry*, Marc Micale and Roy Porter, eds. (Oxford: Oxford University Press, 1994).

99 *Encyclopedia of Erotic Literature*, Gaëtan Brulotte and John Phillips, eds. (New York: Routledge, 2006), vol. I, x.

100 Roudinesco, *Histoire*, 41.

101 See my article 'Naturalisme, sexe et sexologie: Excès catastrophique ou fantaisie médicale?', *Les Cahiers Naturalistes* 85 (2011): 117–33.

102 Paul Moreau, *Des aberrations du sens génésique*, 4th edn (Paris: Asselin, 1887), 7.

103 Richet, preface to Edmund Gurney, Frederic Myers, and Frank Podmore, *Les Hallucinations télépathiques*, 2nd edn, trans. of *Phantasms of the Living* by Léon Marillier (Paris: Alcan, 1892), p. x.

104 Mijolla quotes the letter, *Freud et la France*, 95.

105 Edmond Jaloux, 'Observations sur la psychanalyse', *Le Disque Vert* (1924): 28–37. Text quoted by Mijolla, *Freud et la France*, 276.

106 An earlier French work that covers some of the same ground as Mijolla is Marcel Scheidhauer, *Le Rêve freudien en France: avancées et résistances, 1900–1926* (Paris: Navarin, 1985).

107 Originally published as 'La Psycho-analyse' in the *Journal de Psychologie Normale et Pathologique* 11 (1914) : 1–36, 97–130. My page references are to the reprinted version in Pierre Janet, *La Psychanalyse de Freud*, Serge Nicolas, ed. (Paris: L'Harmattan, 2004), 49–113. This edition also provides the pagination of the original journal article.

108 See Nicolas, *Histoire*, 168. Most of the assessments of Janet's 1913 paper are negative. For a more sympathetic reading, see Paul Brown and Onno van der Hart, 'Memories of Sexual Abuse: Janet's Critique of Freud, a Balanced Approach', *Psychological Reports* 82 (1998): 1027–43.

109 Gauchet and Swain, *Le Vrai Charcot*, 199.

110 Janet, *L'État mental des hystériques* (Paris: Rueff, 1894), 269.

111 Gauchet and Swain, *Le Vrai Charcot*, 199.

112 Roudinesco, *Histoire*, 252.

113 See Mijolla, *Freud et la France*, 144–45, and Roudinesco, *Histoire*, 253–54.

114 Cited by Mijolla, *Freud et la France*, 95.

115 Freud's letter to Marie Bonaparte, 9 April 1937, cited by Mijolla in ibid., 694, and by Roudinesco, *Histoire*, 265–66.

2 Flaubert

1 Lionel Trilling, 'Art and Neurosis', in *The Liberal Imagination. Essays on Literature and Society* (New York: Viking, 1950), 160–80 (169).

2 Corr. 2, 40. References to Flaubert's *Correspondance* in the five-volume Gallimard (Pléiade) edition will henceforth appear in this format, in parentheses in the text.

3 See Gretchen Schultz, 'Gender, Sexuality and the Poetics of Identification', *Nottingham French Studies* 47, 3 (Autumn 2008): 91–102 (94).

4 Jacques Joseph Moreau, *La Psychologie morbide dans ses rapports avec la philosophie de l'histoire* (Paris: Masson, 1859), 481.

5 Zola's letter of 27 June 1870 cited by André de Billy, *Vie des frères Goncourt*, 2 vols. (Monaco: Imprimerie Nationale de Monaco, 1956), 2, 87.

6 Edmond had written a bit earlier, 'M'interrogeant longuement, j'ai la conviction intime qu'il est mort du travail de la forme, *à la peine du style*' ('After long reflexion, I am deeply convinced that he died because of working on literary form, *from the suffering of style*'), *Journal. Mémoires de la vie littéraire*, 4 vols., Robert Ricatte, ed. (Paris: Fasquelle/Flammarion, 1959), vol. 2, 571, 22 June 1870.

7 Edmond Goncourt's letter to Zola quoted by André de Billy, *Vie des frères Goncourt*, 2, 88.

8 Charles Richet, 'Du somnambulisme provoqué', *Journal de l'Anatomie et de la Physiologie* 11 (1875): 348–78.

9 Paul Bourget, *Essais de psychologie contemporaine*, André Guyaux, ed. (Paris: Gallimard, 1993), 103.

10 All references to *Salammbô* are to the edition by Jacques Neefs (Paris: Librairie Générale Française, Livre de Poche Classique, 2011).

11 Baudelaire, *Œuvres complètes* (Paris: Gallimard [Pléiade], 1990), vol. 2, 81.

12 Ibid., 83.

13 Along with reading Hector Landouzy's *Traité complet de l'hystérie* (Paris: Baillière, 1846), it is likely that Flaubert also consulted Jean-Louis Brachet, *Traité de l'hystérie* (Paris: Baillière, 1847), and possibly as well Pierre Briquet, *Traité clinique et thérapeutique de l'hystérie* (Paris: Baillière, 1859).

14 It is incorrect to suggest, as did Benjamin Bart in 'Male Hysteria', 313, that at mid-century hysteria was still exclusively a female disorder.

15 Martine Reid, 'Troubadoureries', in *George Sand, une correspondance*, Nicole Mozet, ed. (St-Cyr-sur-Loire: Christian Pirot, 1994), 261, 266.

16 Quoted by Jan Goldstein, 'The Uses', 157, from Elaine Showalter, 'Critical Cross-Dressing: Male Feminists and the Woman of the Year', *Raritan* 3 (Fall 1983): 130–49.

17 Thaïs E. Morgan, 'Male Lesbian Bodies: The Construction of Alternative Masculinities in Courbet, Baudelaire, and Swinburne', *Genders* 15 (1992): 48–49. Morgan bases her interpretation almost exclusively on one poem, 'Femmes damnées, Delphine et Hippolyte'.

18 Maurras, *L'Avenir de l'intelligence* (Paris: Albert Fontemoing, 1905), 45–46.

19 This text is from Barrès' early periodical, *Les Taches d'encre*, published in *L'Oeuvre de Maurice Barrès*, 20 vols. (Paris: Club de l'Honnête Homme, 1965–69), I, 11.

20 See Jann Matlock, *Scenes of Seduction: Prostitution, Hysteria and Reading Difference in Nineteenth-Century France* (New York: Columbia University Press, 1994), chapter 4, and p. 338, notes 14 and 15.

21 Nicole Edelman, *Les Métamorphoses de l'hystérique. Du début du XIXe siècle à la Grande Guerre* (Paris: Éditions de la La Découverte, 2003), 15.

22 Ibid., 40.

23 Edmond de Goncourt and Jules de Goncourt, *Idées et sensations* (Paris: Librairie Internationale, 1866), 126, 228.

24 In his most cynical moments Flaubert's statements about physical love show utter contempt for the projected partner: 'L'amour est comme un besoin de pisser. Qu'on l'épanche dans un vase d'or ou dans un pot d'argile, il faut que ça sorte. Le hasard seul nous procure des recipients' (Corr. 1, 680). ('Love is like the need to piss. Whether you do it into a golden vase or a clay pot, you have to get it out. It's pure chance that finds us the recipients.')

25 Mark Micale, 'Hysteria Male/Hysteria Female: Reflections on Comparative Gender Construction in Nineteenth-Century France and Britain', in *Science and Sensibility: Essays on Gender and Scientific Enquiry, 1780–1945*, Marina Benjamin, ed. (London: Basil Blackwell, 1991), 200–242 (204–5).

26 See Marie-Christine Desmaret, 'Épileptiques, hystériques, marginaux, fous comme figures protéiformes de l'artiste dans l'œuvre flaubertienne', *Revue Flaubert* 6 (2006): 12–13. Available at http://flaubert.univ-rouen.fr/revue/revue6/.

27 Naomi Schor, 'Male Lesbianism', *GLQ* 7, 3 (2001): 391–99.

28 Hélène Cixous, *La Jeune Née* (Paris: Union Générale d'Éditions ([10/18], 1975), 287–88.

29 Ibid., 12, 15, 36.

30 See for example Michel Weber, 'L'Épilepsie de Gustave Flaubert. Témoignages indirects et directs', *Épilepsies* 18, 3 (2006): 155–59, and H. Gastaut and Y. Gastaut, 'La Maladie de Gustave Flaubert', *Revue Neurologique* 138 (1982), 467–92.

31 On this point, see Pierre-Marc de Biasi, *Gustave Flaubert. Une manière speciale de vivre* (Paris: Grasset, 2009), 133.

32 Landouzy, *Traité*. Flaubert mentions reading Landouzy on a number of occasions, for example, in his dossier 'Sources et méthodes', BnF, N.a.f 23662, fo 154, where he says he consulted the volume 'pour les symptômes graduels du mal de Salammbô'. See Flaubert, *Salammbô*, 103, note 1.

33 I thank Jan Goldstein for providing me with a copy of Flaubert's notes from Landouzy. In her article 'The Uses of Male Hysteria' (1991), she notes (p. 135, note 6) that the Bibliothèque nationale de France had recently acquired a sixty-three-page photocopy of Flaubert's 'Notes de lecture pour *Salammbô*' and that the two pages on Landouzy were numbered 34–35. When a recent request was made to consult this photocopy, under the call number B.N. Manuscrits Don

37287, the Département des manuscrits was unable to match up the acquisition number with any document in its collection.

34 Reading this passage in Landouzy, Flaubert had noted to himself, 'Plusieurs hystériques croient que la constriction de la gorge est opérée par un vers [*sic*] qui remonte de l'estomac pour les ronger et les étouffer.' ('A number of hysterics believe that the constriction in their throat is caused by a worm that ascends from the stomach to gnaw at them and smother them.')

35 Corr. 3, 17. Letter of 18 February 1859.

36 See also *Salammbô*, 388, where soldiers deprived of food and water hallucinate and repeat the same word.

37 Landouzy, 88. The reference is likely to Jean-Baptiste Louyer-Villermay, *Traité des maladies nerveuses ou vapeurs, et particulièrement de l'hystérie et de l'hypocondrie* (Paris: Méquignon l'aîné père, 1816).

38 Corr. 3, 572. Letter to Taine of 1 December 1866.

39 See Landouzy, 65 and ff.

40 Sartre, *L'Idiot de la famille* (Paris: Gallimard (Tel), 1971), vol. 3, 1717.

41 Flaubert, *Les Mémoires d'un fou. Novembre. Pyrénées-Corse. Voyage en Italie*, Claudine Gothot-Mersch, ed. (Paris: Gallimard [Folio], 2001), 198. Gothot-Mersch sees a comic touch in this abrupt intervention and a reference to the structure of Goethe's *Werther*.

42 Proust, CSB, 586. Perhaps in reaction to Proust's discussion of metaphor and style in Flaubert, Albert Thibaudet contends that Flaubert belongs to the race of great creators of images but maintains that it is solely in *Madame Bovary* that images appear in any number. See Thibaudet, *Gustave Flaubert* (Paris: Gallimard, 1935), 227.

43 But feeling skittish about the unconscious elements in mental life may also be related to Bourget's desire to maintain silence about his early homoerotic tendencies. Daniel Ridge, Assistant Director of the W.T. Bandy Center for Baudelaire and Modern French Studies at Vanderbilt University, is preparing a critical edition of Bourget's letters to two youths he admired, Maurice Bouchor and Adrien Juvigny. These letters are part of an archive belonging to Bourget's homosexual college friend Georges Hérelle, held at the Bibliothèque municipale de Troyes. Professor Clive Thomson has recently published a carefully documented study of Hérelle titled *Georges Hérelle: Archéologue de l'inversion sexuelle 'fin-de-siècle'* (Paris: Éditions du Félin, 2014).

44 Goncourts, *Journal*, 2, 845. 9 November 1871.

45 Corr. 2, 243. Letter to Louise Colet of 29 January 1853.

46 Goncourts, *Journal* 2, 974. 1 April 1874.

47 Ibid., 932. 3 May 1873.

48 Jules de Gaultier, 'Le Génie de Flaubert', *Mercure de France* (16 November 1912): 225–60; (1 December 1912): 490–526.

49 Gaultier, 499–500.

50 Corr. 3, 594. Letter of 15 January 1867 from George Sand. Modern-day analysts of hysteria tend to agree with this definition. Julia Kristeva echoes Sand when she writes, 'The hysteric desires both maximum symbolic and physical

jouissance while all the while aware of the impossibility if not the inanity of such a desire', *Les Nouvelles maladies de l'âme* (Paris: Fayard, 1993), 109.

51 See Jules Lemaître, 'Mes Souvenirs (1). Mon arrivée à Paris', *Revue Hebdomadaire* (1 February 1913): 38–58.

52 Quoted from Maxime Du Camp's *Souvenirs littéraires* by Pierre-Marc de Biasi, *Une Manière spéciale*, 134.

53 See Albert Thibaudet, 'Réflexions sur la littérature. Sur le style de Flaubert', *Nouvelle Revue Française* 74 (November 1919): 942–53, and Proust's response, 'À propos du 'style' de Flaubert', *Nouvelle Revue Française* 76 (January–June 1920): 72–90. (References to Proust's article are to the version reprinted in CSB, 586–600). And see Thibaudet's response to Proust, 'Réflexions sur la littérature. Lettre à M. Marcel Proust', *Nouvelle Revue Française* 78 (March 1920): 426–41.

54 Ibid., 436.

55 See CSB, 606–16.

56 Of course, there are some critics, no doubt miffed by what they regard as undiscerning attitudes about Flaubert's nervous condition, who locate his true 'malady' in what they call his lack of conceptual abilities. That is, they speak of Flaubert's inability to 'explain' the psychology of a person, such as Emma, and the absence of explicit acknowledgement of societal context and pressures in *Madame Bovary*. Flaubert, in other words, ought to write more like, say, Sartre in *Les Chemins de la liberté*. See the essay of Jean-Bertrand Pontalis, titled with ironic intent 'La Maladie de Flaubert', in his collection *Après Freud* (Paris: Gallimard, 1968), 293–329. The text first appeared in *Les Temps Modernes*, nos. 100 and 101 (1954).

57 Goncourts, *Journal* 1, 1213. 11 January 1863.

58 Corr. 2, 55. Letter to Louis Colet, 3 March 1852.

59 Corr. 2, 85, note 3. Letter of May 1852. See Jean Bruneau's note on *La Spirale*, Corr. 2, 1067, note 3. Some of these hysteria-related phenomena originating in Landouzy and transferred into *Salammbô* are noted by Niklas Bender: the presence and power of the moon in the narrative, various occasions of the convulsive 'arcs de cercle', the trademark indicator of a hysterical attack. See Bender, *La Lutte des paradigmes. La littérature entre histoire, biologie et médecine (Flaubert, Zola, Fontane)* (Amsterdam: Rodopi, 2010), 47–149, but especially 76–86.

60 See Corr. 2, 290, note 3, for this undertaking to Louise Colet. For a fuller context of Flaubert's thinking about Spirale, see Corr. 2, 85, note 3, and the *Spirale* entry in Flaubert, *Correspondance. Index*, Jean Bruneau and Yvan Leclerc, eds. (Paris: Gallimard, 2007). The text of Flaubert's sketch for *Spirale* is online at http://flaubert.univ-rouen.fr/oeuvres/spirale.php.

61 Quoted by Michael Foucault, *La Bibliothèque fantastique. À propos de 'La Tentation de saint Antoine' de Gustave Flaubert* (Brussels: La Lettre Volée, 1995), 7.

62 Corr. 2, 417. Letter to Louise Colet of 26 August 1853.

63 See Watt, *Reading*, 101–29.

64 Goncourts, *Journal* 2, 1274. 18 May 1863.

65 Ibid., 1070. 4 May 1862.
66 See Corr. 3, 562, letter to Hippolyte Taine of 20 November 1866, and compare his similar comment to the Goncourts, Goncourts, *Journal* 1, 847. 10 December 1860.
67 Corr. 2, 423. Letter to Louise Colet of 2 September 1853.
68 Corr. 2, 891–92. Memento of Louise Colet, 15 August 1852.
69 Corr. 2, 218–19. Letter to Louise Colet of 27 December 1852.
70 Ibid., 377. Letter to Louise Colet of 7 July 1853.
71 Flaubert's remark also recalls, by contrast, the clichéd gender views of mid-nineteenth-century thinkers such as Henri-Frédéric Amiel, who described the ability to identify, if not coalesce, with the other as the essence of femininity. It was the abolition of the individual self, absorbed by a kind of intimate rapture, into the admired object. Under this definition, Flaubert certainly does have a feminine side. See Amiel's *Journal intime de l'année 1866* (Paris: Gallimard, 1959), 310, referred to by Miranda Gill in '*Compagnons de misère*: Melancholic Identification in Nerval and Baudelaire', *Nottingham French Studies* 47, 3 (Autumn 2008): 79–90 (80).
72 Corr. 2, 483. Letter to Louise Colet of 23 December 1853.
73 Quoted from Merleau-Ponty by Marie-Christine Desmaret, *Bizarreries et bigarrures baroques dans 'Salammbô' de Flaubert* (Lille: ANRT, 2005), 11.
74 Corr. 2, 483. Letter to Louise Colet of 23 December 1853.
75 Biasi, *Une Manière spéciale*, 137.
76 Catherine Clément, *La Syncope. Philosophie du ravissement* (Paris: Grasset, 1990).
77 Gérard Genette, 'Silences de Flaubert', in *Figures 1* (Paris: Éditions du Seuil [Points], 1966), 234.
78 Desmaret 'Épileptiques'; Pasetti, 'Hallucinations et création littéraire chez Flaubert', *Revue Flaubert* 12 (2012), available at flaubert.univ.-rouen.fr/revue/article.php?id=103. An early study was that of John C. Lapp, 'Art and Hallucination in Flaubert', *French Studies* 10, 4 (October 1956): 322–34. He concluded that hallucinatory symptoms had been sublimated in Flaubert's style. In Marshall Olds' 'Hallucination and Point of View in *La Tentation de Saint Antoine*', *Nineteenth-Century French Studies*, 17, 1 (Fall–Winter 1998): 170–85, hallucinations are seen as a structuring device in that novel.
79 Flaubert, *Madame Bovary*, Claudine Gothot-Mersch, ed. (Paris: Garnier, 1971), 319–20.
80 *Salammbô*, 274.
81 Desmaret's article 'Épileptiques' provides a rich bibliography on psychoanalytical approaches to Flaubert. See also her *Bizarreries*. Pasetti's bibliography is also wide ranging and informative. She refers to a number of recent medical studies examining Flaubert and hallucination.
82 Desmaret, 'Épileptiques', 5; *Salammbô*, 386 and note.
83 Genette, 'Silences', 232. Genette gives similar examples from *Smarrh* and *Voyage en Corse*.
84 Sartre, *L'Idiot*, vol. 3, 1857.
85 See, for example, Michel Weber, 'L'Épilepsie', 159.

3 Maupassant, Charcot and the Paranormal

1 See Carroy, *Hypnose*, 58.

2 Roudinesco, *Histoire*, 76–84.

3 Quoted from the article 'Une Femme' by Roudinesco, *Histoire*, 76. References to Maupassant's short fiction are to Maupassant, *Contes et nouvelles*, 2 vols., Louis Forestier, ed. (Paris: Gallimard [Pléiade], 1985), but references to the two versions of *Le Horla* are to Maupassant, *Le Horla et autres récits fantastiques*, Mariane Bury, ed. (Paris: Librairie Générale Française/Livre de Poche Classique, 2004).

4 Alexandre Hepp, *Paris-Patraque* (Paris: Dentu, 1884).

5 'Magnétisme' was published in *Gil Blas* on 5 April 1882.

6 Cf. Flaubert's comment to George Sand, mentioned earlier, that even though a man, he is a hysteric and suffers from all the usual symptoms: 'j'ai reconnu tous les symptômes. J'ai la boule, et le clou, à l'occiput' (Corr. 3, 591–92). ('I recognized all the symptoms. I have the ball in the throat, and the feeling of a nail in the back of the head.')

7 From a column entitled 'Les Clientes du docteur' published 22 October 1890 in *L'Écho de Paris*. See Jean Lorrain, *Une Femme par jour*, Michel Desbrouères, ed. (Paris: Christian Pirot, 1983), 139.

8 Marlo Johnston is the latest to indicate such surprise in her *Guy de Maupassant*, 691. Caution on these dates is also expressed in the monumental *Bibliographie des écrivains français. Guy de Maupassant*, Noëlle Benhamou et al., eds. (Rome: Memini, 2008), vol. 2, 717, item 7460. Élisabeth Roudinesco asserts without supporting evidence that Maupassant attended Charcot's demonstrations in 1884–86 (*Histoire*, 78); Pierre Bayard opts rather for 1883–86 (*Maupassant juste avant Freud*), 11; Charcot's biographer Jean Thuillier appears to suggest that Maupassant began visiting La Salpêtrière in 1882 (*Monsieur Charcot*, 164) and says that it was at the beginning of 1888 that Charcot had Maupassant banished from attendance at his lessons (ibid., 239).

9 Bertrand Marquer (*Les Romans*, 83, note 205) refers readers to Léon Daudet, *Souvenirs des milieux littéraires, politiques, artistiques et médicales* (Paris: Nouvelle Librairie Nationale, 1920), vol. 1, 26–28; vol. 2, 39–40, for Maupassant's contacts with Charcot, but Daudet's text does not support the claim that there were such contacts.

10 Axel Munthe, *The Story of San Michele* (London: John Murray, 1955), 200. Munthe, born 31 October 1857, defended his French medical thesis, 'Prophylaxie et traitement des hémorragies post-partum', in August 1880. Charcot and Charles Richet were members of his thesis committee.

11 The consultation is mentioned in a letter to Joseph Primoli. See Johnston, *Guy de Maupassant*, 613.

12 Roudinesco, *Histoire*, 76.

13 *Le Horla*, Bury, 272.

14 Hippolyte Bernheim authored the following three studies on suggestion: *De la suggestion dans l'état hypnotique et dans l'état de veille* (Paris: Doin, 1884), *De la*

suggestion et de ses applications à la thérapeutique (Paris: Doin, 1886), and *Hypnotisme, suggestion, psychothérapie. Études nouvelles* (Paris: Doin, 1891).

15 See, for example, Jules Liégeois, 'Hypnotisme téléphonique. Suggestion à grande distance', in *Mémoire de l'Académie Stanislas* (Nancy: 1885): 133–42.

16 It is Mariane Bury who suggests the Braid connection in her edition of *Le Horla*, 272, note 2.

17 See his column 'La Vie à Paris' in *Le Temps*, 22 March 1881; the article is in part a promotional vehicle for his novel about La Salpêtrière, *Les Amours d'un interne* (Paris: Dentu, 1881), in which certain medical trainees hypnotize women and then revel in the control they can exercise.

18 Ernest Cavailhon, *La Fascination magnétique* (Paris: Dentu, 1882), 31–32.

19 See Paul Ladame, 'Hypnotisme et médecine légale', *Revue de l'Hypnotisme Expérimental et Thérapeutique* 1 (1887): 10–19 (16).

20 See Paul Copin, 'Le Magnétisme et l'hypnotisme dans le roman', *Revue de l'Hypnotisme Expérimental et Thérapeutique* 1 (1887): 313–16, and Copin, 'Un Roman de M. Alphonse [*sic*] Belot: *Alphonsine*', *Revue de l'Hypnotisme Expérimental et Thérapeutique* 2 (1888): 202–8.

21 Copin, 'L'Hypnotisme au Salon de 1887', *Revue de l'Hypnotisme Expérimental et Thérapeutique* 1 (1887): 373–75.

22 See Richet, 'Du somnambulisme provoqué', 348–78.

23 Richet's *À la recherche du bonheur* (1879) features a young woman who reads minds and Lucien/Lucius, an individual with a dual personality. His novella *Soeur Marthe* (1890) is also concerned with mind-reading and dualities.

24 Most sources list Charles Richet's *Possession* as published in 1887 (Paris: Ollendorff), no doubt because the copy held by the Bibliothèque nationale de France is dated 1887, but that copy is a second edition. Paul Ginisty reviewed *Possession* in *Gil Blas* of 16 November 1886; see Ginisty, *L'Année littéraire 1986* (Paris: Charpentier, 1887), 319. It was also reviewed by Ad. Badin in *La Nouvelle Revue* 48, 3 (1 December 1886): 670.

25 Richet, *Possession*, 97.

26 Dostoyevsky, *Les Possédés*, 2 vols. (Paris: Plon-Nourrit, 1886).

27 Camille Lemonnier, *L'Hystérique* (Paris: Charpentier, 1885).

28 *Soeur Jeanne des Anges, supérieure des Ursulines de Loudun (XVIIe siècle): autobiographie d'une hystérique possédée*, Gabriel Légué and Georges Gilles de la Tourette, eds. (Paris: Delahaye & Lecrosnier, 1886). The work, published in the final months of 1886, was reviewed by Paul Ginisty in *Gil Blas* on 11 January 1887. See Ginisty, *L'Année littéraire 1887* (Paris: Charpentier 1888), 7.

29 Lisa Downing, 'Gendered Constructions of the Nightmare in French Nineteenth-Century Medical Writing and Fantastic Fiction', *French Studies* 66, 3 (2012): 331–46 (334). The article is focused on French literature of the Romantic period and does not discuss Maupassant.

30 Pierre Janet, 'Notes sur quelques phénomènes de somnambulisme', *Revue Philosophique* 21 (February 1886): 190–98 (198). See also Janet, 'Deuxième note sur le sommeil provoqué à distance et la suggestion mentale pendant l'état somnambulique', *Revue Philosophique* 22 (July–December 1886): 212–23.

31 Julian Ochorowicz, *De la suggestion mentale* (Paris: Doin, 1887), 133.
32 Dr J. Renaut, 'L'Hypnotisme', *Les Lettres et les Arts* (August 1886): 160–76.
33 Active *magnétiseurs* often had an exotic, foreign origin: Hansen was Danish, Wells Hungarian, Onoffrov an Italian with a Slavic-sounding name, and both Donato and Pickmann were Belgian. See Fernand Bottey, *Le 'Magnétisme animal'. Étude critique et expérimental sur l'hypnotisme ou sommeil nerveux provoqués chez les sujets sains* (Paris: Plon-Nourrit, 1884), 259. For a general review of the magnetism craze, see Michael R. Finn, *Hysteria, Hypnotism, the Spirits and Pornograpy: Fin-de-Siècle Cultural Discourses in the Decadent Rachilde* (Newark: University of Delaware Press, 2009), 94–118.
34 See Léon Tétard, 'La Fascination et l'hypnotisme', *Revue de l'Hypnotisme* 1 (1887): 250.
35 Maupassant, 'Magnétisme', *Contes et nouvelles*, vol. 1, 406.
36 The Belgian-born Jean-Lambert Pickmann apparently began his career as an illusionist under the name Alberti. He later switched to the name Pickman and eventually Pickmann.
37 Article signed only R., 'Pickmann et Donato à Marseille', *La Vie Posthume*, 2e année, no. 10 (April 1887): 226–32. Writing in the same month that *Le Horla* (1887) is appearing, the writer R. seems well informed about thought transmission, mentioning the experiments of medical hypnotists such as Henri Beaunis, Paul Richer and Pierre Janet.
38 Jean Lorrain, *L'Événement* (19 August 1889), quoted by Georges Normandy, *Guy de Maupassant. Recueil de morceaux choisis. Anthologie des auteurs modernes V* (Paris: Méricant [1913]), 44.
39 Santillane, 'La Peur de l'invisible', *Gil Blas*, 11 November 1901, p. 1.
40 Cited by Marlo Johnston, *Guy de Maupassant*, 717.
41 Maupassant, 'Aux bains de mer', *Gil Blas*, 6 September 1887.
42 Gabriel Delanne, *Le Phénomène spirite*, 5th edn (Paris: Chamuel, 1897), 92.
43 Santillane, 'La Peur de l'invisible', p. 1.
44 Letter of a Dr Charles Dont, cited by Johnston, *Guy de Maupassant*, 719–20. Donato's real name was d'Hont: was the supportive Dr Dont the *magnétiseur* himself, or possibly a relative? Dr Dont seems to have been right about Pickmann, who exulted with friends about how easy it was to pull the wool over the eyes of men of science. He ridiculed the credulousness of Lombroso, and also admitted that he had tricked Charles Richet into believing that he could identify cards pulled from a deck after he had been isolated in an adjoining room. See Sofie Lachapelle, *Investigating the Supernatural: From Spiritism and Occultism to Psychical Research and Metapsychics in France, 1853–1931* (Baltimore: Johns Hopkins University Press, 2011), 110–11.
45 Bourget, *Études et portraits III. Sociologie et littérature* (Paris: Plon, 1906), vol. 3, 318.
46 'Aux bains de mer.'
47 From Flammarion's introduction to Félix Fabart, *Histoire philosophique et politique de l'occulte, magie, sorcellerie, spiritisme* (Paris: Marpon and Flammarion, 1885), ix.
48 Joris-Karl Huysmans, *Là-bas* (Paris: Garnier-Flammarion, 1978), 199–200.

49 See Nadine Satiat, *Maupassant* (Paris: Flammarion, 2003), 409.
50 Flammarion also wrote a trio of turgid novels – *Lumen, Uranie* and *Stella* – that might be characterized as spiritualist science fiction.
51 See Eugen Weber, *France, Fin de Siècle*, 236.
52 Richet, preface to Edmund Gurney, Frederic Myers, and Frank Podmore, *Les Hallucinations télépathiques*, trans. of *Phantasms of the Living* by Léon Marillier (Paris: Alcan, 1892 [1890]), 2nd edn, p. x.
53 Paul Bourget, *L'Irréparable. Deuxième amour. Céline Lacoste. Jean Maquenem*, Édn définitive (Paris: Plon, 1901), 4.
54 Article 'Les Subtils', *Gil Blas*, 3 June 1884.
55 'Aux bains de mer'.
56 Léon Chapron, lawyer, journalist at *L'Événement* and author of *Les Coins de Paris* (Paris: Dentu, 1881) died on 17 May 1884. See Johnston, *Guy de Maupassant*, 519–21.
57 Bourget, *Études et portraits III*, vol. 3, 318. Another confidence Maupassant made, supposedly in 1885, underlines again the early nature of his problems. In an article by Mme X . . ., 'Guy de Maupassant intime', *La Grande Revue*, 25 October 1912, Maupassant is described as losing his notion of self if he fixes his gaze for too long on his image in a mirror. See Bernard Pingaud's edition of Maupassant's *Pierre et Jean* (Paris: Gallimard, 1982), 31.
58 Paul Sollier, *Les Phénomènes d'autoscopie* (Paris: Alcan, 1903).
59 Ibid., 10–11, 31.
60 Munthe, *The Story of San Michele*, 201–2.
61 There is no suggestion of a date for these episodes. See Gisèle d'Estoc, *Cahier d'amour* (Paris: Arléa, 1997), 38.
62 Léon Hennique, *Un Caractère* (Paris: Crès, 1923).
63 See Jean-Louis Cabanès, *Le Corps et la maladie*, vol. 2, 118. Bernard Pingaud also sees the fear of loss of identity in Maupassant as a 'dépossession' in his edition of *Pierre et Jean*, 32.
64 Sandra Janssen, 'L'Inquiétante étrangeté', 198, note 9.
65 Text quoted by Janssen (ibid., 196, note 5) from Maupassant, *La Vie errante*.
66 Janssen, 'L'Inquiétante étrangeté', 200, quoting Ribot, *Les Maladies de la personnalité*, 113.
67 Pierre Bayard, *Maupassant juste avant Freud*, 19. I will continue, in spite of Bayard's admonition, to use the term 'unconscious' in a most general sense: it is the idea that certain fundamental workings of thought proceed in their own logic in the absence of our knowledge.
68 Ibid., 54.
69 Roudinesco, *Histoire*, 76.

4 The Unconscious Female/The Female Unconscious

1 From a book review by Raymond Ryckère, '*La Femme criminelle et la prostituée* par C. Lombroso et G. Ferrero', *Archives de l'Anthropologie Criminelle* (1897): 301–21 (307).

2 Andreas Huyssen, *After the Great Divide: Modernism, Mass Culture, Postmodernism* (Bloomington: Indiana University Press, 1986), 52.
3 Cabanès, *Le Corps et la maladie*, vol. 1, 325.
4 Ibid., 326.
5 For much more detail on the focus in fiction on women's 'sickness', 'wounds' and natural functions, see Cabanès, vol. 1, chapter 3, 'Clichés physiologiques et représentations littéraires de la femme', 307–85, and Jacques Noiray, *Le Romancier et la machine. L'image de la machine dans le roman français 1850–1909* (Paris: José Corti, 1981).
6 Nizet, *Suggestion*, 83.
7 See, in Mireille Dottin-Orsini, *Cette Femme qu'ils disent fatale* (Paris: Grasset, 1993), chapter 4, whose subheadings are 'L'Automate, la locomotive, la dame en cire' and 'casser la poupée', 92–112.
8 Most of my examples here come from Noiray, *Le Romancier*, vol. 1, 398–404. See also, in vol. 2 (pp. 243–379), his study of the machine in Villiers de l'Isle-Adam's, *L'Ève future*.
9 Mark Micale, *Approaching Hysteria*, 67.
10 Henri Thulié, *La Femme*. See the critique of his volume in *Revue Philosophique* (November 1885): 538–40.
11 Pierre Bourdieu, *La Domination masculine* (Paris: Seuil, 1998), 21. Bourdieu refers admiringly to Yvonne Knibiehler's article, 'Les Médecins et la 'nature féminine' au temps du Code civil', *Annales. Économies, Sociétés, Civilisations* 31, 4 (1976): 824–45.
12 Pierre-Joseph Proudhon, *De la justice dans la révolution et dans l'église* (Paris: Garnier, 1858), vol. 3, 339.
13 See Micale's reference to this idea, *Approaching Hysteria*, 69, note 1.
14 From an article by Marcel Prévost, 'Le Féminisme', in Victor du Bled et al., eds., *La Femme dans la nature, dans les moeurs, dans la légende, dans la société: tableau de son évolution physique & psychique* (Paris: Bong et Cie., 1908), 4, 323.
15 Sylvain Maréchal, *Projet d'une loi portant défense de lire aux femmes* (Paris: Massé, 1801). References in my text are to the edition by L'Harmattan, 2007, prefaced and annotated by Bernard Jolibert.
16 For an overview of the many early publications that appeared on the subject, see Jolibert's preface, ibid., especially 13–22. A detailed discussion of the debates about education for women, female intellectual powers and the female soul in the late eighteenth and first half of the nineteenth century is available in Geneviève Fraisse, *Muse de la raison. La démocratie exclusive et la différence des sexes* (Aix-en-Provence: Alinéa, 1989).
17 Quoted by Maréchal (96) from François de Callières, *Du Bel Esprit, où sont examinés les sentiments qu'on a d'ordinaire dans le monde* (Paris: J. Anisson, 1695).
18 Evelyne Ender, *Sexing the Mind*, 30. The first chapter of *Sexing the Mind*, 25–65, is a striking account of how female physical weakness was projected onto woman's intellectual abilities. Rachel Mesch also offers a concentrated and carefully referenced summary of the debilitating medico-scientific

discourse that faced female writers of the fin de siècle. See Mesch, *The Hysteric's Revenge: French Women Writers at the Fin de Siècle* (Nashville: Vanderbilt University Press, 2006), 1–24.

19 'Sans vouloir manquer ici de galanterie, je ferai remarquer que la plupart des traits de ce caractère des hystériques ne sont que l'exagération du caractère de la femme. On arrive ainsi à concevoir l'hystérie comme l'exagération du tempérament féminin, *le tempérament féminin devenu névrose*', from the definition of hysteria in *Dictionnaire encyclopédique des sciences médicales*, 4th series, 14 (1889), 331. ('Without wishing to show any lack of gallantry, I would point out that most character traits of hysterics are simply exaggerations of the female character. Thus we arrive at the idea that hysteria is the exaggeration of the female temperament, *the female temperament become neurosis.*')

20 Briquet, *Traité clinique et thérapeutique de l'hystérie*, 50; Ender, *Sexing the Mind*, 37.

21 Claude Burdin and Frédéric Dubois, *Histoire académique du magnétisme animal* (Paris: Baillière, 1846), 92.

22 Brachet, *Traité de l'hystérie*, 68.

23 André Armengaud, *La Population française au XIXe siècle* (Paris: Presses Universitaires de France, 1976), 51. Karen Offen shows how German and English population growth far surpassed French figures during this same period, in 'Depopulation, Nationalism and Feminism in Fin-de-Siècle France', *American Historical Review* 89, 3 (1984): 648–76 (652). See also my article 'Female Sterilization and Artificial Insemination in Fin-de-Siècle France: Facts and Fictions', *Nineteenth-Century French Studies* 39, 3–4 (Spring/Summer 2011): 315–31.

24 See novels such as Jane de La Vaudère, *Les Demi-sexes* (Paris: Ollendorff, 1897), and Armand Dubarry, *Les Femmes eunuques* (Paris: Chamuel, 1899).

25 Charles Livon , *Manuel de vivisections* (Paris: Baillière, 1882).

26 Charles Richet, 'Le Roi des animaux', *Revue des Deux Mondes* 55 (15 February 1883): 817–56 (835).

27 Henri Kleffler, *Les Missions 'humanitaires' des dames anglaises sur le continent. La vivisection, son utilité, sa morale, réponse à la campagne antivivisectionniste de Mme le Dr Anna Kingsford* (Geneva: H. Georg, 1883), 8.

28 Jean-Marie Guyau, *Éducation et hérédité. Étude sociologique* (Paris: Alcan, 1889).

29 J.-P. Dartigues, *De l'amour expérimental ou des causes d'adultère chez la femme au XIXe siècle. Étude d'hygiène et d'économie sociale résultant de l'ignorance, du libertinage et des fraudes dans l'accomplissement des devoirs conjugaux* (Versailles: A. Litzelmann, 1887).

30 Quoted by Jacques Lourbet, *La Femme devant la science contemporaine* (Paris: Alcan, 1896), 120.

31 Fraisse, *Muse de la raison*, 95. See also her remarks on Cabanis and Virey in *La Raison des femmes* (Paris: Plon, 1992), 74–87.

32 Clarke, *Sex in Education.*

33 See Julia Ward Howe, *Sex and Education: A Reply to Dr E. H. Clarke's 'Sex in Education'* (New York: Arno Press, 1972 [1874]).

34 See Bram Dijkstra, *Idols of Perversity: Fantasies of Feminine Evil in Fin-de-Siècle Culture* (Oxford: Oxford University Press, 1986), 160–74.

35 See T. S. Gray's article, 'Herbert Spencer on Women: A Study in Personal and Political Disillusionment', *International Journal of Women's Studies* 7, 3 (1984): 217–31.

36 Otto Weininger, *Sex and Character: An Investigation of Fundamental Principles*, trans. Ladislaus Löb (Bloomington: Indiana University Press, 2005), 90.

37 Alfred Fouillée, 'La Psychologie des sexes', 407.

38 Julie Fette discusses the access of women to the French legal and medical professions in the 1880–1900 period in 'Pride and Prejudice in the Professions: Women Doctors and Lawyers in Third Republic France', *Journal of Women's History* 19, 3 (2007): 60–86, especially 64–67, as does Juliette M. Rogers in *Career Stories: Belle Époque Novels of Professional Development* (University Park: Pennsylvania State University Press, 2007), especially 35–37. Rogers says that both Augusta Klumpke and Blanche Edwards became Paris hospital interns (114, note 3), while Fette states that Edwards was never accepted for an internship (66).

39 It was Mme Céline Renooz, editor of *La Revue Scientifique des Femmes*, who recorded these insulting remarks by Charcot. See 'Charcot dévoilé', *La Revue Scientifique des Femmes* (December 1888): 241–47, and 'Les Nouvelles Doctoresses', *La Revue Scientifique des Femmes* (January 1889): 28–29.

40 Sandra Horvath-Peterson, *Victor Duruy and French Education: Liberal Reform in the Second Empire* (Baton Rouge: Louisiana State University Press, 1984), 39.

41 Ibid., 95.

42 See Bernard Jolibert's preface to Maréchal, *Projet d'une loi* (69), which refers to Françoise Mayeur, *L'Éducation des filles en France au XIXe siècle* (Paris: Hachette, 1979).

43 Olympe Audouard, *M. Barbey d'Aurevilly. Réponse à ses réquisitoires contre les Bas-bleus. Conférence du 11 avril* (Paris: Dentu, 1870), 25–26.

44 Camille Delaville, 'Bacheliers, crétins et filles savantes', *Le Passant* (27 July 1882).

45 Charles Sowerwine, 'Woman's Brain, Man's Brain: Feminism and Anthropology in Late Nineteenth-Century France', *Women's History Review* 12, 2 (2003): 289–307 (290).

46 Ibid., 300–301.

47 For more information on Pascal, see Felicia Gordon, 'French Psychiatry and the New Woman: The Case of Dr Constance Pascal, 1877–1937', *History of Psychiatry* 17, 2 (June 2006): 159–82.

48 Gaston Richard, review of *La Femme devant la science contemporaine*, *Revue Philosophique* (1897): 434–35.

49 Marcel Prévost, 'Le Féminisme', 325.

50 Georges de Peyrebrune, *Une Décadente* (Paris: Frinzine, 1886).

51 For information on Peyrebrune, see Jean-Paul Socard, *Georges de Peyrebrune. Itinéraire d'une femme de lettres, du Périgord à Paris* (Périgueux: ARKA, 2011), and Camille Delaville, *Mes Contemporaines* (Paris: Sévin, 1887).

52 These letters, edited and introduced by Nelly Sanchez, were published in 2010 on-line at www.ccji.cnrs.fr/.

53 It must be pointed out that at the time Adam founded *La Nouvelle Revue*, she was married to the *préfet de police* of Paris: the range of political topics open to her must have felt fairly narrow. On the other hand, she was a lifelong commentator on foreign policy. See Marie-France Hilgar, 'Juliette Adam et la *Nouvelle Revue*', *Rocky Mountain Review of Language and Literature* 51, 2 (1997): 11–18.

54 Roudinesco, *Histoire,* 48.

55 Julia Daudet, *Quand Odile saura lire* (Paris: Crès, 1919), 49.

56 The 28 June 1881 letter of refusal from Adam is held by the Bibliothèque Municipale de Périgueux in its Georges de Peyrebrune archive. Peyrebrune quotes it almost word for word, attributing it to a Mme X, in her novel *Le Roman d'un bas bleu* (Paris: Ollendorff, 1892), 170.

57 See Lesueur, *L'Évolution féminine, ses résultats économiques* (Paris: Lemerre, 1905).

58 Diana Holmes, 'Daniel Lesueur and the Feminist Romance', in *A Belle Époque? Women in French Society and Culture 1890–1914*, Diana Holmes and Carrie Tarr, eds. (New York: Berghahn, 2006), 197–210 (203).

59 *Névrosée* (Paris: Lemerre, 1890). For other female education novels of the period, see Juliette M. Rogers, *Career Stories*, chapter 3, 'Dreams and Disappointments: Women's Education Novels'.

60 The idea of the inferiority of non-European brains was difficult to root out. See Martin S. Staum's wonderfully documented article, 'Ribot, Binet, and the Emergence from the Anthropological Shadow', *Journal of the History of the Behavioural Sciences* 43, 1 (Winter 2007): 1–18.

61 Ryckère, '*La Femme criminelle et la prostituée*', 307.

62 See Michel Pierssens, 'Bas-bleus anonymes: le combat perdu d'Albert Cim', in *Les Romans à clef, Troisième colloque des Invalides*, 3 December 1999 (Tusson: Du Lérot, 2000), 97–103.

63 According to Hepp, *Paris-Patraque*, 19.

64 Gen Doy, *Drapery: Classicism and Barbarism in Visual Culture* (London: I. B. Tauris, 2002), 263, note 84.

65 For a useful discussion of Déga's thesis, see Jacqueline Carroy, 'Le Noviciat de l'hystérie selon *Georgette Déga*', *Psychanalyse à l'Université* 12, 45 (January 1987): 141–52.

66 Hepp, *Paris-Patraque*, 19.

67 Maurice de Fleury, *Introduction à la médecine de l'esprit* (Paris: Alcan, 1897).

68 One reviewer of Fleury's volume found it unreliable and unanalyzable; Fleury was a dilettante: 'Il incarne le journaliste contemporain, ami de tout le monde, informé de toutes choses, incapable d'autonomie intellectuelle et de systématisation philosophique. Médecine, philosophie, littérature, il a tout lu.' ('He is the very incarnation of today's journalist, everyone's friend, knowledgeable about everything, incapable of intellectual autonomy and systematic thinking. Medicine, philosophy, literature, he has read it all.') *Revue de Métaphysique et de Morale*, supplement to September 1897 issue, 8.

69 See the section 'L' Éducation des filles' in Remy de Gourmont, *Sixtine: roman de la vie cérébrale* (Paris: Savine, 1890), 224–25.
70 Rachilde, *Son printemps* (Paris: Mercure de France, 1912), 47.
71 Introduction to her novel *À mort* (Paris: Monnier, 1886), xviii.
72 See Auriant, *Souvenirs sur Madame Rachilde* (À l'Écart, 1889), 31.
73 Rachilde, *Le Mordu* (Paris: Brossier, 1889), 28.
74 Rachilde, *Le Grand Saigneur* (Paris: Flammarion, 1922), 149.
75 See Charles Lasègue, 'Les Cérébraux', in *Études médicales* (Paris: Asselin, 1884), vol. 1, 567–84. Dr Auguste Motet published the story of a fifteen-year-old boy who became an exhibitionist after incurring head injuries in a fall from a horse. See Motet's article 'Outrage à la pudeur', *Annales d'Hygiène Publique et de Médecine Légale* 15 (1886): 202–13.
76 Unpublished manuscript variant from the chapter 'Maurice Barrès, l'immortelle province', in Rachilde's *Portraits d'hommes*, Bibliothèque Municipale de Périgueux. It may be characteristic of Rachilde's diffidence regarding all-out support of women that she did not include this line in *Portraits d'homme.*
77 *Rachilde – Maurice Barrès. Correspondance inédite 1885–1914*, Michael R. Finn, ed. (Brest: Centre d'Étude des Correspondances et Journaux intimes/CNRS, 2002/10), 76.
78 'La Joie d'aimer', ibid., 149.
79 Rachilde, *Pourquoi je ne suis pas féministe*, 10.
80 Rachilde, *Le Dessous* (Paris: Mercure de France, 1904), 13.
81 Rachilde documents, ms. 27433, Fonds Littéraire Jacques Doucet, Paris. It is not without significance that these lines date from a response to a literary questionnaire of 1896, the year Rachilde published *La Princesse des ténèbres*, a novel devoted to the idea of possession.
82 Chabaneix, *Le Subconscient*, 49.
83 See Bourdieu, *La Domination masculine*, 39–48. Bourdieu's idea of corporal dispositions is most interesting, although it goes beyond my discussion here. He argues that such dispositions take an emotional form – shame, humiliation, timidity, anxiety, passion, etc. – and that they can show up in blushing, verbal hesitancy, awkwardness or impotent anger, *all these being signs of submission itself.*

5 Hypnotism, Dual Personalities and the Popular Novel

1 Stubbs, 'Hypnotisme et automatisme', 275.
2 Jules Liégeois, *De la suggestion hypnotique*, 70.
3 Henri Beaunis, 'L'Expérimentation en psychologie par le somnambulisme provoqué', *Revue Philosophique* 20 (July–December 1885): 1.
4 Quoted by Edgar Bérillon in *Histoire de l'hypnotisme expérimental* (Paris: Vigot, 1902), 13.
5 See my article, 'Dogs and Females: Vivisection, Feminists and the Novelist Rachilde', *French Cultural Studies* 23, 3 (August 2012): 190–201. For Bourget's use of the term vivisection, see *Le Disciple*, Antoine Compagnon, ed. (Paris: Librairie Générale Française/Livre de Poche Classique, 2010), 203–4, 224.

6 The story of Delboeuf's visit has been republished in an article by Serge Nicolas, 'L'École de la Salpêtrière en 1885', *Psychologie et Histoire* 1 (2000): 165–207. See also Sofia Kovalevskaya, 'Hypnotism and Medicine in 1888 Paris: Contemporary Observations', trans. Sabine I. Gölz and Oleg V. Timofeyev, *SubStance* 79 (1996): 3–23.
7 There were, as noted previously, à propos of Maupassant, quite a few 'magnétiseurs' active around 1880, many known under just one name: the Dane Hansen; an Italian who had given himself the name Onoffrof; Léon (probably Belgian); Welles, a Hungarian; Henri Delaage (French) and of course Donato and Pickmann.
8 Kovalevskaya, 'Hypnotism and Medicine in 1888 Paris', 16.
9 See in Beaunis, *Le Somnambulisme provoqué* (Paris: Baillière, 1886), the section 'Suggestion à 172 jours d'intervalle', 233–35.
10 Jean-Louis Cabanès, 'Psychologie, histoire, esthétique: les hallucinations à l'entrecroisement des discours', in *Image et pathologie au XIXe siècle, Cahiers de littérature française* VI (Paris: L'Harmattan, 2008), 7–26 (8).
11 Dr Charles Richet may in fact have been the first doctor to have demonstrated 'experimental crimes' committed under posthypnotic suggestion. See Alfred Binet and Charles Féré, *Le Magnétisme animal* (Paris: Alcan, 1887), 280.
12 Claretie, 'La Vie à Paris', *Le Temps*, 22 March 1881.
13 Claretie, 'La Vie à Paris', *Le Temps*, 11 July 1884.
14 Liégeois, *De la suggestion hypnotique.*
15 In his much expanded study, *De la suggestion et du somnambulisme*, his appendix 2 reviews the question of telephone hypnotism.
16 Kovalevskaya, 'Hypnotism and Medicine in 1888 Paris', 9–10.
17 Marc Renneville, *Crime et folie. Deux siècles d'enquêtes médicales et judiciaires* (Paris: Fayard, 2003).
18 Barrès, *Journal de ma vie extérieure*, François Broche and Eric Roussel, eds. (Paris: Julliard, 1994), 354. Original article in *La Vie Moderne*, 20 June 1885.
19 Maurice Barrès, 'La Sensibilité d'Henri Chambige', *Le Figaro*, 11 November 1888, p. 1; Anatole France, 'Un Crime littéraire. L'affaire Chambige', *Le Temps*, 11 November 1888, p. 1.
20 See the extremely interesting article by Jacqueline Carroy and Marc Renneville on Tarde's position in the case, 'Une Cause passionnelle passionnante: Tarde et l'affaire Chambige (1889)', *Champ Pénal*, 34th Congrès Français de Criminologie, available at http://champpenal.revues.org/260.
21 Gabriel Tarde, 'L'Affaire Chambige', *Archives de l'Anthropologie Criminelle* (1889): 94.
22 See, among others, Pierre Drachline, *Le Crime de Pantin. L'Affaire Troppmann* (Paris: Denoël, 1984), and Véronique Gramfort, 'Les Crimes de Pantin: quand Troppmann défrayait la chronique', *Romantisme* 27 (1997): 17–30.
23 See the preface by Charles Virmaître to *Mémoires secrets de Troppmann* (Paris: Duquesne, 1870), 16, and also Michelle Perrot's excerpt of Paris police *préfet* Claude's remarks on Troppmann's hand in *Les Ombres de l'histoire. Crime et châtiment au XIXe siècle* (Paris: Flammarion, 2001), 287–88.

24 See Alexandre Lacassagne's study, *Vacher l'éventreur et les crimes sadiques* (Lyon: Storck; Paris: Masson, 1899).

25 The expression appears in Bernheim's article 'Hypnotisme et suggestion' on page one of the *Supplément* to the 29 January 1891 edition of *Le Temps*, where it had a major public impact. Pierre-Henri Castel notes that the expression also appeared earlier in Bernheim's *Hypnotisme, suggestion, psychothérapie, études nouvelle*. See Castel, *Querelle*, 54 and note 2.

26 Reported by Dr Émile Laurent in *Les Suggestions criminelles* (Paris: Société des Éditions Scientifiques, 1891), 10.

27 Binet and Féré, *Le Magnétisme animal*, 279. Serge Nicolas has dissected the Bompard/Eyraud affair in some detail in *L'Hypnose: Charcot face à Bernheim. L'école de la Salpêtrière et l'école de Nancy* (Paris: L'Harmattan, 2004), esp. 121–32. Georges Gilles de la Tourette provided his own triumphalist summary of the Bompard affair in *L'Épilogue d'un procès célèbre* (Paris: Lecrosnier and Babé, 1891).

28 Castel, *Querelle*, 217, citing Hippolyte Bernheim, *Hypnotisme, suggestion, psychothérapie*, 199.

29 Most of these details are taken from the final report of Brouardel, Motet and Ballet, which is reprinted in Alexandre Lacassagne, *L'Affaire Gouffé* (Lyon: Storck; Paris: Masson, 1891), 67–83.

30 Paul-Émile Garnier, *L'Automatisme somnambulique*, 12.

31 Ibid. 20–21.

32 See the article by Adrien Proust, 'Cas curieux d'automatisme ambulatoire chez un hystérique', *La Tribune Médicale* 13, *Bulletin Hebdomadaire* (27 March 1890): 202–3.

33 Lacassagne, *L'Affaire Gouffé*, 80.

34 See Féré and Binet, 'Hypnotisme et responsabilité', *Revue Philosophique* 19 (January–June 1885): 265–79.

35 Pierre-Henri Castel observes incorrectly that Bompard was acquitted (*Querelle*, 219).

36 See Julien Bogousslavsky, Olivier Walusinski and Denis Veyrunes, 'Crime, Hysteria and *Belle Époque* Hypnotism: The Path Traced by Jean-Martin Charcot and Georges Gilles de la Tourette', *European Neurology* 62 (2009): 193–99. It is these authors who mention the intervention of Dr Jules Voisin in the case; they are also convinced that the three-doctor panel was intent on protecting the position of La Salpêtrière that no crime except rape, and especially not murder, could be the consequence of hypnotism.

37 Gilles de la Tourette, *L'Épilogue d'un procès célèbre*, 3.

38 See the introduction by Sophie Spandonis to the reedition of Alfred Vallette and Raoul Minhar's novel, *À l'écart* (Paris: Champion, 2004).

39 Bertrand Marquer, in part two of his *Les Romans de la Salpêtrière* (pp. 159–287), deals with some of the hysteria-inspired novels that I discuss in this chapter.

40 Edmond de Goncourt, *La Faustin* (Paris: Charpentier, 1882), 53.

41 For a useful discussion of *La Faustin*, see Sylvie Thorel-Cailleteau, *La Tentation du livre sur rien. Naturalisme et décadence* (Mont-de-Marsan: Éditions Interuniversitaires, 1994), 203–11.

42 Jules Claretie, *Jean Mornas* (Paris: Dentu, 1885), and Adolphe Belot, *Alphonsine* (Paris: Dentu, 1887).
43 Cited by Ladame, 'L'Hypnotisme et la médecine légale', 15.
44 Copin, 'Un Roman de M. Alphonse [*sic*] Belot'.
45 Jules Claretie, *L'Obsession (Moi et l'autre)* (Paris: Pierre Lafitte, 1909).
46 Henri Bourru and Ferdinand Burot, *Variations de la personnalité* (Paris: Baillière, 1888). Though this study of multiple personality did not attract as much interest as the famous case of Félida, it did attract much medical attention.
47 Simon Boubée, *Main-de-cire* (Paris: Piaget, 1888).
48 The misshapen assassin's hand appears in Rachilde's *Nono* and *La Marquise de Sade*, in Jean Lorrain's *Monsieur Phocas* and in Paul Bonnetain's last novel, *L'Impasse*.
49 Frédéric Soulié, *Le Magnétiseur*, 2 vols. (Paris: Dumont, 1834).
50 Kovalevskaya, 'Hypnotism and Medicine in 1888 Paris', 21.
51 E. . . T. . ., *L'Écuyer magnétiseur* (Paris and Limoges: Henri-Charles-La Vauzelle, Éditeur Militaire, 1887.)
52 Charles Epheyre, *À la recherche du bonheur* (Paris: Ollendorff, 1879).
53 Georges Maldague, *La Magnétisée* (Paris: Dentu, 1885).
54 Originally published in *La Revue des Deux Mondes* (15 March 1887, 241–302) under the title 'Le Palimpseste', then later in volume form (Paris: Perrin, 1887; second edition, Paris: Armand Colin, 1894). My discussion of the text owes much to Stubbs, 'Hypnotisme et automatisme', 276–77. Anatole France analyzed the story in a column titled 'L'Hypnotisme dans la littérature', *Le Temps* (24 April 1887), later republished as 'L'Hypnotisme dans la littérature. Marfa' in his *Oeuvres complètes illustrées* (Paris: Calmann-Lévy, 1925–35), vol. 6, 111–23.
55 *Possession*, published by Ollendorff and dated 1887, was already being reviewed in journals in late 1886. See *La Nouvelle Revue* 48, 3 (1 December 1886): 670.
56 'La Vie à Paris', *Le Temps*, 22 March 1881.
57 See Jules Huret, *Enquête*, 260.
58 I thank Frédéric Da Silva, who is preparing a biography of Paul Bonnetain, for his advice and for pointing me toward some of the writer's short publications that have paranormal themes.
59 Paul Bonnetain, 'Maternité', *L'Illustration* (2 February 1889).
60 See, in Alfred Binet, *Les Altérations de la personnalité* (Paris: Alcan, 1892), the chapter entitled 'Le Dédoublement de la personnalité et le spiritisme', 295–311.
61 Thorel-Cailleteau, *La Tentation*, 396.
62 André Godard, *L'Agence spirite* (Paris: Retaux et Fils, 1892).
63 Paul Guiraud, *La Conversion de Gaston Ferney. Roman spirite* (Paris: Flammarion, 1897).
64 J.-H. Rosny, *L'Initiation de Diane. Roman spirite* (Paris: Flammarion, 1930).
65 Flammarion, *Mémoires biographiques*, 235.
66 See Thorel-Cailletau, *La Tentation*, 389–96, and the text by C. Nautet quoted by Estrella de la Torre Giménez in '*Suggestion* de Henri Nizet: Un "roman hystérique"', in *L'Hystérie de la Belgité. L'hystérie dans la littérature belge de langue française de la fin du XIXe au début du XXe siècle*, Ana Pano Alaman, ed. (Bologna: CLUEB, 2003), 201–15 (206).

67 The very use of the term 'fellatrice' in Nizet's novel was dangerous. In 1888, a work by Dr Luiz (Paul Devaux) titled *Les Fellatores. Mœurs de la décadence* (Paris: Union des Bibliophiles) was prosecuted for obscenity, its author receiving a sentence of a year in jail and a 2000 franc fine.
68 It seems likely that Nizet borrowed this unusual medical problem from real life, probably hearing about it in relation to fellow naturalist novelist Paul Bonnetain, whose wife suffered from the condition. The gossipy Edmond de Goncourt was one of Bonnetain's confidants and wrote of Mme Bonnetain, 'cette femme sans esprit, sans intelligence, qui n'a pas même un cul à sa disposition, [est] occupée à tous moments par les chirurgiens.' *Journal* 3, 1153. 1 April 1890 ('this woman, lacking wit, lacking intelligence, who doesn't even have a c*** at her disposal, is busy with surgeons every moment of the day').
69 Bertrand Marquer's discussion of *Suggestion* is excellent, highlighting the role of hysteria in the novel. See *Les Romans de la Salpêtrière*, esp. 340–43, 357–58, 373–74, 376–77.
70 Paul Bourget, 'Un Roman d'analyse', *Journal des Débats* (3 April 1888), 2–3.
71 See François Caradec, *Willy: le père des Claudine* (Paris: Fayard, 2003), 172.
72 Micale, *The Mind of Modernism*, 76.
73 Prévost, *L'Automne*. Ellenberger refers to Prévost's novel more than once (*Discovery*, 167, 348–49, 766), and one wonders if it was his interest in the work that contributed to placing it so high in Mark Micale's estimation.
74 Ellenberger, *Discovery*, 766–67.
75 Marcel Prévost, *Le Jardin secret* (Paris: Lemerre, 1904 [1897]).
76 See *La Psychologie des sentiments* (Paris: Alcan, 1896), 140–70. Ribot's first article on the subject appeared in the *Revue Philosophique* in October 1894. He returned to the question of affective memory in *Problèmes de psychologie affective* (Paris: Alcan, 1910).
77 Bourget, *Essais*, 456.
78 Bourget, *L'Irréparable*, 4.
79 The metaphysician of the first edition of *L'Irréparable* was named only M.R. ***. In the definitive 1901 version he became Adrien Sixte, who was a central character in Bourget's great success, *Le Disciple* (1889).
80 See my discussion of Ribot's impact on Proust in *Proust, the Body*, esp. 49–56.
81 See, for example, Pierre Macherey, 'Peut-on encore aujourd'hui lire *Le Disciple* de Paul Bourget?', *Le Trimestre Psychanalytique* 2 (1993): 63–70.
82 Edition consulted, *De l'intelligence*, 6th edn, 2 vols. (Paris: Hachette, 1892).
83 Michel Mansuy, *Un Moderne: Paul Bourget, de l'enfance au 'Disciple'* (Paris: Les Belles Lettres, 1960), 501.
84 See *Le Disciple*, 52–53.

6 Proust, the Intellect and the Unconscious

1 In this chapter, double page references are provided (in parentheses, with volume and page number) for all quotations from *À la recherche du temps perdu*, except for those taken from Proust's manuscript sketches (esquisses). The first

reference (e.g., IV, 58) is to the French text in four volumes (Paris: Gallimard [Pléiade], 1987–89) and the second (e.g., 5, 88) to the six-volume English translation by C. K. Scott Moncrieff and Terence Kilmartin, revised by D. J. Enright (New York: Modern Library, 1998). Quotations from Proust's *Contre Sainte-Beuve* (Paris: Gallimard [Pléiade], 1971) are abbreviated CSB, and those from the English translation by John Sturrock, *Against Sainte-Beuve and Other Essays* (Penguin), are abbreviated ASB. Not all of the material in CSB is translated in ASB. Text from *Jean Santeuil* (Paris: Gallimard [Pléiade], 1971) is marked JS. Quotations from Proust's *Correspondance*, 21 vols., Philip Kolb, ed. (Paris: Plon, 1970–1993), are abbreviated Corr.

2 Marcel Proust, *Le Carnet de 1908*, Philip Kolb, ed. (Paris: Gallimard, 1976), 71.

3 Ibid., 100.

4 Robin MacKenzie, *The Unconscious in Proust's 'À la recherche du temps perdu'* (New York : Peter Lang, 2000), 15. MacKenzie's first chapter provides a wide-ranging and very useful overview of works on Proust and the unconscious, up until 2000. Among such studies, I would single out in particular Malcolm Bowie's *Freud, Proust and Lacan: Theory as Fiction* (Cambridge University Press, 1987) and Julia Kristeva's *Le Temps sensible*. Mireille Naturel reminds us of essays such as Jean Bellemin-Noël's 'Psychanalyser le rêve de Swann?', *Poétique* 8 (1971): 447–69, and more recent studies such as that of Edward Bizub, *Proust et le moi divisé. 'La Recherche': creuset de la psychologie expérimentale* (Genève: Droz, 2006). Pierre Pachet has written a brief, waggish article where he takes Proust to task for not reading the dreams in his work in true Freudian fashion. See 'Comment Proust évite la notion de l'inconscient', *Textuel* 45, *Surprises de la recherche* (2004): 227–32.

5 Jacques Rivière, *Quelques progrès dans l'étude du cœur humain*. Cahiers Marcel Proust 13 (Paris: Gallimard, 1985 [1927]), 107; Jean-Yves Tadié, *Marcel Proust. Biographie I* (Paris: Gallimard [Folio], 1996), 765.

6 See *Journal de l'abbé Mugnier*, Ghislain de Diesbach, ed. (Paris: Mercure de France, 1985), 309.

7 Luc Fraisse is one such reader. See *Le Processus de la création chez Marcel Proust. Le fragment expérimental* (Paris: José Corti, 1988), 242–57.

8 The main French translations of Freud date from the mid-1920s. The first French version of *Traumdeutung* held by the Bibiothèque nationale de France appears to be *Le Rêve et son interprétation* (1925), translated by Hélène Legros from the seventh German edition. Elisabeth Roudinesco lists *La Science des rêves*, trans. I. Meyerson (Paris: Alcan, 1926), as the first translation of Freud's dream theories. See her *Histoire*, 477. One of the first Freudian investigations of *À la recherche* appeared only shortly before Proust's death, in 1922, when René Rousseau, apparently buoyed by a reading of Freud's *Interpretation of Dreams* in German, wrote a long, incisive essay in the *Mercure de France* on Freudian themes in *À la recherche*, 'Marcel Proust et l'esthétique de l'inconscient'.

9 Proust, *Le Carnet de 1908*, 61.

10 Huret, *Enquête*, 252.

11 Ibid., 230, 413.

12 Ibid., 415.
13 Charles Morice, *La Littérature de tout à l'heure* (Paris: Perrin, 1889). See especially 355.
14 Fleury, *Médecine de l'esprit*, 159. Fleury was a columnist for *Le Figaro* in the 1890s.
15 Émile Faguet, *Je sais tout*, September 1907, quoted in *La Vie littéraire à la Belle Époque*, Géraldi Leroy and Julie Bertrand-Sabiani, eds. (Paris: Presses Universitaires de France, 1998), 285, note 2.
16 *Le Carnet de 1908*, 61.
17 Théodule Ribot, *La Philosophie de Schopenhauer* (Paris: Baillière, 1874), 150.
18 Lalande, *Vocabulaire technique et critique de la philosophie, Bulletin de la Société Française de Philosophie* (Paris, 1902). This dictionary was published gradually from 1902 until 1912. I have used the 1960 edition (Paris: Presses Universitaires de France).
19 Lalande (259) cited by Citti, *La Mésintelligence*, 95–96.
20 *Le Disciple*, 52–53. Bourget's biographer sees the novelist's anti-intellectualism and belief in intuition coalescing earlier, around 1886, with his attraction to religion, at a time when Tolstoy and Dostoyevsky were making an impression on French writers; when the neo-Christianism of Édouard Rod, de Vogüé and Paul Desjardin was in vogue; and at the same time esoteric works of Péladan and Stanislas de Guaïta were appearing. See Michel Mansuy, *Paul Bourget*, 432–33.
21 Zola's famous *J'accuse* was published on 13 January 1898 and Barrès' primary attack on the intellectuals was a front-page article in *Le Journal* of 1 February 1898, 'La Protestation des intellectuels?'; see also Brunetière, 'Après le procès', *Revue des Deux Mondes* (15 March 1898): 428–46. Lucien Herr's tranquil counterattack is devastating for Barrès; see Herr, 'À M. Maurice Barrès', *La Revue Blanche* 15 (15 February 1898): 241–45. For a discussion of the Affair and intellectuals, see Vincent Duclert, 'Anti-intellectualisme et intellectuels pendant l'affaire Dreyfus', *Mil Neuf Cent* 15 (1997): 69–83.
22 Weber, *France Fin de Siècle*, 124 and note 55.
23 Remy de Gourmont, *La Culture des idées*, 91.
24 Citti, *Mésintelligence*, 96.
25 Edward J. Hughes, *Proust, Class and Nation* (Oxford: Oxford University Press, 2011). See in particular 19–42.
26 See Corr. XVIII: 334, 19 July 1919. Proust later writes to Halévy of the danger of adopting false ideas simply because those who espouse them have positive qualities (ibid., 369, 11 August 1919). Arguments about the manifesto continued in the *Nouvelle Revue Française*. See Jacques Rivière, 'Le Parti de l'intelligence', *Nouvelle Revue Française* 72 (June–December 1919): 612–18, and a response by Henri Ghéon, 'Réflexions sur le rôle actuel de l'Intelligence française', *Nouvelle Revue Française* 72 (June-December 1919): 953–64.
27 Poincaré, *La Valeur de la science* (Paris: Flammarion, 1905), and *Science et méthode* (Paris: Flammarion, 1908).
28 Proust praises Ribot's book as a 'fine study' (see CSB, 179, note). I have discussed at length what elements in Ribot's volume seem to have made an impact on Proust in Finn, *Proust, the Body*, 45–56.

29 *Les Maladies de la volonté*, 139.
30 Tony James notes that Ribot stood out among French philosophers as the only one to devote a complete study to the creative imagination. See James, *Dream*, 262–65.
31 *La Psychologie des sentiments*, 153.
32 Ibid., 324.
33 Ribot returns to the subject of affective memory in *Problèmes de psychologie affective* and, after Proust's novel had begun to appear, in his *La Vie inconsciente et les mouvements* (Paris: Alcan, 1914).
34 Charles Richet, 'Psychologie. Le génie et la folie', *Revue Scientifique* (January–June 1889): 85.
35 Poincaré, *La Valeur*, 20.
36 Luckhurst, *Science and Structure*, esp. 226–35.
37 Poincaré, *Science et méthode*, 51.
38 Proust, CSB, 413. The text cited was probably written not much later than 1898 (the death of Mallarmé in that year is mentioned).
39 Elena Lozinsky, *L'Intertexte fin-de-siècle dans 'À la recherche du temps perdu' de Marcel Proust. Les carafes dans la Vivonne* (Paris: Honoré Champion, 2013). See chapter 2, 69–95.
40 Marcel Proust, *Sésame et les lys*, 9th edn (Paris: Mercure de France, 1935 [1906]), 150, note 1.
41 Proust asked Reynaldo Hahn to get him a copy of *La Vie des abeilles* in February 1904 (Corr. 4, 58). There are a few mostly article-length texts on Maeterlinck and Proust: Leighton Hodson, 'The Presence of Maeterlinck in Proust's Style and Thought', in *Essays in French Literature* (University of West Australia, 21 November 1984), 38–61; Richard Bales, 'Proust au seuil de la Recherche: La contribution de Maeterlinck essayiste', in *Présence/Absence de Maurice Maeterlinck*, Marc Quaghebeur, ed. (Brussels: Archives et Musée de la littérature, 2002), 369–80; Michael R. Finn, 'Proust, Maeterlinck, les arbres et les clochers', *Bulletin Marcel Proust* 54 (2004): 127–33.
42 *Le Temple enseveli* (Paris: Fasquelle, 1903), 21.
43 See Antoine Compagnon's notes on these sources in *À la recherche* (III, 1271, note, and 1286–89).
44 Marcel Muller, 'Sodome I ou la naturalisation de Charlus', *Poétique* 8 (1971): 470–78.
45 *L'Intelligence des fleurs* (Paris: Fasquelle, 1922 [1907]), p. 4.
46 *Sésame et les lys*, 79, note 1.
47 Ibid.
48 *Le Carnet de 1908*, 97. In the same text Proust writes that while Sainte-Beuve is intelligent and understands nuance, he doesn't accord enough importance to the irrational.
49 W. L. Hodson, 'The Presence', 43.
50 See Proust, '*Les Éblouissements* par la comtesse de Noailles', CSB, 533–45, esp. 537–38.
51 *L'Intelligence des fleurs*, 93–95, emphasis added.

52 Proust, *Le Carnet de 1908*, 52.
53 *L'Intelligence des fleurs*, 95, emphasis added.
54 I, 179–80; 1, 255–56. As we know, the first version of the Martinville spires passage was published not as fiction but as an article describing church steeples in Caen in *Le Figaro* of 19 November 1907. The article was titled 'Impressions de route en automobile' (see CSB, 63–69).
55 See William C. Carter, *Proust: A Life* (New Haven: Yale University Press, 2000), 71.
56 Taine, *De l'intelligence*, 1, 131, emphasis added.
57 Quoted by Léon Dumont, 'L'Action réflexe cérébrale', 32, from Luys' *Études de physiologie et de pathologie cérébrales.*
58 *Le Carnet de 1908*, 114.
59 *La Psychologie des sentiments*, 159.
60 Ribot, *La Vie inconsciente*, 51.
61 Ribot, *Les Maladies de la volonté*, 105. See Finn, *Proust, the Body*, 42–56.
62 Julian Barnes, 'The Profile of Félix Fénéon', in *Through the Window* (Toronto: Vintage Canada, 2012), 133.
63 Pierre Bayard has written a study on 'le plagiat par anticipation', an expression that does not have quite the same meaning as Proust's 'anticipation inconsciente'. Bayard says he heard the notion spoken of at meetings of the Oulipo, but it seems likely that one of the Oulipo group (Bayard himself?) had been reading Proust. See Bayard, *Le Plagiat par anticipation* (Paris: Éditions de Minuit, 2008), 21.
64 A work that must be consulted in any discussion of Proust's philosophical influences is Luc Fraisse, *L'Éclectisme philosophique de Marcel Proust* (Paris: Presses de l'Université Paris-Sorbonne, 2013). A sample of his sensitive, penetrating analysis is his discussion (307–55) of Anne Henry's much-challenged *Marcel Proust – théories pour une esthétique*. Fraisse finds both negative and positive outcomes from Henry's aggressive argument about Proust's supposedly deliberate philosophical structuring of *À la recherche*.
65 *Le Carnet de 1908*, 101.
66 Marcel Proust, *Matinée chez la princesse de Guermantes*, Henri Bonnet and Bernard Brun, eds. (Paris: Gallimard, 1982), 142, note 1.
67 Anne Henry, 'Proust du côté de Schopenhauer', in *Schopenhauer et la création littéraire en Europe* (Paris: Méridiens Klincksieck, 1989), 149–64.
68 Jean-Yves Tadié, *Marcel Proust. Biographie I*, passim.
69 Julia Kristeva, *Le Temps sensible.*
70 Joyce Megay, *Bergson et Proust* (Paris: Vrin, 1976).
71 I borrow the expression 'critique d'identification' from Claude Pichois. See Baudelaire, *Oeuvres complètes*, 2, 1071.
72 Henri Bergson, 'Introduction à la métaphysique', *Revue de Métaphysique et de Morale* (January 1903): 1–36 (3). Quoted by Dominique Parodi, *Philosophie contemporaine*, 256.
73 These two texts are quoted by Françoise Leriche, 'Du nouveau sur le Cahier 14', *Bulletin d'Informations Proustiennes* 21 (1990): 7–10. An earlier reading of

part of the second passage by Jean Milly is slightly different. See Milly, *Les Pastiches de Proust* (Paris: Colin, 1970), 46–47.

74 Georges Poulet, *Études sur le temps humain*, vol. 1 (Paris: Plon, 1952), 386.

Postscript

1 This evolution has been remarked upon in Hacking, *Rewriting the Soul*, 163.

2 *Du hachisch et de l'aliénation mentale* (Paris: Fortin/Masson, 1845), 379.

3 *Le Petit Robert*, 1993, p. 2037.

4 Coriat, *Abnormal Psychology*, 10.

5 Pierre Janet, *De l'angoisse à l'extase. Études sur les croyances et les sentiments*, 2 vols. (Paris: Société Pierre Janet, 1975 [1926–28]), 2, 222.

Bibliography

Amiel, Henri-Frédéric. *Fragments d'un journal intime*, 7th edn. Geneva: Georg, 1897.

Journal intime de l'année 1866. Paris: Gallimard, 1959.

Armengaud, André. *La Population française au XIXe siècle*. Paris: Presses Universitaires de France, 1976.

Audouard, Olympe. *M. Barbey d'Aurevilly. Réponse à ses réquisitoires contre les Bas-bleus. Conférence du 11 avril*. Paris: Dentu, 1870.

Augustin-Thierry, Gilbert. *Marfa*. Paris: Perrin, 1887.

Auriant. *Souvenirs sur Madame Rachilde*. À l'Écart, 1889.

Azam, Eugène. *Hypnotisme et double conscience: origine de leur étude et divers travaux sur des sujets analogues*. Paris: Alcan, 1893.

Bales, Richard. 'Proust au seuil de la Recherche. La contribution de Maeterlinck essayiste'. In *Présence/Absence de Maurice Maeterlinck*. Marc Quaghebeur, ed. Brussels: Archives et Musée de la littérature, 2002. 369–80.

Barnes, Julian. *Through the Window*. Toronto: Vintage Canada, 2012.

Barrès, Maurice. *Journal de ma vie extérieure*. François Broche and Eric Roussel, eds. Paris: Julliard, 1994.

L'Oeuvre de Maurice Barrès. 20 vols. Paris: Club de l'Honnête Homme, 1965–69.

'La Protestation des intellectuels?' *Le Journal* (1 February 1898).

'La Sensibilité d'Henri Chambige'. *Le Figaro* (11 November 1888), 1.

Bart, Benjamin. 'Male Hysteria in *Salammbô*'. *Nineteenth-Century French Studies* 12 (1984): 313–21.

Baudelaire, Charles. *Oeuvres complètes*. 2 vols. Claude Pichois, ed. Paris: Gallimard (Pléiade), 1990.

Bayard, Pierre. *Maupassant juste avant Freud*. Paris: Éditions de Minuit, 1994.

Le Plagiat par anticipation. Paris: Éditions de Minuit, 2008.

Beaton, Alan, and Peter Mariën. 'Language, Cognition and the Cerebellum: Grappling with an Enigma'. *Cortex* 46 (2010): 811–20.

Beaunis, Henri. 'Comment fonctionne mon cerveau. Essai de psychologie introspective'. *Revue Philosophique* 67 (January 1909): 29–40.

'L'Expérimentation en psychologie par le somnambulisme provoqué'. *Revue Philosophique* 20 (July–December 1885): 1–36.

Les Sensations internes. Paris: Alcan, 1889.

Le Somnambulisme provoqué. Paris: Baillière, 1887.

Bellemin-Noël, Jean. '"Psychanalyser' le rêve de Swann'. *Poétique* 8 (1971): 447–69.
Belot, Adolphe. *Alphonsine*. Paris: Dentu, 1887.
Bender, Niklas. *La Lutte des paradigmes. La littérature entre histoire, biologie et médecine (Flaubert, Zola, Fontane)*. Amsterdam: Rodopi, 2010.
Benhamou, Noëlle, et al., eds. *Bibliographie des écrivains français. Guy de Maupassant*. Rome: Memini, 2008.
Bergson, Henri. 'Introduction à la métaphysique'. *Revue de Métaphysique et de Morale* (January 1903): 1–36.
Bérillon, Edgar. *Histoire de l'hypnotisme expérimental*. Paris: Vigot, 1902.
Hypnotisme expérimental. La dualité cérébrale et l'indépendance fonctionnelle des deux hémisphères cérébraux. Paris: Delahaye & Lecrosnier, 1884.
Bernheim, Hippolyte. *De la suggestion dans l'état hypnotique et dans l'état de veille*. Paris: Doin, 1884.
De la suggestion et de ses applications à la thérapeutique. Paris: Doin, 1886.
Hypnotisme, suggestion, psychothérapie. Études nouvelles. Paris: Doin, 1891.
Biasi, Jean-Marc de. *Gustave Flaubert. Une manière spéciale de vivre*. Paris: Grasset, 2009.
Billy, André de. *Vie des frères Goncourt*. 2 vols. Monaco: Imprimerie Nationale de Monaco, 1956.
Binet, Alfred. *Les Altérations de la personnalité*. Paris: Alcan, 1892.
Études de psychologie expérimentale. Paris: Doin, 1888.
Binet, Alfred, and Charles Féré. *Le Magnétisme animal*. Paris: Alcan, 1887.
Biran, Maine de. *Oeuvres*. Paris: Vrin, 1984.
Bizub, Edward. *Proust et le moi divisé. 'La Recherche', creuset de la psychologie expérimentale (1874–1914)*. Geneva: Droz, 2006.
Bogousslavsky, Julien, Olivier Walusinski and Denis Veyrunes. 'Crime, Hysteria and *Belle Époque* Hypnotism: The Path Traced by Jean-Martin Charcot and Georges Gilles de la Tourette'. *European Neurology* 62 (2009): 193–99.
Bonnetain, Paul. 'Maternité'. *L'Illustration*, 2 February 1889.
Bottey, Fernand. *Le 'Magnétisme animal'. Étude critique et expérimentale sur l'hypnotisme ou sommeil nerveux provoqués chez les sujets sains (léthargie, catalepsie, somnambulisme, etc.)*. Paris: Plon-Nourrit, 1884.
Boubée, Simon. *Main-de-cire*. Paris: Piaget, 1888.
Bourdieu, Pierre. *La Domination masculine*. Paris: Seuil, 1998.
Bourget, Paul. *Le Disciple*. Antoine Compagnon, ed. Paris: Librairie Générale Française/Livre de Poche Classique, 2010.
Essais de psychologie contemporaine. André Guyaux, ed. Paris: Gallimard, 1993.
'Guy de Maupassant'. In *Études et portraits III. Sociologie et littérature*. Paris: Plon, 1906. 290–319.
L'Irréparable. Deuxième amour. Céline Lacoste. Jean Maquenem. Paris: Plon [1901].
'Un Roman d'analyse'. *Journal des Débats* (3 April 1888), 2–3.
Bourru, Henri, and Ferdinand Burot. *Variations de la personnalité*. Paris: Baillière, 1888.

Bowie, Malcolm. *Freud, Proust and Lacan: Theory as Fiction*. Cambridge: Cambridge University Press, 1987.

Brachet, Jean-Louis. *Traité de l'hystérie*. Paris: Baillière, 1847.

Braid, James. *Neurypnology, or the Rationale of Nervous Sleep, considered in relation to Animal Magnetism*. London: John Churchill, 1843.

Briquet, Pierre. *Traité clinique et thérapeutique de l'hystérie*. Paris: Baillière, 1859.

Bronfen, Elisabeth. *The Knotted Subject: Hysteria and Its Discontents*. Princeton: Princeton University Press, 1998.

Brown, Paul, and Onno van der Hart. 'Memories of Sexual Abuse: Janet's Critique of Freud, a Balanced Approach'. *Psychological Reports* 82 (1998): 1027–43.

Brulotte, Gaëtan, and John Phillips, eds. *Encylopedia of Erotic Literature*. 2 vols. New York: Routledge, 2006.

Brunetière, Fernand. 'Après le procès'. *Revue des Deux Mondes* (15 March 1898): 428–46.

Brunschvicg, Léon. Review of Théophile Desdouits' *La Philosophie de l'inconscient*. Paris: Roger and Chernoviz, 1892. *Revue de Métaphysique et Morale* (1893): 405–10.

Burdin, Claude, and Frédéric Dubois. *Histoire académique du magnétisme animal*. Paris: Baillière, 1846.

Cabanès, Jean-Louis. *Le Corps et la maladie dans les récits réalistes (1856–1893)*. 2 vols. Paris: Klincksieck, 1991.

'Psychologie, histoire, esthétique: les hallucinations à l'entrecroisement des discours'. *Image et pathologie au XIXe siècle. Cahiers de littérature française VI*. Paris: L'Harmattan, 2008. 7–26.

Cabanès, Jean-Louis, Didier Philippot and Paolo Tortonese, eds. *Paradigmes de l'âme. Littérature et aliénisme au XIXe siècle*. Paris: Presses Sorbonne Nouvelle, 2012.

Caradec, François. *Willy: le père des Claudine*. Paris: Fayard, 2003.

Carpenter, William. *Principles of Mental Physiology*, 2nd edn. London: Henry S. King, 1875.

Carroy, Jacqueline. *Hypnose, suggestion et psychologie. L'invention de sujets*. Paris: Presses Universitaires de France, 1991.

'Le Noviciat de l'hystérie selon Georgette Déga'. *Psychanalyse à l'Université* 12, 45 (January 1987): 141–52.

Les Personnalités doubles et multiples. Entre science et fiction. Paris: Presses Universitaires de France, 1993.

Carroy, Jacqueline, and Régine Plas. 'La Volonté et l'involontaire: l'exemple de l'automatisme'. In Jean-Louis Cabanès, Didier Philippot and Paolo Tortonese, eds., *Paradigmes de l'âme. Littérature et aliénisme au XIXe siècle*. Paris: Presses Sorbonne Nouvelle, 2012. 23–37.

Carroy, Jacqueline, and Marc Renneville. 'Une Cause passionnelle passionnante: Tarde et l'affaire Chambige (1889)'. *Champ Pénal*, 34th Congrès français de criminologie, available at http://champpenal.revues.org/260.

Carter, William C. *Proust. A Life*. New Haven: Yale University Press, 2000.

Castel, Pierre-Henri. *La Querelle de l'hystérie. La formation du discours psychopathologique en France 1881–1913*. Paris: Presses Universitaires de France, 1998.

Cavailhon, Ernest. *La Fascination magnétique*. Paris: Dentu, 1882.

Chabaneix, Dr Paul. *Le Subconscient chez les artistes, les savants et les écrivains*. Paris: Baillière, 1897.

Chapron, Léon. *Les Coins de Paris*. Paris: Dentu, 1881.

Charcot, Jean-Martin. 'Physiologie pathologique. Sur les divers états nerveux déterminés par l'hypnotisation chez les hystériques'. *Comptes-rendus hebdomadaires de l'Académie des Sciences* 94 (1882): 403–5.

Charcot, Jean-Martin, and Paul Richer. *Les Démoniaques dans l'art*. Paris: Delahaye & Lecrosnier, 1887.

Citti, Pierre. *Contre la décadence. Histoire de l'imagination française dans le roman 1890–1914*. Paris: Presses Universitaires de France, 1987.

La Mésintelligence. Essais d'histoire de l'intelligence française du symbolisme à 1914. Saint-Etienne: Éditions des Cahiers Intempestifs, 2000.

Cixous, Hélène. *La Jeune Née*. Paris: Union Générale d'Éditions [10/18], 1975.

Claretie, Jules. *Les Amours d'un interne*. Paris: Dentu, 1881.

Jean Mornas. Paris: Dentu, 1885.

L'Obsession (Moi et l'autre). Paris: Pierre Lafitte, 1909.

'La Vie à Paris'. *Le Temps*, 22 March 1881.

'La Vie à Paris'. *Le Temps*, 11 July 1884.

Clarke, Edward Hammond. *Sex in Education: A Fair Chance for Girls*. New York: Arno Press, 1972 (1873).

Clément, Catherine. *La Syncope. Philosophie du ravissement*. Paris: Grasset, 1990.

Colsenet, Edmond. *Études sur la vie inconsciente de l'esprit*. Paris: Baillière, 1880.

Copin, Paul. 'L'Hypnotisme au Salon de 1887'. *Revue de l'Hypnotisme Expérimental et Thérapeutique* 1 (1887): 373–75.

'Le Magnétisme et l'hypnotisme dans le roman'. *Revue de l'Hypnotisme Expérimental et Thérapeutique* 1 (1887): 313–16.

'Un Roman de M. Alphonse [*sic*] Belot, *Alphonsine*'. *Revue de l'Hypnotisme Expérimental et Thérapeutique* 2 (1888): 202–8.

Coriat, Isador. *Abnormal Psychology*, 2nd edn. London: Moffat, Yard and Co., 1917.

Cullerre, Dr Alexandre. *Magnétisme et hypnotisme*. Paris: Baillière, 1886.

Dartigues, J.-P. *De l'amour expérimental ou des causes d'adultère chez la femme au XIXe siècle. Étude d'hygiène et d'économie sociale résultant de l'ignorance, du libertinage et des fraudes dans l'accomplissement des devoirs conjugaux*. Versailles: A. Litzelmann, 1887.

Daudet, Julia. *Quand Odile saura lire*. Paris: Crès, 1919.

Daudet, Léon. *Souvenirs des milieux littéraires, politiques, artistiques et médicales*. Paris: Nouvelle Librairie Nationale, 1920.

Déga, Georgette. *Essai sur la cure préventive de l'hystérie féminine par l'éducation*. Paris: Alcan, 1898.

Delanne, Gabriel. *Le Phénomène spirite*, 5th edn. Paris: Chamuel, 1897.

Delaville, Camille. 'Bacheliers, crétins et filles savantes'. *Le Passant*, 27 July 1882.
Mes Contemporaines. Paris: Sévin, 1887.
Descourtis, Gabriel. *Du fractionnement des opérations cérébrales et en particulier de leur dédoublement dans les psychopathies*. Paris, medical thesis 194, 1882.
Desdouits, Théophile. *La Philosophie de l'inconscient*. Paris: Roger and Chernoviz, 1892.
Desmaret, Marie-Christine. *Bizarreries et bigarrures baroques dans 'Salammbô' de Flaubert*. (Lille: ANRT, 2005).
'Épileptiques, hystériques, marginaux, fous comme figures protéiformes de l'artiste dans l'œuvre flaubertienne'. *Revue Flaubert* 6 (2006), available at http://flaubert.univ-rouen.fr/revue/revue6/.
Despine, Prosper. *Étude scientifique sur le somnambulisme, sur les phénomènes qu'il présente et sur son action thérapeutique dans certaines maladies nerveuses*. Paris: Savy, 1880.
Devarieux, Anne. *Maine de Biran: L'individualité persévérante*. Grenoble: Jérôme Millon, 2004.
Devaux, Paul (alias Dr Luiz). *Les Fellatores. Moeurs de la décadence*. Paris: Union des Bibliophiles, 1888.
Dijkstra, Bram. *Idols of Perversity: Fantasies of Feminine Evil in Fin-de-Siècle Culture*. Oxford: Oxford University Press, 1986.
Dostoevsky, Fyodor. *Les Possédés*. 2 vols. Paris: Plon-Nourrit, 1886.
Dottin-Orsini, Mireille. *Cette femme qu'ils disent fatale*. Paris: Grasset, 1993.
Downing, Lisa. 'Gendered Constructions of the Nightmare in French Nineteenth-Century Medical Writing and Fantastic Fiction'. *French Studies* 66, 3 (July 2012): 331–46.
Doy, Gen. *Drapery: Classicism and Barbarism in Visual Culture*. London: I. B. Tauris, 2002.
Drachline, Pierre. *Le Crime de Pantin. L'Affaire Troppmann*. Paris: Denoël, 1984.
Dubarry, Armand. *Les Femmes eunuques*. Paris: Chamuel, 1899.
Duclert, Vincent. 'Anti-intellectualisme et intellectuels pendant l'affaire Dreyfus'. *Mil Neuf Cent* 15 (1997): 69–83.
Dumont, M. 'L'Action réflexe cérébrale. MM. Laycock, Carpenter, Luys'. *Revue Scientifique de la France et de l'Étranger* 28 (8 January 1876): 25–33.
E. . .T. . . *L'Écuyer magnétiseur*. Paris and Limoges: Henri-Charles-La Vauzelle, Éditeur Militaire, 1887.
Edelman, Nicole. *Les Métamorphoses de l'hystérique. Du début de XIXe siècle à la Grande Guerre*. Paris: Éditions de la Découverte, 2003.
Ellenberger, Henri. *Beyond the Unconscious. Essays of Henri Ellenberger in the History of Psychiatry*. Mark Micale, ed. Princeton: Princeton University Press, 1993.
The Discovery of the Unconscious: The History and Evolution of Dynamic Psychiatry. New York: Basic Books, 1970.
Ender, Evelyne. *Sexing the Mind: Nineteenth-Century Fictions of Hysteria*. Ithaca: Cornell University Press, 1995.
Epheyre, Charles (pseudonym of Charles Richet). *Possession*. Paris: Ollendorff, 1887.

À la recherche du bonheur. Paris: Ollendorff, 1879
Soeur Marthe. Paris: Ollendorff, 1890.
Estoc, Gisèle d'. *Cahier d'amour*. Paris: Arléa, 1997.
Fabart, Félix. *Histoire philosophique et politique de l'occulte: magie, sorcellerie, spiritisme*. Paris: Marpon and Flammarion, 1885.
Féré, Charles, and Alfred Binet. 'Hypnotisme et responsabilité'. *Revue Philosophique* 19 (January–June 1885): 265–79.
Fette, Julie. 'Pride and Prejudice in the Professions: Women Doctors and Lawyers in Third Republic France'. *Journal of Women's History* 19, 3 (2007): 60–86.
Finn, Michael R. 'Dogs and Females: Vivisection, Feminists and the Novelist Rachilde'. *French Cultural Studies* 23, 3 (August 2012): 190–201.
'Female Sterilization and Artificial Insemination in Fin-de-Siècle France: Facts and Fictions'. *Journal of the History of Sexuality* 18, 1 (January 2009): 26–43.
Hysteria, Hypnosis, the Spirits and Pornography: Fin-de-Siècle Cultural Discourses in the Decadent Rachilde. Newark: University of Delaware Press, 2009.
'Naturalisme, sexe et sexologie. Excès catastrophique ou fantaisie médicale'. *Les Cahiers Naturalistes* 85 (2011): 117–33.
'Physiological Fictions and the Fin-de-Siècle Female Brain'. *Nineteenth-Century French Studies* 39, 3–4 (Spring–Summer 2011): 315–31.
Proust, the Body and Literary Form. Cambridge: Cambridge University Press, 1999/2006.
'Proust, Maeterlinck, les arbres et les clochers'. *Bulletin Marcel Proust* 54 (2004): 127–33.
Flammarion, Camille. *Mémoires biographiques et philosophiques d'un astronome*. Paris: Flammarion [1912].
Flaubert, Gustave. *Correspondance*. 5 vols. Paris: Gallimard (Pléiade), 1973–2007.
Correspondance. Index. Jean Bruneau and Yvan Leclerc, eds. Paris: Gallimard, 2007.
Madame Bovary. Claudine Gothot-Mersch, ed. Paris: Garnier, 1971.
Les Mémoires d'un fou. Novembre. Pyrénées-Corse. Voyage en Italie. Claudine Gothot-Mersch, ed. Paris: Gallimard (Folio), 2001.
Salammbô. Jacques Neefs, ed. Paris: Librairie Générale Française (Livre de Poche Classique), 2011.
La Tentation de saint Antoine. Claudine Gothot-Mersch, ed. Paris: Gallimard (Folio), 1983.
Fleury, Maurice de. *Introduction à la médecine de l'esprit*, 2nd edn. Paris: Alcan, 1897.
Foucault, Michel. *Les Anormaux. Cours au Collège de France. 1974–1975*. Paris: Gallimard/Seuil, 1999.
La Bibliothèque fantastique. À propos de 'La Tentation de saint-Antoine' de Gustave Flaubert. Brussels: La Lettre Volée, 1995.
Fouillée, Alfred. *La Pensée et les nouvelles écoles anti-intellectualistes*. Paris: Alcan, 1911.
'La Psychologie des sexes et ses fondements physiologiques'. *Revue des Deux Mondes* (15 September 1893): 397–429.

Fraisse, Geneviève. *Muse de la raison. La démocratie exclusive et la différence des sexes*. Aix-en-Provence: Alinéa, 1989.

La Raison des femmes. Paris: Plon, 1992.

Fraisse, Luc. *L'Éclectisme philosophique de Marcel Proust*. Paris: Presses de l'Université Paris-Sorbonne, 2013.

Le Processus de la création chez Marcel Proust. Le fragment expérimental. Paris: José Corti, 1988.

France, Anatole. 'Un Crime littéraire. L'affaire Chambige'. *Le Temps* (11 November 1888), 1.

'L'Hypnotisme dans la littérature. Marfa'. In *Oeuvres complètes illustrées*. Paris: Calmann-Lévy, 1925–35, vol. 6, 111–23.

Garnier, Paul-Émile. *L'Automatisme somnambulique devant les tribunaux*. Paris: Baillière, 1887.

Gastaut, H., and Y. Gastaut. 'La Maladie de Gustave Flaubert'. *Revue Neurologique* 138 (1982): 467–92.

Gauchet, Marcel. *L'Inconscient cérébral*. Paris: Éditions du Seuil, 1992.

Gauchet, Marcel, and Gladys Swain. *Le Vrai Charcot. Les chemins imprévus de l'inconscient*. Paris: Calmann-Lévy, 1997.

Gaultier, Jules de. 'Le Génie de Flaubert'. *Mercure de France* (16 November 1912): 225–60; (1 December 1912): 490–526.

Géley, Gustave. *De l'inconscient au conscient*. Paris: Alcan, 1919.

Genette, Gérard. 'Silences de Flaubert'. In *Figures I*. Paris: Éditions du Seuil (Points), 1966. 223–43.

Ghéon, Henri. 'Réflexions sur le rôle actuel de l'intelligence française'. *Nouvelle Revue Française* 72 (June–December 1919): 953–64.

Gill, Miranda. '*Compagnons de misère*: Melancholic Identification in Nerval and Baudelaire'. *Nottingham French Studies* 47, 3 (Autumn 2008): 79–90.

Gilles de la Tourette, Georges. *L'Épilogue d'un procès célèbre (Affaire Eyraud-Bompard)*. Paris: Lescrosnier and Babé, 1891.

Godard, André. *L'Agence spirite*. Paris: Retaux et Fils, 1892.

Goldstein, Jan. 'The Uses of Male Hysteria: Medical and Literary Discourse in Nineteenth-Century France'. *Representations* 34 (Spring 1991): 134–65.

Goncourt, Edmond de. *La Faustin*. Paris: Charpentier, 1882.

Goncourt, Edmond de, and Jules de Goncourt. *Idées et sensations*. Paris: Librairie Internationale, 1866.

Journal. Mémoires de la vie littérature. 4 vols. Robert Ricatte, ed. Paris: Fasquelle/Flammarion, 1959.

Gordon, Felicia. 'French Psychiatry and the New Woman: The Case of Dr Constance Pascal 1877–1937'. *History of Psychiatry* 17, 2 (June 2006): 159–82.

Gourmont, Remy de. *La Culture des idées. Du style ou de l'écriture, la création subconsciente, la dissociation des idées*. Paris: Mercure de France, 1964 [1900].

Sixtine: roman de la vie cérébrale. Paris: Savine, 1890.

Gramfort, Véronique. 'Les Crimes de Pantin: quand Troppmann défrayait la chronique'. *Romantisme* 27 (1997): 17–30.

Gray, T. S. 'Herbert Spencer on Women: A Study in Personal and Political Disillusionment'. *International Journal of Women's Studies* 7, 3 (1984): 217–31.

Guiraud, Paul. *La Conversion de Gaston Ferney. Roman spirite*. Paris: Flammarion, 1897.

Gurney, Edmund, Frederic Myers and Frank Podmore, *Les Hallucinations télépathiques*, 2nd edn. Trans. of *Phantasms of the Living* by Léon Marillier, preface by Charles Richet. Paris: Alcan, 1892.

Guyau, Jean-Marie. *Éducation et hérédité. Étude sociologique*. Paris: Alcan, 1889.

Hacking, Ian. *Rewriting the Soul: Multiple Personality and the Sciences of Memory*, 2nd edn. Princeton: Princeton University Press, 1995.

Hall, Marshall. 'On the Reflex Function of the Medulla Oblongata and Medulla Spinalis'. *Philosophical Transactions of the Royal Society*. 130 (1833): 635–65.

Harrington, Anne. *The Cure Within: A History of Mind-Body Medicine*. New York: Norton, 2008.

Medicine, Mind and the Double Brain: A Study in Nineteenth Century Thought. Princeton: Princeton University Press, 1987.

Hartmann, Eduard von. *La Philosophie de l'inconscient*. 2 vols. Paris: Baillière, 1877.

Hennique, Léon. *Un Caractère*. Paris: Crès, 1923 [1889].

Henry, Anne. 'Proust du côté de Schopenhauer'. In *Schopenhauer et la création littéraire en Europe*. Paris: Méridiens Klincksieck, 1989. 149–64.

Hepp, Alexandre. *Paris-Patraque*. Paris: Dentu, 1884.

Héricourt, Jules. 'L'Activité inconsciente de l'esprit'. *Revue Scientifique* (31 August 1889): 257–68.

Herr, Lucien. 'À M. Maurice Barrès'. *La Revue Blanche* 15 (15 February 1898): 241–45.

Hilgar, Marie-France. 'Juliette Adam et la *Nouvelle Revue*'. *Rocky Mountain Review of Language and Literature* 51, 2 (1997): 11–18.

Hodson, W. L. 'The Presence of Maeterlinck in Proust's Style and Thought'. *Essays in French Literature*. University of West Australia (21 November 1984): 38–61.

Holmes, Diana. 'Daniel Lesueur and the Feminist Romance'. In *A 'Belle Époque? Women in French Society and Culture 1890–1914*. Diana Holmes and Carrie Tarr, eds. New York: Berghahn, 2006. 197–210.

Horvath-Peterson, Sandra. *Victor Duruy and French Education: Liberal Reform in the Second Empire*. Baton Rouge: Louisiana State University Press, 1984.

Howe, Julia Ward. *Sex and Education: A Reply to Dr E. H. Clarke's 'Sex in Education'*. New York: Arno Press, 1972 (1874).

Hughes, Edward J. *Proust, Class and Nation*. Oxford: Oxford University Press, 2011.

Huret, Jules. *Enquête sur l'évolution littéraire*. Daniel Grojnowski, ed. Paris: José Corti, 1999 [1891].

Huysmans, Joris-Karl. *À rebours*. Paris: Garnier-Flammarion, 1978.

Là-bas. Paris: Garnier-Flammarion, 2003.

Huyssen, Andreas. *After the Great Divide: Modernism, Mass Culture, Post-Modernism*. Bloomington: Indiana University Press, 1986.

Jaloux, Edmond. 'Observations sur la psychanalyse'. *Le Disque Vert* (1924): 28–37.

James, Tony. *Dream, Creativity and Madness in Nineteenth-Century France.* Oxford: Clarendon Press, 1995.

Janet, Pierre. 'À propos de la Métapsychique'. *Revue Philosophique* (July–December 1923): 5–32.

L'Automatisme psychologique, essai de psychologie expérimentale sur les formes inférieures de l'activité humaine, 2nd edn. Paris: Alcan, 1894 (1889).

De l'angoisse à l'extase. Études sur les croyances et les sentiments. 2 vols. Paris: Société Pierre Janet, 1975 [1926].

'Deuxième note sur le sommeil provoqué à distance et la suggestion mentale pendant l'état somnambulique'. *Revue Philosophique* 22 (July–December 1886): 212–23.

L'État mental des hystériques. Paris: Rueff, 1894.

La Médecine psychologique. Paris: Flammarion, 1980 [1923].

'Notes sur quelques phénomènes du somnambulisme'. *Revue Philosophique* 21 (February 1886): 190–98.

'La Psycho-analyse'. *Journal de Psychologie Normale et Pathologique* 11 (1914): 1–36; 97–130.

Janssen, Sandra. 'L'Inquiétante étrangeté de la physiologie nerveuse. Parasitisme mental, illusionnisme et fantastique chez Maupassant'. In *Paradigmes de l'âme. Littérature et aliénisme*, Jean-Louis Cabanès, Didier Philippot and Paolo Tortonese, eds. Paris: Presses Sorbonne Nouvelle, 2012. 195–212.

Jastrow, Joseph. *La Subconscience.* Preface by Pierre Janet. Paris: Alcan, 1908.

Jeanne des Anges. *Soeur Jeanne des Anges, supérieure des Ursulines de Loudun (XVIIe siècle): autobiographie d'une hystérique possédée.* Gabriel Légué and Georges Gilles de la Tourette, eds. Paris: Delahaye & Lecrosnier, 1886.

Johnston, Marlo. *Guy de Maupassant.* Paris: Fayard, 2012.

Kleffler, Henri. *Les Missions 'humanitaires' des dames anglaises sur le continent. La vivisection, son utilité, sa morale, réponse à la campagne antivivisectionniste de Mme le Dr Anna Kingsford.* Geneva: H. Georg, 1883.

Knibiehler, Yvonne. 'Les Médecins et la "nature féminine" au temps du Code civil'. *Annales. Économies, Sociétés, Civilisations* 31, 4 (1976): 824–45.

Kovalevskaya, Sofia. 'Hypnotism and Medicine in 1888 Paris: Contemporary Observations'. Trans. Sabine I. Gölz and Oleg V. Timofeyev. *SubStance* 79 (1996): 3–23.

Kristeva, Julia. *Les Nouvelles maladies de l'âme.* Paris: Fayard, 1993.

Le Temps sensible. Proust et l'expérience littéraire. Paris: Gallimard, 1994.

Lacassagne, Alexandre. *L'Affaire Gouffé.* Lyon/Paris: Storck/Masson, 1891.

Vacher l'éventreur et les crimes sadiques. Lyon: Storck/Paris: Masson, 1899.

Lachapelle, Sofie. *Investigating the Supernatural: From Spiritism and Occultism to Psychical Research and Metapsychics in France, 1853–1931.* Baltimore: Johns Hopkins University Press, 2011.

Ladame, Paul-Louis. 'L'Hypnotisme et la médecine légale'. *Revue de l'Hypnotisme Expérimental et Thérapeutique* 1 (1887): 10–19.

Lalande, André. *Vocabulaire technique et critique de la philosophie.* Paris: Presses Universitaires de France, 1960.

Landouzy, Hector. *Traité complet de l'hystérie*. Paris: Baillière, 1846.

Lapp, John C. 'Art and Hallucination in Flaubert'. *French Studies* 10, 4 (October 1956): 322–34.

Lasègue, Charles. 'Les Cérébraux'. In *Études médicales I*. Paris: Asselin, 1884. 567–84.

Laurent, Émile. *Les Suggestions criminelles*. Paris: Société des Éditions Scientifiques, 1891.

La Vaudère, Jane de. *Les Demi-sexes*. Paris: Ollendorff, 1897.

Laycock, Thomas. 'On the Reflex Function of the Brain'. *British and Foreign Medical Journal* 19 (1845): 298–311.

'Reflex, Automatic and Unconscious Cerebration. A History and a Criticism'. *The Journal of Mental Science* 21 (January 1876): 477–98.

Le Bon, Gustave. *La Psychologie des foules*. Paris: Alcan, 1895.

Le Guennec, Jean. *États de l'inconscient dans le récit fantastique 1800–1900*. Paris: L'Harmattan, 2002.

Raison et déraison dans le récit fantastique au XIXe siècle. Paris: L'Harmattan, 2003.

Legrand du Saulle, Henri. *Les Hystériques. État physique et mental. Actes insolites, délictueux et criminels*. Paris: Baillière, 1883.

Lemaître, Jules. 'Mes Souvenirs (1). Mon arrivée à Paris'. *Revue Hebdomadaire* (1 February 1913): 38–58.

Lemonnier, Camille. *L'Hystérique*. Paris: Charpentier, 1885.

Leriche, Françoise. 'Du nouveau sur le Cahier 14'. *Bulletin d'informations proustiennes* 21 (1990): 7–10.

Leroy, Géraldi, and Julie Bertrand-Sabiani, eds. *La Vie littéraire à la Belle Époque*. Paris: Presses Universitaires de France, 1998.

Lesueur, Daniel. *L'Évolution féminine, ses résultats économiques*. Paris: Lemerre, 1905.

Névrosée. Paris: Lemerre, 1890.

Liégeois, Jules. *De la suggestion et du somnambulisme dans leurs rapports avec la jurisprudence et la médecine légale*. Paris: Doin, 1889.

De la suggestion hypnotique dans ses rapports avec le droit civil et le droit criminel. Paris: Alphonse Picard, 1884.

'Hypnotisme téléphonique. Suggestion à grande distance'. *Mémoire de l'Académie Stanislas*. Nancy, 1885. 133–42.

Livon, Charles. *Manuel de vivisections*. Paris: Baillière, 1882.

Lorrain, Jean. 'Les Clientes de docteur'. In *Une Femme par jour*. Michel Desbrouères, ed. Paris: Christian Pirot, 1983.

Lourbet, Jacques. *La Femme devant la science contemporaine*. Paris: Alcan, 1896.

Louyer-Villermay, Jean-Baptiste. *Traité des maladies nerveuses ou vapeurs, et particulièrement de l'hystérie et de l'hypocondrie*. Paris: Méquignon l'aîné père, 1816.

Lozinsky, Elena. *L'Intertexte fin-de-siècle dans 'À la recherche du temps perdu' de Marcel Proust. Les carafes dans la Vivonne*. Paris: Honoré Champion, 2013.

Luckhurst, Nicola. *Science and Structure in Proust's 'À la recherche du temps perdu'*. Oxford: Oxford University Press, 2000.

Luys, Jules. *Études de physiologie et de pathologie cérébrales. Des actions réflexes du cerveau dans les conditions normales et pathologiques de leur fonctionnement.* Paris: Baillière, 1874.

Études sur le dédoublement des opérations cérébrales et sur le rôle isolé de chaque hémisphère dans les phénomènes de la pathologie mentale. Paris: Masson, 1879.

Macherey, Pierre. 'Peut-on encore lire aujourd'hui *Le Disciple* de Paul Bourget?' *Le Trimestre Psychanalytique* 2 (1993): 63–70.

MacKenzie, Robin. *The Unconscious in Proust's 'À la recherche du temps perdu'.* New York: Peter Lang, 2000.

Maeterlinck, Maurice. *L'Intelligence des fleurs.* Paris: Fasquelle, 1922 [1907].

Le Temple enseveli. Paris: Fasquelle, 1903.

Magnan, Valentin. *Recherches sur les centres nerveux: alcoolisme, folie des héréditaires dégénérés, paralysie générale, médecine légale* (Paris: Masson, 1893).

Maldague, Georges. *La Magnétisée.* Paris: Dentu, 1885.

Mansuy, Michel. *Un Moderne: Paul Bourget, de l'enfance au 'Disciple'.* Paris: Les Belles Lettres, 1960.

Maréchal, Sylvain. *Projet d'une loi portant défense d'apprendre à lire aux femmes.* Bernard Jolibert, ed. Paris: L'Harmattan, 2007 [1801].

Marion, Henri. *Études de psychologie féminine. L'Éducation des jeunes filles.* Paris: Colin, 1902.

Marquer, Bertrand. *Les 'Romans' de la Salpêtrière. Réception d'une scénographie clinique: Jean-Martin Charcot dans l'imaginaire fin-de-siècle.* Geneva: Droz, 2008.

Matlock, Jann. *Scenes of Seduction: Prostitution, Hysteria and Reading Difference in Nineteenth-Century France.* New York: Columbia University Press, 1994.

Maupassant, Guy de. 'Aux bains de mer'. *Gil Blas*, 6 September 1887.

Contes et nouvelles. 2 vols. Louis Forestier, ed. Paris: Gallimard (Pléiade), 1985.

'Une Femme'. *Gil Blas*, 16 August 1882.

Le Horla et autres récits fantastiques. Mariane Bury, ed. Paris: Librairie Générale Française/Livre de Poche Classique, 2004.

Pierre et Jean. Bernard Pingaud, ed. Paris: Gallimard, 1982.

Maurras, Charles. *L'Avenir de l'intelligence.* Paris: Albert Fontemoing, 1905.

Mayeur, Françoise. *L'Éducation des filles en France au XIXe siècle.* Paris: Hachette, 1979.

Megay, Joyce. *Bergson et Proust.* Paris: Vrin, 1976.

Mesch, Rachel. *The Hysteric's Revenge: French Women Writers at the Fin de Siècle.* Nashville: Vanderbilt University Press, 2006.

Micale, Mark. *Approaching Hysteria: Disease and Its Interpretations.* Princeton: Princeton University Press, 1995.

'Charcot and the Idea of Hysteria in the Male: Gender, Mental Science and Diagnosis in Late Nineteenth-Century France'. *Medical History* 34, 4 (1990): 363–411.

'Hysteria Male/Hysteria Female: Reflections on Comparative Gender Construction in Nineteenth-Century France and Britain'. In *Science and Sensibility: Essays on Gender and Scientific Enquiry, 1780–1945.* Marina Benjamin, ed. London: Basil Blackwell, 1991. 200–242.

ed. *The Mind of Modernism: Medicine, Psychology, and the Cultural Arts in Europe and America 1880–1940*. Stanford: Stanford University Press, 2004.

Micale, Mark, and Roy Porter, eds. *Discovering the History of Psychiatry*. Oxford: Oxford University Press, 1994.

Mijolla, Alain de. *Freud et la France*. Paris: Presses Universitaires de France, 2010.

Milly, Jean. *Les Pastiches de Proust*. Paris: Colin, 1970.

Mme X... 'Guy de Maupassant intime'. *La Grande Revue* (25 October 1912).

Moreau, Paul. *Des aberrations du sens génésique*, 4th edn. Paris: Asselin, 1887.

Moreau de Tours, Jacques Joseph. *Un Chapitre oublié de la pathologie mentale*. Paris: Masson, 1850.

La Psychologie morbide dans ses rapports avec la philosophie de l'histoire. Paris: Masson, 1859.

Morgan, Thaïs E. 'Male Lesbian Bodies: The Construction of Alternative Masculinities in Courbet, Baudelaire, and Swinburne'. *Genders* 15 (1992): 37–57.

Morice, Charles. *La Littérature de tout à l'heure*. Paris: Perrin, 1889.

Motet, Auguste. 'Outrage à la pudeur'. *Annales d'Hygiène Publique et de Médecine Légale* 15 (1886): 202–13.

Mugnier, Arthur. *Journal de l'abbé Mugnier*. Ghislain de Diesbach, ed. Paris: Mercure de France, 1985.

Müller, Johannes. *Handbuch der Physiologie des Menschen für Vorlesungen*. 2 vols. Koblenz: J. Hölscher, 1833–40.

Muller, Marcel. 'Sodome I ou la naturalisation de Charlus'. *Poétique* 8 (1971): 470–78.

Munthe, Axel. *The Story of San Michele*. London: John Murray, 1955.

Nicholls, Angus, and Martin Liebscher, eds. *Thinking the Unconscious: Nineteenth-Century German Thought*. Cambridge: Cambridge University Press, 2010.

Nicolas, Serge. 'L'École de la Salpêtrière en 1885'. *Psychologie et Histoire* 1 (2000): 165–207.

Histoire de la psychologie française. Naissance d'une nouvelle science. Paris: In Press Éditions, 2002.

L'Hypnose: Charcot face à Bernheim. L'école de la Salpêtrière et l'école de Nancy. Paris: L'Harmattan, 2004.

ed. *La Psychanalyse de Freud*. Paris: L'Harmattan, 2004.

Nizet, Henri. *Suggestion*. Paris: Tresse and Stock, 1891.

Noiray, Jacques. *Le Romancier et la machine. L'image de la machine dans le roman français 1850–1909*. 2 vols. Paris: José Corti, 1981.

Normandy, Georges. *Guy de Maupassant. Recueil de morceaux choisis. Anthologie des auteurs modernes, V*. Paris: Méricant [1913].

Ochorowicz, Julian. *De la suggestion mentale*. Paris: Doin, 1887.

Offen, Karen. 'Depopulation, Nationalism and Feminism in Fin-de-Siècle France'. *American Historical Review* 89, 3 (1984): 648–76.

Olds, Marshall. 'Hallucination and Point of View in *La Tentation de Saint Antoine*'. *Nineteenth-Century French Studies*, 17,1 (Fall–Winter 1998): 170–85.

Pachet, Pierre. 'Comment Proust évite la notion de l'inconscient'. *Textuel* 45, *Surprises de la recherche* (2004): 227–32.

'Peut-on encore lire aujourd'hui *Le Disciple* de Paul Bourget?' *Le Trimestre Psychanalytique* 2 (1993): 63–70.

Parodi, Dominique. 'L'Inconscient dans la vie mentale'. *Bulletin de la Société Française de Philosophie*, 10th year, 2 (February 1910): 17–51.

La Philosophie contemporaine en France, 2nd edn. Paris: Alcan, 1920 [1919].

Pasetti, Chiara. 'Hallucinations et création littéraire chez Flaubert'. *Revue Flaubert* 12 (2012). Available at flaubert.univ-rouen.fr/revue/article.php?id=103.

Perrot, Michelle, ed. *Les Ombres de l'histoire. Crime et châtiment au XIXe siècle.* Paris: Flammarion, 2001.

Peyrebrune, Georges de. *Une Décadente*. Paris: Frinzine, 1886.

Le Roman d'un bas bleu. Paris: Ollendorff, 1892.

Les Vierges de feu et la décroissance de la population. Paris: En vente chez tous les libraires, 1876.

Pierce, Arthur. 'Subliminal Self or Unconscious Cerebration?' *Proceedings of the Society for Psychical Research* 11 (1895): 317–25.

Pierrot, Jean. *L'Imaginaire décadent 1880–1900*. Paris: Presses Universitaires de France, 1977.

Pierssens, Michel. 'Bas-bleus anonymes: le combat perdu d'Albert Cim'. In *Romans à clef.* Troisième colloque des Invalides (3 December 1999). Tusson, Charentes: Du Lérot, 2000. 97–103.

Pontalis, Jean-Bertrand. 'La Maladie de Flaubert'. In *Après Freud*, Paris: Gallimard, 1968. 293–329.

Poulet, Georges. *Études sur le temps humain*. Paris: Plon, 1952.

'Pour un parti de l'intelligence'. *Le Figaro. Supplément littéraire* (19 July 1919): 1.

Prévost, Marcel. *L'Automne d'une femme*. Paris: Lemerre, 1893.

'Le Féminisme'. In Victor du Bled et al., *La Femme dans la nature, dans les moeurs, dans la légende, dans la société: tableau de son évolution physique & psychique*. Paris: Bong et Cie., 1908, 4: 319–48.

Le Jardin secret [Paris: Lemerre, 1904; [1897].

Prochasson, Christophe. *Les Années électriques, 1880–1910*. Paris: Éditions de la Découverte, 1991.

Proudhon, Pierre-Joseph. *De la justice dans la révolution et dans l'église*. Paris: Garnier frères, 1858.

Proust, Adrien. 'Cas curieux d'automatisme ambulatoire chez un hystérique'. *La Tribune Médicale* 13, *Bulletin Hebdomadaire* (27 March 1890): 202–3.

Proust, Marcel. *À la recherche du temps perdu*. 4 vols. Paris: Gallimard (Pléiade), 1987–89.

Le Carnet de 1908. Philip Kolb, ed. Paris: Gallimard, 1976.

Contre Sainte-Beuve. Paris: Gallimard (Pléiade), 1971.

Jean Santeuil. Paris: Gallimard (Pléiade), 1971.

Matinée chez la princesse de Guermantes. Henri Bonnet and Bernard Brun, eds. Paris: Gallimard, 1982.

'À propos du 'style' de Flaubert'. In *Contre Sainte-Beuve*. Paris: Gallimard (Pléiade), 1971. 586–600.

Sésame et les lys, 9th edn. Paris: Mercure de France, 1935 [1906]).

R. 'Pickmann et Donato à Marseille'. *La Vie Posthume*, 2e année, no. 10 (April 1887): 226–32.
Rachilde. *À mort*. Paris: Monnier, 1886.
Le Dessous. Paris: Mercure de France, 1904.
Le Grand Saigneur. Paris: Flammarion, 1922.
La Marquise de Sade. Paris: Gallimard (L'Imaginaire), 1996 [1887].
Monsieur Vénus. Paris: Flammarion, 1977 [1884].
Le Mordu. Paris: Brossier, 1889.
Pourquoi je ne suis pas féministe. Paris: Éditions de France, 1928.
Son printemps. Paris: Mercure de France, 1912.
Rachilde and Maurice Barrès. *Rachilde – Maurice Barrès. Correspondance inédite 1885–1914*. Michael R. Finn, ed. Brest: Centre d'Étude des Correspondances et Journaux intimes/CNRS, 2002/10.
Rainey, Lawrence. 'Shock Effects: Marinetti, Pathology and Italian Avant-Garde Poetics'. In *The Mind of Modernism: Medicine, Psychology, and the Cultural Arts in Europe and America 1880–1940*. Marc Micale, ed. Stanford: Stanford University Press, 2004. 197–213.
Rand, Nicolas. 'The Hidden Soul: The Growth of the Unconscious in Philosophy, Psychology, Medicine and Literature, 1750–1900'. *American Imago* 61, 3 (2004): 257–89.
Régis, Emmanuel, and Angelo Hesnard. *La Psychoanalyse des névroses et des psychoses: ses applications médicales et extra-médicales*. Paris: Alcan, 1914.
Reid, Martine. 'Troubadoureries'. In *George Sand, une correspondance*. Nicole Mozet, ed. St-Cyr-sur-Loire: Christian Pirot, 1994. 254–68.
Renaut, Dr J. 'L'Hypnotisme'. *Les Lettres et les Arts* (August 1886): 160–76.
Renneville, Marc. *Crime et folie. Deux siècles d'enquêtes médicales et judiciaires*. Paris: Fayard, 2003.
Renooz, Céline. 'Charcot dévoilé. '*Revue Scientifique des Femmes* 6 (December 1888): 241–47.
'Les Nouvelles Doctoresses'. *Revue Scientifique des Femmes* 1 (January 1889): 28–29.
Ribot, Théodule. *Essai sur l'imagination créatrice*. Paris: Alcan, 1900.
Les Maladies de la mémoire. Paris: Baillière, 1881.
Les Maladies de la personnalité. Paris: Alcan, 1885.
Les Maladies de la volonté. Paris: Alcan, 1883.
La Philosophie de Schopenhauer. Paris: Baillière, 1874.
Problèmes de psychologie affective. Paris: Alcan, 1910.
La Psychologie des sentiments. Paris: Alcan, 1896.
La Vie inconsciente et les mouvements. Paris: Alcan, 1914.
Richard, Gaston. Review of Jacques Lourbet, *La Femme devant la science contemporaine*. *Revue Philosophique* (1897): 434–35.
Richet, Charles (see also Charles Epheyre). 'Psychologie. Le génie et la folie'. *Revue Scientifique* (January–June 1889): 83–85.
'Le Roi des animaux'. *Revue des Deux Mondes* 55 (15 February 1883): 817–56.
'Du somnambulisme provoqué'. *Journal de l'Anatomie et de la Physiologie* 11 (1875): 348–78.

Souvenirs d'un psychologue. Paris: Peyronnet, 1933.

Traité de métapsychique. Paris: Alcan, 1922.

Rigoli, Juan. *Lire le délire. Aliénisme, rhétorique et littérature en France au XIXe siècle*. Paris: Fayard, 2001.

Rivière, Jacques. 'Le Parti de l'intelligence'. *Nouvelle Revue Française* 72 (June–December 1919): 612–18.

Quelques progrès dans l'étude du cœur humain. Cahiers Marcel Proust 13. Paris: Gallimard, 1985 [1927].

Rogers, Juliette M. *Career Stories: Belle Époque Novels of Professional Development*. University Park: Pennsylvania State University Press, 2007.

Rosny, J.-H. *L'Initiation de Diane. Roman spirite*. Paris: Flammarion, 1930.

Roudinesco, Élisabeth. *Histoire de la psychanalyse en France 1, 1885–1939*. Paris: Fayard, 1994.

Roudinesco, Élisabeth, and Michel Plon. *Dictionnaire de la psychanalyse*. Paris: Libraire Générale Française/Fayard, 2011.

Rousseau, René. 'Marcel Proust et l'esthétique de l'inconscient'. *Mercure de France* (15 January 1922): 361–86.

Ryckère, Raymond. 'La Femme criminelle et la prostituée par C. Lombroso et G. Ferrero'. *Archives de l'Anthropologie Criminelle* (1897): 301–21.

Santillane. 'La Peur de l'invisible'. *Gil Blas*, 11 November 1901, p. 1.

Sartre, Jean-Paul. *L'Idiot de la famille. Gustave Flaubert de 1821 à 1857*. 3 vols. Paris: Gallimard (Collection Tel), 1971.

Satiat, Nadine. *Maupassant*. Paris: Flammarion, 2003.

Scheidhauer, Marcel. *Le Rêve freudien en France: avancées et résistances, 1900–1926*. Paris: Navarin, 1985.

Schor, Naomi. 'Male Lesbianism'. *GLQ* 7, 3 (2001): 391–99.

Schultz, Gretchen. 'Gender, Sexuality and the Poetics of Identification'. *Nottingham French Studies* 47, 3 (Autumn 2008): 91–102.

Sédat, Jacques. 'La Réception de Freud en France durant la première moitié du XXe siècle. Le freudisme à l'épreuve de l'esprit latin'. *Topique* 2, 115 (2011): 51–68.

Showalter, Elaine. 'Critical Cross-Dressing: Male Feminists and the Woman of the Year'. *Raritan* 3 (Fall 1983): 130–49.

Socard, Jean-Paul. *Georges de Peyrebrune. Itinéraire d'une femme de lettres, du Périgord à Paris*. Périgueux: ARKA, 2011.

Sollier, Paul. *Les Phénomènes d'autoscopie*. Paris: Alcan, 1903.

Soulié, Frédéric. *Le Magnétiseur*. 2 vols. Paris: Dumont, 1834.

Sowerwine, Charles. 'Woman's Brain, Man's Brain: Feminism and Anthropology in Late Nineteenth-Century France'. *Women's History Review* 12, 2 (2003): 289–307.

Staum, Martin S. 'Ribot, Binet and the Emergence from the Anthropological Shadow'. *Journal of the History of the Behavioural Sciences* 43, 1 (Winter 2007): 1–18.

Stubbs, Jeremy. 'Between Medicine and Hermeticism: "The" Unconscious in *fin-de-siècle* France'. In *Symbolism, Decadence and the Fin de Siècle: French and European Perspectives*. Patrick McGuinness, ed. Exeter: University of Exeter Press, 2000. 144–72.

'Hypnotisme et automatisme dans la fiction fin-de-siècle'. In *Le Champ littéraire 1860–1900. Études offertes à Michael Pakenham*. Keith Cameron and James Kearns, eds. Amsterdam: Rodopi, 1996. 275–83.

Tadié, Jean-Yves. *Le Lac inconnu. Entre Proust et Freud*. Paris: Gallimard, 2012.

Marcel Proust. Biographie. 2 vols. Paris: Gallimard [Folio], 1996.

Taine, Hippolyte. *De l'intelligence*, 6th edn, 2 vols. Paris: Hachette, 1892 (1870).

Tarde, Gabriel. 'L'Affaire Chambige'. *Archives de l'Anthropologie Criminelle* (1889): 92–108.

Tétard, Léon. 'La Fascination et l'hypnotisme. Conférence faite par Donato à la Salle des Capucines'. *Revue de l'Hypnotisme* 1 (1887): 249–51.

Thibaudet, Albert. *Gustave Flaubert*. Paris: Gallimard, 1935.

'Réflexions sur la littérature. Lettre à M. Marcel Proust'. *Nouvelle Revue Française* 78 (March 1920): 426–41.

'Réflexions sur la littérature. Sur le style de Flaubert.' *Nouvelle Revue Française* 74 (November 1919): 942–53.

Thomson, Clive. *Georges Hérelle. Archéologie de l'inversion sexuelle 'fin-de-siècle'*. Paris: Le Félin, 2014.

Thorel-Cailleteau, Sylvie. *La Tentation du livre sur rien. Naturalisme et décadence*. Mont-de-Marsan: Éditions Interuniversitaires, 1994.

Thuillier, Jean. *Monsieur Charcot de la Salpêtrière*. Paris: Laffont, 1993.

Thulié, Henri. *La Femme, essai de sociologie physiologique*. Paris: Delahaye and Lescrosnier, 1885.

Torre Giménez, Estrella de la. '*Suggestion* de Henri Nizet: Un "roman hystérique"'. In *L'Hystérie de la 'Belgité'. L'hystérie dans la littérature belge de langue française de la fin du XIXe au début du XXe siècle*. Ana Pano Alaman, ed. Bologna: CLUEB, 2003. 201–15.

Trilling, Calvin. 'Art and Neurosis.' In *The Liberal Imagination. Essays on Literature and Society*. New York: Viking, 1950. 160–80.

Troubetzkoy, Vladimir, ed. *La Figure du double*. Paris: Didier, 1995.

L'Ombre et la différence. Le double en Europe. Paris: Presses Universitaires de France, 1996.

Vallette, Alfred, and Raoul Minhar. *À l'écart*. Paris: Champion, 2004 [1891].

Villiers de l'Isle-Adam, Auguste. *L'Ève future*. Alan Raitt, ed. Paris: Gallimard (Folio classique), 1993.

Virmaître, Charles. *Mémoires secrets de Troppmann*. Paris: Dequesne, 1870.

Watt, Adam. *Reading in Proust's 'À la recherche': 'le délire de la lecture'*. Oxford: Oxford University Press, 2009.

Weber, Eugen. *France, Fin de Siècle*. Cambridge: Harvard University Press, 1986.

Weber, Michel. 'L'Épilepsie de Gustave Flaubert. Témoignages directs et indirects'. *Épilepsies* 18, 3 (2006): 155–59.

Weininger, Otto. *Sex and Character: An Investigation of Fundamental Principles*. Trans. Ladislaus Löb. Bloomington: Indiana University Press, 2005.

Whyte, Lancelot. *The Unconscious before Freud*, 2nd edn. New York: St. Martin's, 1978.

Index